U.S. COIN Digest

The Complete Guide to Current Market Values

Edited by
Dave Harper & Harry Miller

©2008 Krause Publications

Published by

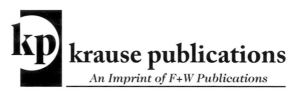

krause publications

An Imprint of F+W Publications

700 East State Street • Iola, WI 54990-0001
715-445-2214 • 888-457-2873

Our toll-free number to place an order or obtain
a free catalog is (800) 258-0929.

ISSN 1544-8517

ISBN-13: 978-0-89689-628-4
ISBN-10: 0-89689-628-5

Designed by Sandra Morrison
Edited by Dave Harper

Printed in China

Contents

Preface

Since 1952, Krause Publications has built its business and reputation by serving the needs of coin collectors. Three questions dominate every collector's thinking. The first is: "What is it?" We hope the photographs in this price guide will help you identify the coins you own. The second question is: "What's it worth? The prices contained in this volume are intended to serve as a retail guide. That means if you want to buy a specific coin in a specific grade, the price listed will be approximately what you would have to pay at the time this book was compiled. The prices listed are neither an offer to buy nor an offer to sell the coins listed. They are simply a guide assembled for your convenience by the authors. Remember that prices fluctuate. What dealers will pay to buy coins from you is a question beyond the scope of this book. The third question is: "How do I buy one (a specific coin)?" There are several thousand coin dealers across America who are ready, willing, and able to serve your needs. To find them, you can consult the phone book in your local area, but beyond that, there is a whole hobby world out there and newspapers and magazines that feature advertisements by dealers who want to fill your needs. Take a look at the Krause Web site to discover the many other fine products that the firm offers.

Photo Credits

We wish to thank the following auction houses and individuals for the fabulous color images contained within these pages.

Mike Locke   **Jay M. Galst, M.D.**

Chester L. Krause

Heritage Numismatic Auctions, Inc.   **Stack's**
3500 Maple Avenue   123 West 57th Street
17th Floor   New York, NY 10019-2280
Dallas, Texas 75219   www.stacks.com
www.HeritageCoins.com

Ken Potter
P.O. Box 760232
Lathrup Village, MI 48076
www.koinpro.com

Introduction

The authors have organized this book a manner that we hope you will find both logical and useful.

Value listings

Values listed in the following price guide are average retail prices. These are the approximate prices collectors can expect to pay when purchasing coins from dealers. They are not offers to buy or sell. The pricing section should be considered a guide only; actual selling prices will vary.

The values were compiled by Krause Publications' independent staff of market analysts. They derived the values listed by monitoring auction results, business on electronic dealer trading networks, and business at major shows, and in consultation with a panel of dealers. For rare coins, when only a few specimens of a particular date and mintmark are known, a confirmed transaction may occur only once every several years. In those instances, the most recent auction result is listed.

Grading

Values are listed for coins in various states of preservation, or grades. Standards used in determining grade for U.S. coins are those set by the American Numismatic Association (www.money.org). See Chapter 4 for more on grading.

Precious metal content

Throughout this book precious metal content is indicated in troy ounces. One troy ounce equals 480 grains, or 31.103 grams. This is followed by ASW or AGW, which stand for Actual Silver (Gold) Weight.

Dates and mintmarks

The dates listed are the individual dates that appear on each coin. The letter that follows the date is the mintmark and indicates where the coin was struck: "C" – Charlotte, N.C. (1838-1861); "CC" – Carson City, Nev. (1870-1893); "D" – Dahlonega, Ga. (1838-1861), and Denver (1906-present); "O" – New Orleans (1838-1909); "P" – Philadelphia (1793-present), coins without mintmarks also were struck at Philadelphia; "S" – San Francisco (1854-present); and "W" – West Point, N.Y. (1984-present).

A slash mark in a date indicates an overdate. This means a new date was engraved on a die over an old date. For example, if the date is listed as "1899/8," an 1898 die had a 9 engraved over the last 8 in the date. Portions of the old numeral are still visible on the coin.

A slash mark in a mintmark listing indicates an overmintmark (example: "1922-P/D"). The same process as above occurred, but this time a new mintmark was engraved over an old.

See Chapter 3, "U.S. Minting Varieties and Errors," for more information on overdates and overmintmarks.

1 American Coin History

U.S. Mint founded in 1792

At peak production, the U.S. Mint strikes nearly 30 billion coins a year. Who would have thought it possible at its founding? In July 1792, a site for the new U.S. Mint not yet having been secured, 1,500 silver half dismes were struck on a small screw press in the cellar of a Philadelphia building owned by sawmaker John Harper. Though some have since categorized these early emissions of the fledgling U.S. Mint as patterns, it is clear that first President George Washington – who is said to have deposited the silver from which the coins were struck – considered this small batch of half dismes to be the first official U.S. coins.

The law establishing the Mint dates to April 2, 1792. From that early legislative birth has flowed the coins that have underpinned the workings of U.S. commerce for over two centuries. It must be remembered that the Mint was born in chaos. It was a time shortly after the Revolutionary War and as hard as it was to win independence from Great Britain, setting up American government finances on a sound basis was to prove almost as daunting.

At first a cumbersome system was proposed by Robert Morris, a Revolutionary War financier and first superintendent of finance. Refinements tendered by Thomas Jefferson and Alexander Hamilton then firmly placed the nation on an easily understood decimal system of coinage. They were working with a hodgepodge system that grew up in the Colonial period. Despite a dire need for coinage in the Colonies, Great Britain considered it a royal right and granted franchises sparingly. Much of the Colonial economy, therefore, revolved around barter, with food staples, crops, and goods serving as currency. Indian wampum or bead money also was used, first in the fur trade and later as a form of money for Colonial use.

Copper pieces were produced around 1616 for Sommer Islands (now Bermuda), but coinage within the American Colonies apparently didn't begin until 1652, when John Hull struck silver threepence, sixpence and shillings under authority of the General Court of Massachusetts. This coinage continued, with design changes (willow, oak, and pine trees), through 1682. Most of the coins were dated 1652, apparently to avoid legal problems with England.

In 1658 Cecil Calvert, second Lord Baltimore, commissioned coins to be struck in England for use in Maryland. Other authorized and unauthorized coinages – including those of Mark Newby, John Holt, William Wood, and Dr. Samuel Higley – all became part of the landscape of circulating coins. In the 1780s there were influxes of counterfeit British halfpence and various state coinages.

The Articles of Confederation had granted individual states the right to produce copper coins. Many states found this to be appealing, and merchants in the mid-1780s traded copper coins of Vermont, Connecticut, Massachusetts, New Jersey, and New York. Not all were legal issues; various entrepreneurs used this as an invitation to strike imitation state coppers and British halfpence. Mutilated and worn foreign coins also circulated in abundance. Included among these were coins of Portugal, Great Britain, and France, with the large majority of the silver arriving from Spain.

The accounting system used by the states was derived from the British system of pounds, shillings, and pence. Each state was allowed to set its own rates at which foreign gold and silver coins would trade in relation to the British pound.

In 1782 Robert Morris, newly named superintendent of finance, was appointed to head a committee to determine the values and weights of the gold and silver coins in circulation. Asked simply to draw up a table of values, Morris took the opportunity to propose the establishment of a federal mint. In his Jan. 15, 1782, report (largely prepared by his assistant, Gouverneur Morris), Morris noted that the exchange rates between the states were complicated.

He observed that a farmer in New Hampshire would be hard-pressed if asked to determine the value of a bushel of wheat in South Carolina. Morris recorded that an amount of wheat worth four shillings in his home state of New Hampshire would be worth 21 shillings and eightpence under the accounting system used in South Carolina.

Morris claimed these difficulties plagued not only farmers, but that "they are perplexing to most Men and troublesome to all." Morris further pressed for the adoption of an American coin to solve the problems of the need for small change and debased foreign coinages in circulation.

In essence, what he was advocating was a monometallic system based on silver. He said that gold and silver had fluctuated throughout history. Because these fluctuations resulted in the more valuable metal leaving the country, any nation that adopted a bimetallic coinage was doomed to have its gold or silver coins disappear from circulation.

Gouverneur Morris calculated the rate at which the Spanish dollar traded to the British pound in the various states. Leaving out South Carolina, because it threw off his calculations, Gouverneur Morris arrived at a common denominator of 1,440. Robert Morris, therefore, recommended a unit of value of 1/1,440, equivalent to a quarter grain of silver. He suggested the striking of a silver 100-unit coin, or cent; a silver 500-unit coin, or quint; a silver 1,000-unit coin, or mark; and two copper coins, one of eight units and the other of five units.

On Feb. 21, 1782, the Grand Committee of Congress approved the proposal and directed Morris to press forward and report with a plan to establish a mint. Morris had already done so. Apparently feeling confident that Congress would like his coinage ideas, Morris (as shown by his diary) began efforts at the physical establishment prior to his January 1782 report. He had already engaged Benjamin Dudley to acquire necessary equipment for the mint and hoped to have sample coins available to submit with his original report to Congress.

It wasn't until April 23, 1783, that Morris was able to send his Nova Constellatio patterns to Congress and suggest that he was ready to report on establishing a mint. Apparently nothing came of Morris' efforts. Several committees looked into the matter, but nothing was accomplished. Dudley was eventually discharged as Morris' hopes dimmed.

Thomas Jefferson was the next to offer a major plan. Jefferson liked the idea of a decimal system of coinage, but disliked Morris' basic unit of value. As chairman of the Currency Committee, Jefferson reviewed Morris' plan and formulated his own ideas.

To test public reaction, Jefferson gave his "Notes on Coinage" to The Providence Gazette, and Country Journal, which published his plan in its July 24, 1784, issue. Jefferson disagreed with Morris' suggestion for a 1/1,440 unit of value and instead proposed a decimal coinage based on the dollar, with the lowest unit of account being the mil, or 1/1,000.

"The most easy ratio of multiplication and division is that by ten," Jefferson wrote. "Every one knows the facility of Decimal Arithmetic."

Jefferson argued that although Morris' unit would have eliminated the unwanted fraction that occurred when merchants converted British farthings to dollars, this was of little significance. After all, the original idea of establishing a mint was to get rid of foreign currencies.

Morris' unit, Jefferson said, was too cumbersome for use in normal business transactions. According to Jefferson, under Morris' plan a horse valued at 80 Spanish dollars would require a notation of six figures and would be shown as 115,200 units.

Jefferson' coinage plan suggested the striking of a dollar, or unit; half dollar, or five-tenths; a double tenth, or fifth of a dollar, equivalent to a pistareen; a tenth, equivalent to a Spanish bit; and a one-fifth copper coin, relating to the British farthing. He also wanted a gold coin of $10, corresponding to the British double guinea; and a copper one-hundredth coin, relating to the British halfpence.

In reference to his coinage denominations, Jefferson said, it was important that the coins "coincide in value with some of the known coins so nearly, that the people may by quick reference in the mind, estimate their value." The Spanish dollar was the most commonly used coin in trade, so it was natural basis for the new U.S. silver dollar. In the Spanish system, the coin was called an eight reales, or piece of eight.

More than a year, however, passed without any further action on his plan or that proposed by Morris. In a letter to William Grayson, a member of the Continental Congress, Washington expressed concern for the establishment of a national coinage system, terming it "indispensably necessary." Washington also complained of the coinage in circulation: "A man must travel with a pair of scales in his pocket, or run the risk of receiving gold at one-fourth less than it counts."

On May 13, 1785, the 13-member Grand Committee, to whom Jefferson's plan had been submitted, filed its report, generally favoring Jefferson's coinage system. The committee did, however, make slight alterations, including the elimination of the gold $10 coin, the addition of a gold $5 coin, and the dropping of Jefferson's double tenth, which it replaced with a quarter dollar. The committee also added a coin equal to 1/200 of a dollar (half cent). On July 6, 1785, Congress unanimously approved the Grand Committee's plan. It failed, however, to set a standard weight for the silver dollar or to order plans drawn up for a mint.

Several proposals were offered for a contract coinage. On April 21, 1787, the board accepted a proposal by James Jarvis to strike 300 tons of copper coin at the federal standard. Jarvis, however, delivered slightly less than 9,000 pounds of his contract. The contract was voided the following year for his failure to meet scheduled delivery times, but helped to delay further action on a mint. Concerted action on a coinage system and a mint would wait until the formation of the new government.

Alexander Hamilton, named in September 1789 to head the new Treasury, offered three different methods by which the new nation could achieve economic stability, including the funding of the national debt, establishment of the Bank of North America and the founding of the U.S. Mint. On Jan. 21, 1791, Hamilton submitted to Congress a "Report on the Establishment of a Mint."

Hamilton agreed with Jefferson that the dollar seemed to be best suited to serve as the basic unit, but believed it necessary to establish a proper weight and fineness for the new coin. To do so, Hamilton had several Spanish coins assayed to determine the fine weight of the Spanish dollar. He also watched the rate at which Spanish dollars traded for fine gold (24 3/4 grains per dollar) on the world market.

From his assays and observations he determined that the Spanish dollar contained 371 grains of silver. He then multiplied 24 3/4 by 15 (the gold value of silver times his suggested bimetallic ratio) and arrived at 371 1/4 as the proper fine silver weight for the new silver dollar.

The Spanish dollar actually contained 376 grains of pure silver when new, 4 3/4 grains more than Hamilton's proposed silver dollar.

Hamilton also wanted a bimetallic ratio of 15-to-1. Hamilton said his ratio was closer to Great Britain's, which would be important for trade, and Holland's, which would be important for repaying loans from that country.

His report suggested the striking of a gold $10; gold dollar; silver dollar; silver tenth, or disme; and copper one-hundredth and half-hundredth. Hamilton felt the last of these, the half cent, was necessary because it would enable merchants to lower their prices, which would help the poor.

Congress passed the act establishing the U.S. Mint April 2, 1792. It reinstated several coin denominations left out by Hamilton and dropped his gold dollar. In gold, the act authorized at $10 coin, or "eagle"; a $5 coin, or "half eagle"; and a $2.50 coin, or "quarter eagle." In silver were to be a dollar, half dollar, quarter dollar, disme, and half disme, and in copper a cent and half cent.

Though it established a sound system of U.S. coinage, the act failed to address the problem of foreign coins in circulation. It was amended in February 1793 to cancel their legal-tender status within three years of the mint's opening.

Coinage totals at the first mint in Philadelphia were understandably low. Skilled coiners, assayers and others who could handle the mint's daily operations were in short supply in the United States. Also in want were adequate equipment and supplies of metal for coinage. Much of the former had to be built or imported. Much of the latter was also imported or salvaged from various domestic sources, including previously struck tokens and coins, and scrap metal.

Coinage began in earnest in 1793 with the striking of half cents and cents at the new mint located at Seventh Street between Market and Arch streets in Philadelphia. Silver coinage followed in 1794, with half dimes, half dollars, and dollars. Gold coinage did not begin until 1795 with the minting of the first $5 and $10 coins. Silver dimes and quarters and gold $2.50 coins did not appear until 1796.

Under the bimetallic system of coinage by which gold and silver served as equal representations of the unit of value, much of the success and failure of the nation's coinage to enter and remain in circulation revolved around the supply and valuation of precious metals. From the Mint's beginning, slight miscalculations in the proper weight for the silver dollar and a proper bimetallic ratio led gold and silver to disappear from circulation. The U.S. silver dollar traded at par with Spanish and Mexican dollars, but because the U.S. coin was lighter, it was doomed to be exported.

A depositor at the first mint could make a profit at the mint's expense by sending the coins to the West Indies. There they could be traded at par for the heavier Spanish or Mexican eight reales, which were then shipped back to the United States for recoinage. As a result, few early silver dollars entered domestic circulation; most failed to escape the melting pots.

Gold fared no better. Calculations of the bimetallic ratio by which silver traded for gold on the world market were also askew at first and were always subject to fluctuations. Gold coins either disappeared quickly after minting or never entered circulation, languishing in bank vaults. These problems led President Jefferson to halt coinage of the gold $10 and the silver dollar in 1804.

The gold $10 reappeared in 1838 at a new, lower weight standard. The silver dollar, not coined for circulation since 1803, returned in 1836 with a limited mintage. Full-scale coinage waited until 1840.

Nor was the coinage of copper an easy matter for the first mint. Severe shortages of the metal led the mint to explore various avenues of obtaining sufficient supplies for striking cents and half cents.

Witness, for example, the half-cent issues of 1795 and 1797 struck over privately issued tokens of the New York firm of Talbot, Allum & Lee because of a shortage of copper for the federal issue. Rising copper prices and continued shortages forced the mint to lower the cent's weight from 208 grains to 168 grains in 1795.

In 1798, because of the coinage shortage, the legal-tender status of foreign coins was restored. Several more extensions were given during the 1800s, ending with the withdrawal of legal-tender status for Spanish coins in 1857.

A new law made the mint lower the standard weight of all gold coins in 1834. This reflected market conditions and in effect recognized a higher gold price when bought with silver coins. For example, $5 in silver coins bought a new, lighter $5 gold piece, meaning the buyer got less gold. This led to the melting of great numbers of the older, heavier gold coins as speculators grabbed a 4.7 percent profit.

By the 1850s discovery of gold in California made silver more expensive in terms of gold. All silver quickly disappeared from circulation. Congress reacted in 1853 by lowering the weight of the silver half dime, dime, quarter, and half dollar, hoping to keep silver in circulation. A new gold coin of $20 value, the "double eagle," was introduced to absorb a great amount of the gold from Western mines.

Not long after, silver was discovered in Nevada. By the mid-1870s the various mines that made up what was known as the Comstock Lode (named after its colorful early proprietor, Henry P. Comstock) had hit the mother lode. Large supplies of silver from the Comstock, combined with European demonetization, caused a severe drop in its value.

Silver coins were made heavier as a result in 1873.

Also, it was believed that the introduction of a heavier, 420-grain silver dollar in 1873, known as the Trade dollar, would create a market for much of the Comstock silver, bolster its price, and at the same time wrest control from Great Britain of lucrative trade with the Orient. It didn't. Large numbers of Trade dollars eventually flooded back into the United States. They were demonetized in 1887.

Morgan dollars were introduced in 1878 as a panacea to the severe economic problems following the Civil War. Those who proudly carried the banner of free silver contended that by taking the rich output of the Comstock mines and turning it into silver dollars, a cheaper, more plentiful form of money would become available. This was supposed to give the economy a boost.

The Free Silver Movement reached its peak in 1896 when William Jennings Bryan attempted to gain the White House on a plank largely based on restoration of the free and unlimited coinage of the standard 412.5-grain silver dollar. He failed. Silver failed. In 1900 the United States officially adopted a gold standard.

Silver continued to be a primary coinage metal until 1964, when rising prices led the Mint to remove it from the dime and quarter. Mintage of the silver dollar had ended in 1935. The half dollar continued to be coined through 1970 with a 40 percent silver composition. It, too, was then made of copper-nickel clad metal.

Gold coinage ended in 1933 and exists today only in commemorative issues and American Eagle bullion coins with fictive face values. A clad composition of copper and nickel is now the primary coinage metal. Even the cent is no longer all copper; a copper-coated zinc composition has been used since 1982.

Precious-metal supplies were also linked to the opening of additional mints, which served the parent facility in Philadelphia. The impact of gold discoveries in the 1820s in the southern Appalachian Mountains was directly tied to the construction of branch mints in Dahlonega, Ga., and Charlotte, N.C., in 1838. These new mints struck only gold coins. New Orleans also became the site of a branch mint in the same year as Dahlonega and Charlotte. It took in some of the outflow of gold from Southern mines, but also struck silver coins.

Discovery of gold in California in the late 1840s created a gold rush, and from it sprang a great western migration. Private issues of gold coinage, often of debased quality, were prevalent, and the cost of shipping the metal eastward for coinage at Philadelphia was high. A call for an official branch mint was soon heard and heeded in 1852 with the authorization of the San Francisco Mint, which began taking deposits in 1854.

The discovery of silver in the Comstock Lode led to yet another mint. Located only a short distance via Virginia & Truckee Railroad from the fabulous Comstock Lode, the Carson City mint began receiving bullion in early 1870.

Denver, also located in a mineral-rich region, became the site of an assay office in 1863 when the government purchased the Clark, Gruber & Co. private mint. It became a U.S. branch mint in 1906. Now four mints exist. They are in Denver, Philadelphia, San Francisco and West Point, N.Y. The latter strikes current precious metal coinage for collectors and investors.

2 How Are Coins Made?

Mints are really factories

Copper, nickel, silver, and gold are pretty much the basic coin metals for the United States. When mixed with tin, copper becomes bronze, and this alloy was used in cents. Current cents have a pure zinc core. There have been patterns made of aluminum, but these never were issued for use in circulation. Platinum joined gold and silver as a precious metal used in U.S. coinage starting in 1997.

There are three basic parts of the minting process: (1) the making of the planchet, which is divided into the selection and processing of the metal and the preparation of the planchets, (2) the making of the dies, and (3) the use of the dies to strike the planchets. To help you remember these three parts, think of "P," "D," and "S" for planchet, die, and striking.

Making the 'blanks'

The piece of metal that becomes a coin is known as a "blank." This is a usually round, flat piece that has been punched or cut from a sheet or strip of coin metal.

Before a blank can become a coin it has to be processed, cleaned, softened, and given what is known as an "upset edge" – a raised ridge or rim around both sides. The blank then becomes a "planchet" and is ready to be struck into a coin by the dies. First they go through what looks like a monstrous cement mixer. A huge cylinder revolves slowly as the planchets are fed in at one end and spiral their way through. This is an annealing oven, which heats the planchets to soften them. When they come out the end, they fall into a bath where they are cleaned with a diluted acid or soap solution. As the final step, they go through the upsetting mill, the machine that puts the raised rim on the blank and turns it into a planchet, ready to be struck. In a different department the process of making the dies used to strike the coins has already begun.

Preparing the dies

For those who haven't studied metallurgy, the concept of hard metal flowing about is pretty hard to swallow, but this is actually what happens. It is basically the same process as the one used in an auto plant to turn a flat sheet of steel into a fender with multiple curves and sharp bends. The cold metal is moved about by the pressure applied.

To make the metal move into the desired design, there has to be a die. Actually, there have to be two dies, because one of the laws of physics is that for every action there has to be an equal and opposite reaction. You cannot hold a piece of metal in midair and strike one side of it. Instead you make two dies, fix one, and drive the other one against it – with a piece of metal in between to accept the design from each die.

A die is a piece of hard metal, like steel, with a design on its face that helps to form a mirror image on the struck coin. Early dies were made by hand. Engravers used hand tools, laboriously cutting each letter, each digit, and each owl or eagle or whatever design was being used into the face of the die. Notice that this is "into" the surface of the die. Each part of the die design is a hole or cavity of varying shape and depth.

This is because we want a mirror image on the coin, but we want it raised, or in "relief." To make a relief image on a coin, the image on the die has to be recessed into the face of the die, or "incuse." Of course, if we want an incuse image on the coin, such as the gold $2.50 and $5 coins of 1908-1929, the design on the die face would have to be in relief.

To fully understand this, take a coin from your pocket and a piece of aluminum foil. Press the foil down over the coin design and rub it with an eraser. When you take the foil off and look at the side that was in contact with the coin, you have a perfect copy of a die. Everywhere there is a relief design on the coin there is an incuse design on your foil "die."

From sketchbook to coin

The design process begins with an artist's sketch. This is translated into a three-dimensional relief design that is hand-carved from plaster or, in recent years, from a form of plastic.

The plaster or plastic design is then transformed into a "galvano," which is an exact copy of the design that has been plated with a thin layer of copper. This is used as a template or pattern in a reducing lathe, which cuts the design into a die blank.

This die becomes the master die, from which all of the following steps descend. The process can be reversed so that the designs will be cut in relief, forming a tool called a "hub," which is simply a piece of steel with the design in relief, exactly the same as the relief design on the intended coin.

To make working dies, pieces of special steel are prepared, with one end shaped with a slight cone. The die blank is softened by heating it. Then the hub is forced into the face of the die, forming the incuse, mirror-image design in the face of the die.

The process usually has to be repeated because the die metal will harden from the

A galvano of the 1976 half dollar goes on the reducing lathe.

pressure. The die is removed, softened, and returned to the hubbing press for a second impression from the hub. As you can imagine, it takes several hundred tons per square inch to force the hub into the die. Logically, this process is called "hubbing" a die.

The advantage of hubbing a die is that thousands of working dies can be made from a single hub, each one for all practical purposes as identical as the proverbial peas in a pod. This enables, for example, U.S. mints to strike billions of one-cent coins each year, each with the identical design.

Die making has come a long way from the early days. Philadelphia used to make all dies and then shipped them to the branch mints. Now Denver has its own die shop and creates dies of its own.

Striking the coin

Yesterday's die might strike only a few hundred coins. Today it is not unusual for a die to strike well over a million coins.

The coin press used to strike modern coins is a complicated piece of equipment that consists basically of a feed system to place the planchets in position for the stroke of the hammer die to form a coin. This process takes only a fraction of a second, so the press has to operate precisely to spew out the hundreds of coins that are struck every minute.

The end of the early hammered coinage came with the introduction of the collar, which often is called the "third" die. The collar is nothing more than a steel plate with a hole in it. This hole is the exact diameter of the intended coin and often is lined with carbide to prolong its life. It surrounds the lower, or fixed, die. Its sole purpose is to contain the coin metal to keep it from spreading too far sideways under the force of the strike.

If the intended coin has serrations, or "reeds," on the edge, then the collar has the matching design. The strike forces the coin metal against the serrations in the collar, forming the reeded edge at the same time that the two dies form the front and back, or obverse and reverse, of the coin.

A binful of blanks are ready for the coin press.

Lettered-edge coins are produced usually by running the planchets through an edge-lettering die, or by using a segmented collar that is forced against the edge of the planchet during the strike by hydraulic pressure.

Several hundred tons were required to drive a hub into a die. Not as much but still significant amounts of force are needed to strike coins. A cent requires about 30 tons per square inch. A silver dollar took 150 tons. Other denominations fall between.

Modern coin presses apply pressure in a variety of ways. A ram, carrying the moving or "hammer" die, is forced against the planchet. Most commonly this is with the mechanical advantage of a "knuckle" or connected pieces to which pressure is applied from the side. When the joint straightens – like straightening your finger – the ram at the end of the piece is driven into the planchet. Once the strike is complete, at the final impact of the die pair, the coin has been produced. It is officially a coin now, and it's complete and ready to be spent.

Making proof coins

Proof coins started out as special presentation pieces. They were and still are struck on specially prepared planchets with specially prepared dies. Today the definition of a proof coin also requires that it be struck two or more times.

Currently all proof versions of circulating U.S. coins are struck at the San Francisco Mint, but some of the proof commemorative coins have been struck at the other mints. West Point currently strikes proof American Eagles of silver, gold, and platinum, and they carry a "W" mintmark.

After the proof blanks are punched from the strip, they go through the annealing oven, but on a conveyor belt rather than being tumbled in the revolving drum. After cleaning and upsetting they go into a huge vibrating machine where they are mixed with steel pellets that look like tiny footballs. The movement of the steel pellets against the planchets burnishes, or smooths, the surface so any scratches and gouges the planchets pick up during processing are smoothed over.

Proof dies get an extra polishing before the hubbing process. They are made at Philadelphia and shipped to the branch mints. When the proof dies arrive at San Francisco, they are worked on by a team of specialists who use diamond dust and other polishing agents to turn the fields of the proof dies into mirrorlike surfaces. The incuse design is sandblasted to make the surface rough, producing what is known as a "frosted" design. Because collectors like the frosted proofs, the design is periodically swabbed with acid to keep the surface rough and increase the number of frosted proofs from each die. This process has been around about a quarter century, so frosted examples of earlier proofs are considerably scarcer.

The presses that strike proof coins usually are hand-operated rather than automatic. Some of the newer presses use equipment such as vacuum suction devices to pick up the planchets, place them in the coining chamber, and then remove the struck coins. This avoids handling the pieces any more than necessary.

On a hand-operated press, the operator takes a freshly washed and dried planchet and, using tongs, places it in the collar. The ram with the die descends two or more times before the finished coin is removed from the collar and carefully stored in a box for transport to storage or the packaging line. After each strike the operator wipes the dies to make sure that lint or other particles don't stick to the dies and damage the coins as they are struck.

Proof dies are used for only a short time. Maximum die life is usually less than 10,000 coins, varying with the size of the coin and the alloy being struck.

3 U.S. Minting Varieties and Errors

Most are common, some are rare

Introduction

The P.D.S. cataloging system used here to list minting varieties was originally compiled by Alan Herbert in 1971. PDS stands for the three main divisions of the minting process, "planchet," "die" and "striking." Two more divisions cover collectible modifications after the strike, as well as non-collectible alterations, counterfeits and damaged coins.

This listing includes 445 classes, each a distinct part of the minting process or from a specific non-mint change in the coin. Classes from like causes are grouped together. The PDS system applies to coins of the world, but is based on U.S. coinage with added classes for certain foreign minting practices.

Price ranges are based on a U.S. coin in MS-60 grade (uncirculated.) The ranges may be applied in general to foreign coins of similar size or value although collector values are not usually as high as for U.S. coins. Prices are only a guide as the ultimate price is determined by a willing buyer and seller.

To define minting varieties, "A coin which exhibits a variation of any kind from the normal, as a result of any portion of the minting process, whether at the planchet stage, as a result of a change or modification of the die, or during the striking process. It includes those classes considered to be intentional changes, as well as those caused by normal wear and tear on the dies or other minting equipment and classes deemed to be "errors."

The three causes are represented as follows:
1. (I) = Intentional Changes
2. (W) = Wear and Tear
3. (E) = Errors
Note: A class may show more than one cause and could be listed as (IWE).

Rarity level

The rarity ratings are based on the following scale:

1 - Very Common. Ranges from every coin struck down to 1,000,000.

2 - Common. From 1,000,000 down to 100,000.

3 - Scarce. From 100,000 down to 10,000.

4 - Very Scarce. From 10,000 down to 1,000.

5 - Rare. From 1,000 down to 100.

6 - Very Rare. From 100 down to 10.

7 - Extremely Rare. From 10 down to 1.

Unknown: If there is no confirmed report of a piece fitting a particular class, it is listed as Unknown. Reports of finds by readers would be appreciated in order to update future presentations.

An Unknown does not mean that your piece automatically is very valuable. Even a Rarity 7 piece, extremely rare, even unique, may have a very low collector value because of a lack of demand or interest in that particular class.

Classes, definitions and price ranges are based on material previously offered in Alan Herbert's book, The Official Price Guide to Minting Varieties and Errors and in Coin Prices Magazine.

Pricing information has also been provided by John A. Wexler and Ken Potter, with special pricing and technical advice from Del Romines.

Also recommended is the Cherrypicker's Guide to Rare Die Varieties by Bill Fivaz and J.T. Stanton. Check your favorite coin shop, numismatic library or book seller for availability of the latest edition.

For help with your coin questions, to report significant new finds and for authentication of your minting varieties, include a loose first class stamp and write to Alan Herbert, 700 E. State St., Iola, WI 54990-0001. Don't include any numismatic material until you have received specific mailing instructions from me.

Quick check index

If you have a coin and are not sure where to look for the possible variety:

If your coin shows doubling, first check V-B-I.

Then try II-A, II-B, II-C, II-I (4 & 5), III-J, III-L, or IV-C.

If part of the coin is missing, check III-B, III-C, or III-D.

If there is a raised line of coin metal, check II-D, II G.

If there is a raised area of coin metal, check II-E, II-F, or III-F.

If the coin is out of round, and too thin, check III-G.

If coin appears to be the wrong metal, check III-A, III-E, III-F-3 and III-G.

If the die appears to have been damaged, check II-E, II-G. (Damage to the coin itself usually is not a minting variety.)

If the coin shows incomplete or missing design, check II-A, II-E, III-B-3, III-B-5 or III-D.

If only part of the planchet was struck, check III-M.

If something was struck into the coin, check III-J and III-K.

If something has happened to the edge of the coin, check II-D-6, II-E-10, III-I, III-M and III-O.

If your coin shows other than the normal design, check II-A or II-C.

If a layer of the coin metal is missing, or a clad layer is missing, check III-B and III-D.

If you have an unstruck blank, or planchet, check I-G.

If your coin may be a restrike, check IV-C.

If your coin has a counterstamp, countermark, additional engraving or apparent official modifications, check IV-B and V-A-8.

Do not depend on the naked eye to examine your coins. Use a magnifying lens whenever possible, as circulation damage, wear and alterations frequently can be mistaken for legitimate minting varieties.

The planchet varieties

DIVISION I

The first division of the PDS System includes those minting varieties that occur in the manufacture of the planchet upon which the coins will ultimately be struck and includes classes resulting from faulty metallurgy, mechanical damage, faulty processing, or equipment or human malfunction prior to the actual coin striking.

●PLANCHET ALLOY MIX (I–A)

This section includes those classes pertaining to mixing and processing the various metals which will be used to make a coin alloy.

I-A-1 Improper Alloy Mix (WE), Rarity Level: 3-4, Values: $5 to $10.

I-A-2 Slag Inclusion Planchet (WE), Rarity Level: 5-6, Values: $25 up.

●DAMAGED AND DEFECTIVE PLANCHETS (I–B)

To be a class in this section the blank, or planchet, must for some reason not meet the normal standards or must have been damaged in processing. The classes cover the areas of defects in the melting, rolling, punching and processing of the planchets up to the point where they are sent to the coin presses to be struck.

I-B-1 Defective Planchet (WE), Rarity Level: 6, Values: $25 up.

I-B-2 Mechanically Damaged Planchet (WE), Rarity Level: –, Values: No Value. (See values for the coin struck on a mechanically damaged planchet.)

I-B-3 Rolled Thin Planchet (WE), Rarity Level: 6 - (Less rare on half cents of 1795, 1797 and restrikes of 1831-52.) Values: $10 up.

I-B-4 Rolled Thick Planchet (WE), Rarity Level: 7 - (Less rare in Colonial copper coins. Notable examples occur on the restrike half cents of 1840-52.) Values: $125 up.

I-B-5 Tapered Planchet (WE), Rarity Level: 7, Values: $25 up.

I-B-6 Partially Unplated Planchet (WE), Rarity Level: 6, Values: $15 up.

I-B-7 Unplated Planchet (WE), Rarity Level: 6-7, Values: $50 up.

I-B-8 Bubbled Plating Planchet (WE), Rarity Level: 1, Values: No Value.

I-B-9 Included Gas Bubble Planchet (WE), Rarity Level: 6-7, Values: $50 up.

I-B-10 Partially Unclad Planchet (WE), Rarity Level: 6, Values: $20 up.

I-B-11 Unclad Planchet (WE), Rarity Level: 6-7, Values: $50 up.

I-B-12 Undersize Planchet (WE), Rarity Level: 7, Values: $250 up.

I-B-13 Oversize Planchet (WE), Rarity Level: 7, Values: $250 up.

I-B-14 Improperly Prepared Proof Planchet (WE), Rarity Level: 7, Values: $100 up.

I-B-15 Improperly Annealed Planchet (WE), Rarity Level: - , Values: No Value.

I-B-16 Faulty Upset Edge Planchet (WE), Rarity Level: 5-6, Values: $10 up.

I-B-17 Rolled-In Metal Planchet (WE), Rarity Level: 6-7, Values: $50 up.

I-B-18 Weld Area Planchet (WE), Rarity Level: Unknown, Values: No Value Established. (See values for the coins struck on weld area planchets.)

I-B-19 Strike Clip Planchet (WE), Rarity Level: 7, Values: $150 up.

I-B-20 Unpunched Center-Hole Planchet (WE), Rarity Level: 5-7, Values: $5 and up.

I-B-21 Incompletely Punched Center-Hole Planchet (WE), Rarity Level: 6-7, Values: $15 up.

I-B-22 Uncentered Center-Hole Planchet (WE), Rarity Level: 6-7, Values: $10 up.

I-B-23 Multiple Punched Center-Hole Planchet (WE), Rarity Level: 7, Values: $35 up.

I-B-24 Unintended Center-Hole Planchet (WE), Rarity Level: Unknown, Values: -.

I-B-25 Wrong Size or Shape Center-Hole Planchet (IWE), Rarity Level: 5-7, Values: $10 up.

●CLIPPED PLANCHETS (I–C)

Clipped blanks, or planchets, occur when the strip of coin metal fails to move forward between successive strokes of the gang punch to clear the previously punched holes, in the same manner as a cookie cutter overlapping a previously cut hole in the dough. The size of the clip is a function of the amount of overlap of the next punch.

The overlapping round punches produce a missing arc with curve matching the outside circumference of the blanking punch. Straight clips occur when the punch overlaps the beginning or end of a strip which has had the end sheared or sawed off. Ragged clips occur in the same manner when the ends of the strip have been left as they were rolled out.

The term "clip" as used here should not be confused with the practice of clipping or shaving small pieces of metal from a bullion coin after it is in circulation.

I-C-1 Disc Clip Planchet (WE), Rarity Level: 3-5, Values: $5 up.

I-C-2 Curved Clip Planchet - (To 5%) (WE), Rarity Level: 5-6, Values: $5 up.

I-C-3 Curved Clip Planchet - (6 to 10%) (WE), Rarity Level: 6, Values: $10 up.

I-C-4 Curved Clip Planchet - (11 to 25%) (WE), Rarity Level: 5-6, Values: $15 up.

I-C-5 Curved Clip Planchet - (26 to 60%) (WE), Rarity Level: 6-7, Values: $25 up.

I-C-6 Double Curved Clip Planchet (WE), Rarity Level: 6, Values: $10 up.

I-C-7 Triple Curved Clip Planchet (WE), Rarity Level: 5-6, Values: $25 up.

I-C-8 Multiple Curved Clip Planchet (WE), Rarity Level: 6-7, Values: $35 up.

I-C-9 Overlapping Curved Clipped Planchet (WE), Rarity Level: 6-7, Values: $50 up.

I-C-10 Incompletely Punched Curved Clip Planchet (WE), Rarity Level: 6, Values: $35 up.

I-C-11 Oval Curved Clip Planchet (WE), Rarity Level: 6-7, Values: $50 up.

I-C-12 Crescent Clip Planchet - (61% or more) (WE), Rarity Level: 7, Values: $200 up.

I-C-13 Straight Clip Planchet (WE), Rarity Level: 6, Values: $30 up.

I-C-14 Incompletely Sheared Straight Clip Planchet (WE), Rarity Level: 6, Values: $50 up.

I-C-15 Ragged Clip Planchet (WE), Rarity Level: 6-7, Values: $35 up.

I-C-16 Outside Corner Clip Planchet (E), Rarity Level: -, Values: No Value.

I-C-17 Inside Corner Clip Planchet (E), Rarity Level: -, Values: No Value.

I-C-18 Irregularly Clipped Planchet (E) Rarity Level: -, Values: Value not established.

I-C-19 Incompletely Punched Scalloped or Multi-Sided Planchet (E), Rarity Level: 7, Values: $25 up.

I-C-2

●LAMINATED, SPLIT, OR BROKEN PLANCHET (I-D)

For a variety of reasons the coin metal may split into thin layers (delaminate) and either split completely off the coin, or be retained. Common causes are included gas or alloy mix problems. Lamination cracks usually enter the surface of the planchet at a very shallow angle or are at right angles to the edge. The resulting layers differ from slag in that they appear as normal metal.

Lamination cracks and missing metal of any size below a split planchet are too common in the 35 percent silver 1942-1945 nickels to be collectible or have any significant value.

I-D-1 Small Lamination Crack Planchet (W), Rarity Level: 4-5, Values: $1 up.

I-D-2 Large Lamination Crack Planchet (W), Rarity Level: 3-4, Values: $5 up.

I-D-3 Split Planchet (W), Rarity Level: 5-6, Values: $15 up.

I-D-4 Hinged Split Planchet (W), Rarity Level: 6-7, Values: $75 up.

I-D-5 Clad Planchet With a Clad Layer Missing (W), Rarity Level: 5-6, Values: $35 up.

I-D-6 Clad Planchet With Both Clad Layers Missing (W), Rarity Level: 6-7, Values: $75 up.

I-D-7 Separated Clad Layer (W), Rarity Level: 5, Values: $25 up.

I-D-8 Broken Planchet (WE), Rarity Level: 3-4, Values: $5 up.

●WRONG STOCK PLANCHET (I-E)

The following classes cover those cases where the wrong coin metal stock was run through the blanking press, making blanks of the correct diameter, but of the wrong thickness, alloy or metal or a combination of the wrong thickness and the wrong metal.

I-E-1 Half Cent Stock Planchet (IE), Rarity Level: Unknown, Values: No Value Established.

I-E-2 Cent Stock Planchet (IE), Rarity Level: Unknown, Values: No Value Established.

I-E-3 Two Cent Stock Planchet (E), Rarity Level: Unknown, Values: No Value Established.

I-E-4 Three Cent Silver Stock Planchet (E), Rarity Level: Unknown, Values: No Value Established.

I-E-5 Three Cent Nickel Stock Planchet (E), Rarity Level: Unknown, Values: No Value Established.

I-E-6 Half Dime Stock Planchet (E), Rarity Level: Unknown, Values: No Value Established.

I-E-7 Dime Stock Planchet (E), Rarity Level: 7, Values: $200 up.

I-E-8 Twenty Cent Stock Planchet (E), Rarity Level: Unknown, Values: No Value Established.

I-E-9 Quarter Stock Planchet (E), Rarity Level: Unknown, Values: No Value Established.

I-E-10 Half Dollar Stock Planchet (E), Rarity Level: Unknown, Values: No Value Established.

I-E-11 Dollar Stock Planchet (E), Rarity Level: 7, Values: $300 up.

I-E-12 Token or Medal Stock Planchet (E), Rarity Level: Unknown, Values: No Value Established.

I-E-13 Wrong Thickness Spoiled Planchet (IWE), Rarity Level: Unknown, Values: No Value Established.

I-E-14 Correct Thickness Spoiled Planchet (IWE), Rarity Level: Unknown, Values: No Value Established.

I-E-15 Cut Down Struck Token Planchet (IWE), Rarity Level: Unknown, Values: No Value Established.

I-E-16 Experimental or Pattern Stock Planchet (IE), Rarity Level: Unknown, Values: No Value Established.

I-E-17 Proof Stock Planchet (IE), Rarity Level: Unknown, Values: No Value Established.

I-E-18 Adjusted Specification Stock Planchet (IE), Rarity Level: 7, Values: $25 up.

I-E-19 Trial Strike Stock Planchet (IE), Rarity Level: Unknown, Values: No Value Established.

I-E-20 U.S. Punched Foreign Stock Planchet (E), Rarity Level: 7, Values: $75 up.

I-E-21 Foreign Punched Foreign Stock Planchet (E), Rarity Level: 7, Values: $75 up.

I-E-22 Non-Standard Coin Alloy Planchet (IE), Rarity Level: 7, Values: Unknown.

● EXTRA METAL ON A BLANK, OR PLANCHET (I–F)

True extra metal is only added to the blank during the blanking operation. This occurs as metal is scraped off the sides of the blanks as they are driven down through the thimble, or lower die in the blanking press. The metal is eventually picked up by a blank passing through, welded to it by the heat of friction.

A second form of extra metal has been moved to this section, the sintered coating planchet, the metal deposited on the planchet in the form of dust during the annealing operation.

I-F-1 Extra Metal on a Type 1 Blank (W), Rarity Level: 7, Values: $50 up.

I-F-2 Extra Metal on a Type 2 Planchet (W), Rarity Level: 6-7, Values: $75 up.

I-F-3 Sintered Coating Planchet (W), Rarity Level: 7, Values: $75 up.

● NORMAL OR ABNORMAL PLANCHETS (I–G)

This section consists of the two principal forms – the blank as it comes from the blanking press – and in the form of a planchet after it has passed through the upsetting mill. It also includes a class for purchased planchets and one for planchets produced by the mint.

I-G-1 Type I Blank (IWE), Rarity Level: 3-5, Values: $2 up.

I-G-2 Type II Planchet (IWE), Rarity Level: 3-4, Values: 50 up.

I-G-3 Purchased Planchet (I), Rarity Level: 1, Values: No Value.

I-G-4 Mint Made Planchet (I), Rarity Level: 1, Values: No Value.

I-G-5 Adjustment-Marked Planchet (I), Rarity Level: Unknown, Values: No Value.

I-G-6 Hardness Test-Marked Planchet (I), Rarity Level: -, Values: No Value Established.

Note: There are no classes between I-G-6 and I-G-23

I-G-23 Proof Planchet (IE), Rarity Level: 6-7, Values: $1 up.

● COIN METAL STRIP (I–H)

When the coin metal strip passes through the blanking press it goes directly to a chopper. This cuts the remaining web into small pieces to be sent back to the melting furnace. Pieces of the web or the chopped up web may escape into the hands of collectors.

I-H-1 Punched Coin Metal Strip (IWE), Rarity Level: 4-6, Values: $5 up, depending on size, denomination and number of holes showing.

I-H-2 Chopped Coin Metal Strip (IE), Rarity Level: 3-5, Values: $5 up.

The die varieties

DIVISION II

Die varieties may be unique to a given die, but will repeat for the full life of the die unless a further change occurs. Anything that happens to the die will affect the appearance of the struck coin. This includes all the steps of the die making:

- Cutting a die blank from a tool steel bar.
- Making the design.
- Transferring it to a model.
- Transferring it to the master die or hub.
- The hubbing process of making the die.
- Punching in the mintmark.
- Heat treating of the die.

The completed dies are also subject to damage in numerous forms, plus wear and tear during the striking process and repair work done with abrasives. All of these factors can affect how the struck coin looks.

●ENGRAVING VARIETIES (II–A)

In all cases in this section where a master die, or master hub is affected by the class, the class will affect all the working hubs and all working dies descending from it.

Identification as being on a master die or hub depends on it being traced to two or more of the working hubs descended from the same master tools.

II-A-1 Overdate (IE), Rarity Level: 1-7, Values: $1 up.

II-A-2 Doubled Date (IE), Rarity Level: 1-7, Values: $1 up.

II-A-3 Small Date (IE), Rarity Level: 2-5, Values: $1 up.

II-A-4 Large Date (IE), Rarity Level: 2-5, Values: $1 up.

II-A-5 Small Over Large Date (IE), Rarity Level: 4-6, Values: $15 up.

II-A-6 Large Over Small Date (IE), Rarity Level: 3-5, Values: $10 up.

II-A-7 Blundered Date (E), Rarity Level: 6-7, Values: $50 up.

II-A-8 Corrected Blundered Date (IE), Rarity Level: 3-5, Values: $5 up.

II-A-9 Wrong Font Date Digit (IE), Rarity Level: 5-6, Values: Minimal.

II-A-10 Worn, Broken or Damaged Punch (IWE), Rarity Level: 5-6, Values: $5 up.

II-A-11 Expedient Punch (IWE), Rarity Level: 5-6, Values: $10 up.

II-A-12 Blundered Digit (E), Rarity Level: 4-5, Values: $50 up.

II-A-13 Corrected Blundered Digit (IE), Rarity Level: 3-6, Values: $10 up.

II-A-14 Doubled Digit (IWE), Rarity Level: 2-6, Values: $2 up.

II-A-15 Wrong Style or Font Letter or Digit (IE), Rarity Level: 3-5, Values: Minimal.

II–A–1

II–A–2

II–A–2

II-A-16 One Style or Font Over Another (IE), Rarity Level: 4-6, Values: $10 up.

II-A-17 Letter Over Digit (E), Rarity Level: 6-7, Values: $25 up.

II-A-18 Digit Over Letter (E), Rarity Level: 6-7, Values: $25 up.

II-A-19 Omitted Letter or Digit (IWE), Rarity Level: 4-6, Values: $5 up.

II-A-20 Blundered Letter (E), Rarity Level: 6-7, Values: $50 up.

II-A-21 Corrected Blundered Letter (IE), Rarity Level: 1-3, Values: $10 up.

II-A-22 Doubled Letter (IWE), Rarity Level: 2-6, Values: $2 up.

II-A-23 Blundered Design Element (IE), Rarity Level: 6-7, Values: $50 up.

II-A-24 Corrected Blundered Design Element (IE), Rarity Level: 3-5, Values: $10 up.

II-A-25 Large Over Small Design Element (IE), Rarity Level: 4-6, Values: $2 up.

II-A-26 Omitted Design Element (IWE), Rarity Level: 5-7, Values: $10 up.

II-A-27 Doubled Design Element (IWE), Rarity Level: 2-6, Values: $2 up.

II-A-28 One Design Element Over Another (IE), Rarity Level: 3-6, Values: $5 up.

II-A-29 Reducing Lathe Doubling (WE), Rarity Level: 6-7, Values: $50 up.

II-A-30 Extra Design Element (IE), Rarity Level: 3-5, Values: $10 up.

II-A-31 Modified Design (IWE), Rarity Level: 1-5, Values: No Value up.

II-A-32 Normal Design (I), Rarity Level: 1, Values: No Extra Value.

II-A-33 Design Mistake (IE), Rarity Level: 2-6, Values: $1 up.

II-A-34 Defective Die Design (IWE), Rarity Level: 1, Values: No Value.

II-A-35 Pattern (I), Rarity Level: 6-7, Values: $100 up.

II-A-36 Trial Design (I), Rarity Level: 5-7, Values: $100 up.

II-A-37 Omitted Designer's Initial (IWE), Rarity Level: 3-7, Values: $1 up.

II-A-38 Layout Mark (IE), Rarity Level: 5-7, Values: Minimal.

II-A-39 Abnormal Reeding (IWE), Rarity Level: 2-5, Values: $1 up.

II-A-40 Modified Die or Hub (IWE), Rarity Level: 1-5, Values: No Value up.

II-A-41 Numbered Die (I), Rarity Level: 3-5, Values: $5 up.

II-A-42 Plugged Die (IW), Rarity Level: 5-6, Values: Minimal.

II-A-43 Cancelled Die (IE), Rarity Level: 3-6, Values: No Value up.

II-A-44 Hardness Test Marked Die (IE), Rarity Level: 7, Values: $100 up.

II-A-45 Coin Simulation (IE), Rarity Level: 6-7, Values: $100 up, but may be illegal to own.

II-A-46 Punching Mistake (IE), Rarity Level: 2-6, Values: $1 up.

II-A-47 Small Over Large Design (IE), Rarity Level: 4-6, Values: $5 up.

II-A-48 Doubled Punch (IE), Rarity Level: 5-7, Values: $5 up.

II-A-49 Mint Display Sample (I) Rarity Level: 7, Values not established.

II-A-50 Center Dot, Stud or Circle (IE) Rarity Level: 7, much more common on early cents, Values not established

●HUB DOUBLING VARIETIES (II−B)

This section includes eight classes of hub doubling. Each class is from a different cause, described by the title of the class. At the latest count over 2,500 doubled dies have been reported in the U.S. coinage, the most famous being examples of the 1955, 1969-S and 1972 cent dies.

II-B-I Rotated Hub Doubling (WE), Rarity Level: 3-6, Values: $1 up

II-B-II Distorted Hub Doubling (WE), Rarity Level: 3-6, Values: $1 up.

II-B-III Design Hub Doubling (IWE), Rarity Level: 3-6, Values: $1 up to five figure amounts.

II-B-IV Offset Hub Doubling (WE), Rarity Level: 4-6, Values: $15 up.

II-B-V Pivoted Hub Doubling (WE), Rarity Level: 3-6, Values: $10 up.

II-B-VI Distended Hub Doubling (WE), Rarity Level: 2-5, Values: $1 up.

II-B-VII Modified Hub Doubling (IWE), Rarity Level: 2-5, Values: $1 up.

II-B-VIII Tilted Hub Doubling (WE), Rarity Level: 4-6, Values: $5 up.

●MINTMARK VARIETIES (II−C)

Mintmarks are punched into U.S. coin dies by hand (Up to 1985 for proof coins, to 1990 for cents and nickels and 1991 for other denominations). Variations resulting from mistakes in the punching are listed in this section. Unless exceptionally mispunched, values are usually estimated at 150 percent of numismatic value. Slightly tilted or displaced mintmarks have no value.

II-C-1 Doubled Mintmark (IE), Rarity Level: 2-6, Values: 50 cents up.

II-C-2 Separated Doubled Mintmark (IE), Rarity Level: 5-6, Values: $15 up.

II-C-3 Over Mintmark (IE), Rarity Level: 3-6, Values: $2 up.

II-C-4 Tripled Mintmark (IE), Rarity Level: 3-5, Values: 50 up.

II-C-5 Quadrupled Mintmark (IE), Rarity Level: 4-6, Values: $1 up.

II-C-6 Small Mintmark (IE), Rarity Level: 2-5, Values: No Extra Value up.

II-C-7 Large Mintmark (IE), Rarity Level: 2-5, Values: No Extra Value up.

II-C-8 Large Over Small Mintmark (IE), Rarity Level: 2-5, Values: $2 up.

II-C-9 Small Over Large Mintmark (IE), Rarity Level: 3-6, Values: $5 up.

II-C-10 Broken Mintmark Punch (W), Rarity Level: 5-6, Values: $5 up.

II-C-11 Omitted Mintmark (IWE), Rarity Level: 4-7, Values: $125 up.

II-C-12 Tilted Mintmark (IE), Rarity Level: 5-7, Values: $5 up.

II-C-13 Blundered Mintmark (E), Rarity Level: 4-6, Values: $5 up.

II-C-14 Corrected Horizontal Mintmark (IE), Rarity Level: 4-6, Values: $5 up.

II-C-15 Corrected Upside Down Mintmark (IE), Rarity Level: 4-6, Values: $5 up.

II-C-16 Displaced Mintmark (IE), Rarity Level: 4-6, Values: $5 to $10.

II-C-17 Modified Mintmark (IWE), Rarity Level: 1-4, Values: No Extra Value up.

II-C-18 Normal Mintmark (I), Rarity Level: 1, Values: No Extra Value.

II-C-19 Doubled Mintmark Punch (I), Rarity Level: 6-7, Values: No Extra Value up.

II-C-20 Upside Down Mintmark (E) Rarity Level 6-7, Values: $5 up.

II-C-21 Horizontal Mintmark (E) Rarity Level 6-7, Values: $5 up.

II-C-22 Wrong Mintmark (E) Rarity Level 6-7, Values $15 up. (Example has a D mintmark in the date, but was used at Philadelphia.)

II-C-3

II-C-3

II-C-1

II-C-4

●DIE, COLLAR AND HUB CRACKS (II–D)

Cracks in the surface of the die allow coin metal to be forced into the crack during the strike, resulting in raised irregular lines of coin metal above the normal surface of the coin. These are one of the commonest forms of die damage and wear, making them easily collectible.

Collar cracks and hub cracks are added to this section because the causes and effects are similar or closely associated.

Die cracks, collar cracks and hub cracks are the result of wear and tear on the tools, with intentional use assumed for all classes.

II-D-1 Die Crack (W), Rarity Level: 1-3, Values: 10 to $1, $25 up on a proof coin with a rarity level of 6-7.

II-D-2 Multiple Die Cracks (W), Rarity Level: 1-3, Values: 25 cents to $2.

II-D-3 Head-To-Rim Die Crack (Lincoln Cent) (W), Rarity Level: 2-6, Values: 25 to $10 for multiple die cracks.

II-D-4 Split Die (W), Rarity Level: 5-6, Values: $10 up.

II-D-5 Rim-To-Rim Die Crack (W), Rarity Level: 2-5, Values: $1 up.

II-D-6 Collar Crack (W), Rarity Level: 4-6, Values: $10 up.

II-D-7 Hub Crack (W), Rarity Level: 3-5, Values: $1-$2.

●DIE BREAKS (II–E)

Breaks in the surface of the die allow coin metal to squeeze into the resulting holes, causing raised irregular areas above the normal surface of the coin. Die chips and small die breaks are nearly as common as the die cracks, but major die breaks, which extend in from the edge of the coin, are quite rare on the larger coins.

If the broken piece of the die is retained, the resulting design will be above or below the level of the rest of the surface.

II-E-1 Die Chip (W), Rarity Level: 1-2, Values: 10 to $1.

II-E-2 Small Die Break (W), Rarity Level: 1-3, Values: 10 to $2.

II-E-3 Large Die Break (W), Rarity Level: 3-5, Values: $1 to $50 and up.

II-E-4 Rim Die Break (W), Rarity Level: 2-3, Values: 25 cents to $5.

II-E-5 Major Die Break (WE), Rarity Level: 3-6, Values: $5 to $100 and up.

II-E-6 Retained Broken Die (W), Rarity Level: 3-5, Values: $1 to $10 and up.

II-E-7 Retained Broken Center of the Die (W), Rarity Level: 6-7, Values: $100 up.

II-E-8 Laminated Die (W), Rarity Level: 3-5, Values: 10 cents to $5.

II-E-9 Chipped Chrome Plating (W), Rarity Level: 4-5, Values: $10 to $25 on proofs.

II-E-10 Collar Break (W), Rarity Level: 4-6, Values: $5 to $25 and up.

II-E-11 Broken Letter or Digit on an Edge Die (W), Rarity Level: 4-6, Values: Minimal.

II-E-12 "Bar" Die Break (W), Rarity Level: 3-5, Values: 25 to $20.

II-E-13 Hub Break (W), Rarity Level: 4-6, Values: 50 to $10 and up.

●"BIE" VARIETIES (II–F)

A series of small die breaks or die chips in the letters of "LIBERTY" mostly on the wheat-reverse Lincoln cent are actively collected. The name results from the resemblance to an "I" between the "B" and "E" on many of the dies, but they are found between all of the letters in different cases. Well over 1,500 dies are known and cataloged. Numerous more recent examples are known.

II-F-1 ILI Die Variety (W), Rarity Level: 4-5, Values: 25 cents to $10.

II-F-2 LII Die Variety (W), Rarity Level: 3-5, Values: 50 cents to $15.

II-F-3 IIB Die Variety (W), Rarity Level: 3-5, Values: 50 cents to $15.

II-F-4 BIE Die Variety (W), Rarity Level: 3-5, Values: $1 to $20.

II-F-5 EIR Die Variety (W), Rarity Level: 3-5, Values: 50 to $15.

II-F-6 RIT Die Variety (W), Rarity Level: 4-5, Values: $2 to $25.

II-F-7 TIY Die Variety (W), Rarity Level: 4-5, Values: $5 to $30.

II-F-8 TYI Die Variety (W), Rarity Level: 4-5, Values: $2 to $25.

●WORN AND DAMAGED DIES, COLLARS AND HUBS (II–G)

Many dies are continued deliberately in service after they have been damaged, dented, clashed or show design transfer, since none of these classes actually affect anything but the appearance of the coin. The root cause is wear, but intent or mistakes may enter the picture.

II-G-1 Dented Die, Collar or Hub (IWE), Rarity Level: 3-5, Values: 25 to $5.

II-G-2 Damaged Die, Collar or Hub (IWE), Rarity Level: 3-5, Values: 25 to $5.

II-G-3 Worn Die, Collar or Hub (IWE), Rarity Level: 2-3, Values: No Extra Value to Minimal Value.

II-G-4 Pitted or Rusted Die, Collar or Hub (IWE), Rarity Level: 3-4, Values: No Extra Value, marker only.

II-G-5

II-G-5 Heavy Die Clash (IWE), Rarity Level: 4-5, Values: $1 to $10 and up.

II-G-6 Heavy Collar Clash (IWE), Rarity Level: 3-4, Values: $1 to $5 and up.

II-G-7 Heavy Design Transfer (IWE), Rarity Level: 3-4, Values: 10 cents to $1.

● DIE PROGRESSIONS (II–H)

The progression section consists of three classes. These are useful as cataloging tools for many different die varieties, but especially the die cracks and die breaks which may enlarge, lengthen or increase in number.

II-H-1 Progression (W), Rarity Level: 3-5, Values: $1 up.

II-H-2 Die Substitution (IW), Rarity Level: 2-4, Values: No Extra Value to Minimal Value.

II-H-3 Die Repeat (I), Rarity Level: 2-4, Values: No Extra Value to Minimal Value.

● DIE SCRATCHES, POLISHED AND ABRADED DIES (II–I)

This section consists of those classes having to do with the use of an abrasive in some form to intentionally polish proof dies, or repair the circulating die surface. Several classes which previously were referred to as "polished" now are listed as "abraded."

II-I-1 Die Scratch (IW), Rarity Level: 1-2, Values: No Extra Value to 10 cents to 25 cents, as a marker.

II-I-2 Polished (proof) Die (IW), Rarity Level: 1, Values: No Extra Value.

II-I-3 Abraded (Circulation) Die (IW), Rarity Level: 1-2, Values: No Extra Value up to $10.

II-I-4 Inside Abraded Die Doubling (IW), Rarity Level: 1-3, Values: No Extra Value to $1.

II-I-5 Outside Abraded Die Doubling (IW), Rarity Level: 1-3, Values: No Extra Value to $1.

II-I-6 Lathe Marks (IW), Rarity Level: 5-7, Values: No Extra Value, marker only.

Striking varieties

DIVISION III

Once the dies are made and the planchets have been prepared, they are struck by a pair of dies and become a coin. In this division, we list the misstrikes resulting from human or mechanical malfunction in the striking process. These are one-of-a-kind varieties, but there may be many similar coins that fall in a given class.

Multiples and combinations of classes must be considered on a case by case basis. The first several sections match the planchet sections indicated in the title.

● STRUCK ON DEFECTIVE ALLOY MIX PLANCHETS (III–A)

This section includes those classes of coins struck on planchets that were made from a defective alloy.

III-A-1 Struck on an Improper Alloy Mix Planchet (IE), Rarity Level: 2-3, Values: 10 cents to $2.

III-A-2 Struck on a Planchet With Slag Inclusions(IE), Rarity Level: 5-6, Values: $10 up.

● STRUCK ON DAMAGED, DEFECTIVE OR ABNORMAL PLANCHET (III–B)

Coins get struck on many strange objects. The more common of course are planchets which have been damaged in some way in the production process. In most of the classes in this section intent is at least presumed, if not specifically listed as a cause.

III-B-1 Struck on a Defective Planchet (IWE), Rarity Level: 4-6, Values: $5 to $10 and up.

III-B-2 Struck on a Mechanically Damaged Planchet (IWE), Rarity Level: 5-6, Values: $10 to $20 and up.

III-B-3 Struck on a Rolled Thin Planchet (IWE), Rarity Level: 5-6, Values: $2 to $5 and up.

III-B-4 Struck on a Rolled Thick Planchet (IWE), Rarity Level: 5-6, Values: $35 to $50 and up.

III-B-5 Struck on a Tapered Planchet (WE), Rarity Level: 4-6, Values: $2 to $5 and up.

III-B-6 Struck on a Partially Unplated Planchet (WE), Rarity Level: 5, Values: $10 up.

III-B-7 Struck on an Unplated Planchet (WE), Rarity Level: 6-7, Values: $100 up.

III-B-11

III-B-19

III-B-29

III-B-8 Struck on a Bubbled Plating Planchet (IWE), Rarity Level: 1, Values: No Value.

III-B-9 Struck on an Included Gas Bubble Planchet (WE), Rarity Level: 5-6, Values: $5 up.

III-B-10 Struck on a Partially Unclad Planchet (WE), Rarity Level: 5-6, Values: $5 up.

III-B-11 Struck on an Unclad Planchet (WE), Rarity Level: 4-5, Values: $5 and up.

III-B-12 Struck on an Undersize Planchet (WE), Rarity Level: 4-6, Values: Minimal.

III-B-13 Struck on an Oversize Planchet (WE), Rarity Level: 6-7, Values: Minimal.

III-B-14 Struck on an Improperly Prepared Proof Planchet (IWE), Rarity Level: 3-5, Values: $5 up.

III-B-15 Struck on an Improperly Annealed Planchet (IWE), Rarity Level: 4-5, Values: $5 up.

III-B-16 Struck on a Faulty Upset Edge Planchet (IWE), Rarity Level: 4-5, Values: $1 to $2.

III-B-17 Struck on a Rolled In Metal Planchet (WE), Rarity Level: 4-6, Values: $2 up.

III-B-18 Struck on a Weld Area Planchet (WE), Rarity Level: 6, Values: $25 to $50.

III-B-19 Struck on a Strike Clip Planchet (W), Rarity Level: 6-7, Values: $25 up.

III-B-20 Struck on an Unpunched Center Hole Planchet (WE), Rarity Level: 4-6, Values: $1 and up.

III-B-21 Struck on an Incompletely Punched Center Hole Planchet (WE), Rarity Level: 6-7, Values: $5 up.

III-B-22 Struck on an Uncentered Center Hole Planchet (WE), Rarity Level: 6-7, Values: $10 up.

III-B-23 Struck on a Multiple Punched Center Hole Planchet (WE), Rarity Level: 7, Values: $25 up.

III-B-24 Struck on an Unintended Center Hole Planchet (WE), Rarity Level: 6-7, Values: $25 and up.

III-B-25 Struck on a Wrong Size or Shape Center Hole Planchet (WE), Rarity Level: 5-7, Values: $5 up.

III-B-26 Struck on Scrap Coin Metal (E), Rarity Level: 4-6, Values: $10 up.

III-B-27 Struck on Junk Non Coin Metal (E), Rarity Level: 4-6, Values: $15 up.

III-B-28 Struck on a False Planchet (E), Rarity Level: 3-5, Values: $35 up.

III-B-29 Struck on Bonded Planchets (E), Rarity Level: 6-7, Values: $50 up.

●STRUCK ON A CLIPPED PLANCHET (III–C)

Coins struck on clipped blanks, or planchets, exhibit the same missing areas as they did before striking, modified by the metal flow from the strike which rounds the edges and tends to move metal into the missing areas. Values for blanks will run higher than planchets with similar clips.

III-C-3

III-C-1 Struck on a Disc Clip Planchet (WE), Rarity Level: 4-5, Values: $1 on regular coins, $20 and up for clad coins.

III-C-2 Struck on a Curved Clip Planchet - to 5% (WE), Rarity Level: 3-5, Values: 50 cents up.

III-C-3 Struck on a Curved Clip Planchet - (6 to 10%) (WE), Rarity Level: 4-5, Values: $1 up.

III-C-4 Struck on a Curved Clip Planchet - (11 to 25%) (WE), Rarity Level: 4-5, Values: $2 up.

III-C-5 Struck on a Curved Clip Planchet - (26 to 60%) (WE), Rarity Level: 4-6, Values: $10 up.

III-C-6 Struck on a Double Curved Clip Planchet (WE), Rarity Level: 3-4, Values: $2 up.

III-C-7 Struck on a Triple Curved Clip Planchet (WE), Rarity Level: 4-5, Values: $5 up.

III-C-8 Struck on a Multiple Curved Clip Planchet (WE), Rarity Level: 4-6, Values: $5 up.

III-C-9 Struck on an Overlapping Curved Clipped Planchet (WE), Rarity Level: 5-6, Values: $15 up.

III-C-10 Struck on an Incomplete Curved Clip Planchet (WE), Rarity Level: 4-5, Values: $10 up.

III-C-11 Struck on an Oval Clip Planchet (WE), Rarity Level: 5-6, Values: $20 up.

III-C-12 Struck on a Crescent Clip Planchet - (61% or more) (WE), Rarity Level: 6-7, Values: $100 up.

III-C-13 Struck on a Straight Clip Planchet (E), Rarity Level: 4-6, Values: $10 up.

III-C-14 Struck on an Incomplete Straight Clip Planchet (WE), Rarity Level: 5-6, Values: $20 up.

III-C-15 Struck on a Ragged Clip Planchet (E), Rarity Level: 4-6, Values: $15 up.

III-C-16 Struck on an Outside Corner Clip Planchet (E), Rarity Level: 7, Values: $100 up.

III-C-17 Struck on an Inside Corner Clip Planchet (E), Rarity Level: Unknown outside mint., Values: -.

III-C-18 Struck on an Irregularly Clipped Planchet (E), Rarity Level: 6-7, Values: $20 up.

III-C-19 Struck on an Incompletely Punched Scalloped or Multi-Sided Planchet (E), Rarity Level: 7, Values: $20 up.

III-C-15

●STRUCK ON A LAMINATED, SPLIT OR BROKEN PLANCHET (III–D)

This section has to do with the splitting, cracking or breaking of a coin parallel to the faces of the coin, or at least very nearly parallel, or breaks at right angles to the faces of the coin.

Lamination cracks and missing metal of any size below a split planchet are too common in the 35-percent silver 1942-1945 nickels to be collectible or have any significant value.

III-D-1 Struck on a Small Lamination Crack Planchet (W), Rarity Level: 3-4, Values: 10 up.

III-D-2 Struck on a Large Lamination Crack Planchet (W), Rarity Level: 3-6, Values: $1 up.

III-D-3 Struck on a Split Planchet (W), Rarity Level: 4-6, Values: $5 up.

III-D-4 Struck on a Hinged Split Planchet (W), Rarity Level: 5-6, Values: $35 up.

III-D-5 Struck on a Planchet With a Clad Layer Missing (W), Rarity Level: 4-5, Values: $15 up.

III-D-6 Struck on a Planchet With Both Clad Layers Missing (W), Rarity Level: 4-5, Values: $25 up.

III-D-7

III-E-2

III-D-7 Struck on a Separated Clad Layer or Lamination (W), Rarity Level: 6-7, Values: $75 up.

III-D-8 Struck on a Broken Planchet Before the Strike (W), Rarity Level: 3-5, Values: $10 up.

III-D-9 Broken Coin During or After the Strike (W), Rarity Level: 4-6, Values: $20 up.

III-D-10 Struck Coin Fragment Split or Broken During or After the Strike (W), Rarity Level: 3-5, Values: $5 up.

III-D-11 Reedless Coin Broken During or After the Strike (W), Rarity Level: Unknown, Values: -.

●STRUCK ON WRONG STOCK PLANCHETS (III-E)

These classes cover those cases where the wrong stock was run through the blanking press, making planchets of the correct diameter, but of the wrong thickness, alloy or metal or a combination of incorrect thickness and metal.

III-E-1 Struck on a Half Cent-Stock Planchet (IE), Rarity Level: Unknown, Values: No Value Established.

III-E-2 Struck on a Cent-Stock Planchet (IE), Rarity Level: Unknown, Values: No Value Established.

III-E-3 Struck on a Two-Cent-Stock Planchet (E), Rarity Level: Unknown, Values: -.

III-E-4 Struck on a Three-Cent-Silver Stock Planchet (E), Rarity Level: Unknown, Values: -.

III-E-5 Struck on a Three-Cent-Nickel Stock Planchet (E), Rarity Level: Unknown, Values: -.

III-E-6 Struck on a Half Dime-Stock Planchet (E), Rarity Level: Unknown, Values: -.

III-E-7 Struck on a Dime-Stock Planchet (E), Rarity Level: 5-6, Values: $20 up.

III-E-8 Struck on a Twenty-Cent-Stock Planchet (E), Rarity Level: Unknown, Values: -.

III-E-9 Struck on a Quarter-Stock Planchet (E), Rarity Level: 6, Values: $50 up.

III-E-10 Struck on a Half Dollar-Stock Planchet (E), Rarity Level: 6-7, Values: $100 up.

III-E-11 Struck on a Dollar-Stock Planchet (E), Rarity Level: 6-7, Values: $300 up.

III-E-12 Struck on a Token/Medal-Stock Planchet (E), Rarity Level: 7, Values: No Value Established.

III-E-13 Struck on a Wrong Thickness Spoiled Planchet (IWE), Rarity Level: 7, Values: $50 up.

III-E-14 Struck on a Correct Thickness Spoiled Planchet (IWE), Rarity Level: Unknown, Values: No Value Established.

III-E-15 Struck on a Cut Down Struck Token (IWE), Rarity Level: 6-7, Values: $50 up.

III-E-16 Struck on an Experimental or Pattern-Stock Planchet (IE), Rarity Level: 7, Values: $50 up.

III-E-17 Struck on a Proof-Stock Planchet (IE), Rarity Level: 7, Values: $100 up.

III-E-18 Struck on an Adjusted Specification-Stock Planchet (IE), Rarity Level: 3-7, Values: No Value to $5 and up.

III-E-19 Struck on a Trial Strike-Stock Planchet (IE), Rarity Level: Unknown, Values: No Value Established.

III-E-20 U.S. Coin Struck on a Foreign-Stock Planchet. (E), Rarity Level: 5, Values: $35 up.

III-E-7

III-G-18

III-E-21 Foreign Coin Struck on a Foreign-Stock Planchet (E), Rarity Level: 5-6, Values: $25 up.

III-E-22 Struck on a Non-Standard Coin Alloy (IE), Rarity Level: 4-7, Values: $20 up.

●Extra metal (III-F)

The term "extra metal" for the purpose of this section includes both extra metal added to the blank during the blanking operation and metal powder added to the planchet during the annealing operation.

III-F-1 Struck on a Type 1 Blank With Extra Metal (W), Rarity Level: Unknown, Values: -.

III-F-2 Struck on a Type 2 Planchet With Extra Metal (W), Rarity Level: 4-5, Values: $10 up.

III-F-3 Struck on a Sintered Coating Planchet (W), Rarity Level: 6-7, Values: $35 up.

●Struck on normal or abnormal blanks, or planchets (III-G)

This section includes coins struck on either a blank, as it comes from the blanking press, or as a planchet that has passed through the upsetting mill. Added to this section are those planchets which are normal until they are struck by the wrong dies. These differ from the wrong stock planchets because the wrong stock planchets are already a variety before they are struck.

III-G-1 Struck on a Type 1 Blank (IWE), Rarity Level: 4-6, Values: $10 up.

III-G-2 Struck on a Type 2 Planchet (I), Rarity Level: 1, Values: No Extra Value.

III-G-3 Struck on a Purchased Planchet (I), Rarity Level: 1, Values: No Extra Value.

III-G-4 Struck on a Mint-Made Planchet (I), Rarity Level: 1, Values: No Extra Value.

III-G-5 Struck on an Adjustment-Marked

Planchet (I), Rarity Level: 4-7, Values: Minimal, and may reduce value of coin in some cases.

III-G-6 Struck on a Hardness Test-Marked Planchet (I), Rarity Level: 6-7, Values: $10 up.

III-G-7 Wrong Planchet or Metal on a Half Cent Planchet (IE), Rarity Level: 5-7, Values: $100 up.

III-G-8 Wrong Planchet or Metal on a Cent Planchet (IE), Rarity Level: 3-6, Values: $25 up.

III-G-9 Wrong Planchet or Metal on a Nickel Planchet (E), Rarity Level: 4-6, Values: $35 up

III-G-10 Wrong Planchet or Metal on a Dime Planchet (E), Rarity Level: 4-6, Values: $50 up.

III-G-11 Wrong Planchet or Metal on a Quarter Planchet (E), Rarity Level: 4-6. Values: $100 up.

III-G-12 Wrong Planchet or Metal on a Half Dollar Planchet (E), Rarity Level: 6-7, Values: $500 up.

III-G-13 Wrong Planchet or Metal on a Dollar Planchet (E), Rarity Level: 7, Values: $500 up.

III-G-14 Wrong Planchet or Metal on a Gold Planchet (E), Rarity Level: 7, Values: $1000 up.

III-G-15 Struck on a Wrong Series Planchet (IE), Rarity Level: 6-7, Values: $1500 up.

III-G-16 U.S. Coin Struck on a Foreign Planchet (E), Rarity Level: 5-7, Values: $35 up.

III-G-17 Foreign Coin Struck on a U.S. Planchet (E), Rarity Level: 6-7, Values: $50 up.

III-G-18 Foreign Coin Struck on a Wrong Foreign Planchet (E), Rarity Level: 6-7, Values: $50 up.

III-G-19 Struck on a Medal Planchet (E), Rarity Level: 6-7, Values: $100 up.

III-G-20 Medal Struck on a Coin Planchet (IE), Rarity Level: 3-5, Values: $10 up.

III-G-21 Struck on an Official Sample Planchet (IE), Rarity Level: Unknown, Values: No Value Established.

III-G-22 Struck Intentionally on a Wrong Planchet (I), Rarity Level: 6-7, Values: Mainly struck as Presentation Pieces, full numismatic value.

III-G-23 Non-Proof Struck on a Proof Planchet (IE), Rarity Level: 6-7, Values: $500 up.

●STRUCK ON COIN METAL STRIP (III–H)

Pieces of the coin metal strip do manage at times to escape into the coin press.

III-H-1 (See I-H-1 Punched Coin Metal Strip), Rarity Level: Impossible, Values: -.

III-H-2 Struck on Chopped Coin Metal Strip (E), Rarity Level: 6-7, Values: $25 up.

●DIE ADJUSTMENT STRIKES (III–I)

As the dies are set up and adjusted in the coin press, variations in the strike occur until the dies are properly set. Test strikes are normally scrapped, but on occasion reach circulation.

III-I-1 Die Adjustment Strike (IE), Rarity Level: 5-6, Values: $35 up.

III-I-2 Edge Strike (E), Rarity Level: 5-6, Values: $10 to $20 and up.

III-I-3 Weak Strike (W), Rarity Level: 1, Values: No Extra Value.

III-I-4 Strong Strike (IWE), Rarity Level: 1, Values: No value except for the premium that might be paid for a well struck coin.

III-I-5 Jam Strike (IE), Rarity Level: 7, Values: $50 up.

III-I-6 Trial Piece Strike (I), Rarity Level: 6-7, Values: $100 up.

III-I-7 Edge-Die Adjustment Strike (I), Rarity Level: 5-7, Values: $5 up.

III-I-8 Uniface Strike (I), Rarity Level 7, Values: $50 up.

III-I-3

●INDENTED, BROCKAGE AND COUNTER–BROCKAGE STRIKES (III–J)

Indented and uniface strikes involve an extra unstruck planchet between one of the dies and the planchet being struck. Brockage strikes involve a struck coin between one of the dies and the planchet and a counter-brockage requires a brockage coin between one of the dies and the planchet.

A cap, or capped die strike results when a coin sticks to the die and is squeezed around it in the shape of a bottle cap.

III-J-1 Indented Strike (W), Rarity Level: 3-6, Values: $5 up.

III-J-2 Uniface Strike (W), Rarity Level: 3-5, Values: $15 up.

III-J-3 Indented Strike By a Smaller Planchet (WE), Rarity Level: 5-7, Values: $100 up.

III-J-4 Indented Second Strike (W), Rarity Level: 3-5, Values: $10 up, about the same as a regular double strike of comparable size.

III-J-5 Partial Brockage Strike (W), Rarity Level: 3-6, Values: $15 up.

III-J-6 Full Brockage Strike (W), Rarity Level: 3-6, Values: $5 up.

III-J-7 Brockage Strike of a Smaller Coin (WE), Rarity Level: 6-7, Values: $200 up.

III-J-8 Brockage Strike of a Struck Coin Fragment (WE), Rarity Level: 4-6, Values: $5 up.

III-J-9 Brockage Second Strike (WE), Rarity Level: 3-5, Values: $5 up.

III-J-10 Partial Counter-Brockage Strike (WE), Rarity Level: 3-5, Values: $10 up.

III-J-11 Full Counter-Brockage Strike (WE), Rarity Level: 5-7, Values: $100 up.

III-J-12 Counter-Brockage Second Strike (WE), Rarity Level: 4-6, Values: $10 up.

III-J-13 Full Brockage-Counter-Brockage Strike (WE), Rarity Level: 6-7, Values: $150 up.

III-J-14 Multiple Brockage or Counter-Brockage Strike (WE), Rarity Level: 5-7, Values: $100 up.

III-J-15 Capped Die Strike (WE), Rarity Level: 6-7, Values: $500 up.

III-J-16 Reversed Capped Die Strike (WE), Rarity Level: 7, Values: $1,000 up.

III-J-1

III-J-3

III-J-4

III-J-6

●Struck Through Abnormal Objects (III–K)

This section covers most of the objects or materials which might come between the planchet and the die and be struck into the surface of the coin. Unless noted, the materials - even the soft ones - are driven into the surface of the coin.

III-K-1 Struck Through Cloth (IWE), Rarity Level: 3-6, Values: $35 up.

III-K-2 Struck Through Wire (IWE), Rarity Level: 3-6, Values: $5 up.

III-K-3 Struck Through Thread (IWE), Rarity Level: 3-6, Values: $5 up.

III-K-4 Struck Through Dirt-and-Grease-Filled Die (IWE), Rarity Level: 1-4, Values: 10 cents to 25 cents up, but no value on a worn or circulated coin.

III-K-5 Struck Through a Dropped Filling (IWE), Rarity Level: 5-6, Values: $10 up.

III-K-6 Struck Through Wrong Metal Fragments (IWE), Rarity Level: 4-6, Values: $1 up.

III-K-7 Struck Through an Unstruck Planchet Fragment (IWE), Rarity Level: 3-5, Values: $1 up.

III-K-1

III-K-7

III-K-7

III-K-8

III-K-8

III-K-8 Struck Through a Rim Burr (IWE), Rarity Level: 3-5, Values: $1 to $2 and up.

III-K-9 Struck Through plit-Off Reeding (IWE), Rarity Level: 5-6, Values: $25 up.

III-K-10 Struck Through a Feed Finger (IWE), Rarity Level: 5-7, Values: $25 to $50 and up.

III-K-11 Struck Through Miscellaneous Objects (IWE), Rarity Level: 4-6, Values: $1 up.

III-K-12 Struck Through Progression (IWE), Rarity Level: 4-6, Values: $1 up.

Note: Some 1987 through 1994 quarters are found without mintmarks, classed as III-K-4, a Filled Die. Values depend on market conditions. Filled dies have value ONLY on current, uncirculated grade coins.

●DOUBLE STRIKES (III-L)

Only coins which receive two or more strikes by the die pair fall in this section and are identified by the fact that both sides of the coin are affected. Unless some object interferes, an equal area of both sides of the coin will be equally doubled.

The exception is the second strike with a loose die, which will double only one side of a coin, but is a rare form usually occurring only on proofs. A similar effect is flat field doubling from die chatter.

III-L-1 Close Centered Double Strike (WE), Rarity Level: 4-6, Values: $15 up.

III-L-2 Rotated Second Strike Over a Centered First Strike (WE), Rarity Level: 4-6, Values: $15 up.

III-L-3 Off-Center Second Strike Over a Centered First Strike (WE), Rarity Level: 4-6, Values: $15 up.

III-L-4 Off-Center Second Strike Over an Off-Center First Strike (WE), Rarity Level: 4-6, Values: $10 up.

III-L-5 Off-Center Second Strike Over a Broadstrike (WE), Rarity Level: 5-6, Values: $20 up.

III-L-6 Centered Second Strike Over an Off-Center First Strike (WE), Rarity Level: 5-6, Values: $50 up.

III-L-7 Obverse Struck Over Reverse (WE), Rarity Level: 5-6, Values: $25 up.

III-L-8 Nonoverlapping Double Strike (WE), Rarity Level: 5-6 Values: $20 up.

III-L-9 Struck Over a Different Denomination or Series (WE), Rarity Level: 6, Values: $300 and up.

III-L-10 Chain Strike (WE), Rarity Level: 6, Values: $300 up for the pair of coins that were struck together.

III-L-11 Second-Strike Doubling From a Loose Die (W), Rarity Level: 6-7, Values: $200 up.

III-L-12 Second-Strike Doubling From a Loose Screw Press Die (W), Rarity Level: 5-6, Values: $100 up.

III-L-13 Second Strike on an Edge Strike (WE), Rarity Level: 5-6, Values: $20 up.

III-L-14 Folded Planchet Strike (WE), Rarity Level: 5-7, Values: $100 up.

III-L-15 Triple Strike (WE), Rarity Level: 6-7, Values: $100 up.

III-L-16 Multiple Strike (WE), Rarity Level: 6-7, Values: $200 up.

III-L-17 U.S. Coin Struck Over a Struck Foreign Coin (WE), Rarity Level: 6-7, Values: $300 up.

III-L-18 Foreign Coin Struck Over a Struck U.S. Coin (WE), Rarity Level: 6-7, Values: $400 up.

III-L-19 Foreign Coin Struck Over a Struck Foreign Coin (WE), Rarity Level: 7, Values: $500 up.

III-L-20 Double Strike on Scrap or Junk (E), Rarity Level: 6, Values: $50 up.

III-L-21 Struck on a Struck Token or Medal (E), Rarity Level: 5-6, Values: $100 up.

III-L-22 Double-Struck Edge Motto or Design (E), Rarity Level: 6-7, Values: $200 up.

III-L-23 One Edge Motto or Design Struck Over Another (E), Rarity Level: 7, Values: $300 up.

III-L-24 Flat Field Doubling (W), Rarity Level: 2-3, Values: $1 to $5.

III-L-25 Territorial Struck over Struck U.S. Coin: (I) Rarity Level: 6-7, Values: $200 up.

III-L-26 Pattern Struck over Struck U.S. Coin: (I) Rarity Level: 6-7, Values: $200 up.

III-L-27 Pattern Struck over Struck Pattern:(I) Rarity Level 6-7, Values: $200 up.

III-L-28 Pattern Struck Over Foreign Coin:(I) Rarity Level 6-7, Values - $200 up.

●COLLAR STRIKING VARIETIES (III-M)

The collar is often referred to as the "Third Die," and is involved in a number of forms of misstrikes. The collar normally rises around the planchet, preventing it from squeezing sideways between the dies and at the same time forming the reeding on reeded coins.

If the collar is out of position or tilted, a partial collar strike results; if completely missing, it causes a broadstrike; if the planchet is not entirely between the dies, an off-center strike.

III-M-1 Flanged Partial Collar Strike (WE), Rarity Level: 5-6, Values: $20 up.

III-M-2 Reversed Flanged Partial Collar Strike (WE), Rarity Level: 6-7, Values: $35 up.

III-M-3 Tilted Partial Collar Strike (WE), Rarity Level: 5-6, Values: $20 up.

III-M-4 Centered Broadstrike (WE), Rarity Level: 5-6, Values: $5 up.

III-L-3

III-L-3

III-L-4

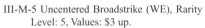

III–M–5   III–M–8

III-M-5 Uncentered Broadstrike (WE), Rarity Level: 5, Values: $3 up.

III-M-6 Reversed Broadstrike (WE), Rarity Level: 6, Values: $10 up.

III-M-7 Struck Off-Center 10-30% (W), Rarity Level: 3-6, Values: $3 up.

III-M-8 Struck Off-Center 31-70% (W), Rarity Level: 4-6, Values: $5 up.

III-M-9 Struck Off-Center 71% or More (W), Rarity Level: 3-5, Values: $2 up.

III-M-10 Rotated Multi-sided Planchet Strike (W), Rarity Level: 5-6, Values: $10 up.

III-M-11 Wire Edge Strike (IWE), Rarity Level: 1-2, Values: No Extra Value.

III-M-12 Struck With the Collar Too High (WE), Rarity Level: 6-7, Values: $20 up.

III-M-13 Off-Center Slide Strike (W), Rarity Level:3-6 $4 up.

●MISALIGNED AND ROTATED (DIE) STRIKE VARIETIES (III–N)

One (rarely both) of the dies may be Offset Misaligned, off to one side, or may be tilted (Vertically Misaligned). One die may either have been installed so that it is turned in relation to the other die, or may turn in the holder, or the shank may break allowing the die face to rotate in relation to the opposing die.

Vertical misaligned dies are rarely found, and like rotated dies, find only limited collector interest. Ninety and 180 degree rotations are the most popular. Rotations of 14 degrees or less have no value. The 1989-D Congress dollar is found with a nearly 180 degree rotated reverse, currently retailing for around $2,000. Only about 30 have been reported to date.

III-N-1 Offset Die Misalignment Strike (WE), Rarity Level: 3-5, Values: $2 up.

III-N-2 Vertical Die Misalignment Strike (WE), Rarity Level: 4-6, Values: $1 up.

III-N-3 Rotated Die Strike - 15 to 45 Degrees (IWE), Rarity Level: 4-6, Values: $2 up.

III-N-4 Rotated Die Strike - 46 to 135 Degrees (IWE), Rarity Level: 5-6, Values: $10 up.

III-N-5 Rotated Die Strike - 136 to 180 Degrees (IWE), Rarity Level: 5-6, Values: $25 up.

●LETTERED AND DESIGN EDGE STRIKE VARIETIES (III–O)

Early U.S. coins and a number of foreign coins have either lettered edges, or designs on the edge of the coin. Malfunctions of the application of the motto or design to the edge fall in this section.

III-O-1 Overlapping Edge Motto or Design (WE), Rarity Level: 3-4, Values: $5 to $10 and up.

III-O-2 Wrong Edge Motto or Design (WE), Rarity Level: 5-6-7, Values: $50 up.

III-O-3 Missing Edge Motto, Design or Security Edge (IWE), Rarity Level: 5-6-7, Values: $50 up.

III-O-4 Jammed Edge Die Strike (W), Rarity Level: 6, Values: $10 up.

III-O-5 Misplaced Segment of an Edge Die (E), Rarity Level: 4-7, Values: $25 up.

III-O-6 Reeded Edge Struck Over a Lettered Edge (IE), Rarity Level: 3-6, Values: No Extra Value up.

●DEFECTIVE STRIKES AND MISMATCHED DIES (III–P)

The final section of the Striking Division covers coins which are not properly struck for reasons other than those in previous classes, such as coins struck with mismatched (muled) dies. The mismatched die varieties must be taken on a case by case basis, while the otherclasses presently have little collector demand or premium.

III-P-1 Defective Strike (WE), Rarity Level: 1, Values: No Extra Value.

III-P-2 Mismatched Die Strike (E), Rarity Level: 4-7, Values: $25 up.

III-P-3 Single-Strike Proof (WE), Rarity Level: 4-5, Values: Minimal.

III-P-4 Single Die-Proof Strike (IE), Rarity Level: 5-6, Values: $100 up.

III-P-5 Reversed Die Strike (I), Rarity Level: 4-5, Values: No Extra Value to Minimal.

Official Mint modifications

DIVISION IV

Several mint produced varieties occur after the coin has been struck, resulting in the addition of the fourth division to my PDS System. Since most of these coins are either unique or are special varieties, each one must be taken on a case by case basis. All classes listed here are by definition intentional.

I have not listed values as the coins falling in these classes which are sold through regular numismatic channels, are cataloged with the regular issues or are covered in specialized catalogs in their particular area.

●MATTE PROOFS (IV-A)

Matte proofs as a section include several of the forms of proof coins which have the striking characteristics of a mirror proof but have been treated AFTER striking to give them a grainy, non-reflective surface.

IV-A-1 Matte Proof (I), Rarity Level: 3-5, Values: Normal Numismatic Value.

IV-A-2 Matte Proof on One Side (I), Rarity Level: 7, Values: Normal Numismatic Value.

IV-A-3 Sandblast Proof (I), Rarity Level: 4-6, Values: Normal Numismatic Value.

●ADDITIONAL ENGRAVING (IV-B)

This section includes any added markings which are placed on the struck coin and struck coins which later were cut into pieces for various purposes. The warning is repeated: Anything done to a coin after the strike is extremely difficult to authenticate and is much easier to fake than a die struck coin.

IV-B-1 Counterstamp and Countermark (I), Rarity Level: 3-6, Values: Normal Numismatic Value.

IV-B-2 Perforated and Cut Coins (I), Rarity Level: 4-6, Values: Normal Numismatic Value.

●RESTRIKES (IV-C)

Restrikes cover a complicated mixture of official use of dies from a variety of sources. Whether or not some were officially sanctioned is always a problem for the collector.

IV-C-1 Restrike on the Same Denomination Planchet (I), Rarity Level: 4-6, Values: Normal Numismatic Value.

IV-C-2 Restrike on a Different Denomination or Series Planchet (I), Rarity Level: 4-6, Values: Normal Numismatic Value.

IV-C-3 Restrike on a Foreign Coin (I), Rarity Level: 6-7, Values: Normal Numismatic Value.

IV-C-4 Restrike on a Token or Medal (I), Rarity Level: 5-6, Values: Normal Numismatic Value.

IV-C-5 Restruck With the Original Dies (I), Rarity Level: 4-6, Values: Normal Numismatic Value.

IV-C-6 Restruck With Mismatched Dies (I), Rarity Level: 4-6, Values: Normal Numismatic Value.

IV-C-7 Copy Strike With New Dies (I), Rarity Level: 3-5, Values. Normal Numismatic Value.

IV-C-8 Fantasy Strike (I), Rarity Level: 4-6, Values: Normal Numismatic Value.

After strike modifications

DIVISION V

This division includes both modifications that have value to collectors – and those that don't. I needed a couple of divisions to cover other things that happen to coins to aid in cataloging them. This avoids the false conclusion that an unlisted coin is quite rare, when the exact opposite is more likely to be the case.

●COLLECTIBLE MODIFICATIONS AFTER STRIKE (V-A)

This section includes those classes having to do with deliberate modifications of the coin done with a specific purpose or intent which makes them of some value to collectors. Quite often these pieces were made specifically to sell to collectors, or at least to the public under the guise of being collectible.

V-A-1 Screw Thaler, Rarity Level: 5-6, Values: Normal Numismatic Value.

V-A-2 Love Token, Rarity Level: 3-6, Values: $10 up.

V-A-3 Satirical or Primitive Engraving, Rarity Level: 6-7, Values: $5 up.

V-A-4 Elongated Coin, Rarity Level: 2-7, Values: 50 cents to $1 and up.

V-A-5 Coin Jewelry, Rarity Level: 2-5, Values: $1 up.

V-A-6 Novelty Coin, Rarity Level: 1-3, Values: No Value up to $5 to $10.

V-A-7 Toning, Rarity Level: 3-6, Values: No value up, depending on coloration. Easily faked.

V-A-8 Mint Modification, Rarity Level: 4-7, Values: $5 up. Easily faked.

V-A-9 Mint Packaging Mistake, Rarity Level: 5-7, Values: Nominal $1. Very easily faked.

●ALTERATIONS AND DAMAGE AFTER THE STRIKE(V-B)

This section includes those changes in a coin which have no collector value. In most cases their effect on the coin is to reduce or entirely eliminate any collector value - and in the case of counterfeits they are actually illegal to even own.

V-B-1 Machine Doubling Damage: NOTE: Machine doubling damage is defined as: "Damage to a coin after the strike, due to die bounce or chatter or die displacement, showing on the struck coin as scrapes on the sides of the design elements, with portions of the coin metal in the relief elements either displaced sideways or downward, depending on the direction of movement of the loose die." Machine doubling damage, or MDD, is by far the most common form of doubling found on almost any coin in the world. Rarity Level: 0, Values: Reduces the coin's value.

V-B-2 Accidental or Deliberate Damage, Rarity Level: 0, Values: Reduces the coin's value.

V-B-3 Test Cut or Mark, Rarity Level: 0, Values: Reduces value of coin to face or bullion value.

V-B-4 Alteration, Rarity Level: 0, Values: Reduces value to face or bullion value.

V-B-5 Whizzing, Rarity Level: 0, Values: Reduces value sharply and may reduce it to face or bullion value.

V-B-6 Counterfeit, Copy, Facsimile, Forgery or Fake, Rarity Level: 0, Values: No Value and may be illegal to own.

V-B-7 Planchet Deterioration. Very common on copper-plated zinc cents. Rarity level: 0, Values: No Value.

How to Grade

Better condition
equals better value

Grading is one of the most important factors in buying and selling coins as collectibles. Unfortunately, it's also one of the most controversial. Since the early days of coin collecting in the United States, buying through the mail has been a convenient way for collectors to acquire coins. As a result, there has always been a need in numismatics for a concise way to classify the amount of wear on a coin and its condition in general.

A look back

In September 1888, Dr. George Heath, a physician in Monroe, Mich., published a four-page pamphlet titled *The American Numismatist*. Publication of subsequent issues led to the founding of the American Numismatic Association, and *The Numismatist*, as it's known today, is the association's official journal. Heath's first issues were largely devoted to selling world coins from his collection. There were no formal grades listed with the coins and their prices, but the following statement by Heath indicates that condition was a consideration for early collectors:

"The coins are in above average condition," Heath wrote, "and so confident am I that they will give satisfaction, that I agree to refund the money in any unsatisfactory sales on the return of the coins."

As coin collecting became more popular and *The Numismatist* started accepting paid advertising from others, grading became more formal. The February 1892 issue listed seven "classes" for the condition of coins (from worst to best): mutilated, poor, fair, good, fine, uncirculated, and proof. Through the years, the hobby has struggled with developing a grading system that would be accepted by all and could apply to all coins. The hobby's growth was accompanied by a desire for more grades, or classifications, to more precisely define a coin's condition. The desire for more precision, however, was at odds with the basic concept of grading: to provide a concise method for classifying a coin's condition.

For example, even the conservatively few classifications of 1892 included fudge factors.

"To give flexibility to this classification," *The Numismatist* said, "such modification of find, good and fair, as 'extremely,' 'very,' 'almost,' etc., are used to express slight variations from the general condition."

The debate over grading continued for decades in *The Numismatist*. A number of articles and letters prodded the ANA to write grading guidelines and endorse them as the association's official standards. Some submitted specific suggestions for terminology and accompanying standards for each grade. But grading remained a process of "instinct" gained through years of collecting or dealing experience.

A formal grading guide in book form finally appeared in 1958, but it was the work of two individuals rather than the ANA, *A Guide to the Grading of United States Coins* by Martin R. Brown and John W. Dunn was a break-through in the great grading debate. Now collectors had a reference that gave them specific guidelines for specific coins and could be studied and restudied at home.

The first editions of Brown and Dunn carried text only, no illustrations. For the fourth edition, in 1964, publication was assumed by Whitman Publishing Co. of Racine, Wis., and line drawings were added to illustrate the text.

The fourth edition listed six principal categories for circulated coins (from worst to best): good, very good, fine, very fine, extremely fine, and about uncirculated. But again, the desire for more precise categories were evidenced. In the book's introduction, Brown and Dunn wrote, "Dealers will sometimes advertise coins that are graded G-VG, VG-F, F-VF, VF-XF. Or the description may be ABT. G. or VG plus, etc. This means that the coin in question more than meets minimum standards for the lower grade but is not quite good enough for the higher grade."

When the fifth edition appeared, in 1969, the "New B & D Grading System" was introduced. The six principal categories for circulated coins were still intact, but variances within those categories were now designated by up to four letters: "A," "B," "C" or "D." For example, an EF-A coin was "almost about uncirculated." An EF-B was "normal extra fine" within the B & D standards. EF-C had a "normal extra fine" obverse, but the reverse was "obviously not as nice as obverse due to poor strike or excessive wear." EF-D had a "normal extra fine" reverse but a problem obverse.

But that wasn't the end. Brown and Dunn further listed 29 problem points that could appear on a coin – from No. 1 for an "edge bump" to No. 29 for "attempted re-engraving outside of the Mint." The number could be followed by the letter "O" or "R" to designate whether the problem appeared on the obverse or reverse and a Roman numeral corresponding to a clock face to designate where the problem appears on the obverse or reverse. For example, a coin described as "VG-B-9-O-X" would grade "VG-B"; the "9" designated a "single rim nick"; the "O" indicated the nick was on the obverse; and the "X" indicated it appeared at the 10 o'clock position, or upper left, of the obverse.

The author's goal was noble – to create the perfect grading system. They again, however, fell victim to the age-old grading-system problem: Precision comes at the expense of brevity. Dealer Kurt Krueger wrote in the January 1976 issues of *The Numismatist*, "Under the new B & D system, the numismatist must contend with a minimum of 43,152 different grading combinations! Accuracy is apparent, but simplicity has been lost." As a result, the "New B & D Grading System" never caught on in the marketplace.

The 1970s saw two important grading guides make their debut. The first was

Photograde by James F. Ruddy. As the title implies, Ruddy uses photographs instead of line drawings to show how coins look in the various circulated grades. Simplicity is also a virtue of Ruddy's book. Only seven circulated grades are listed (about good, good, very good, fine, very fine, extremely fine, and about uncirculated), and the designations stop there.

In 1977 the longtime call for the ANA to issue grading standards was met with the release of *Official A.N.A. Grading Standards for United States Coins*. Like Brown and Dunn, the first edition of the ANA guide used line drawings to illustrate coins in various states of wear. But instead of using adjectival descriptions, the ANA guide adopted a numerical system for designating grades.

The numerical designations were based on a system used by Dr. William H. Sheldon in his book *Early American Cents*, first published in 1949. He used a scale of 1 to 70 to designate the grades of large cents.

"On this scale," Sheldon wrote, "1 means that the coin is identifiable and not mutilated – no more than that. A 70-coin is one in flawless Mint State, exactly as it left the dies, with perfect mint color and without a blemish or nick."

(Sheldon's scale also had its pragmatic side. At the time, a No. 2 large cent was worth about twice a No. 1 coin; a No. 4 was worth about twice a No. 2, and so on up the scale.)

With the first edition of its grading guide, the ANA adopted the 70-point scale for grading all U.S. coins. It designated 10 categories of circulated grades: AG-3, G-4, VG-8, F-12, VF-20, VF-30, EF-40, EF-45, AU-50, and AU-55. The third edition, released in 1987, replaced the line drawings with photographs, and another circulated grade was added: AU-58. A fourth edition was released in 1991.

Grading circulated U.S. coins

Dealers today generally use either the ANA guide or Photograde when grading circulated coins for their inventories. (Brown and Dunn is now out of print.) Many local coin shops sell both books. Advertisers in *Numismatic News*, *Coins* Magazine, and *Coin Prices* must indicate which standards they are using in grading their coins. If the standards are not listed, they must conform to ANA standards.

Following are some general guidelines, accompanied by photos, for grading circulated U.S. coins. Grading even circulated pieces can be subjective, particularly when attempting to draw the fine line between, for example, AU-55 and AU-58. Two long-time collectors or dealers can disagree in such a case.

But by studying some combination of the following guidelines, the ANA guide, and *Photograde*, and by looking at a lot of coins at shops and shows, collectors can gain enough grading knowledge to buy circulated coins confidently from dealers and other collectors. The more you study, the more knowledge and confidence you will gain. When you decide which series of coins you want to collect, focus on the guidelines for that particular series. Read them, reread them, and then refer back to them again and again.

AU-50

AU-50 (about uncirculated): Just a slight trace of wear, result of brief exposure to circulation or light rubbing from mishandling, may be evident on elevated design areas. These imperfections may appear as scratches or dull spots, along with bag marks or edge nicks. At least half of the original mint luster generally is still evident.

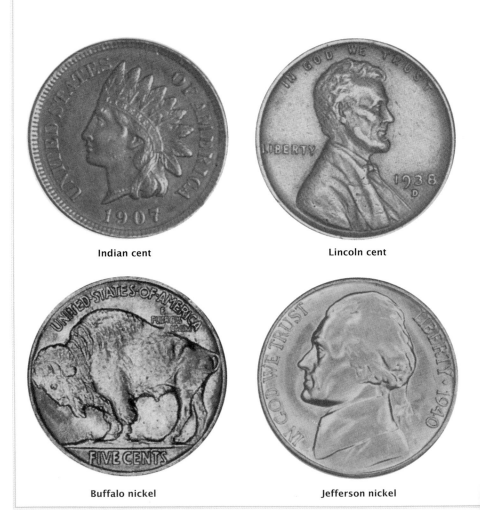

Indian cent

Lincoln cent

Buffalo nickel

Jefferson nickel

Mercury dime

Standing Liberty quarter

Washington quarter

Walking Liberty half dollar

Morgan dollar

Barber coins

XF-40

XF–40 (extremely fine): The coin must show only slight evidence of wear on the highest points of the design, particularly in the hair lines of the portrait on the obverse. The same may be said for the eagle's feathers and wreath leaves on the reverse of most U.S. coins. A trace of mint luster may still show in protected areas of the coin's surface.

Indian cent

Lincoln cent

Buffalo nickel

Jefferson nickel

Mercury dime

Standing Liberty quarter

Washington quarter

Walking Liberty half dollar

Morgan dollar

Barber coins

VF-20

VF-20 (very fine): The coin will show light wear at the fine points in the design, though they may remain sharp overall. Although the details may be slightly smoothed, all lettering and major features must remain sharp.

Indian cent: All letters in "Liberty" are complete but worn. Headdress shows considerable flatness, with flat spots on the tips of the feathers.

Lincoln cent: Hair, cheek, jaw, and bow-tie details will be worn but clearly separated, and wheat stalks on the reverse will be full with no weak spots.

Buffalo nickel: High spots on hair braid and cheek will be flat but show some detail, and a full horn will remain on the buffalo.

Jefferson nickel: Well over half of the major hair detail will remain, and the pillars on Monticello will remain well defined, with the triangular roof partially visible.

Mercury dime: Hair braid will show some detail, and three-quarters of the detail will remain in the feathers. The two diagonal bands on the fasces will show completely but will be worn smooth at the middle, with the vertical lines sharp.

Standing Liberty quarter: Rounded contour of Liberty's right leg will be flattened, as will the high point of the shield.

Washington quarter: There will be considerable wear on the hair curls, with feathers on the right and left of the eagle's breast showing clearly.

Indian cent

Lincoln cent

Buffalo nickel

Jefferson nickel

Walking Liberty half dollar: All lines of the skirt will show but will be worn on the high points. Over half the feathers on the eagle will show.

Morgan dollar: Two-thirds of the hair lines from the forehead to the ear must show. Ear should be well defined. Feathers on the eagle's breast may be worn smooth.

Barber coins: All seven letters of "Liberty" on the headband must stand out sharply. Head wreath will be well outlined from top to bottom.

Mercury dime

Standing Liberty quarter

Washington quarter

Walking Liberty half dollar

Morgan dollar

Barber coins

F-12

F–12 (fine): Coins show evidence of moderate to considerable but generally even wear on all high points, though all elements of the design and lettering remain bold. Where the word "Liberty" appears in a headband, it must be fully visible. On 20th century coins, the rim must be fully raised and sharp.

Indian cent

Lincoln cent

Buffalo nickel

Jefferson nickel

Mercury dime

Standing Liberty quarter

Washington quarter

Walking Liberty half dollar

Morgan dollar

Barber coins

VG-8

VG-8 (very good): The coin will show considerable wear, with most detail points worn nearly smooth. Where the word "Liberty" appears in a headband, at least three letters must show. On 20th century coins, the rim will start to merge with the lettering.

Indian cent

Lincoln cent

Buffalo nickel

Jefferson nickel

Mercury dime

Standing Liberty quarter

Washington quarter

Walking Liberty half dollar

Morgan dollar

Barber coins

G-4

G-4 (good): Only the basic design remains distinguishable in outline form, will all points of detail worn smooth. The word "Liberty" has disappeared, and the rims are almost merging with the lettering.

About good or fair: The coin will be identifiable by date and mint but otherwise badly worn, with only parts of the lettering showing. Such coins are of value only as fillers in a collection until a better example of the date and mintmark can be obtained. The only exceptions would be rare coins.

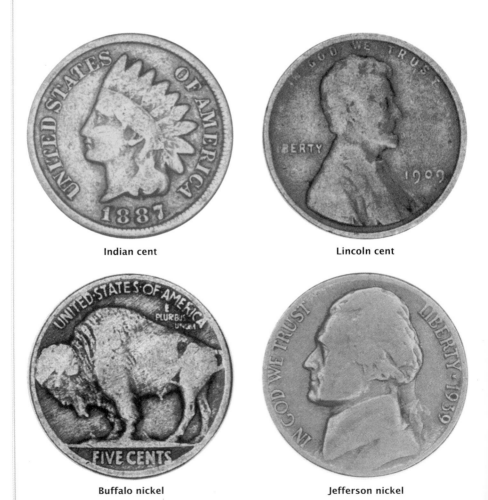

Indian cent

Lincoln cent

Buffalo nickel

Jefferson nickel

Mercury dime

Standing Liberty quarter

Washington quarter

Walking Liberty half dollar

Morgan dollar

Barber coins

Grading uncirculated U.S. coins

The subjectivity of grading and the trend toward more classifications becomes more acute when venturing into uncirculated, or mint-state, coins. A minute difference between one or two grade points can mean a difference in value of hundreds or even thousands of dollars. In addition, the standards are more difficult to articulate in writing and illustrate through drawings or photographs. Thus, the possibilities for differences of opinion on one or two grade points increase in uncirculated coins.

Back in Dr. George Heath's day and continuing through the 1960s, a coin was either uncirculated or it wasn't. Little distinction was made between uncirculated coins of varying condition, largely because there was little if any difference in value. When *Numismatic News* introduced its value guide in 1962 (the forerunner of today's Coin Market section in the *News*), it listed only one grade of uncirculated for Morgan dollars.

But as collectible coins increased in value and buyers of uncirculated coins became more picky, distinctions within uncirculated grade started to surface. In 1975 *Numismatic News* still listed only one uncirculated grade in Coin Market, but added this note: "Uncirculated and proof specimens in especially choice condition will also command proportionately higher premiums than these listed."

The first edition of the ANA guide listed two grades of uncirculated, MS-60 and MS-65, in addition to the theoretical but non-existent MS-70 (a flawless coin). MS-60 was described as "typical uncirculated" and MS-65 as "choice uncirculated." *Numismatic News* adopted both designations for Coin Market. In 1981, when the second edition of the ANA grading guide was released, MS-67 and MS-63 were added. In 1985 *Numismatic News* started listing six grades of uncirculated for Morgan dollars: MS-60, MS-63, MS-65, MS-65+, and MS-63 prooflike.

Then in 1986, a new entity appeared that has changed the nature of grading and trading uncirculated coins ever since. A group of dealers led by David Hall of Newport Beach, Calif., formed the Professional Coin Grading Service. For a fee, collectors could submit a coin through an authorized PCGS dealer and receive back a professional opinion of its grade.

The concept was not new; the ANA

Collectors have a variety of grading services to choose from. This set of Arkansas half dollars that appeared in an Early American History Auctions sale used two of the services.

had operated an authentication service since 1972 and a grading service since 1979. A collector or dealer could submit a coin directly to the service and receive a certificate giving the service's opinion on authenticity and grade. The grading service was the source of near constant debate among dealers and ANA officials. Dealers charged that ANA graders were too young and inexperienced, and that their grading was inconsistent.

Grading stability was a problem throughout the coin business in the early 1980s, not just with the ANA service. Standards among uncirculated grades would tighten during a bear market and loosen during a bull market. As a result, a coin graded MS-65 in a bull market may have commanded only MS-63 during a bear market.

PCGS created several innovations in the grading business in response to these problems:

1. Coins could be submitted through PCGS-authorized dealers only.

2. Each coin would be graded by at least three members of a panel of "top graders," all prominent dealers in the business. (Since then, however, PCGS does not allow its graders to also deal in coins.)

3. After grading, the coin would be encapsulated in an inert, hard-plastic holder with a serial number and the grade indicated on the holder.

4. PCGS-member dealers pledged to make a market in PCGS-graded coins and honor the grades assigned.

5. In one of the most far-reaching moves, PCGS said it would use all 11 increments of uncirculated on the 70-point numerical scale: MS-60, MS-61, MS-62, MS-63, MS-64, MS-65, MS-66, MS-67, MS-68, MS-69, and MS-70.

Numerous other commercial grading services followed in the steps of PCGS and third-party grading is an accepted part of the hobby.

How should a collector approach the buying and grading of uncirculated coins? Collecting uncirculated coins worth thousands of dollars implies a higher level of numismatic expertise by the buyer. Those buyers without that level of expertise should cut their teeth on more inexpensive coins, just as today's experienced collectors did. Inexperienced collectors can start toward that level by studying the guidelines for mint-state coins in the ANA grading guide and looking at lots of coins at shows and shops.

Study the condition and eye appeal of a coin and compare it to other coins of the same series. Then compare prices. Do the more expensive coins look better? If so, why? Start to make your own judgments concerning relationships between condition and value. Experience remains the best teacher in the field of grading.

Grading U.S. proof coins

Because proof coins are struck by a special process using polished blanks, they receive their own grading designation. A coin does not start out being a proof and then become mint state if it becomes worn. Once a proof coin, always a proof coin.

In the ANA system, proof grades use the same numbers as circulated and uncirculated grades, and the amount of wear on the coin corresponds to those grades. But the number is preceded by the word "proof." For example, Proof-65, Proof-55, Proof-45, and so on. In addition, the ANA says a proof coin with many marks, scratches or other defects should be called an "impaired proof."

5 Organization is Key

Sets worth more than accumulations

There are two major ways to organize a collection: by type, and by date and mint-mark. By following either method, you will create a logically organized set that other collectors perceive as having a value greater than a random group of similar coins

Let's take collecting by type first. Look at a jar of coins, or take the change out of your pocket. You find Abraham Lincoln and the Lincoln Memorial on current cents. You find Thomas Jefferson and his home, Monticello, on the nickel. Franklin D. Roosevelt and a torch share the dime. George Washington and the eagle, or the more recent state designs, appear on the quarter. John F. Kennedy and the presidential seal are featured on the half dollar.

Each design is called a "type." If you took one of each and put the five coins in a holder, you would have a type set of the coins that are currently being produced for circulation by the U.S. Mint.

With just these five coins, you can study various metallic compositions. You can evaluate their states of preservation and assign a grade to each. You can learn about the artists who designed the coins, and you can learn of the times in which these designs were created.

As you might have guessed, many different coin types have been used in the United States over the years. You may remember seeing some of them circulating. These designs reflect the hopes and aspirations of people over time. Putting all of them together forms a wonderful numismatic mosaic of American history.

George Washington did not mandate that his image appear on the quarter. Quite the contrary. He would have been horrified. When he was president, he headed off those individuals in Congress who thought the leader of the country should have his image on its coins. Washington said it smacked of monarchy and would have nothing to do with it.

Almost a century and a half later, during the bicentennial of Washington's birth in 1932, a nation searching for its roots during troubled economic times decided that it needed his portrait on its coins as a reminder of his great accomplishments and as reassurances that this nation was the same place it had been in prosperous days.

In its broadest definition, collecting coins by type requires that you obtain an example of every design that was struck by the U.S. Mint since it was founded in 1792. That's a tall order. You would be looking for denominations like the half cent, two-cent piece, three-cent piece, and 20-cent piece, which have not been produced in over a century. You would be looking for gold coins ranging in face value from $1 to $50.

But even more important than odd-sounding denominations or high face values is the question of rarity. Some of the pieces in this two-century type set are rare and expensive. That's why type collectors often divide the challenge into more digestible units.

Type collecting can be divided into 18th, 19th, 20th and 21st century units. Starting type collectors can focus on 20th century coin designs, which are easily obtainable. The fun and satisfaction of putting the 20th or 21st century set together then creates the momentum to continue backward in time. In the process of putting a 20th century type set together, one is also learning how to grade, learning hobby jargon, and discovering how to obtain coins from dealers, the U.S. Mint, and other collectors. All of this knowledge is then refined as the collector increases the challenge to himself.

This book is designed to help. How many dollar types were struck in the 20th century? Turn to the price-guide section and check it out. We see the Morgan dollar, Peace dollar, Eisenhower dollar, and Anthony dollar. The Sacagawea dollar arrived in 2000. Hobbyists could also add the Ike dollar with the Bicentennial design of 1976 and the silver American Eagle bullion coin struck since 1986. One can also find out their approximate retail prices from the listings. The beauty of type collecting is that one can choose the most inexpensive example of each type. There is no need to select a 1903-O Morgan when the 1921 will do just as well. With the 20th century type set, hobbyists can dodge some truly big-league prices.

As a collector's hobby confidence grows, he can tailor goals to fit his desires. He can take the road less traveled if that is what suits him. Type sets can be divided by denomination. You can choose two centuries of one-cent coins. You can take just obsolete denominations or copper, silver or gold denominations.

You can even collect by size. Perhaps you would like to collect all coin types larger than 30 millimeters or all coins smaller than 20 millimeters. Many find this freedom of choice stimulating.

Type collecting has proven itself to be enduringly popular over the years. It provides a maximum amount of design variety while allowing collectors to set their own level of challenge.

The second popular method of collecting is by date and mintmark. What this means, quite simply, is that a collector picks a given type – Jefferson nickels, for example – and then goes after an example of every year, every mintmark, and every type of manufacture that was used with the Jefferson design.

Looking at this method of collecting brings up the subject of mintmarks. The "U.S. Mint" is about as specific as most non-collectors get in describing the government agency that provides everyday coins. Behind that label are the various production facilities that actually do the work.

In two centuries of U.S. coinage, there have been eight such facilities. Four are still in operation. Those eight in alphabetical order are Carson City, Nev., which used a "CC" mintmark to identify its work; Charlotte, N.C. ("C"); Dahlonega, Ga. ("D"); Denver (also uses a "D," but it opened long after the Dahlonega Mint closed, so there was never any confusion); New Orleans ("O"); Philadelphia (because it was the primary mint, it used no mintmark for much of its history, but currently uses a "P"); San Francisco ("S"); and West Point, N.Y. ("W").

A person contemplating the collecting of Jefferson nickels by date and mintmark will find that three mints produced them: San Francisco, Denver and Philadelphia. Because the first two are branch mints serving smaller populations, their output has tended over time to be smaller than that of Philadelphia. This fact, repeated in other series, has helped give mintmarks quite an allure to collectors. It provides one of the major attractions in collecting coins by date and mintmark.

The key date for Jeffersons is the 1950-D when using mintages as a guide. In that year, production was just 2.6 million pieces. Because collectors of the time were aware of the coin's low mintage, many examples were saved. As a result, prices are reasonable.

The Depression-era 1939-D comes in as the most valuable regular-issue Jefferson nickel despite a mintage of 3.5 million – almost 1 million more than the 1950-D. The reason: Fewer were saved for later generations of coin collectors.

Date and mintmark collecting teaches hobbyists to use mintage figures as a guide but to take them with a grain of salt. Rarity, after all, is determined by the number of surviving coins, not the number initially created.

The Jefferson series is a good one to collect by date and mintmark, because the mintmarks have moved around, grown in size, and expanded in number.

When the series was first introduced, the Jefferson nickel was produced at the three mints previously mentioned. In 1942, because of a diversion of certain metals to wartime use, the coin's alloy of 75 percent copper and 25 percent nickel was changed. The new alloy was 35 percent silver, 56 percent copper, and 9 percent manganese.

To denote the change, the mintmarks were moved and greatly enlarged. The pre-1942 mintmarks were small and located to the right of Monticello; the wartime mintmarks were enlarged and placed over the dome. What's more, for the first time in American history, the Philadelphia Mint used a mintmark ("P").

The war's end restored the alloy and mintmarks to their previous status. The "P" disappeared. This lasted until the 1960s, when a national coin shortage saw all mintmarks removed for three years (1965-1967) and then returned, but in a different location. Mintmarks were placed on the obverse, to the right of Jefferson's portrait near the date in 1968. In 1980 the "P" came back in a smaller form and is still used.

Another consideration arises with date and mintmark collecting: Should the hobbyist include proof coins in the set? This can be argued both ways. Suffice to say that anyone who has the desire to add proof coins to the set will have a larger one. It is not necessary nor is it discouraged.

Some of the first proof coins to carry mintmarks were Jefferson nickels. When proof coins were made in 1968 after lapsing from 1965 to 1967, production occurred at San Francisco instead of Philadelphia. The "S" mintmark was placed on the proof coins of that year, including the Jefferson nickel, to denote the change. Since that time, mintmarks used on proof examples of various denominations have included the "P," "D," "S," and "W."

For all of the mintmark history that is embodied in the Jefferson series, prices are reasonable. For a first attempt at collecting coins by date and mintmark, it provides excellent background for going on to the more expensive and difficult types. After all, if you are ever going to get used to the proper handling of a coin, it is far better to experiment on a low-cost coin than a high-value rarity.

As one progresses in date and mintmark collecting and type collecting, it is important to remember that all of the coins should be of similar states of preservation. Sets look slapdash if one coin is VG and another is MS-65 and still another is VF. Take a look at the prices of all the coins in the series before you get too far, figure out what you can afford, and then stick to that grade or range of grades.

Sure, there is a time-honored practice of filling a spot with any old example until a better one comes along. That is how we got the term "filler." But if you get a few placeholders, don't stop there. By assembling a set of uniform quality, you end up with a more aesthetically pleasing and more valuable collection.

The date and mintmark method used to be the overwhelmingly dominant form of collecting. It still has many adherents. Give it a try if you think it sounds right for you.

Before we leave the discussion of collecting U.S. coins, it should be pointed out that the two major methods of organizing a collection are simply guidelines. They are not hard-and-fast rules that must be followed without questions. Collecting should be satisfying to the hobbyist. It should never be just one more item in the daily grind. Take the elements of these aproaches that you like and ignore the rest.

It should also be pointed out that U.S. coinage history does not start with 1792 nor do all of the coins struck since that time conform precisely to the two major organizational approaches. But these two areas are good places to start.

There are coins and tokens from the American Colonial period (1607-1776) that are just as fascinating and collectible as regular U.S. Mint issues. There are federal issues struck before the Mint was actually established. See the Colonial price-guide section in this book. There are error coins covered in Chapter 3.

There are special coins called commemoratives, which have been struck by the U.S. Mint since 1892 to celebrate some aspect of American history or a contemporary event. They are not intended for circulation. There was a long interruption between 1954 and 1982, but currently numerous commemoratives are being offered for sale directly to collectors by the Mint.

Collecting commemoratives has always been considered something separate from collecting regular U.S. coinage. It is, however, organized the same way. Commemoratives can be collected by date and mintmark or by type.

Current commemoratives can be purchased from the U.S. Mint. Check the Web site at www.usmint.gov or telephone (800) USA-MINT.

Buying coins from the Mint can be considered a hobby pursuit in its own right. Some collectors let the Mint organize their holdings for them. They buy complete sets and put them away. They never buy anything from anywhere else.

Admittedly, this is a passive form of collecting, but there are individuals around the world who enjoy collecting at this level without ever really going any deeper. They like acquiring every new issue as it comes off the Mint's presses.

Once done, there is a certain knowledge that one has all the examples of the current year. Obviously, too, collectors by date and mintmark of the current types would have to buy the new coins each year, but, of course, they do not stop there.

6 Glossary

Adjustment marks: Marks made by use of a file to correct the weight of overweight coinage planchets prior to striking. Adjusting the weight of planchets was a common practice at the first U.S. Mint in Philadelphia and was often carried out by women hired to weigh planchets and do any necessary filing of the metal.

Altered coin: A coin that has been changed after it left the mint. Such changes are often to the date or mintmark of a common coin in an attempt to increase its value by passing to an unsuspecting buyer as a rare date or mint.

Alloy: A metal or mixture of metals added to the primary metal in the coinage composition, often as a means of facilitating hardness during striking. For example, most U.S. silver coins contain an alloy of 10 percent copper.

Anneal: To heat in order to soften. In the minting process planchets are annealed prior to striking.

Authentication: The act of determining whether a coin, medal, token or other related item is a genuine product of the issuing authority.

Bag marks: Scrapes and impairments to a coin's surface obtained after minting by contact with other coins. The term originates from the storage of coins in bags, but such marks can occur as coins leave the presses and enter hoppers. A larger coin is more susceptible to marks, which affect its grade and, therefore, its value.

Base metal: A metal with low intrinsic value.

Beading: A form of design around the edge of a coin. Beading once served a functional purpose of deterring clipping or shaving parts of the metal by those looking to make a profit and then return the debased coin to circulation.

Blank: Often used in reference to the coinage planchet or disc of metal from which the actual coin is struck. Planchets or blanks are punched out of a sheet of metal by what is known as a blanking press.

Business strike: A coin produced for circulation.

Cast copy: A copy of a coin or medal made by a casting process in which molds are used to produce the finished product. Casting imparts a different surface texture to the finished product than striking and often leaves traces of a seam where the molds came together.

Center dot: A raised dot at the center of a coin caused by use of a compass to aid the engraver in the circular positioning of die devices, such as stars, letters, and dates. Center dots are prevalent on early U.S. coinage.

Chop mark: A mark used by Oriental merchants as a means of guaranteeing the silver content of coins paid out. The merchants' chop marks, or stamped insignia, often obliterated the original design of the host coin. U.S. Trade dollars, struck from 1873 through 1878 and intended for use in trade with China, are sometimes found bearing multiple marks.

Clash marks: Marks impressed in the coinage dies when they come together without a planchet between them. Such marks will affect coins struck subsequently by causing portions of the obverse design to appear in raised form on the reverse, and vice versa.

Clipping: The practice of shaving or cutting small pieces of metal from a coin in circulation. Clipping was prevalent in Colonial times as a means of surreptitiously extracting precious metal from a coin before placing it back into circulation. The introduction of beading and a raised border helped to alleviate the problem.

Coin alignment: U.S. coins are normally struck with an alignment by which, when a coin is held by the top and bottom edge and rotated from side-to-side, the reverse will appear upside down.

Collar: A ring-shaped die between which the obverse and reverse coinage dies are held during striking. The collar contains the outward flow during striking and can be used to produce edge reeding.

Commemorative: A coin issued to honor a special event or person. United States commemorative coins have historically been produced for sale to collectors and not placed in circulation, though the 50-states quarters are circulating commemoratives.

Copy: A replica of an original issue. Copies often vary in quality and metallic composition from the original. Since passage of the Hobby Protection Act (Public Law 93-167) of Nov. 29, 1973, it has been illegal to produce or import copies of coins or other numismatic items that are not clearly and permanently marked with the word "Copy."

Counterfeit: A coin or medal or other numismatic item made fraudulently, either for entry into circulation or sale to collectors.

Denticles: The toothlike pattern found around a coin's obverse or reverse border.

Die: A cylindrical piece of metal containing an incuse image that imparts a raised image when stamped into a planchet.

Die crack: A crack that develops in a coinage die after extensive usage, or if the die is defective or is used to strike harder metals. Die cracks, which often run through border lettering, appear as raised lines on the finished coin.

Device: The principal design element.

Double eagle: Name adopted by the Act of March 3, 1849, for the gold coin valued at 20 units or $20.

Eagle: Name adopted by the Coinage Act of 1792 for a gold coin valued at 10 units or $10. Also a name used to refer to gold, silver, and platinum coins of the American Eagle bullion coinage program begun in 1986.

Edge: The cylindrical surface of a coin between the two sides. The edge can be plain, reeded, ornamented, or lettered.

Electrotype: A copy of a coin, medal, or token made by electroplating.

Exergue: The lower segment of a coin, below the main design, generally separated by a line and often containing the date, designer initials, and mintmark.

Face value: The nominal legal-tender value assigned to a given coin by the governing authority.

Fasces: A Roman symbol of authority consisting of a bound bundle of rods and an axe.

Field: The flat area of a coin's obverse or reverse, devoid of devices or inscriptions.

Galvano: A reproduction of a proposed design from an artist's original model produced in plaster or other substance and then electroplated with metal. The galvano is then used in a reducing lathe to make a die or hub.

Glory: A heraldic term for stars, rays or other devices placed as if in the sky or luminous.

Grading: The largely subjective practice of providing a numerical or adjectival ranking of the condition of a coin, token, or medal. The grade is often a major determinant of value.

Gresham's law: The name for the observation made by Sir Thomas Gresham, 16th century English financier, that when two coins with the same face value but different intrinsic values are in circulation at the same time, the one with the lesser intrinsic value will remain in circulation while the other is hoarded.

Half eagle: Name adopted by the Coinage Act of 1792 for a gold coin valued at five units or $5.

Hub: A piece of die steel showing the coinage devices in relief. The hub is used to produce a die that, in contrast, has the relief details incuse. The die is then used to produce the final coin, which looks much the same as the hub. Hubs may be reused to make new dies.

Legend: A coin' principal lettering, generally shown along its outer perimeter.

Lettered edge: Incuse or raised lettering on a coin's edge.

Matte proof: A proof coin on which the surface is granular or dull. On U.S. coins this type of surface was used on proofs of the early 20th century. The process has since been abandoned.

Magician's coin: A term sometimes used to describe a coin with two heads or two tails. Such a coin is considered impossible in normal production due to physical differences in obverse and reverse die mountings, though as of 2001 two have been certified as genuine by professional coin authenticators. The vast majority are products made outside the Mint as novelty pieces.

Medal: Made to commemorate an event or person. Medals differ from coins in that a medal is not legal tender and, in general, is not produced with the intent of circulating as money.

Medal alignment: Medals are generally struck with the coinage dies facing the same direction during striking. When held by the top and bottom edge and rotated from side-to-side, a piece struck in this manner will show both the obverse and reverse right side up.

Mintage: The total number of coins struck during a given time frame, generally one year.

Mintmark: A letter or other marking on a coin's surface to identify the mint at which the coin was struck.

Mule: The combination of two coinage dies not intended for use together.

Numismatics: The science, study or collecting of coins, tokens, medals, paper money, and related items.

Obverse: The front or "heads" side of a coin, medal, or token.

Overdate: Variety produced when one or more digits of the date are re-engraved over an old date on a die at the Mint, generally to save on dies or correct an error. Portions of the old date can still be seen under the new one.

Overmintmark: Variety created at the Mint when a different mintmark is punched over an already existing mintmark, generally done to make a coinage die already punched for one mint usable at another. Portions of the old mintmark can still be seen under the new one.

Overstrike: A coin, token or medal struck over another coin, token, or medal.

Pattern: A trial strike of a proposed coin design, issued by the Mint or authorized agent of a governing authority. Patterns can be in a variety of metals, thicknesses, and sizes.

Phrygian cap: A close-fitting, egg-shell-shaped hat placed on the head of a freed slave when Rome was in its ascendancy. Hung from a pole, it was a popular symbol of freedom during the French Revolution and in 18th century United States.

Planchet: A disc of metal or other material on which the image of the dies are impressed, resulting in a finished coin. Also sometimes called a blank.

Proof: A coin struck twice or more from specially polished dies and polished planchets. Modern proofs are prepared with a mirror finish. Early 20th century proofs were prepared with a matte surface.

Prooflike: A prooflike coin exhibits some of the characteristics of a proof despite having been struck by regular production processes. Many Morgan dollars are found with prooflike surfaces. The field will have a mirror background similar to that of a proof, and design details are frosted like some proofs.

Quarter eagle: Name adopted by the Coinage Act of 1792 for a gold coin valued at 2.5 units or $2.50.

Reeding: Serrated (toothlike) ornamentation applied to the coin's edge during striking.

Relief: The portion of a design raised above the surface of a coin, medal, or token.

Restrike: A coin, medal or token produced from original dies at a later date, often with the purpose of sale to collectors.

Reverse: The backside or "tails" side of a coin, medal or token, opposite from the principal figure of the design or obverse.

Rim: The raised area bordering the edge and surrounding the field.

Series: The complete group of coins of the same denomination and design and representing all issuing mints.

Token: A privately issued piece, generally in metal, with a represented value in trade or offer of service. Tokens are also produced for advertising purposes.

Type coin: A coin from a given series representing the basic design. A type coin is collected as an example of a particular design rather than for its date and mint-mark.

Variety: Any coin noticeably different in dies from another of the same design, date and mint. Overdate and overmintmarks are examples of varieties.

Wire edge: Created when coinage metal flows between the coinage die and collar, producing a thin flange of coin metal at the outside edge or edges of a coin.

7 Treasures in Your Set?

Discover hidden value in ultra grades

If you like treasure hunts or believe in second chances, the dealer market is signaling it is time for both. Due to a shift in grading interpretations by commercial third-party grading services, modern commemorative coins that you bought 10 or 15 years ago from the U.S. Mint might now be worth more than you think. So get out your sets and start checking. It is even affecting Lincoln cents previously thought common.

Consider the 1986-W Statue of Liberty $5 gold piece. The proof version was sold to collectors for $170 each during the pre-issue discount period and the uncirculated version was sold for $160. They nearly tripled in price in trading on the secondary market in early 1986 before collapsing to $90, barely more than bullion value. Prices have stayed below issue price for many years. Even now, if you wanted to buy the coins on the ordinary secondary market, you probably wouldn't have to pay much more than $100 for either one. They look nice, housed as they are in the Mint's original acrylic plastic capsule. But what a difference it makes housed in a plastic slab with a new desirable grade of MS-70 or Proof-70 ultra cameo attached to it from a reputable third-party grading service. An MS-70 is retailing for $295, according to advertisements in *Numismatic News*, a popular weekly hobby newspaper. A Proof-70 UCAM is $350. With those kind of prices, it might be worth your while to pull out your coins and see if they might get the big money. The key, of course, is sending them in to third-party grading services. These services have rules you must follow and fees you must pay. In the end, your coins might not measure up to the new ultra-high grades.

What makes this new grading phenomenon so startling is that it applies to numerous commemorative issues that for many years had been considered common. Take the 1987-W Constitution $5 gold piece. This issue holds the mintage record for the gold $5 commemorative series. There are 214,225 uncirculated pieces and 651,659 proofs. In the original Mint holders they are trading for around $100, but put one in a slab with MS-70 or Proof-70 on it and the price becomes $260.

In effect, by checking over coins that you may have purchased years ago, you get a second shot at the brass ring of profit. After seeing the Statue of Liberty $5 coins soar, more than a few collectors ordered the 1987-W Constitution in hopes of a repeat performance. That didn't happen, but 16 years later, it might now be time to try again.

Throw in another factor, such as a much lower mintage, and prices go even higher. The 1997-W Franklin Delano Roosevelt $5 gold commemoratives are trading at hardly more than issue price in the $230-$250 range. But that's still more than double the ordinary Statue of Liberty and Constitution prices, reflecting the fact that mintages were lower. The uncirculated FDR $5 has a mintage of 11,805. The proof version is 29,233. Add the ultra-grade factor and the price of an MS-70 FDR $5 is $650. Do you have one in your set?

Even impatient people can get a reward. An issue as recent as the 2001-W Capitol Visitors Center $5 trades at $1,350. Its mintage is even lower than the FDR commemorative coins. The uncirculated version has a mintage of 6,761. The proof mintage is 27,652.

There is not enough space on these pages to list every single modern commemorative issue's turbocharged price in an ultra grade, but it is fair to generalize that these higher grades tend to raise the price significantly across the board. Even in the ultra grades, mintage numbers mean something. Lower mintages tend to mean higher prices.

It is also fair to say that this is a new hobby happening. When the 2003 edition of this book was assembled, nobody had ever heard of ultra-grade modern commemoratives. Condition rarity was something that was usually confined to older collector coins. Collectors, however, are nothing if not ingenious. If the concept can apply to Morgan dollars and Walking Liberty half dollars, why not the modern commemorative coins that have been struck since 1982? If the American Numismatic Association-created and sanctioned numerical grading system includes numbers up to 70, why not use them? It doesn't seem to matter that when the numerical grading system was introduced in 1977 the top numerical designation was considered to be nothing short of perfection. That accounts for the fact that for many years it was never assigned. That psychological barrier has been broken and the use of higher numbers with high price tags attached are now a fact of numismatic life.

A January 2003 auction saw a Proof-70 Deep Cameo 1963 cent sell for $39,100. The Proof-65 price is $1. With over three million 1963 proof sets to search, it is like a lottery. Will you be a prize winner?

So, what are you waiting for? If you are a loyal U.S. Mint customer with some of these issues put away, it is time to get them out and have them professionally evaluated to see if there are any ultra-grade treasures in your possession. It also pays to know that ultra grades are being applied to American Eagle gold and silver bullion coins, which have been struck since 1986, and to the 50-state quarter coins that began in 1999, and even to Roosevelt dimes. Because the hobby never stands still, it probably pays to keep an eye on every other coin series in your collection, for if it hasn't happened yet, the ultra grades will probably soon be applied to them also. For the long-suffering owner of a Statue of Liberty $5, the opportunity to more than double its value is in fact a hobby second chance.

UNITED STATES MINT ISSUES

HALF CENT

Liberty Cap. Head facing left.

KM# 10 Designer: Henry Voigt. **Diameter:** 22 **Weight:** 6.7400 g. **Composition:** Copper

Date	Mintage	G-4	VG-8	F-12	VF-20	XF-40	MS-60
1793	35,334	2,200	3,400	6,750	10,000	17,000	35,000

Head facing right.

KM# 14 Designer: Robert Scot (1794) and John Smith Gardner (1795). **Diameter:** 23.5 **Composition:** Copper **Weight:** 6.74 g. (1794-95) and 5.44 g. (1795-97) **Notes:** The "lettered edge" varieties have "Two Hundred for a Dollar" inscribed around the edge. The "pole" varieties have a pole upon which the cap is hanging, resting on Liberty's shoulder. The "punctuated date" varieties have a comma after the 1 in the date. The 1797 "1 above 1" variety has a second 1 above the 1 in the date.

Date	Mintage	G-4	VG-8	F-12	VF-20	XF-40	MS-60
1794	81,600	400	650	900	1,600	3,500	18,000
1795 lettered edge, pole	25,600	450	700	950	1,500	4,250	17,500
1795 plain edge, no pole	109,000	375	475	800	1,400	3,500	16,000
1795 lettered edge, punctuated date	Inc. above	475	700	1,000	1,600	3,750	20,000
1795 plain edge, punctuated date	Inc. above	350	450	750	1,200	3,000	27,500
1796 pole	5,090	16,000	20,000	23,500	30,000	35,000	—
1796 no pole	1,390	27,000	32,500	47,500	90,000	—	—
1797 plain edge	119,215	400	575	950	1,900	6,000	27,500
1797 lettered edge	Inc. above	1,700	2,700	4,000	8,000	25,000	—
1797 1 above 1	Inc. above	375	475	950	1,600	3,250	20,000
1797 gripped edge	Inc. above	16,000	37,500	48,000	60,000	70,000	—

Draped Bust Half Cent.
Draped bust right, date at angle below. Value within thin wreath.

KM# 33 Designer: Robert Scot. **Diameter:** 23.5 **Weight:** 5.4400 g. **Composition:** Copper **Notes:** The wreath on the reverse was redesigned slightly in 1802, resulting in "reverse of 1800" and "reverse of 1802" varieties. The "stems" varieties have stems extending from the wreath above and on both sides of the fraction on the reverse. On the 1804 "crosslet 4" variety, a serif appears at the far right of the crossbar on the 4 in the date. The "spiked chin" variety appears to have a spike extending from Liberty's chin, the result of a damaged die. Varieties of the 1805 strikes are distinguished by the size of the 5 in the date. Varieties of the 1806 strikes are distinguished by the size of the 6 in the date.

Stemless   Stems

Date	Mintage	G-4	VG-8	F-12	VF-20	XF-40	MS-60
1800	211,530	50.00	75.00	100.00	200	500	2,500
1802/0 rev. 1800	14,366	15,000	22,000	30,000	—	—	—
1802/0 rev. 1802	Inc. above	800	1,400	2,750	6,500	17,000	—
1803	97,900	45.00	70.00	125	275	950	7,000
1804 plain 4, stemless wreath	1,055,312	50.00	60.00	85.00	130	250	1,400
1804 plain 4, stems	Inc. above	45.00	75.00	125	250	1,500	12,000
1804 crosslet 4, stemless	Inc. above	50.00	75.00	85.00	125	250	1,350
1804 crosslet 4, stems	Inc. above	47.00	75.00	110	175	300	1,200
1804 spiked chin	Inc. above	60.00	90.00	125	175	325	1,200
1805 small 5, stemless	814,464	50.00	75.00	90.00	135	400	3,500
1805 small 5, stems	Inc. above	800	1,200	2,400	4,500	8,000	—
1805 large 5, stems	Inc. above	49.00	65.00	85.00	125	400	3,000

Date	Mintage	G-4	VG-8	F-12	VF-20	XF-40	MS-60
1806 small 6, stems	356,000	200	325	600	1,000	2,750	—
1806 small 6, stemless	Inc. above	50.00	65.00	85.00	125	235	1,350
1806 large 6, stems	Inc. above	50.00	65.00	85.00	125	250	1,200
1807	476,000	50.00	80.00	120	175	300	1,400
1808/7	400,000	300	400	600	1,200	6,000	27,500
1808	Inc. above	50.00	65.00	90.00	135	350	5,000

Classic Head Half Cent. Classic head left, flanked by stars, date below. Value within wreath.

KM# 41 Designer: John Reich. **Diameter:** 23.5 **Weight:** 5.4400 g. **Composition:** Copper **Notes:** Restrikes listed were produced privately in the mid-1800s. The 1831 restrikes have two varieties with different-size berries in the wreath on the reverse. The 1828 strikes have either 12 or 13 stars on the obverse.

Date	Mintage	G-4	VG-8	F-12	VF-20	XF-40	MS-60
1809/6	1,154,572	60.00	80.00	110	150	215	1,000
1809	Inc. above	32.00	40.00	55.00	80.00	215	800
1809 circle in 0	—	35.00	45.00	60.00	110	250	2,100
1810	215,000	45.00	60.00	120	200	600	3,250
1811	63,140	225	375	750	1,800	4,000	—
1811 restrike, reverse of 1802, uncirculated	—	—	—	—	—	—	27,500
1825	63,000	45.00	60.00	75.00	110	200	950
1826	234,000	40.00	55.00	75.00	90.00	200	750
1828 13 stars	606,000	40.00	60.00	75.00	85.00	110	300
1828 12 stars	Inc. above	50.00	80.00	120	175	250	850
1829	487,000	40.00	55.00	70.00	100.00	150	500
1831 original	2,200	5,500	7,500	11,000	16,500	22,500	—
1831 1st restrike, lg. berries, reverse of 1836	—	—	—	—	—	—	6,500
1831 2nd restrike, sm. berries, reverse of 1840, proof	—	—	—	—	—	—	25,000
1832	154,000	39.00	50.00	70.00	95.00	130	350
1833	120,000	39.00	50.00	70.00	95.00	130	350
1834	141,000	39.00	50.00	70.00	95.00	130	350
1835	398,000	39.00	50.00	70.00	95.00	130	350
1836 original, proof	—	—	—	—	—	—	6,000
1836 restrike, reverse of 1840, proof	—	—	—	—	—	—	20,000

Braided Hair Half Cent. Head left, braided hair, within circle of stars, date below. Value within wreath.

KM# 70 Designer: Christian Gobrecht. **Diameter:** 23 **Weight:** 5.4400 g. **Composition:** Copper **Notes:** 1840-1849 and 1852 strikes, both originals and restrikes, are known in proof only; mintages are unknown. The small-date varieties of 1849, both originals and restrikes are known in proof only. The Restrikes were produced clandestinely by Philadelphia Mint personnel in the mid-1800s.

Date	Mintage	G-4	VG-8	F-12	VF-20	XF-40	MS-60	Prf-60
1840 original	—	1,000	1,200	1,500	2,000	3,000	—	5,500
1840 1st restrike	—	1,000	1,200	1,500	2,000	3,000	—	6,500
1840 2nd restrike	—	1,000	1,200	1,500	2,000	3,000	—	5,500
1841 original	—	1,000	1,200	1,500	2,000	3,000	—	5,500
1841 1st restrike	—	1,000	1,200	1,500	2,000	3,000	—	6,500
1841 2nd restrike	—	1,000	1,200	1,500	2,000	3,000	—	6,000
1842 original	—	1,000	1,200	1,500	2,000	3,000	—	6,000
1842 1st restrike	—	1,000	1,200	1,500	2,000	3,000	—	6,000
1842 2nd restrike	—	1,000	1,200	1,500	2,000	3,000	—	6,000
1843 original	—	1,000	1,200	1,500	2,000	3,000	—	6,500
1843 1st restrike	—	1,000	1,200	1,500	2,000	3,000	—	6,000
1843 2nd restrike	—	1,000	1,200	1,500	2,000	3,000	—	6,500
1844 original	—	1,000	1,200	1,500	2,000	3,000	—	6,000
1844 1st restrike	—	1,000	1,200	1,500	2,000	3,000	—	6,000
1844 2nd restrike	—	1,000	1,200	1,500	2,000	3,000	—	6,000
1845 original	—	1,000	1,200	1,500	2,000	3,000	—	6,000
1845 1st restrike	—	1,000	1,200	1,500	2,000	3,000	—	6,000

Date	Mintage	G-4	VG-8	F-12	VF-20	XF-40	MS-60	Prf-60
1845 2nd restrike	—	1,000	1,200	1,500	2,000	3,000	—	6,000
1846 original	—	1,000	1,200	1,500	2,000	3,000	—	6,000
1846 1st restrike	—	1,000	1,200	1,500	2,000	3,000	—	6,500
1846 2nd restrike	—	1,000	1,200	1,500	2,000	3,000	—	6,000
1847 original	—	1,000	1,200	1,500	2,000	3,000	—	6,000
1847 1st restrike	—	3,000	4,000	4,500	5,000	5,500	—	8,000
1847 2nd restrike	—	1,000	1,200	1,500	2,000	3,000	—	6,000
1848 original	—	1,000	1,200	1,500	2,000	3,000	—	6,000
1848 1st restrike	—	1,000	1,200	1,500	2,000	3,000	—	6,000
1848 2nd restrike	—	1,000	1,200	1,500	2,000	3,000	—	6,000
1849 original, small date	—	1,000	1,200	1,500	2,000	3,000	—	6,500
1849 1st restrike small date	—	1,000	1,200	1,500	2,000	3,000	—	6,000
1849 large date	39,864	50.00	70.00	90.00	125	175	325	—
1850	39,812	45.00	60.00	90.00	150	200	400	—
1851	147,672	45.00	60.00	75.00	90.00	120	175	—
1852 original	—	12,000	25,000	30,000	35,000	40,000	—	90,000
1852 1st restrike	—	1,000	1,200	1,500	2,000	3,000	—	5,000
1852 2nd restrike	—	1,000	1,200	1,500	2,000	3,000	—	7,000
1853	129,694	50.00	75.00	90.00	125	160	300	—
1854	55,358	50.00	75.00	90.00	125	160	300	—
1855	56,500	50.00	75.00	90.00	125	160	300	—
1856	40,430	50.00	75.00	90.00	125	160	300	—
1857	35,180	80.00	100.00	200	250	300	500	—

CENT

Flowing Hair Cent. Chain.

KM# 11 **Designer:** Henry Voigt. **Diameter:** 26-27
Weight: 13.4800 g. **Composition:** Copper

Date	Mintage	G-4	VG-8	F-12	VF-20	XF-40	MS-60
1793	36,103	7,750	11,000	15,000	23,000	33,000	135,000

Flowing Hair Cent. Wreath.

KM# 12 **Designer:** Henry Voigt. **Diameter:** 26-28
Weight: 13.4800 g. **Composition:** Copper

Date	Mintage	G-4	VG-8	F-12	VF-20	XF-40	MS-60
1793	63,353	1,700	2,500	4,000	8,000	12,000	30,000

Liberty Cap Cent.

KM# 13 **Designer:** Joseph Wright (1793-1795)
and John Smith Gardner (1795-1796). **Diameter:**
29 **Composition:** Copper **Weight:** 13.48 g. (1793-
95) and 10.89 g. (1795-96) **Notes:** The heavier
pieces were struck on a thicker planchet. The Liberty
design on the obverse was revised slightly in 1794,
but the 1793 design was used on some 1794 strikes.
A 1795 "lettered edge" variety has "One Hundred for
a Dollar" and a leaf inscribed on the edge.

Date	Mintage	G-4	VG-8	F-12	VF-20	XF-40	MS-60
1793 cap	11,056	5,000	6,000	9,000	20,000	26,000	—
1794	918,521	350	485	750	1,200	3,750	9,000
1794 head '93	Inc. above	1,500	2,600	4,000	7,900	12,000	—
1795	501,500	350	485	650	1,000	2,000	4,750

Liberty Cap Cent.

KM# 13a Designer: Joseph Wright (1793-1795) and John Smith Gardner (1795-1796). **Diameter:** 29 **Weight:** 10.8900 g. **Composition:** Copper

Date	Mintage	G-4	VG-8	F-12	VF-20	XF-40	MS-60
1795 lettered edge, "One Cent" high in wreath	37,000	400	550	900	1,750	4,000	15,000
1796	109,825	350	500	800	1,400	3,750	21,000

Draped Bust Cent.
Draped bust right, date at angle below. Value within wreath.

KM# 22 Designer: Robert Scot. **Diameter:** 29 **Weight:** 10.9800 g. **Composition:** Copper **Notes:** The 1801 "3 errors" variety has the fraction on the reverse reading "1/000," has only one stem extending from the wreath above and on both sides of the fraction on the reverse, and "United" in "United States of America" appears as "Iinited."

Stemless   Stems

Date	Mintage	G-4	VG-8	F-12	VF-20	XF-40	MS-60
1796	363,375	350	600	850	1,800	3,400	—
1797	897,510	130	175	250	335	1,150	3,300
1797 stemless	Inc. above	300	495	600	910	3,200	—
1798	1,841,745	90.00	130	200	350	1,300	3,100
1798/7	Inc. above	200	300	375	1,200	3,900	—
1799	42,540	3,500	5,000	8,500	16,000	35,000	—
1800	2,822,175	50.00	95.00	200	400	1,750	—
1801	1,362,837	60.00	87.00	180	325	1,000	—
1801 3 errors	Inc. above	225	500	925	1,750	5,500	—
1802	3,435,100	50.00	75.00	150	250	775	2,250
1803	2,471,353	50.00	80.00	150	250	775	2,250
1804	96,500	1,400	2,000	2,600	3,200	7,000	—
1804 Restrike of 1860	—	400	500	700	900	1,100	1,500
1805	941,116	60.00	90.00	160	300	875	2,450
1806	348,000	70.00	100.00	150	375	1,100	4,700
1807	727,221	60.00	80.00	160	300	800	2,250
1807/6 large 7/6	—	60.00	80.00	160	350	1,275	—
1807/6 small 7/6	—	1,900	2,900	4,200	6,000	19,000	—

Classic Head Cent.
Classic head left, flanked bt stars, date below. Value within wreath.

KM# 39 Designer: John Reich. **Diameter:** 29 **Weight:** 10.8900 g. **Composition:** Copper

Date	Mintage	G-4	VG-8	F-12	VF-20	XF-40	MS-60
1808	1,109,000	125	200	325	575	1,200	3,600
1809	222,867	250	350	600	1,200	2,650	6,300
1810	1,458,500	75.00	95.00	210	550	1,100	3,850
1811	218,025	110	175	400	1,000	1,500	7,000
1811/10	Inc. above	130	200	440	1,200	2,200	—
1812	1,075,500	48.00	83.00	200	525	975	2,800
1813	418,000	60.00	175	400	800	1,200	—
1814	357,830	45.00	80.00	200	530	975	2,800

Coronet Cent. Coronet head left, within circle of stars, date below. Value within wreath.

KM# 45 **Designer:** John Reich. **Diameter:** 28-29 **Weight:** 10.8900 g. **Composition:** Copper **Notes:** The 1817 strikes have either 13 or 15 stars on the obverse.

Date	Mintage	G-4	VG-8	F-12	VF-20	XF-40	MS-60
1816	2,820,982	25.00	35.00	50.00	100.00	175	420
1817 13 stars	3,948,400	25.00	35.00	45.00	75.00	145	500
1817 15 stars	Inc. above	35.00	50.00	90.00	225	500	1,600
1818	3,167,000	25.00	30.00	35.00	60.00	125	270
1819	2,671,000	25.00	30.00	35.00	63.00	120	285
1820	4,407,550	25.00	30.00	35.00	65.00	120	300
1821	389,000	40.00	75.00	250	400	1,500	6,000
1822	2,072,339	25.00	35.00	50.00	100.00	195	750
1823 Included in 1824 mintage	—	90.00	200	310	690	2,750	—
1823/22 Included in 1824 mintage	—	80.00	110	300	675	2,450	—
1823 Restrike	—	600	750	850	1,000	1,200	2,000
1824	1,262,000	25.00	26.00	38.00	160	350	950
1824/22	Inc. above	35.00	45.00	100.00	400	975	3,600
1825	1,461,100	25.00	35.00	50.00	110	300	960
1826	1,517,425	25.00	35.00	40.00	84.00	175	750
1826/25	Inc. above	30.00	40.00	75.00	175	600	2,000
1827	2,357,732	25.00	35.00	40.00	75.00	160	750
1828	2,260,624	25.00	35.00	40.00	90.00	175	450
1829	1,414,500	25.00	35.00	40.00	90.00	175	475
1830	1,711,500	25.00	35.00	40.00	90.00	175	400
1831	3,359,260	25.00	35.00	40.00	80.00	175	315
1832	2,362,000	25.00	35.00	40.00	80.00	175	380
1833	2,739,000	25.00	35.00	40.00	80.00	175	300
1834	1,855,100	25.00	35.00	40.00	80.00	175	375
1835	3,878,400	25.00	35.00	40.00	80.00	200	300
1836	2,111,000	25.00	35.00	40.00	80.00	175	350
1837	5,558,300	25.00	30.00	40.00	80.00	175	300
1838	6,370,200	25.00	30.00	45.00	80.00	175	300
1839	3,128,661	30.00	40.00	65.00	90.00	175	350
1839/36	Inc. above	425	700	850	1,500	3,900	—

Braided Hair Cent. Head left, braided hair, within circle of stars, date below. Value within wreath.

KM# 67 **Designer:** Christian Gobrecht. **Diameter:** 27.5 **Weight:** 10.8900 g. **Composition:** Copper **Notes:** 1840 and 1842 strikes are known with both small and large dates, with little difference in value. 1855 and 1856 strikes are known with both slanting and upright 5s in the date, with little difference in value. A slightly larger Liberty head and larger reverse lettering were used beginning in 1843. One 1843 variety uses the old obverse with the new reverse.

Date	Mintage	G-4	VG-8	F-12	VF-20	XF-40	MS-60
1840	2,462,700	20.00	30.00	40.00	50.00	70.00	475
1841	1,597,367	20.00	30.00	40.00	50.00	80.00	440
1842	2,383,390	20.00	30.00	40.00	50.00	70.00	425
1843	2,425,342	20.00	30.00	40.00	50.00	75.00	445
1843 obverse 1842 with reverse of 1844	Inc. above	20.00	30.00	40.00	50.00	80.00	400
1844	2,398,752	20.00	30.00	40.00	50.00	75.00	300
1844/81	Inc. above	65.00	125	225	300	400	850
1845	3,894,804	20.00	30.00	40.00	50.00	75.00	250
1846	4,120,800	20.00	30.00	40.00	50.00	75.00	250
1847	6,183,669	20.00	30.00	40.00	50.00	75.00	250
1848	6,415,799	20.00	30.00	40.00	50.00	75.00	250
1849	4,178,500	20.00	30.00	40.00	50.00	75.00	325
1850	4,426,844	20.00	30.00	40.00	50.00	75.00	250
1851	9,889,707	20.00	30.00	40.00	50.00	75.00	200
1851/81	Inc. above	50.00	75.00	125	175	290	600
1852	5,063,094	20.00	30.00	40.00	50.00	75.00	200

Date	Mintage	G-4	VG-8	F-12	VF-20	XF-40	MS-60
1853	6,641,131	20.00	30.00	40.00	50.00	75.00	200
1854	4,236,156	20.00	30.00	40.00	50.00	75.00	200
1855	1,574,829	20.00	30.00	40.00	50.00	75.00	200
1856	2,690,463	20.00	30.00	40.00	50.00	75.00	200
1857	333,456	150	175	200	225	300	600

Flying Eagle Cent. Flying eagle above date. Value within wreath.

KM# 85   Designer: James B. Longacre. **Diameter:** 19 **Weight:** 4.6700 g. **Composition:** Copper-Nickel
Notes: On the large-letter variety of 1858, the "A" and "M" in "America" are connected at their bases; on the small-letter variety, the two letters are separated.

Large letters

Small letters

Date	Mintage	G-4	VG-8	F-12	VF-20	XF-40	AU-50	MS-60	MS-65	Prf-65
1856	Est. 2,500	6,250	7,250	9,000	12,500	14,000	13,500	17,500	100,000	28,500
1857	17,450,000	26.00	37.50	40.00	46.00	130	200	320	4,000	30,000
1858/7	—	65.00	92.50	180	400	790	1,500	3,400	60,000	—
1858 large letters	24,600,000	27.00	39.50	42.00	57.50	150	225	350	4,000	24,500
1858 small letters	Inc. above	26.00	37.50	40.00	50.00	135	175	310	3,850	30,000

Indian Head Cent. Indian head with headdress left above date. Value within wreath.

KM# 87   Designer: James B. Longacre. **Diameter:** 19 **Weight:** 4.6700 g. **Composition:** Copper-Nickel

Date	Mintage	G-4	VG-8	F-12	VF-20	XF-40	AU-50	MS-60	MS-65	Prf-65
1859	36,400,000	12.50	15.00	22.50	50.00	100.00	175	250	4,000	5,200

Indian Head Cent. Indian head with headdress left above date. Value within wreath, shield above.

KM# 90   Designer: James B. Longacre. **Diameter:** 19 **Weight:** 4.6700 g. **Composition:** Copper-Nickel

Date	Mintage	G-4	VG-8	F-12	VF-20	XF-40	AU-50	MS-60	MS-65	Prf-65
1860 Rounded Bust	20,566,000	11.00	15.00	22.00	40.00	70.00	110	200	1,200	3,800
1860 Pointed Bust	Inc. above	20.00	30.00	40.00	60.00	100.00	160	300	6,000	
1860	(1,000)	—	—	—	—	—	—	—	—	7,500
1861	10,100,000	20.00	30.00	41.00	60.00	95.00	160	200	1,200	7,250
1862	28,075,000	11.00	11.50	12.00	14.50	30.00	60.00	100.00	1,000	2,350
1863	49,840,000	7.50	9.00	10.00	12.50	28.00	57.00	100.00	1,200	3,100
1864	13,740,000	16.00	28.00	35.00	62.00	110	160	210	1,750	3,200

Indian Head Cent. Indian head with headdress left above date. Value within wreath, shield above.

KM# 90a   Designer: James B. Longacre. **Diameter:** 19 **Weight:** 3.1100 g. **Composition:** Bronze **Notes:** The 1864 "L" variety has the designer's initial in Liberty's hair to the right of her neck.

1864 "L"

Date	Mintage	G-4	VG-8	F-12	VF-20	XF-40	AU-50	MS-60	MS-65	Prf-65
1864	39,233,714	7.00	19.00	24.00	45.00	70.00	85.00	90.00	375	4,300
1864 L Pointed bust	Inc. above	52.50	65.00	130	185	275	325	400	1,750	110,000
1865	35,429,286	6.00	10.00	17.50	23.00	40.00	55.00	80.00	450	1,550
1866	9,826,500	40.00	56.00	75.00	110	195	250	250	1,900	950
1867	9,821,000	50.00	62.00	90.00	115	195	240	265	1,900	1,050
1867/1867	—	60.00	85.00	130	190	275	385	—	—	—
1868	10,266,500	37.50	42.00	70.00	120	180	245	230	1,200	985
1869/9	6,420,000	190	375	525	750	865	1,000	1,100	2,500	—
1869	Inc. above	72.50	100.00	230	335	450	560	510	1,750	950

Date	Mintage	G-4	VG-8	F-12	VF-20	XF-40	AU-50	MS-60	MS-65	Prf-65
1870	5,275,000	55.00	90.00	225	285	410	510	515	1,750	1,075
1871	3,929,500	77.50	100.00	280	325	450	525	575	3,000	1,100
1872	4,042,000	90.00	160	375	440	625	775	775	4,100	1,100
1873 closed 3	11,676,500	30.00	50.00	85.00	130	235	300	400	1,500	850
1873 open 3	Inc. above	20.00	30.00	58.00	80.00	175	215	235	—	—
1873 Double Liberty die 1	Inc. above	185	365	800	1,400	2,400	4,250	7,500	—	—
1873 Double Liberty die 2	Inc. above	—	—	450	900	1,650	2,800	—	—	—
1874	14,187,500	15.00	22.00	40.00	57.50	112	150	170	800	800
1875	13,528,000	16.00	27.50	53.50	70.00	120	165	175	800	1,500
1876	7,944,000	27.00	35.00	70.00	130	230	295	315	1,500	925
1877	852,500	850	1,000	1,650	2,250	2,850	3,250	3,800	13,000	6,750
1878	5,799,850	26.00	35.00	65.00	135	245	300	315	1,000	490
1879	16,231,200	7.00	10.00	16.00	33.00	75.00	90.00	100.00	450	450
1880	38,964,955	4.00	6.00	8.00	11.00	28.00	48.00	60.00	450	435
1881	39,211,575	4.00	5.00	7.00	10.00	23.00	30.00	40.00	350	425
1882	38,581,100	4.00	6.00	7.00	10.00	22.00	30.00	40.00	350	425
1883	45,589,109	3.00	4.50	6.00	8.00	18.00	30.00	45.00	350	425
1884	23,261,742	4.00	5.00	7.00	13.00	29.00	40.00	65.00	500	425
1885	11,765,384	6.50	8.00	12.00	26.00	62.00	84.00	95.00	750	425
1886 Type 1 obverse	17,654,290	4.00	6.00	19.00	55.00	140	175	240	1,250	500
1886 Type 2 obverse	Inc. above	7.00	10.00	35.00	90.00	200	250	325	—	—
1887	45,226,483	2.50	3.00	4.00	7.00	19.00	28.00	65.00	400	475
1888	37,494,414	2.60	3.25	5.00	8.00	21.00	28.00	75.00	950	525
1889	48,869,361	2.25	2.75	3.50	6.00	12.00	26.00	50.00	450	450
1890	57,182,854	2.10	2.50	3.00	6.00	10.00	23.00	40.00	400	500
1891	47,072,350	2.25	2.75	3.25	6.00	13.00	23.00	40.00	400	520
1892	37,649,832	2.40	2.85	3.50	6.00	18.00	25.00	40.00	400	525
1893	46,642,195	2.10	2.75	3.25	6.00	10.00	22.00	40.00	350	540
1894	16,752,132	4.00	5.50	12.00	20.00	50.00	65.00	80.00	375	525
1894/94	Inc. above	24.00	30.00	80.00	150	275	440	750	—	—
1895	38,343,636	2.10	2.40	3.50	5.00	11.00	23.00	35.00	275	475
1896	39,057,293	1.95	2.50	3.00	5.00	13.00	26.00	35.00	275	425
1897	50,466,330	1.95	2.40	2.75	4.00	10.00	23.00	35.00	175	425
1898	49,823,079	1.95	2.40	2.75	4.00	10.00	23.00	35.00	275	425
1899	53,600,031	1.95	2.20	2.60	4.00	10.00	23.00	35.00	175	415
1900	66,833,764	1.95	2.20	2.50	4.00	12.00	23.00	30.00	225	425
1901	79,611,143	1.85	2.20	2.50	4.00	11.00	23.00	30.00	200	425
1902	87,376,722	1.85	2.20	2.50	4.00	10.00	22.00	30.00	200	425
1903	85,094,493	1.85	2.20	2.50	4.00	10.00	21.00	30.00	200	425
1904	61,328,015	1.75	2.20	2.50	4.00	10.00	21.00	30.00	200	475
1905	80,719,163	1.75	2.20	2.50	3.50	9.00	20.00	30.00	175	475
1906	96,022,255	1.75	2.20	2.50	3.50	9.00	21.00	30.00	175	395
1907	108,138,618	1.75	2.20	2.50	3.50	8.50	20.00	30.00	175	485
1908	32,327,987	1.75	2.30	2.50	3.50	9.00	20.00	30.00	145	395
1908S	1,115,000	62.50	65.00	75.00	88.00	170	200	300	750	—
1909	14,370,645	11.50	12.00	12.25	12.50	18.00	27.00	30.00	150	400
1909S	309,000	500	535	575	615	750	850	800	2,000	—

Lincoln Cent. Wheat Ears.

KM# 132   Designer: Victor D. Brenner. **Diameter:**
19 **Weight:** 3.1100 g. **Composition:** Bronze **Notes:**
The 1909 "VDB" varieties have the designer's initials
inscribed at the 6 o'clock position on the reverse.
The initials were removed until 1918, when they
were restored on the obverse • MS60 prices are for
Brown coins and MS65 prices are for coins that are at
least 90% original red.

1922 no "D"

Date	Mintage	G-4	VG-8	F-12	VF-20	XF-40	AU-50	MS-60	MS-65	Prf-65
1909 VDB	27,995,000	11.50	12.00	12.50	13.00	14.00	16.00	18.00	100.00	6,000
1909 VDB Doubled Die Obverse	Inc. above	—	—	55.00	75.00	100.00	120	150	1,900	—
1909S VDB	484,000	750	800	900	1,100	1,200	1,300	1,500	6,800	—
1909	72,702,618	2.25	2.50	2.75	3.50	6.00	12.00	15.00	85.00	520
1909S	1,825,000	100.00	105	120	165	235	255	325	1,300	—
1909S/S S over horizontal S	Inc. above	115	120	135	180	255	280	350	1,600	—
1910	146,801,218	.50	.60	.75	1.00	4.00	9.00	17.50	250	700
1910S	6,045,000	15.00	17.00	18.00	25.00	40.00	67.00	85.00	800	—
1911	101,177,787	.60	.80	2.00	2.50	4.50	9.00	20.00	375	600
1911D	12,672,000	5.25	6.00	10.00	15.00	40.00	65.00	80.00	1,550	—
1911S	4,026,000	27.00	30.00	33.00	38.00	70.00	95.00	175	3,300	—
1912	68,153,060	1.75	2.00	2.50	6.00	12.00	21.00	30.00	550	950
1912D	10,411,000	7.00	10.00	12.00	25.00	68.00	110	150	2,800	—
1912S	4,431,000	22.00	24.00	27.00	34.00	70.00	100.00	160	4,400	—
1913	76,532,352	1.00	1.20	1.75	3.25	13.50	20.00	33.50	400	550
1913D	15,804,000	3.00	3.50	4.00	1.50	42.00	61.00	90.00	2,100	—
1913S	6,101,000	13.00	16.00	18.50	24.00	46.00	95.00	180	6,250	—

Date	Mintage	G-4	VG-8	F-12	VF-20	XF-40	AU-50	MS-60	MS-65	Prf-65
1914	75,238,432	.75	1.10	2.25	5.50	14.00	34.00	47.50	415	600
1914D	1,193,000	210	250	385	440	800	1,350	1,900	22,000	—
1914S	4,137,000	22.00	23.00	26.00	36.00	80.00	170	285	11,500	—
1915	29,092,120	1.75	2.00	3.75	15.00	50.00	70.00	80.00	1,150	600
1915D	22,050,000	1.75	2.00	3.50	6.50	21.00	42.00	70.00	1,250	—
1915S	4,833,000	18.00	21.00	23.00	25.00	70.00	90.00	175	4,800	—
1916	131,833,677	.35	.60	1.25	2.60	6.00	11.50	18.00	200	1,650
1916D	35,956,000	1.75	2.25	3.00	6.00	13.00	27.50	65.00	3,300	—
1916S	22,510,000	2.25	3.25	4.50	7.00	23.00	36.00	80.00	8,500	—
1917	196,429,785	.35	.45	.55	2.00	4.50	10.00	16.00	450	—
1917 Doubled Die Obverse	Inc. above	90.00	110	175	350	900	1,750	2,500	25,000	—
1917D	55,120,000	1.50	1.75	2.50	5.50	28.00	36.00	60.00	3,000	—
1917S	32,620,000	.80	1.20	1.75	2.50	9.50	22.00	58.00	7,200	—
1918	288,104,634	.35	.40	.50	1.25	4.50	8.00	13.00	385	—
1918D	47,830,000	1.60	2.00	2.65	5.50	15.00	29.00	70.00	3,500	—
1918S	34,680,000	.50	1.20	1.75	3.65	10.00	32.00	61.00	7,800	—
1919	392,021,000	.30	.40	.50	.80	1.75	4.25	8.50	175	—
1919D	57,154,000	1.25	1.60	2.00	4.00	10.00	30.00	50.00	2,700	—
1919S	139,760,000	.40	.70	1.80	2.65	6.00	16.00	40.00	4,300	—
1920	310,165,000	.35	.40	.90	1.50	2.80	7.00	13.50	225	—
1920D	49,280,000	1.25	1.65	2.80	5.50	16.00	31.00	62.50	2,750	—
1920S	46,220,000	.90	1.00	1.50	2.75	10.00	32.50	90.00	9,000	—
1921	39,157,000	.60	1.00	1.25	2.80	10.00	20.00	41.50	375	—
1921S	15,274,000	1.65	2.10	2.85	6.00	33.00	68.00	100.00	6,700	—
1922D	7,160,000	17.00	18.00	20.00	24.00	35.00	70.00	100.00	2,350	—
1922D Weak Rev	Inc. above	15.00	15.00	17.00	20.00	30.00	60.00	90.00	1,750	—
1922D Weak D	Inc. above	30.00	44.00	60.00	100.00	220	285	550	—	—
1922 No D Die 2 Strong Rev	Inc. above	675	800	1,275	1,700	3,300	6,600	10,350	200,000	—
1922 No D Die 3 Weak Rev	Inc. above	275	375	650	850	1,750	3,500	8,500	—	—
1923	74,723,000	.60	.80	1.00	1.35	4.50	8.00	13.50	480	—
1923S	8,700,000	2.50	3.50	4.50	7.75	30.00	80.00	195	15,500	—
1924	75,178,000	.35	.50	.60	1.00	4.50	8.00	20.00	390	—
1924D	2,520,000	33.00	37.00	42.00	54.00	110	160	255	9,500	—
1924S	11,696,000	1.75	2.00	2.80	5.00	30.00	66.00	115	11,000	—
1925	139,949,000	.30	.40	.50	.70	2.50	6.00	8.50	100.00	—
1925D	22,580,000	1.50	2.00	3.00	5.00	15.00	27.50	60.00	5,000	—
1925S	26,380,000	1.20	1.50	2.00	2.75	11.00	30.00	80.00	9,000	—
1926	157,088,000	.25	.40	.50	.70	1.65	4.40	7.00	75.00	—
1926D	28,020,000	1.50	1.70	2.80	4.50	13.50	32.50	80.00	4,350	—
1926S	4,550,000	8.00	9.00	11.00	14.00	30.00	65.00	130	100,000	—
1927	144,440,000	.20	.30	.40	.70	1.60	4.50	7.00	95.00	—
1927D	27,170,000	1.50	1.75	2.25	3.35	7.00	23.00	58.50	2,000	—
1927S	14,276,000	1.50	1.85	3.00	4.65	11.50	32.50	62.50	6,500	—
1928	134,116,000	.20	.30	.40	.70	1.25	3.75	7.50	90.00	—
1928D	31,170,000	1.10	1.40	2.00	3.00	6.50	14.00	34.00	1,100	—
1928S Small S	17,266,000	1.20	1.65	2.60	3.50	8.00	25.00	71.50	4,650	—
1928S Large S	Inc. above	2.00	2.85	4.00	6.00	15.00	40.00	135	5,500	—
1929	185,262,000	.20	.30	.40	.60	1.00	4.25	6.00	85.00	—
1929D	41,730,000	.70	1.20	1.50	2.35	4.65	11.00	21.50	625	—
1929S	50,148,000	.80	1.25	1.75	2.50	4.00	6.75	17.50	550	—
1930	157,415,000	.20	.30	.40	.60	1.25	2.25	3.75	32.50	—
1930D	40,100,000	.35	.45	.65	.90	2.00	4.00	10.50	95.00	—
1930S	24,286,000	.35	.45	.60	.80	1.50	6.00	10.00	50.00	—
1931	19,396,000	.70	.80	1.30	2.00	2.75	8.00	19.00	135	—
1931D	4,480,000	4.85	6.00	6.50	7.00	12.50	37.50	52.00	950	—
1931S	866,000	110	115	120	125	130	135	140	750	—
1932	9,062,000	1.50	1.85	2.75	3.50	5.75	12.50	19.00	100.00	—
1932D	10,500,000	1.40	2.00	2.50	2.85	4.15	9.60	17.50	150	—
1933	14,360,000	1.40	1.80	2.50	2.85	4.25	9.50	17.50	100.00	—
1933D	6,200,000	3.25	4.00	4.75	6.25	11.50	16.00	23.00	135	—
1934	219,080,000	.20	.30	.40	.60	1.25	4.00	8.00	30.00	—
1934D	28,446,000	.35	.50	.80	1.50	3.00	9.00	20.00	52.00	—
1935	245,338,000	.20	.30	.40	.55	.90	1.50	3.50	28.00	—
1935D	47,000,000	.15	.20	.30	.40	.95	2.50	4.50	30.00	—
1935S	38,702,000	.25	.35	.60	1.75	3.00	5.00	12.00	55.00	—
1936 (Proof in Satin Finish)	309,637,569	.20	.30	.40	.55	.85	1.40	2.00	7.50	1,200
1936 Brilliant Proof	Inc. above	—	—	—	—	—	—	—	—	—
1936D	40,620,000	.20	.30	.40	.55	.90	1.50	3.50	22.00	—
1936S	29,130,000	.20	.30	.45	.60	1.00	1.75	3.00	18.00	—
1937	309,179,320	.20	.30	.40	.55	.85	1.40	1.60	20.00	125
1937D	50,430,000	.20	.30	.40	.60	.95	1.00	2.20	24.00	—
1937S	34,500,000	.20	.30	.40	.55	.90	1.25	2.40	22.50	—
1938	156,696,734	.20	.30	.40	.55	.85	1.20	3.00	16.50	85.00
1938D	20,010,000	.20	.30	.45	.60	1.00	1.50	3.50	17.00	—
1938S	15,180,000	.30	.40	.50	.70	1.00	2.00	2.80	26.00	—
1939	316,479,520	.20	.40	.40	.55	.75	.90	1.00	15.00	78.00

Date	Mintage	G-4	VG-8	F-12	VF-20	XF-40	AU-50	MS-60	MS-65	Prf-65
1939D	15,160,000	.35	.50	.50	.60	.85	1.90	2.50	20.00	—
1939S	52,070,000	.30	.50	.50	.60	.80	1.10	2.00	19.00	—
1940	586,825,872	.10	.30	.30	.40	.50	.75	1.00	17.00	70.00
1940D	81,390,000	.20	.40	.40	.55	.75	.50	1.20	11.50	—
1940S	112,940,000	.20	.40	.40	.55	.90	1.25	1.40	14.00	—
1941	887,039,100	.10	.30	.30	.40	.50	.70	.85	17.00	65.00
1941 Doubled Die Obv	Inc. above	35.00	70.00	70.00	80.00	95.00	135	200	2,800	—
1941D	128,700,000	.20	.40	.40	.55	.75	1.25	2.25	20.00	—
1941S	92,360,000	.20	.40	.40	.55	.75	1.75	2.75	23.50	—
1942	657,828,600	.10	.30	.30	.40	.50	.70	.85	17.00	78.00
1942D	206,698,000	.20	.30	.30	.35	.40	.50	.65	22.00	—
1942S	85,590,000	.25	.45	.45	.85	1.25	2.50	4.50	26.00	—

Lincoln Cent. Wheat Ears.

KM# 132a Designer: Victor D. Brenner.
Diameter: 19 **Weight:** 2.7000 g. **Composition:**
Zinc Coated Steel

Date	Mintage	G-4	VG-8	F-12	VF-20	XF-40	AU-50	MS-60	MS-65	Prf-65
1943	684,628,670	.25	.30	.35	.45	.60	.85	1.25	4.75	—
1943D	217,660,000	.35	.40	.45	.50	.70	1.00	1.25	8.50	—
1943D/D RPM	—	30.00	38.00	50.00	65.00	90.00	125	200	—	—
1943S	191,550,000	.45	.45	.50	.65	.90	1.40	3.00	13.50	—

Lincoln Cent. Wheat Ears.

KM# A132 Designer: Victor D. Brenner.
Diameter: 19 **Weight:** 3.1100 g. **Composition:**
Copper-Zinc **Notes:** KM#132 design and
composition resumed • MS60 prices are for Brown
coins and MS65 prices are for coins that are at least
90% original red.

1955 Double-die

Date	Mintage	XF-40	MS-65	Prf-65
1944	1,435,400,000	.40	8.00	—
1944D	430,578,000	.50	12.50	—
1944D/S Type 1	Inc. above	235	3,750	—
1944D/S Type 2	Inc. above	175	1,600	—
1944S	282,760,000	.40	12.00	—
1945	1,040,515,000	.40	15.00	—
1945D	226,268,000	.40	13.50	—
1945S	181,770,000	.40	12.00	—
1946	991,655,000	.30	13.00	—
1946D	315,690,000	.30	6.00	—
1946S	198,100,000	.30	5.50	—
1946S/D	—	70.00	600	—
1947	190,555,000	.45	16.00	—
1947D	194,750,000	.40	10.00	—
1947S	99,000,000	.35	12.00	—
1948	317,570,000	.40	14.00	—
1948D	172,637,000	.40	6.75	—
1948S	81,735,000	.40	6.50	—
1949	217,775,000	.40	15.00	—
1949D	153,132,000	.40	12.00	—
1949S	64,290,000	.50	10.00	—
1950	272,686,386	.40	13.50	40.00
1950D	334,950,000	.35	9.00	—
1950S	118,505,000	.40	8.00	—
1951	295,633,500	.40	14.00	40.00
1951D	625,355,000	.30	8.00	—
1951S	136,010,000	.40	10.00	—
1952	186,856,980	.40	16.00	34.00
1952D	746,130,000	.30	8.00	—
1952S	137,800,004	.60	9.00	—
1953	256,883,800	.30	18.00	28.00
1953D	700,515,000	.30	11.00	—

Date	Mintage	XF-40	MS-65	Prf-65
1953S	181,835,000	.40	11.50	—
1954	71,873,350	.25	17.50	9.00
1954D	251,552,500	.25	10.00	—
1954S	96,190,000	.25	12.00	—
1955	330,958,000	.25	15.00	13.00
1955 doubled die	Inc. above	1,425	40,000	—

Note: The 1955 "doubled die" has distinct doubling of the date and lettering on the obverse.

Date	Mintage	XF-40	MS-65	Prf-65
1955D	563,257,500	.20	12.00	—
1955S	44,610,000	.35	7.50	—
1956	421,414,384	.20	16.00	3.00
1956D	1,098,201,100	.20	8.00	—
1957	283,787,952	.20	9.00	2.00
1957D	1,051,342,000	.20	8.00	—
1958	253,400,652	.20	9.00	3.00
1958D	800,953,300	.20	8.00	—

Lincoln Cent. Lincoln Memorial.

KM# 201   Rev. Designer: Frank Gasparro.
Weight: 3.1100 g. **Composition:** Copper-Zinc
Notes: MS65 prices are for coins that are at least
90% original red. The dates were modified in 1960,
1970 and 1982, resulting in large-date and small-
date varieties for those years. The 1972 "doubled
die" shows doubling of "In God We Trust." The
1979-S and 1981-S Type II proofs have a clearer mint
mark than the Type I proofs of those years. Some
1982 cents have the predominantly copper
composition; others have the predominantly zinc
composition. They can be distinguished by weight.

Small date

Large date

Large date

Small date

Date	Mintage	XF-40	MS-65	Prf-65
1959	610,864,291	—	18.00	1.50
1959D	1,279,760,000	—	16.00	—
1960 small date, low 9	588,096,602	2.10	12.00	16.00
1960 large date, high 9	Inc. above	—	10.00	1.25
1960D small date, low 9	1,580,884,000	—	10.00	—
1960D large date	Inc. above	—	11.00	—
1960D/D small over large date	—	—	300	—
1961	756,373,244	—	6.50	1.00
1961D	1,753,266,700	—	15.00	—
1962	609,263,019	—	8.00	1.00
1962D	1,793,148,400	—	14.00	—
1963	757,185,645	—	10.00	1.00
1963D	1,774,020,400	—	12.00	—
1964	2,652,525,762	—	6.50	1.00
1964D	3,799,071,500	—	7.00	—
1965	1,497,224,900	—	10.00	—
1965 SMS	—	—	7.50	—
1966	2,188,147,783	—	10.00	—
1966 SMS	—	—	8.00	—
1967	3,048,667,100	—	10.00	—
1967 SMS	—	—	8.00	—
1968	1,707,880,970	—	12.00	—
1968D	2,886,269,600	—	12.00	—
1968S	261,311,510	—	8.00	1.00
1969	1,136,910,000	—	6.50	—
1969D	4,002,832,200	—	10.00	—
1969S	547,309,631	—	8.00	1.10
1969S Double Die Obverse	—	—	—	—
1970	1,898,315,000	—	8.00	—
1970D	2,891,438,900	—	6.00	—
1970S	693,192,814	—	.40	1.20
1970S small date, level 7	Inc. above	—	75.00	60.00
1970S large date, low 7	Inc. above	—	16.00	—
1970S double die obverse	Inc. above	—	—	—
1971	1,919,490,000	—	25.00	—
1971D	2,911,045,600	—	5.50	—
1971S	528,354,192	—	6.00	1.20
1971S double die obverse	—	—	—	—
1972	2,933,255,000	—	6.00	—

Date	Mintage	XF-40	MS-65	Prf-65
1972 doubled die	—	285	800	—
1972D	2,665,071,400	—	10.00	—
1972S	380,200,104	—	30.00	1.15
1973	3,728,245,000	—	8.00	—
1973D	3,549,576,588	—	11.00	—
1973S	319,937,634	—	8.00	0.80
1974	4,232,140,523	—	12.00	—
1974D	4,235,098,000	—	12.00	—
1974S	412,039,228	—	10.00	0.75
1975	5,451,476,142	—	8.00	—
1975D	4,505,245,300	—	13.50	—
1975S	(2,845,450)	—	—	5.50
1976	4,674,292,426	—	18.00	—
1976D	4,221,592,455	—	20.00	—
1976S	(4,149,730)	—	—	5.00
1977	4,469,930,000	—	14.00	—
1977D	4,149,062,300	—	14.00	—
1977S	(3,251,152)	—	—	3.00
1978	5,558,605,000	—	14.00	—
1978D	4,280,233,400	—	12.00	—
1978S	(3,127,781)	—	—	3.50
1979	6,018,515,000	—	12.00	—
1979D	4,139,357,254	—	8.00	—
1979S type I, proof	(3,677,175)	—	—	4.00
1979S type II, proof	Inc. above	—	—	4.25
1980	7,414,705,000	—	0.50	—
1980D	5,140,098,660	—	10.00	—
1980S	(3,554,806)	—	—	2.25
1981	7,491,750,000	—	7.50	—
1981S type II, proof	Inc. above	—	—	60.00
1981D	5,373,235,677	—	9.00	—
1981S type I, proof	(4,063,083)	—	—	3.50
1982 large date	10,712,525,000	—	6.00	—
1982 small date	Inc. above	—	8.00	—
1982D large date	6,012,979,368	—	6.00	—
1982S	3,857,479	—	—	—

Lincoln Cent. Lincoln Memorial.

KM# 201a **Diameter:** 19 **Weight:** 2.5000 g.
Composition: Copper Plated Zinc **Notes:** MS65
prices are for coins that are at least 90% original red.

Date	Mintage	XF-40	MS-65	Prf-65
1982 large date	—	—	6.00	—
1982 small date	—	—	9.00	—
1982D large date	—	—	8.00	—
1982D small date	—	—	6.00	—

Lincoln Cent. Lincoln Memorial.

KM# 201b **Diameter:** 19 **Composition:** Copper
Plated Zinc **Notes:** MS65 prices are for coins that are
at least 90% original red. The 1983 "doubled die
reverse" shows doubling of "United States of
America." The 1984 "doubled die" shows doubling
of Lincoln's ear on the obverse.

Date	Mintage	XF-40	MS-65	Prf-65
1982S	(3,857,479)	—	—	3.00
1983	7,752,355,000	—	7.00	—
1983 doubled die	Inc. above	—	400	—
1983D	6,467,199,428	—	5.50	—
1983S	(3,279,126)	—	—	4.00
1984	8,151,079,000	—	7.50	—

Date	Mintage	XF-40	MS-65	Prf-65
1984 doubled die	Inc. above	—	275	—
1984D	5,569,238,906	—	5.50	—
1984S	(3,065,110)	—	—	4.50
1985	5,648,489,887	—	4.50	—
1985D	5,287,399,926	—	4.50	—
1985S	(3,362,821)	—	—	6.00
1986	4,491,395,493	—	5.00	—
1986D	4,442,866,698	—	8.00	—
1986S	(3,010,497)	—	—	7.50
1987	4,682,466,931	—	8.50	—
1987D	4,879,389,514	—	6.00	—
1987S	(4,227,728)	—	—	5.00
1988	6,092,810,000	—	8.50	—
1988D	5,253,740,443	—	5.50	—
1988S	(3,262,948)	—	—	4.00
1989	7,261,535,000	—	5.00	—
1989D	5,345,467,111	—	5.00	—
1989S	(3,220,194)	—	—	6.00
1990	6,851,765,000	—	5.00	—
1990D	4,922,894,533	—	5.00	—
1990S	(3,299,559)	—	—	5.00
1990 no S, Proof only	Inc. above	—	—	2,750
1991	5,165,940,000	—	6.00	—
1991D	4,158,442,076	—	5.00	—
1991S	(2,867,787)	—	—	5.00
1992	4,648,905,000	—	5.50	—
1992D	4,448,673,300	—	5.50	—
1992D Close AM, Proof Reverse Die	Inc. above	—	—	—
1992S	(4,176,560)	—	—	5.00
1993	5,684,705,000	—	5.50	—
1993D	6,426,650,571	—	5.50	—
1993S	(3,394,792)	—	—	7.00
1994	6,500,850,000	—	10.00	—
1994D	7,131,765,000	—	5.50	—
1994S	(3,269,923)	—	—	4.00
1995	6,411,440,000	—	4.50	—
1995 Doubled Die Obverse	Inc. above	20.00	50.00	—
1995D	7,128,560,000	—	5.00	—
1995S	(2,707,481)	—	—	9.50
1996	6,612,465,000	—	5.00	—
1996D	6,510,795,000	—	5.00	—
1996S	(2,915,212)	—	—	6.50
1997	4,622,800,000	—	5.00	—
1997D	4,576,555,000	—	5.00	—
1997S	(2,796,678)	—	—	11.50
1998	5,032,155,000	—	5.00	—
1998 Wide AM Reverse For Proof Die	Inc. above	—	—	—
1998D	5,255,353,500	—	5.00	—
1998S	(2,957,286)	—	—	9.50
1999	5,237,600,000	—	5.00	—
1999 Wide AM Reverse For Proof Die	Inc. above	—	—	—
1999D	6,360,065,000	—	5.00	—
1999S	(3,362,462)	—	—	5.00
2000 Wide AM Reverse For Proof Die	Inc. above	—	—	—
2000	5,503,200,000	—	4.00	—
2000D	8,774,220,000	—	4.00	—
2000S	(4,063,361)	—	—	4.00
2001	4,959,600,000	—	4.00	—
2001D	5,374,990,000	—	4.00	—
2001S	(3,099,096)	—	—	4.00
2002	3,260,800,000	—	4.00	—
2002D	4,028,055,000	—	4.00	—
2002S	(3,157,739)	—	—	4.00
2003	3,300,000,000	—	3.50	—
2003D	3,548,000,000	—	3.50	—
2003S	(3,116,590)	—	—	4.00
2004	3,379,600,000	—	3.50	—
2004D	3,456,400,000	—	3.50	—
2004S	2,992,069	—	—	4.00
2005	3,935,600,000	—	3.50	—
2005D	3,764,450,000	—	3.50	—
2005S	3,273,000	—	—	4.00
2006	4,290,000,000	—	2.00	—
2006D	3,944,000,000	—	2.50	—
2006S	2,923,105	—	—	4.00
2007	—	—	1.50	—
2007D	—	—	1.50	—
2007S	—	—	—	4.00

2 CENTS

Shield in front of crossed arrows, banner above, date below. Value within wheat wreath.

KM# 94 Designer: James B. Longacre. **Diameter:** 23 **Weight:** 6.2200 g. **Composition:** Copper-Tin-Zinc
Notes: The motto "In God We Trust" was modified in 1864, resulting in small-motto and large-motto varieties for that year.

Small letters in motto

Large letters in motto

Date	Mintage	G-4	VG-8	F-12	VF-20	XF-40	AU-50	MS-60	MS-65	Prf-65
1864 small motto	19,847,500	125	185	265	400	595	675	900	3,000	45,000
1864 large motto	Inc. above	15.00	16.00	22.00	28.50	38.50	67.50	85.00	520	1,400
1865	13,640,000	15.00	16.00	22.00	28.50	38.50	67.50	85.00	520	850
1866	3,177,000	15.00	19.00	23.00	28.50	38.50	67.50	85.00	660	850
1867	2,938,750	17.50	22.00	36.00	46.00	60.00	96.00	130	550	850
1868	2,803,750	17.50	22.00	37.50	47.50	62.50	100.00	145	625	850
1869	1,546,000	18.50	23.00	40.00	50.00	71.00	120	160	650	850
1870	861,250	25.00	32.50	46.00	65.00	115	160	255	775	850
1871	721,250	34.00	41.50	55.00	82.50	130	195	270	750	850
1872	65,000	325	375	470	650	850	960	1,400	4,300	900
1873 proof	Est. 1,100	1,250	1,350	1,500	1,600	1,750	2,000	—	—	4,350

SILVER 3 CENTS

Silver 3 Cents - Type 1. Shield within star, no outlines in star. Roman numeral in designed C, within circle of stars.

KM# 75 **Designer:** James B. Longacre. **Diameter:** 14 **Weight:** 0.8000 g. **Composition:** 0.7500 Silver, 0.0193 oz. ASW.

Date	Mintage	G-4	VG-8	F-12	VF-20	XF-40	AU-50	MS-60	MS-65	Prf-65
1851	5,447,400	25.00	41.50	42.50	45.00	65.00	155	185	975	—
1851O	720,000	38.50	47.50	55.00	100.00	160	250	340	2,600	—
1852	18,663,500	25.00	41.50	42.50	45.00	65.00	155	180	975	—
1853	11,400,000	25.00	41.50	42.50	45.00	65.00	155	180	975	—

Silver 3 Cents - Type 2. Shield within star, three outlines in star. Roman numeral in designed C, within circle of stars.

KM# 80 **Designer:** James B. Longacre. **Diameter:** 14 **Weight:** 0.7500 g. **Composition:** 0.9000 Silver, 0.0217 oz. ASW.

Date	Mintage	G-4	VG-8	F-12	VF-20	XF-40	AU-50	MS-60	MS-65	Prf-65
1854	671,000	26.00	42.50	44.00	50.00	105	230	350	3,450	33,500
1855	139,000	44.00	57.50	75.00	125	205	340	550	8,500	15,000
1856	1,458,000	30.00	45.00	46.00	65.00	125	205	275	4,500	15,500
1857	1,042,000	28.50	42.50	45.00	62.50	130	240	300	3,300	13,500
1858	1,604,000	27.50	42.50	44.00	55.00	110	200	240	3,300	6,400

Silver 3 Cents - Type 3. Shield within star, two outlines in star. Roman numeral in designed C, within circle of stars.

KM# 88 **Designer:** James B. Longacre. **Diameter:** 14 **Weight:** 0.7500 g. **Composition:** 0.9000 Silver, 0.0217 oz. ASW.

Date	Mintage	G-4	VG-8	F-12	VF-20	XF-40	AU-50	MS-60	MS-65	Prf-65
1859	365,000	30.00	44.00	50.00	62.50	82.50	170	195	975	2,150
1860	287,000	30.00	44.00	45.00	60.00	80.00	170	195	975	4,000
1861	498,000	30.00	44.00	45.00	60.00	80.00	170	195	975	1,800
1862	343,550	38.50	51.00	50.00	70.00	82.50	195	230	975	1,400
1863	21,460	340	375	400	445	480	625	780	2,250	1,350
1863/62 proof only; Rare	Inc. above	—	—	—	—	—	—	—	—	5,400
1864	12,470	340	375	400	445	480	625	780	1,700	1,350
1865	8,500	400	440	475	520	550	600	750	1,700	1,350
1866	22,725	340	375	400	445	495	550	650	1,900	1,325
1867	4,625	400	440	475	520	550	600	720	2,750	1,300
1868	4,100	400	445	480	520	575	625	740	5,750	1,400
1869	5,100	400	445	480	520	575	625	720	2,350	1,400
1869/68 proof only; Rare	Inc. above	—	—	—	—	—	—	—	—	—
1870	4,000	420	450	495	550	595	670	900	5,500	1,350
1871	4,360	400	440	480	520	575	625	750	1,700	1,450
1872	1,950	420	450	495	550	595	675	795	5,500	1,350
1873 proof only	600	650	685	730	800	890	980	—	—	2,500

NICKEL 3 CENTS

Coronet head left, date below. Roman numeral value within wreath.

KM# 95 **Designer:** James B. Longacre. **Diameter:** 17.9 **Weight:** 1.9400 g. **Composition:** Copper-Nickel

Date	Mintage	G-4	VG-8	F-12	VF-20	XF-40	AU-50	MS-60	MS-65	Prf-65
1865	11,382,000	15.00	16.00	17.50	24.50	35.00	57.50	105	700	6,500
1866	4,801,000	15.00	16.00	17.50	24.50	35.00	57.50	105	700	1,725
1867	3,915,000	15.00	16.00	17.50	24.50	35.00	57.50	105	750	1,575

Date	Mintage	G-4	VG-8	F-12	VF-20	XF-40	AU-50	MS-60	MS-65	Prf-65
1868	3,252,000	15.00	16.00	17.50	24.50	35.00	57.50	105	700	1,400
1869	1,604,000	16.00	17.50	19.00	26.00	37.50	62.50	120	775	1,000
1870	1,335,000	17.50	18.50	20.50	28.50	40.00	65.00	135	825	2,300
1871	604,000	17.50	19.00	22.50	30.00	41.50	70.00	150	850	1,200
1872	862,000	19.00	22.50	25.00	32.50	44.00	75.00	170	1,100	880
1873	1,173,000	16.00	18.50	22.50	27.50	40.00	65.00	140	1,400	1,050
1874	790,000	17.50	20.50	22.50	30.00	41.50	72.50	155	1,050	950
1875	228,000	19.00	22.50	26.00	34.00	48.50	90.00	190	850	1,700
1876	162,000	20.50	23.50	28.50	38.50	52.50	105	220	1,700	1,000
1877 proof	Est. 900	1,100	1,150	1,175	1,250	1,300	1,350	—	—	3,750
1878 proof	2,350	615	645	720	770	795	825	—	—	1,200
1879	41,200	65.00	75.00	96.00	105	115	170	320	850	580
1880	24,955	100.00	115	130	155	185	230	375	800	630
1881	1,080,575	15.00	16.00	19.00	25.00	37.50	60.00	100.00	715	580
1882	25,300	130	150	180	205	250	200	425	1,100	625
1883	10,609	200	225	260	305	355	415	480	4,350	580
1884	5,642	415	445	550	595	645	730	800	5,800	600
1885	4,790	470	520	645	700	745	790	900	2,300	650
1886 proof	4,290	320	330	345	385	385	415	—	—	700
1887/6 proof	7,961	350	390	415	450	460	515	—	—	975
1887	Inc. above	305	355	395	430	455	495	540	1,350	1,350
1888	41,083	52.50	62.50	71.50	82.50	100.00	170	315	725	580
1889	21,561	90.00	115	140	180	215	250	320	800	580

HALF DIME

Flowing Hair Half Dime.

KM# 15   Designer: Robert Scot. **Diameter:** 16.5
Weight: 1.3500 g. **Composition:** 0.8920 Silver,
0.0387 oz. ASW.

Date	Mintage	G-4	VG-8	F-12	VF-20	XF-40	MS-60
1794	86,416	1,000	1,250	1,750	2,700	4,800	13,500
1795	Inc. above	700	900	1,350	2,000	4,000	9,500

Draped Bust Half Dime. Small eagle.

KM# 23   Designer: Robert Scot. **Diameter:** 16.5
Weight: 1.3500 g. **Composition:** 0.8920 Silver,
0.0387 oz. ASW. **Notes:** Some 1796 strikes have
"Liberty" spelled as "Likerty." The 1797 strikes have
either 13, 15 or 16 stars on the obverse.

Date	Mintage	G-4	VG-8	F-12	VF-20	XF-40	MS-60
1796	10,230	1,000	1,350	2,000	3,500	6,000	13,500
1796 "Likerty"	Inc. above	1,100	1,400	2,100	3,750	6,250	14,500
1796/5	Inc. above	1,000	1,350	2,200	4,000	7,000	25,000
1797 13 stars	44,527	1,750	2,300	3,000	5,500	9,000	25,000
1797 15 stars	Inc. above	1,000	1,250	1,900	3,250	5,750	12,500
1797 16 stars	Inc. above	1,050	1,350	2,100	3,650	6,250	13,750

Draped Bust Half Dime. Draped bust right, flanked by stars, date at angle below. Heraldic eagle.

KM# 34   Designer: Robert Scot. **Diameter:** 16.5
Weight: 1.3500 g. **Composition:** 0.8920 Silver,
0.0387 oz. ASW.

Date	Mintage	G-4	VG-8	F-12	VF-20	XF-40	MS-60
1800	24,000	575	750	1,500	2,500	4,250	9,000
1800 "Libekty"	Inc. above	600	800	1,575	2,650	4,400	9,300
1801	33,910	775	1,150	1,600	2,800	5,000	15,000
1802	13,010	17,500	25,000	40,000	65,000	85,000	185,000
1803 Large 8	37,850	750	950	1,300	2,000	4,000	9,000
1803 Small 8	Inc. above	950	1,400	1,900	3,000	5,500	11,500
1805	15,600	900	1,250	1,650	2,500	5,500	27,500

Liberty Cap Half Dime. Classic head left, flanked by stars, date below. Eagle with arrows in talons, banner above.

KM# 47 **Designer:** William Kneass. **Diameter:** 15.5 **Weight:** 1.3500 g. **Composition:** 0.8920 Silver, 0.0387 oz. ASW. **Notes:** Design modifications in 1835, 1836 and 1837 resulted in variety combinations with large and small dates, and large and small "5C." inscriptions on the reverse.

Date	Mintage	G-4	VG-8	F-12	VF-20	XF-40	AU-50	MS-60	MS-65
1829	1,230,000	27.50	36.00	48.00	80.00	140	250	350	2,650
1830	1,240,000	25.00	36.00	48.00	75.00	140	250	350	2,650
1831	1,242,700	25.00	36.00	48.00	75.00	140	250	350	2,600
1832	965,000	25.00	36.00	48.00	75.00	140	250	350	2,600
1833	1,370,000	25.00	36.00	48.00	75.00	140	250	350	2,650
1834	1,480,000	25.00	36.00	48.00	75.00	140	250	350	2,600
1835 lg. dt., lg. 5C.	2,760,000	25.00	36.00	48.00	75.00	140	250	350	2,600
1835 lg. dt., sm. 5C	Inc. above	25.00	36.00	48.00	75.00	140	250	350	2,600
1835 sm. dt., lg. 5C	Inc. above	25.00	36.00	48.00	75.00	140	250	350	2,600
1835 sm. dt., sm. 5C	Inc. above	25.00	36.00	48.00	75.00	140	250	350	2,600
1836 lg. 5C.	1,900,000	25.00	36.00	48.00	75.00	140	250	350	2,600
1836 sm. 5C.	Inc. above	25.00	36.00	48.00	75.00	140	250	350	2,600
1837 lg. 5C.	2,276,000	27.50	36.00	48.00	80.00	140	250	350	3,500
1837 sm. 5C.	Inc. above	33.00	40.00	55.00	100.00	200	450	950	8,750

Seated Liberty Half Dime. Seated Liberty, no stars around border, date below. Value within wreath.

KM# 60 **Designer:** Christian Gobrecht. **Diameter:** 15.5 **Weight:** 1.3400 g. **Composition:** 0.9000 Silver, 0.0388 oz. ASW. **Notes:** A design modification in 1837 resulted in small-date and large-date varieties for that year.

Date	Mintage	G-4	VG-8	I-12	VF-20	XF-40	AU-50	MS-60	MS-65
1837 small date	Inc. above	30.00	42.00	62.50	115	190	485	800	3,900
1837 large date	Inc. above	34.00	46.00	70.00	125	200	375	625	3,250
1838O	70,000	95.00	125	250	475	975	1,450	2,500	25,000

Seated Liberty Half Dime. Seated Liberty, stars around top 1/2 of border, date below. Value within wreath.

KM# 62.1 **Designer:** Christian Gobrecht. **Diameter:** 15.5 **Weight:** 1.3400 g. **Composition:** 0.9000 Silver, 0.0388 oz. ASW. **Notes:** The two varieties of 1838 are distinguished by the size of the stars on the obverse. The 1839-O with reverse of 1838-O was struck from rusted reverse dies. The result is a bumpy surface on this variety's reverse.

Date	Mintage	G-4	VG-8	F-12	VF-20	XF-40	AU-50	MS-60	MS-65
1838 large stars	2,255,000	15.00	17.50	20.00	27.50	70.00	150	250	2,250
1838 small stars	Inc. above	18.00	27.50	45.00	100.00	175	315	650	3,850
1839	1,069,150	16.00	18.50	21.00	30.00	75.00	160	250	2,500
1839O	1,034,039	17.50	20.00	25.00	35.00	93.50	185	550	5,500
1839O reverse 1838O	—	500	700	1,200	1,750	3,000	—	—	—
1840	1,344,085	16.00	18.50	21.00	30.00	75.00	160	250	2,100
1840O	935,000	20.00	25.00	35.00	70.00	110	250	700	17,000

Seated Liberty Half Dime. Seated Liberty, stars around top 1/2 of border, date below.

for the 1848 Philadelphia strikes are distinguished by the size of the numerals in the date.

KM# 62.2 **Designer:** Christian Gobrecht. **Diameter:** 15.5 **Weight:** 1.3400 g. **Composition:** 0.9000 Silver, 0.0388 oz. ASW. **Notes:** In 1840 drapery was added to Liberty's left elbow. Varieties

Date	Mintage	G-4	VG-8	F-12	VF-20	XF-40	AU-50	MS-60	MS-65
1840	Inc. above	25.00	40.00	75.00	125	225	350	450	300

Date	Mintage	G-4	VG-8	F-12	VF-20	XF-40	AU-50	MS-60	MS-65
1840O	Inc. above	35.00	60.00	115	225	450	1,250	6,500	—
1841	1,150,000	15.00	17.50	21.00	28.50	56.00	115	160	1,250
1841O	815,000	17.50	20.00	30.00	50.00	125	300	650	6,500
1842	815,000	15.00	17.50	20.00	27.50	55.00	115	160	1,750
1842O	350,000	30.00	45.00	75.00	250	550	1,250	2,500	—
1843	1,165,000	15.00	17.50	20.00	27.50	55.00	110	160	1,350
1844	430,000	17.50	20.00	22.50	31.50	56.00	115	175	1,150
1844O	220,000	75.00	105	175	450	1,000	2,250	5,400	25,000
1845	1,564,000	15.00	17.50	20.00	33.50	56.00	110	160	1,150
1845/1845	Inc. above	16.00	20.00	22.50	35.00	60.00	115	160	1,200
1846	27,000	375	550	850	1,250	2,250	3,600	8,500	—
1847	1,274,000	15.00	17.50	20.00	27.50	55.00	110	160	1,150
1848 medium date	668,000	17.50	20.00	23.50	30.00	57.50	125	230	2,850
1848 large date	Inc. above	22.50	30.00	45.00	65.00	135	275	450	4,000
1848O	600,000	19.00	25.00	33.00	65.00	135	265	400	1,950
1849/8	1,309,000	28.50	35.00	47.50	62.50	125	250	625	2,600
1849/6	Inc. above	20.00	26.00	30.00	52.50	105	200	400	2,500
1849	Inc. above	16.00	18.50	27.50	50.00	65.00	125	180	1,700
1849O	140,000	29.00	40.00	95.00	225	475	1,100	1,950	14,000
1850	955,000	17.50	20.00	23.50	31.50	60.00	115	165	1,400
1850O	690,000	18.50	22.50	35.00	65.00	125	280	675	4,250
1851	781,000	15.00	17.50	20.00	27.50	56.00	110	160	1,500
1851O	860,000	17.50	20.00	25.00	41.50	110	220	500	4,350
1852	1,000,500	15.00	17.50	20.00	27.50	56.00	110	160	1,150
1852O	260,000	25.00	40.00	70.00	135	275	475	750	10,000
1853	135,000	35.00	50.00	75.00	135	220	385	750	3,000
1853O	160,000	250	325	450	850	1,800	3,500	5,250	25,000

Seated Liberty Half Dime. Seated Liberty, stars around top 1/2 of border, arrows at date. Value within wreath.

KM# 76   Designer: Christian Gobrecht. Weight: 1.2400 g. Composition: 0.9000 Silver, 0.0359 oz. ASW.

Date	Mintage	G-4	VG-8	F-12	VF-20	XF-40	AU-50	MS-60	MS-65	Prf-65
1853	13,210,020	13.50	16.00	17.50	21.00	50.00	120	190	1,850	35,000
1853O	2,200,000	13.50	16.00	17.50	21.00	65.00	135	275	3,500	—
1854	5,740,000	13.50	16.00	17.50	21.00	45.00	110	185	1,850	16,000
1854O	1,560,000	13.50	16.00	17.50	21.00	60.00	145	250	4,250	—
1855	1,750,000	13.50	16.00	17.50	21.00	47.00	115	190	1,950	18,000
1855O	600,000	15.00	20.00	30.00	55.00	135	235	600	4,000	—

Seated Liberty Half Dime. Seated Liberty, stars around top 1/2 of border, date below. Value within wreath.

KM# A62.2   Designer: Christian Gobrecht. Weight: 1.2400 g. Composition: 0.9000 Silver, 0.0359 oz. ASW. Notes: On the 1858/inverted date variety, the date was engraved into the die upside down and then re-engraved right side up. Another 1858 variety has the date doubled.

Date	Mintage	G-4	VG-8	F-12	VF-20	XF-40	AU-50	MS-60	MS-65	Prf-65
1856	4,880,000	13.50	16.00	17.50	23.50	50.00	115	170	1,650	15,000
1856O	1,100,000	16.00	18.50	20.00	46.00	95.00	250	550	2,000	—
1857	7,280,000	13.50	16.00	17.50	23.50	50.00	110	170	1,550	5,500
1857O	1,380,000	15.00	16.00	18.50	37.50	60.00	185	325	1,800	—
1858	3,500,000	13.50	16.00	17.50	23.50	55.00	175	300	1,700	5,500
1858 inverted date	Inc. above	30.00	43.50	62.50	90.00	185	275	675	3,000	—
1858 double date	Inc. above	45.00	60.00	90.00	175	285	425	700	—	—
1858O	1,660,000	15.00	16.00	20.00	42.50	75.00	135	265	1,600	—
1859	340,000	16.00	17.50	21.50	34.00	70.00	135	225	1,550	4,000
1859O	560,000	17.50	20.00	28.50	43.50	115	200	260	1,850	—

Seated Liberty Half Dime. Seated Liberty, date below. Value within wreath.

KM# 91 Designer: Christian Gobrecht. **Weight:** 1.2400 g. **Composition:** 0.9000 Silver, 0.0359 oz. ASW. **Notes:** In 1860 the legend "United States of America" replaced the stars on the obverse.

Date	Mintage	G-4	VG-8	F-12	VF-20	XF-40	AU-50	MS-60	MS-65	Prf-65
1860	799,000	13.50	16.00	17.50	21.00	40.00	72.50	125	1,150	1,850
1860O	1,060,000	13.50	16.00	18.50	25.00	43.50	93.50	180	1,450	—
1861	3,361,000	13.50	16.00	17.50	21.00	40.00	72.50	125	1,175	2,500
1861/0	Inc. above	25.00	32.50	59.00	125	260	435	560	4,000	—
1862	1,492,550	20.00	25.00	33.50	43.50	55.00	93.50	160	1,150	1,650
1863	18,460	225	250	300	400	475	550	700	1,650	1,700
1863S	100,000	35.00	45.00	70.00	95.00	165	300	700	2,500	—
1864	48,470	375	475	575	750	950	1,100	1,350	2,250	1,750
1864S	90,000	60.00	75.00	115	175	250	450	700	3,750	—
1865	13,500	375	475	575	750	950	1,100	1,200	1,950	1,750
1865S	120,000	29.00	40.00	60.00	85.00	145	375	800	—	—
1866	10,725	375	475	550	700	875	1,000	1,250	2,550	1,700
1866S	120,000	29.00	40.00	60.00	85.00	145	285	450	5,000	—
1867	8,625	575	650	775	900	1,100	1,200	1,400	2,250	1,750
1867S	120,000	29.00	40.00	60.00	85.00	150	325	550	3,850	—
1868	89,200	70.00	90.00	190	225	300	425	570	2,400	1,750
1868S	280,000	20.00	25.00	35.00	40.00	55.00	125	300	3,250	—
1869	208,600	20.00	25.00	35.00	40.00	55.00	125	235	1,500	1,750
1869S	230,000	18.00	22.00	30.00	35.00	50.00	115	325	4,000	—
1870	536,600	18.00	22.00	30.00	35.00	50.00	125	175	1,200	1,650
1870S unique	—	—	—	—	—	—	—	—	—	—

Note: 1870S, Superior Galleries, July 1986, brilliant uncirculated, $253,000.

Date	Mintage	G-4	VG-8	F-12	VF-20	XF-40	AU-50	MS-60	MS-65	Prf-65
1871	1,873,960	14.00	16.00	17.50	21.00	37.50	75.00	125	1,250	1,650
1871S	161,000	25.00	30.00	45.00	60.00	90.00	175	250	2,450	—
1872	2,947,950	14.00	16.00	17.50	21.00	37.50	75.00	125	1,200	1,650
1872S mint mark in wreath	837,000	14.00	16.00	17.50	21.00	37.50	75.00	125	1,200	—
1872S mint mark below wreath	Inc. above	14.00	16.00	17.50	21.00	37.50	75.00	125	1,200	—
1873	712,600	14.00	16.00	17.50	21.00	37.50	75.00	125	1,300	1,750
1873S	324,000	20.00	25.00	30.00	39.00	50.00	90.00	150	1,350	—

5 CENTS

Shield Nickel. Draped garland above shield, date below. Value within center of rays between stars.

KM# 96 Designer: James B. Longacre. **Diameter:** 20.5 **Weight:** 5.0000 g. **Composition:** Copper-Nickel

Date	Mintage	G-4	VG-8	F-12	VF-20	XF-40	AU-50	MS-60	MS-65	Prf-65
1866	14,742,500	27.50	38.50	50.00	75.00	155	235	260	2,700	3,850
1867	2,019,000	37.50	50.00	67.50	100.00	200	295	350	4,150	75,000

Shield Nickel. Draped garland above shield, date below. Value within circle of stars.

KM# 97 Weight: 5.0000 g. **Composition:** Copper-Nickel

Date	Mintage	G-4	VG-8	F-12	VF-20	XF-40	AU-50	MS-60	MS-65	Prf-65
1867	28,890,500	18.00	21.00	28.00	37.50	60.00	120	160	900	3,450
1868	28,817,000	18.00	21.00	28.00	37.50	60.00	120	160	975	1,500
1869	16,395,000	18.00	21.00	28.00	37.50	60.00	120	160	775	1,000
1870	4,806,000	27.00	34.00	52.00	65.00	90.00	145	200	1,700	1,250
1871	561,000	70.00	90.00	125	170	265	325	375	2,100	1,100
1872	6,036,000	35.00	42.00	70.00	80.00	115	150	235	1,350	820
1873 Open 3	4,550,000	28.00	36.00	52.00	65.00	80.00	135	200	2,400	840
1873 Closed 3	—	34.00	42.00	65.00	90.00	150	220	350	3,250	—
1874	3,538,000	29.00	39.00	70.00	82.00	105	140	225	1,500	1,000
1875	2,097,000	40.00	55.00	80.00	110	145	190	250	2,000	1,650

Date	Mintage	G-4	VG-8	F-12	VF-20	XF-40	AU-50	MS-60	MS-65	Prf-65
1876	2,530,000	38.00	50.00	74.00	100.00	135	175	230	1,000	900
1877 proof	Est. 900	1,500	1,650	1,750	2,000	2,150	2,300	—	—	4,300
1878 proof	2,350	800	875	900	1,100	1,300	1,450	—	—	2,150
1879	29,100	415	520	625	675	750	825	970	2,000	840
1879/8	—	—	—	—	—	—	—	—	—	850
1880	19,995	560	620	775	950	1,300	1,750	3,450	47,500	700
1881	72,375	270	340	445	500	600	730	800	1,900	660
1882	11,476,600	18.00	20.00	27.00	36.00	58.00	115	150	750	660
1883	1,456,919	18.00	21.00	32.00	37.50	60.00	118	160	750	660
1883/2	—	210	285	425	650	850	1,000	1,400	4,000	—

Liberty Nickel. Liberty head left, within circle of stars, date below. Roman numeral value within wreath, without "cents" below.

KM# 111 Designer: Charles E. Barber. **Diameter:** 21.2 **Weight:** 5.0000 g. **Composition:** Copper-Nickel

Date	Mintage	G-4	VG-8	F-12	VF-20	XF-40	AU-50	MS-60	MS-65	Prf-65
1883	5,479,519	5.50	6.50	7.00	7.50	8.00	12.50	26.00	310	1,100

Liberty Nickel. Liberty head left, within circle of stars, date below. Roman numeral value within wreath, "Cents" below.

KM# 112 Weight: 5.0000 g. **Composition:** Copper-Nickel

Date	Mintage	G-4	VG-8	F-12	VF-20	XF-40	AU-50	MS-60	MS-65	Prf-65
1883	16,032,983	16.00	27.50	41.50	57.50	90.00	130	170	720	675
1884	11,273,942	21.00	35.00	41.50	60.00	93.50	135	200	2,000	660
1885	1,476,490	600	650	900	1,100	1,350	1,700	2,050	8,400	3,350
1886	3,330,290	290	345	425	520	715	875	1,100	9,000	1,950
1887	15,263,652	12.50	22.00	32.50	45.00	82.50	115	150	1,450	675
1888	10,720,483	30.00	45.00	70.00	130	185	250	305	2,200	765
1889	15,881,361	11.00	16.00	31.00	55.00	82.50	125	160	1,000	675
1890	16,259,272	8.00	20.00	27.50	41.50	68.50	115	170	1,875	685
1891	16,834,350	6.00	11.00	22.00	38.50	62.50	125	160	1,100	675
1892	11,699,642	7.00	11.00	23.00	41.50	65.00	125	165	1,500	675
1893	13,370,195	5.50	11.00	25.00	38.50	62.50	125	155	1,400	675
1894	5,413,132	17.50	31.00	100.00	165	240	315	375	1,600	800
1895	9,979,884	5.75	8.00	25.00	46.00	70.00	125	150	2,900	690
1896	8,842,920	9.50	20.00	41.50	68.50	100.00	160	215	2,500	750
1897	20,428,735	3.00	4.50	12.50	27.50	44.00	74.00	100.00	1,250	675
1898	12,532,087	2.35	4.50	11.00	23.50	41.50	72.00	140	1,250	675
1899	26,029,031	1.85	2.00	8.50	20.00	34.00	69.00	96.00	725	675
1900	27,255,995	1.85	2.50	8.50	19.50	34.00	72.00	90.00	725	675
1901	26,480,213	1.85	2.50	7.50	15.00	34.00	69.00	88.00	720	675
1902	31,480,579	1.85	2.50	4.50	15.00	31.00	69.00	94.00	720	675
1903	28,006,725	1.85	2.50	5.00	15.00	31.00	69.00	85.00	725	675
1904	21,404,984	1.85	2.50	5.00	12.50	29.00	69.00	88.00	750	700
1905	29,827,276	1.85	2.50	4.50	12.50	29.00	69.00	88.00	720	675
1906	38,613,725	1.85	2.50	4.50	12.50	29.00	69.00	88.00	950	675
1907	39,214,800	1.85	2.25	4.50	12.50	29.00	69.00	88.00	1,400	675
1908	22,686,177	1.85	2.25	4.50	12.50	29.00	69.00	93.00	1,300	675
1909	11,590,526	2.20	2.50	4.50	13.50	32.00	85.00	105	1,350	675
1910	30,169,353	1.85	2.25	4.50	11.00	29.00	55.00	72.00	720	675
1911	39,559,372	1.85	2.25	4.50	11.00	29.00	55.00	72.00	720	675
1912	26,236,714	1.85	2.25	4.50	11.00	29.00	55.00	72.00	720	675
1912D	8,474,000	2.70	4.00	12.00	38.00	74.00	175	290	2,600	—
1912S	238,000	175	245	280	500	850	1,350	1,550	7,500	—
1913 5 known	—	—	—	—	—	—	—	—	—	—

Note: 1913, Superior Sale, March 2001, Proof, $1,840,000.

Buffalo Nickel. Buffalo standing on a mound.

KM# 133   Designer: James Earle Fraser.
Diameter: 21.2 **Weight:** 5.0000 g. **Composition:**
Copper-Nickel

Date	Mintage	G-4	VG-8	F-12	VF-20	XF-40	AU-50	MS-60	MS-65	Prf-65
1913	30,993,520	8.00	11.00	11.75	12.50	18.50	25.00	32.50	200	3,500
1913D	5,337,000	16.00	19.50	21.00	25.00	35.00	57.00	62.50	330	—
1913S	2,105,000	43.00	47.00	50.00	60.00	75.00	100.00	125	725	—

Buffalo Nickel. American Bison standing on a line.

KM# 134   Designer: James Earle Fraser.   **Diameter:** 21.2 **Weight:** 5.0000 g. **Composition:** Copper-Nickel
Notes: In 1913 the reverse design was modified so the ground under the buffalo was represented as a line rather than a mound. On the 1937D 3-legged variety, the buffalo's right front leg is missing, the result of a damaged die.

1918/17D

1937D 3-legged

Date	Mintage	G-4	VG-8	F-12	VF-20	XF-40	AU-50	MS-60	MS-65	Prf-65
1913	29,858,700	8.00	11.00	11.50	12.50	18.50	25.00	34.00	375	2,600
1913D	4,156,000	125	155	180	190	205	240	285	1,575	—
1913S	1,209,000	365	425	445	475	575	675	850	4,300	—
1914	20,665,738	17.00	21.00	22.00	23.00	27.50	37.50	49.00	450	2,250
1914/3	Inc. above	150	300	425	525	700	1,050	2,750	24,000	—
1914D	3,912,000	92.00	130	155	220	315	395	450	1,850	—
1914/3D	Inc. above	—	—	—	—	—	—	—	—	—
1914S	3,470,000	26.00	37.50	45.00	62.50	90.00	145	160	2,050	—
1914/3S	Inc. above	250	500	750	1,000	1,450	2,200	4,300	—	—
1915	20,987,270	5.50	7.00	7.75	11.00	21.50	38.50	50.00	325	2,100
1915D	7,569,500	21.50	31.00	41.50	66.00	115	150	225	2,500	—
1915S	1,505,000	47.00	74.00	105	185	320	490	625	3,400	—
1916	63,498,066	5.00	6.40	7.00	8.00	13.50	24.00	43.50	350	3,650
1916/16	Inc. above	2,000	4,250	8,000	12,000	17,000	38,000	55,000	395,000	—
1916D	13,333,000	15.00	26.50	29.00	38.50	82.50	110	150	2,500	—
1916S	11,860,000	11.00	13.50	20.00	35.00	75.00	125	175	2,650	—
1917	51,424,029	5.00	7.00	8.00	10.00	16.00	32.50	60.00	580	—
1917D	9,910,800	20.00	31.00	55.00	80.00	135	255	345	3,750	—
1917S	4,193,000	23.00	42.00	80.00	110	180	285	395	5,250	—
1918	32,086,314	5.00	6.50	8.00	15.00	31.00	48.50	110	1,700	—
1918/17D	8,362,314	1,150	1,650	2,850	6,250	10,000	11,800	28,500	365,000	—
1918D	Inc. above	22.50	39.00	66.00	135	220	330	430	5,000	—
1918S	4,882,000	14.00	27.50	55.00	100.00	175	300	495	28,500	—
1919	60,868,000	2.20	3.40	3.80	7.00	16.00	32.00	60.00	595	—
1919D	8,006,000	15.50	31.00	66.00	115	235	335	570	7,750	—
1919S	7,521,000	8.00	20.00	50.00	110	225	360	540	26,000	—
1920	63,093,000	1.50	2.75	3.25	8.00	16.00	30.00	59.00	850	—
1920D	9,418,000	8.50	19.00	35.00	125	275	340	555	7,600	—
1920S	9,689,000	4.50	12.75	30.00	100.00	200	300	525	28,500	—
1921	10,663,000	3.75	6.25	8.50	25.00	53.50	73.00	125	850	—
1921S	1,557,000	67.50	120	200	545	845	1,100	1,500	8,000	—
1923	35,715,000	1.70	3.25	4.25	7.00	14.00	37.50	60.00	750	—
1923S	6,142,000	8.00	11.00	27.00	125	275	335	595	12,500	—
1924	21,620,000	1.25	2.40	4.50	10.00	19.00	41.00	73.50	950	—
1924D	5,258,000	8.00	12.00	30.00	90.00	215	315	375	5,600	—
1924S	1,437,000	16.50	32.00	96.00	455	1,100	1,700	2,300	13,500	—
1925	35,565,100	2.50	3.00	3.75	8.50	18.00	32.00	44.00	525	—
1925D	4,450,000	10.00	20.00	38.00	80.00	160	240	380	6,400	—
1925S	6,256,000	4.50	9.00	17.50	77.50	170	250	440	42,500	—
1926	44,693,000	1.50	2.00	2.80	5.40	11.50	20.00	31.50	200	—
1926D	5,638,000	10.00	17.50	28.50	100.00	170	295	315	6,400	—
1926S	970,000	20.00	42.00	100.00	450	900	2,750	5,000	125,000	—
1927	37,981,000	1.40	1.75	2.50	4.50	12.50	20.00	35.00	300	—
1927D	5,730,000	3.00	6.00	7.00	27.50	75.00	115	150	9,000	—
1927S	3,430,000	2.00	3.00	6.00	31.00	80.00	160	485	22,500	—
1928	23,411,000	1.40	1.75	2.50	4.50	12.50	25.00	32.50	325	—
1928D	6,436,000	1.90	2.50	3.75	16.00	40.00	46.50	50.00	950	—
1928S	6,936,000	1.75	2.35	3.00	12.00	27.50	105	215	5,350	—

Date	Mintage	G-4	VG-8	F-12	VF-20	XF-40	AU-50	MS-60	MS-65	Prf-65
1929	36,446,000	1.40	1.75	2.50	4.50	13.00	21.00	35.00	375	—
1929D	8,370,000	1.50	1.85	3.00	6.75	32.50	42.50	55.00	1,950	—
1929S	7,754,000	1.50	1.85	2.25	4.00	12.50	25.00	47.50	525	—
1930	22,849,000	1.40	1.75	2.50	4.50	12.00	21.00	32.50	250	—
1930S	5,435,000	1.50	2.00	3.00	4.50	16.00	37.50	55.00	550	—
1931S	1,200,000	16.00	18.00	20.00	22.00	33.00	50.00	65.00	315	—
1934	20,213,003	1.40	1.75	2.50	4.50	11.00	19.00	48.50	425	—
1934D	7,480,000	2.00	3.00	4.75	9.60	22.00	50.00	82.50	1,000	—
1935	58,264,000	1.25	1.60	2.25	3.00	4.00	11.00	20.00	145	—
1935 Double Die Rev.	Inc. above	50.00	75.00	125	250	600	1,800	3,500	35,000	—
1935D	12,092,000	1.60	2.50	3.00	9.00	20.00	48.00	75.00	525	—
1935D/S	Inc. above	—	—	—	—	—	—	—	—	—
1935S	10,300,000	1.35	1.75	2.50	3.50	4.50	17.50	50.00	260	—
1936	119,001,420	1.25	1.60	2.25	3.00	4.00	6.75	15.00	110	1,750
1936 Brilliant	—	—	—	—	—	—	—	—	—	2,800
1936D	24,814,000	1.35	1.75	2.75	4.00	5.35	11.50	35.00	118	—
1936S	14,930,000	1.35	1.75	2.50	3.50	4.50	11.00	35.00	115	—
1937	79,485,769	1.25	1.60	2.25	3.00	4.00	6.75	14.50	74.00	2,100
1937D	17,826,000	1.35	1.75	2.50	3.50	4.50	9.00	30.00	75.00	—
1937D 3-legged	Inc. above	560	650	950	1,100	1,300	1,500	2,650	26,500	—
1937S	5,635,000	1.35	1.75	2.50	3.50	4.50	10.00	27.50	70.00	—
1938D	7,020,000	3.50	3.75	3.90	4.00	4.50	8.00	20.00	70.00	—
1938D/D		4.00	4.50	6.00	8.00	10.00	17.00	28.00	125	—
1938D/S	Inc. above	4.50	6.75	9.00	12.50	19.00	32.50	50.00	185	—

Jefferson Nickel. Monticello, mintmark to right side.

KM# 192 **Designer:** Felix Schlag. **Diameter:** 21.2
Weight: 5.0000 g. **Composition:** Copper-Nickel
Notes: Some 1939 strikes have doubling of the word
"Monticello" on the reverse.

Date	Mintage	VG-8	F-12	VF-20	XF-40	MS-60	MS-65	-65FS	Prf-65
1938	19,515,365	.30	.50	.80	1.25	4.00	8.50	125	130
1938D	5,376,000	.90	1.00	1.25	1.75	3.50	8.00	95.00	—
1938S	4,105,000	1.75	2.00	2.50	3.00	4.75	8.50	165	—
1939 T I	—	—	—	—	—	—	—	300	70.00
1939 T II	120,627,535	—	.20	.25	.30	1.75	3.50	40.00	130
1939 doubled Monticello T II	—	40.00	60.00	90.00	165	300	1,250	2,000	—
1939D T I	—	—	—	—	—	—	—	275	—
1939D T II	3,514,000	4.00	5.00	7.00	12.00	42.00	125	250	—
1939S T I	—	—	—	—	—	—	—	250	—
1939S T II	6,630,000	.45	.60	1.50	2.75	15.00	45.00	275	—
1940	176,499,158	—	—	—	.25	1.00	3.00	35.00	135
1940D	43,540,000	—	.20	.30	.40	1.50	2.75	25.00	—
1940S	39,690,000	—	.20	.25	.50	2.50	6.00	45.00	—
1941	203,283,720	—	—	—	.20	.75	2.50	40.00	130
1941D	53,432,000	—	.20	.30	.50	2.50	6.00	25.00	—
1941S	43,445,000	—	.20	.30	.50	3.75	6.75	60.00	—
1942	49,818,600	—	—	—	.40	5.00	8.50	75.00	115
1942D	13,938,000	1.00	1.50	3.00	5.00	32.00	60.00	70.00	—

Note: Fully Struck Full Step nickels command higher prices. Bright, Fully Struck coins command even higher prices. 1938 thru 1989 - 5 Full Steps. 1990 to date - 6 Full Steps. Without bag marks or nicks on steps.

Jefferson Nickel. Monticello, mint mark above.

KM# 192a **Designer:** Felix Schlag. **Diameter:**
21.2 **Composition:** 0.3500 Copper-Silver-
Manganese **Notes:** War-time composition nickels
have the mint mark above Monticello on the reverse.

1943/2P

Date	Mintage	VG-8	F-12	VF-20	XF-40	MS-60	MS-65	-65FS	Prf-65
1942P	57,900,600	.65	.85	1.00	1.75	8.00	22.50	70.00	205
1942S	32,900,000	.70	1.00	1.10	1.75	14.00	20.00	125	—
1943P	271,165,000	.50	.85	1.00	1.50	4.00	15.00	35.00	—
1943/2P	Inc. above	35.00	50.00	75.00	110	250	650	1,000	—
1943D	15,294,000	.90	1.20	1.50	1.75	5.00	13.00	30.00	—
1943S	104,060,000	.55	.70	1.00	1.50	6.00	13.00	55.00	—
1944P	119,150,000	.50	.70	1.00	1.50	10.00	22.50	100.00	—
1944D	32,309,000	.60	.80	1.00	1.75	10.00	17.50	30.00	—
1944S	21,640,000	.70	1.00	1.25	2.00	7.00	14.00	185	—
1945P	119,408,100	.50	.70	1.00	1.50	6.00	13.50	125	—
1945D	37,158,000	.55	.75	1.00	1.50	5.50	13.00	40.00	—

Date	Mintage	VG-8	F-12	VF-20	XF-40	MS-60	MS-65	-65FS	Prf-65
1945S	58,939,000	.50	.70	.80	.90	5.00	14.00	250	—

Note: Fully Struck Full Step nickels command higher prices. Bright, Fully Struck coins command even higher prices. 1938 thru 1989 - 5 Full Steps. 1990 to date - 6 Full Steps. Without bag marks or nicks on steps.

Jefferson Nickel. Pre-war design resumed.

KM# A192 Designer: Felix Schlag. **Diameter:** 19.53 **Weight:** 5.0000 g. **Composition:** Copper-Nickel **Notes:** KM#192 design and composition resumed. The 1979-S and 1981-S Type II proofs have clearer mint marks than the Type I proofs of those years.

Date	Mintage	VG-8	F-12	VF-20	XF-40	MS-60	MS-65	-65FS	Prf-65
1946	161,116,000	—	—	.20	.25	.80	3.50	40.00	—
1946D	45,292,200	—	—	.25	.35	.95	3.50	30.00	—
1946S	13,560,000	—	—	.30	.40	.50	2.00	45.00	—
1947	95,000,000	—	—	.20	.25	.75	2.00	30.00	—
1947D	37,822,000	—	—	.20	.30	.90	2.50	30.00	—
1947S	24,720,000	—	—	.20	.25	1.00	2.25	55.00	—
1948	89,348,000	—	—	.20	.25	.50	2.50	60.00	—
1948D	44,734,000	—	—	.25	.35	1.20	4.50	30.00	—
1948S	11,300,000	—	—	.25	.50	1.20	3.50	45.00	—
1949	60,652,000	—	—	.25	.30	2.25	6.00	200	—
1949D	36,498,000	—	—	.30	.40	1.25	5.00	75.00	—
1949D/S	Inc. above	—	35.00	40.00	65.00	170	325	1,750	—
1949S	9,716,000	.25	.35	.45	.90	1.50	3.50	145	—
1950	9,847,386	.20	.30	35	.75	1.50	4.75	150	70.00
1950D	2,630,030	12.00	13.00	14.00	15.00	22.00	30.00	45.00	—
1951	28,609,500	—	—	.40	.50	1.50	9.00	90.00	70.00
1951D	20,460,000	.25	.30	.40	.50	3.00	10.00	45.00	—
1951S	7,776,000	.30	.40	.50	1.10	1.75	5.00	150	— —
1952	64,069,980	—	—	.20	.25	.85	4.50	125	37.50
1952D	30,638,000	—	—	.30	.45	2.00	7.00	65.00	—
1952S	20,572,000	—	—	.20	.25	.75	3.50	195	—
1953	46,772,800	—	—	.20	.25	.40	1.50	200	37.50
1953D	59,878,600	—	—	.20	.25	.40	1.50	100.00	—
1953S	19,210,900	—	—	.20	.25	.60	2.50	1,750	—
1954	47,917,350	—	—	— —	—	.60	2.00	95.00	20.00
1954D	117,136,560	—	—	—	—	.35	2.00	175	—
1954S	29,384,000	—	—	—	.20	1.00	3.00	1,000	—
1954S/D	Inc. above	—	9.00	14.00	20.00	50.00	200	—	—
1955	8,266,200	.25	.35	.40	.45	.75	2.00	85.00	13.50
1955D	74,464,100	—	—	—	—	.20	1.00	150	—
1955D/S	Inc. above	—	10.00	16.00	25.00	65.00	135	185	—
1956	35,885,384	—	—	—	—	.30	.70	35.00	2.50
1956D	67,222,940	—	—	—	—	.25	.60	90.00	—
1957	39,655,952	—	—	—	—	.25	.60	40.00	1.50
1957D	136,828,900	—	—	—	—	.25	.60	55.00	—
1958	17,963,652	—	—	.15	.20	.30	.65	80.00	7.00
1958D	168,249,120	—	—	—	—	.25	.60	30.00	—

Note: Fully Struck Full Step nickels command higher prices. Bright, Fully Struck coins command even higher prices. 1938 thru 1989 - 5 Full Steps. 1990 to date - 6 Full Steps. Without bag marks or nicks on steps.

1959	28,397,291	—	—	—	—	.30	.65	30.00	1.25
1959D	160,738,240	—	—	—	—	.25	.55	45.00	—
1960	57,107,602	—	—	—	—	.25	2.00	60.00	1.00
1960D	192,582,180	—	—	—	—	.25	.55	650	—
1961	76,668,244	—	—	—	—	.25	.55	100.00	1.00
1961D	229,342,760	—	—	—	—	.25	.55	800	—
1962	100,602,019	—	—	—	—	.25	1.50	75.00	1.00
1962D	280,195,720	—	—	—	—	.25	.55	600	—
1963	178,851,645	—	—	—	—	.25	.55	45.00	1.00
1963D	276,829,460	—	—	—	—	.25	.55	650	—
1964	1,028,622,762	—	—	—	—	.25	.55	55.00	1.00
1964D	1,787,297,160	—	—	—	—	.25	.50	500	—
1965	136,131,380	—	—	—	—	.25	.50	225	—
1966	156,208,283	—	—	—	—	.25	.50	350	—
1967	107,325,800	—	—	—	—	.25	.50	275	—
1968 none minted		—	—	—	—	—	—	—	—
1968D	91,227,880	—	—	—	—	.25	.50	750	—
1968S	103,437,510	—	—	—	—	.25	.50	300	0.75
1969 none minted	—	—	—	—	—	—	—	—	—
1969D	202,807,500	—	—	—	—	.25	.50	—	—
1969S	123,099,631	—	—	—	—	.25	.50	450	0.75
1970 none minted	—	—	—	—	—	—	—	—	—
1970D	515,485,380	—	—	—	—	.25	.50	500	—
1970S	241,464,814	—	—	—	—	.25	.50	125	0.75
1971	106,884,000	—	—	—	—	.85	2.00	35.00	—

Date	Mintage	VG-8	F-12	VF-20	XF-40	MS-60	MS-65	-65FS	Prf-65
1971D	316,144,800	—	—	—	—	.25	.50	25.00	—
1971S	(3,220,733)	—	—	—	—	—	—	—	2.00
1972	202,036,000	—	—	—	—	.25	.50	35.00	—
1972D	351,694,600	—	—	—	—	.25	.50	25.00	—
1972S	(3,260,996)	—	—	—	—	—	—	—	2.00
1973	384,396,000	—	—	—	—	—	.50	20.00	—
1973D	261,405,000	—	—	—	—	—	.50	20.00	—
1973S	(2,760,339)	—	—	—	—	—	—	—	1.75
1974	601,752,000	—	—	—	—	—	.50	75.00	—
1974D	277,373,000	—	—	—	—	—	.50	50.00	—
1974S	(2,612,568)	—	—	—	—	—	—	—	2.00
1975	181,772,000	—	—	—	—	—	.75	65.00	—
1975D	401,875,300	—	—	—	—	—	.50	60.00	—
1975S	(2,845,450)	—	—	—	—	—	—	—	2.25
1976	367,124,000	—	—	—	—	—	.75	150	—
1976D	563,964,147	—	—	—	—	—	.60	55.00	—
1976S	(4,149,730)	—	—	—	—	—	—	—	2.00
1977	585,376,000	—	—	—	—	—	.40	65.00	—
1977D	297,313,460	—	—	—	—	—	.55	35.00	—
1977S	(3,251,152)	—	—	—	—	—	—	—	1.75
1978	391,308,000	—	—	—	—	—	.40	40.00	—
1978D	313,092,780	—	—	—	—	—	.40	35.00	—
1978S	(3,127,781)	—	—	—	—	—	—	—	1.75
1979	463,188,000	—	—	—	—	—	.40	95.00	—
1979D	325,867,672	—	—	—	—	—	.40	35.00	—
1979S type I, proof	(3,677,175)	—	—	—	—	—	—	—	1.50
1979S type II, proof	Inc. above	—	—	—	—	—	—	—	1.75
1980P	593,004,000	—	—	—	—	—	.40	30.00	—
1980D	502,323,448	—	—	—	—	.25	.40	25.00	—
1980S	(3,554,806)	—	—	—	—	—	—	—	1.50
1981P	657,504,000	—	—	—	—	.25	.40	70.00	—
1981D	364,801,843	—	—	—	—	.25	.40	40.00	—
1981S type I, proof	(4,063,083)	—	—	—	—	—	—	—	2.00
1981S type II, proof	Inc. above	—	—	—	—	—	—	—	2.50
1982P	292,355,000	—	—	—	—	2.00	12.50	80.00	—
1982D	373,726,544	—	—	—	—	1.50	3.50	45.00	—
1982S	(3,857,479)	—	—	—	—	—	—	—	3.50
1983P	561,615,000	—	—	—	—	1.50	4.00	45.00	—
1983D	536,726,276	—	—	—	—	.75	2.50	35.00	—
1983S	(3,279,126)	—	—	—	—	—	—	—	4.00
1984P	746,769,000	—	—	—	—	1.25	3.00	65.00	—
1984D	517,675,146	—	—	—	—	.30	.85	30.00	—
1984S	(3,065,110)	—	—	—	—	—	—	—	5.00
1985P	647,114,962	—	—	—	—	.35	.75	60.00	—
1985D	459,747,446	—	—	—	—	.35	.75	35.00	—
1985S	(3,362,821)	—	—	—	—	—	—	—	4.00
1986P	536,883,483	—	—	—	—	.40	1.00	70.00	—
1986D	361,819,140	—	—	—	—	1.00	2.00	60.00	—
1986S	(3,010,497)	—	—	—	—	—	—	—	7.00
1987P	371,499,481	—	—	—	—	.25	.75	30.00	—
1987D	410,590,604	—	—	—	—	.25	.75	25.00	—
1987S	(4,227,728)	—	—	—	—	—	—	—	3.50
1988P	771,360,000	—	—	—	—	.25	.75	30.00	—
1988D	663,771,652	—	—	—	—	—	.75	25.00	—
1988S	(3,262,948)	—	—	—	—	—	—	—	6.50
1989P	898,812,000	—	—	—	—	.25	.75	75.00	—
1989D	570,842,474	—	—	—	—	.25	.75	25.00	—
1989S	(3,220,194)	—	—	—	—	—	—	—	5.50
1990P	661,636,000	—	—	—	—	.25	.75	25.00	—
1990D	663,938,503	—	—	—	—	.25	.75	25.00	—
1990S	(3,299,559)	—	—	—	—	—	—	—	5.50
1991P	614,104,000	—	—	—	—	.25	.75	25.00	—
1991D	436,496,678	—	—	—	—	.25	.75	25.00	—
1991S	(2,867,787)	—	—	—	—	—	—	—	5.00
1992P	399,552,000	—	—	—	—	.65	2.00	25.00	—
1992D	450,565,113	—	—	—	—	.25	.75	25.00	—
1992S	(4,176,560)	—	—	—	—	—	—	—	4.00
1993P	412,076,000	—	—	—	—	.25	.75	25.00	—
1993D	406,084,135	—	—	—	—	.25	.75	25.00	—
1993S	(3,394,792)	—	—	—	—	—	—	—	4.50
1994P	722,160,000	—	—	—	—	.25	.75	25.00	—
1994P matte proof	(167,703)	—	—	—	—	—	—	—	75.00
1994D	715,762,110	—	—	—	—	.25	.75	25.00	—
1994S	(3,269,923)	—	—	—	—	—	—	—	4.00
1995P	774,156,000	—	—	—	—	.25	.75	25.00	—
1995D	888,112,000	—	—	—	—	.35	.85	25.00	—
1995S	(2,707,481)	—	—	—	—	—	—	—	4.00
1996P	829,332,000	—	—	—	—	.25	.75	25.00	—
1996D	817,736,000	—	—	—	—	.25	.75	25.00	—

Date	Mintage	VG-8	F-12	VF-20	XF-40	MS-60	MS-65	-65FS	Prf-65
1996S	(2,915,212)	—	—	—	—	—	—	—	4.00
1997P	470,972,000	—	—	—	—	.25	.75	25.00	—
1997P matte proof	(25,000)	—	—	—	—	—	—	—	200
1997D	466,640,000	—	—	—	—	.30	2.00	25.00	—
1997S	(1,975,000)	—	—	—	—	.25	—	—	5.00
1998P	688,272,000	—	—	—	—	.25	.80	25.00	—
1998D	635,360,000	—	—	—	—	.25	.80	25.00	—
1998S	(2,957,286)	—	—	—	—	—	—	—	4.50
1999P	1,212,000,000	—	—	—	—	.25	.80	20.00	—
1999D	1,066,720,000	—	—	—	—	.25	.80	20.00	—
1999S	(3,362,462)	—	—	—	—	—	—	—	3.50
2000P	846,240,000	—	—	—	—	.25	.80	20.00	—
2000D	1,509,520,000	—	—	—	—	.25	.80	20.00	—
2000S	(4,063,361)	—	—	—	—	—	—	—	2.00
2001P	675,704,000	—	—	—	—	.25	.50	20.00	—
2001D	627,680,000	—	—	—	—	.25	.50	20.00	—
2001S	(3,099,096)	—	—	—	—	—	—	—	2.00
2002P	539,280,000	—	—	—	—	.25	.50	—	—
2002D	691,200,000	—	—	—	—	.25	.50	—	—
2002S	(3,157,739)	—	—	—	—	—	—	—	2.00
2003P	441,840,000	—	—	—	—	.25	.50	—	—
2003D	383,040,000	—	—	—	—	.25	.50	—	—
2003S	(3,116,590)	—	—	—	—	—	—	—	2.00

Jefferson - Jefferson era peace medal design: two clasped hands, pipe and hatchet.

KM# 360 **Obv. Designer:** Felix Schlag. **Rev. Designer:** Norman E. Nemeth. **Diameter:** 21.2 **Weight:** 5.0000 g. **Composition:** Copper Nickel

Date	Mintage	MS-65	Prf-65
2004P	361,440,000	.50	—
2004D	372,000,000	.50	—
2004S	—	—	13.00

Jefferson - Lewis and Clark's Keelboat.

KM# 361 **Obv. Designer:** Felix Schlag. **Rev. Designer:** Al Maletsky. **Diameter:** 21.2 **Weight:** 5.0000 g. **Composition:** Copper Nickel

Date	Mintage	MS-65	Prf-65
2004P	366,720,000	.50	—
2004D	344,880,000	.50	—
2004S	—	—	13.00

Jefferson large profile - American Bison right.

KM# 368 **Obv. Designer:** Joe Fitzgerald and Don Everhart II. **Rev. Designer:** Jamie Franki and Norman E. Nemeth. **Diameter:** 21.2 **Weight:** 5.0000 g. **Composition:** Copper Nickel

Date	Mintage	MS-65	Prf-65
2005P	448,320,000	.50	—
2005D	487,680,000	.50	—
2005S	—	—	7.50

Jefferson - Pacific coastline.

KM# 369 **Obv. Designer:** Joe Fitzgerald and Don Everhart. **Rev. Designer:** Joe Fitzgerald and Donna Weaver. **Diameter:** 21.2 **Weight:** 5.0000 g. **Composition:** Copper Nickel

Date	Mintage	MS-65	Prf-65
2005P	394,080,000	.50	—
2005D	411,120,000	.50	—
2005S	—	—	6.50

Jefferson large facing portrait - Enhanced Monticello Reverse.

KM# 381 **Obv. Designer:** Jamie N. Franki and Donna Weaver. **Rev. Designer:** Felix Schlag and John Mercanti. **Diameter:** 21 **Weight:** 5.0000 g. **Composition:** Copper-Nickel

Date	Mintage	MS-65	Prf-65
2006	693,120,000	—	—
2006D	809,280,000	—	—
2006S	—	—	4.00
2007P	—	—	—
2007D	—	—	—
2007S	—	—	4.00

DIME

Draped Bust Dime. Small eagle.

KM# 24 **Designer:** Robert Scot. **Diameter:** 19 **Weight:** 2.7000 g. **Composition:** 0.8920 Silver, 0.0774 oz. ASW. **Notes:** 1797 strikes have either 13 or 16 stars on the obverse.

Date	Mintage	G-4	VG-8	F-12	VF-20	XF-40	MS-60
1796	22,135	1,450	2,350	3,350	4,450	6,750	18,500
1797 13 stars	25,261	1,600	2,650	3,650	4,900	8,000	57,500
1797 16 stars	Inc. above	1,650	2,550	3,500	4,700	7,350	29,000

Draped Bust Dime. Draped bust right, date at angle below. Heraldic eagle.

KM# 31 **Designer:** Robert Scot. **Diameter:** 19 **Weight:** 2.7000 g. **Composition:** 0.8920 Silver, 0.0774 oz. ASW. **Notes:** The 1805 strikes have either 4 or 5 berries on the olive branch held by the eagle.

Date	Mintage	G-4	VG-8	F-12	VF-20	XF-40	MS-60
1798 large 8	27,550	575	700	950	1,500	2,750	7,000
1798 small 8	Inc. above	900	1,150	1,700	2,550	4,400	12,500
1798/97 13 stars	Inc. above	1,700	2,850	4,000	5,800	8,650	70,000
1798/97 16 stars	Inc. above	650	800	1,050	1,650	3,850	11,500

Note: The 1798 overdates have either 13 or 16 stars on the obverse; Varieties of the regular 1798 strikes are distinguished by the size of the 8 in the date

Date	Mintage	G-4	VG-8	F-12	VF-20	XF-40	MS-60
1800	21,760	625	875	1,300	2,175	4,500	32,500
1801	34,640	775	1,000	1,500	3,250	5,600	47,500
1802	10,975	1,500	2,000	3,000	4,200	7,500	52,500
1803	33,040	650	950	1,500	2,200	4,850	—
1804 13 stars	8,265	2,000	3,400	6,500	13,500	32,500	—
1804 14 stars	Inc. above	3,500	4,850	7,500	14,000	40,000	—
1805 4 berries	120,780	450	650	800	1,050	2,150	5,000
1805 5 berries	Inc. above	600	9,000	1,200	1,800	2,700	8,000
1807	165,000	450	650	800	1,050	2,150	5,000

Liberty Cap Dime. Draped bust left, flanked by stars, date below. Eagle with arrows in talons, banner above, value below.

KM# 42 **Designer:** John Reich. **Diameter:** 18.8 **Weight:** 2.7000 g. **Composition:** 0.8920 Silver, 0.0774 oz. ASW. **Notes:** Varieties of the 1814, 1821 and 1828 strikes are distinguished by the size of the numerals in the dates. The 1820 varieties are distinguished by the size of the 0 in the date. The 1823 overdates have either large E's or small E's in "United States of America" on the reverse.

Date	Mintage	G-4	VG-8	F-12	VF-20	XF-40	AU-50	MS-60	MS-65
1809	51,065	150	250	450	800	1,400	3,000	4,500	22,500
1811/9	65,180	90.00	165	275	650	1,100	2,000	4,000	22,500
1814 small date	421,500	60.00	70.00	120	475	700	1,000	2,000	8,000
1814 large date	Inc. above	29.00	35.00	55.00	200	400	800	1,100	8,000
1820 large O	942,587	26.00	33.00	55.00	150	375	750	1,050	8,000
1820 small O	Inc. above	26.00	33.00	55.00	175	425	750	1,050	8,000

Date	Mintage	G-4	VG-8	F-12	VF-20	XF-40	AU-50	MS-60	MS-65
1821 large date	1,186,512	26.00	33.00	60.00	150	375	750	1,050	8,000
1821 small date	Inc. above	26.00	33.00	55.00	175	400	750	1,050	8,000
1822	100,000	425	600	1,100	1,700	3,000	6,000	10,000	—
1823/22 large E's	440,000	26.00	33.00	50.00	150	375	750	1,050	8,000
1823/22 small E's	Inc. above	26.00	33.00	50.00	150	375	750	1,050	8,000
1824/22 mintage undetermined	—	30.00	50.00	150	400	750	1,500	2,500	—
1825	510,000	26.00	33.00	50.00	150	450	900	1,250	8,000
1827	1,215,000	26.00	33.00	50.00	140	375	775	1,050	8,000
1828 large date	125,000	80.00	110	175	375	750	1,275	3,000	—

Liberty Cap Dime. Draped bust left, flanked by stars, date below. Eagle with arrows in talons, banner above, value below.

KM# 48 Designer: John Reich. **Diameter:** 18.5 **Composition:** Silver ASW. **Notes:** The three varieties of 1829 strikes and two varieties of 1830 strikes are distinguished by the size of "10C." on the reverse. On the 1833 "high 3" variety, the last 3 in the date is higher than the first 3. The two varieties of the 1834 strikes are distinguished by the size of the 4 in the date.

Date	Mintage	G-4	VG-8	F-12	VF-20	XF-40	AU-50	MS-60	MS-65
1828 small date	Inc. above	30.00	45.00	75.00	195	475	775	1,750	
1829 very large 10C.	770,000	35.00	45.00	85.00	150	375	600	1,500	—
1829 large 10C.	—	26.00	30.00	40.00	75.00	270	400	725	8,000
1829 medium 10C.	Inc. above	26.00	30.00	40.00	70.00	270	400	725	8,000
1829 small 10C.	Inc. above	26.00	30.00	40.00	70.00	270	400	725	8,000
1829 curl base 2	—	3,200	5,000	7,500	—	—	—	—	—
1830 large 10C	510,000	26.00	30.00	38.00	65.00	260	375	675	8,000
1830 small 10C.	Inc. above	26.00	30.00	38.00	65.00	260	375	675	8,000
1830/29	Inc. above	35.00	60.00	115	250	500	775	1,500	—
1831	771,350	26.00	30.00	38.00	65.00	260	375	675	6,000
1832	522,500	26.00	30.00	38.00	65.00	260	375	675	6,500
1833	485,000	26.00	30.00	38.00	65.00	260	375	675	6,700
1834	635,000	26.00	30.00	38.00	65.00	260	375	675	6,500
1835	1,410,000	26.00	30.00	38.00	66.00	280	375	675	6,500
1836	1,190,000	26.00	30.00	38.00	65.00	260	375	675	6,500
1837	1,042,000	26.00	30.00	38.00	65.00	260	375	675	6,600

Seated Liberty Dime. Seated Liberty, date below. Value within wreath.

KM# 61 Designer: Christian Gobrecht. **Diameter:** 17.9 **Weight:** 2.6700 g. **Composition:** 0.9000 Silver, 0.0773 oz. ASW. **Notes:** The two 1837 varieties are distinguished by the size of the numerals in the date.

Date	Mintage	G-4	VG-8	F-12	VF-20	XF-40	AU-50	MS-60	MS-65
1837 small date	Inc. above	40.00	50.00	85.00	290	550	750	1,100	6,500
1837 large date	Inc. above	40.00	50.00	85.00	290	550	750	1,100	6,500
1838O	406,034	40.00	60.00	110	375	725	1,250	3,500	21,000

Seated Liberty Dime. Seated Liberty, stars around top 1/2 of border, date below. Value within wreath.

KM# 63.1 Obv. Designer: Christian Gobrecht. **Diameter:** 17.9 **Weight:** 2.6700 g. **Composition:** 0.9000 Silver, 0.0773 oz. ASW. **Notes:** The two 1838 varieties are distinguished by the size of the stars on the obverse. The 1838 "partial drapery" variety has

drapery on Liberty's left elbow. The 1839-O with reverse of 1838-O variety was struck from rusted dies. This variety has a bumpy surface on the reverse.

No drapery at elbow

Date	Mintage	G-4	VG-8	F-12	VF-20	XF-40	AU-50	MS-60	MS-65
1838 small stars	1,992,500	25.00	30.00	50.00	80.00	165	350	600	—
1838 large stars	Inc. above	17.50	20.00	30.00	37.50	110	215	280	8,500
1838 partial drapery	Inc. above	35.00	50.00	85.00	150	225	350	550	—
1839	1,053,115	16.00	18.50	25.00	35.00	105	195	280	3,000
1839O	1,323,000	18.50	22.50	35.00	60.00	150	365	1,250	6,000
1839O reverse 1838O	—	165	225	375	550	1,150	—	—	—
1840	1,358,580	16.00	18.50	25.00	35.00	105	195	300	4,000
1840O	1,175,000	18.50	22.50	40.00	70.00	105	365	975	6,500

Seated Liberty Dime. Seated Liberty, stars around top 1/2 of border, date below. Value within wreath.

Drapery at elbow

KM# 63.2 **Designer:** Christian Gobrecht. **Diameter:** 17.9 **Weight:** 2.6700 g. **Composition:** 0.9000 Silver, 0.0773 oz. ASW. **Notes:** Drapery added to Liberty's left elbow

Date	Mintage	G-4	VG-8	F-12	VF-20	XF-40	AU-50	MS-60	MS-65
1840	Inc. above	35.00	50.00	95.00	185	350	1,250	—	—
1841	1,622,500	16.00	18.50	21.50	27.50	50.00	175	260	2,700
1841O	2,007,500	18.50	22.50	28.50	45.00	75.00	250	1,500	5,000
1841O large O	Inc. above	600	900	1,200	2,500	—	—	—	—
1842	1,887,500	15.00	17.50	21.50	26.00	45.00	175	260	2,700
1842O	2,020,000	18.50	23.50	30.00	75.00	225	1,350	2,900	—
1843	1,370,000	15.00	17.50	21.50	26.00	45.00	175	260	3,000
1843/1843	—	16.00	18.50	22.50	30.00	75.00	200	295	—
1843O	150,000	50.00	80.00	135	325	1,100	2,250	—	—
1844	72,500	275	350	550	800	1,450	2,200	3,000	—
1845	1,755,000	16.00	18.50	21.50	27.50	45.00	120	260	2,600
1845/1845	Inc. above	17.00	20.00	35.00	55.00	100.00	175	—	—
1845O	230,000	25.00	35.00	95.00	250	750	1,750	—	—
1846	31,300	250	350	500	950	1,750	2,750	5,500	—
1847	245,000	19.00	25.00	40.00	85.00	150	350	950	9,000
1848	451,500	18.50	21.50	25.00	50.00	95.00	250	750	7,000
1849	839,000	17.50	19.50	23.50	33.50	60.00	140	500	4,000
1849O	300,000	21.50	30.00	50.00	135	275	750	2,200	—
1850	1,931,500	17.50	19.50	23.50	32.50	55.00	120	260	5,900
1850O	510,000	21.50	25.00	40.00	90.00	175	475	1,250	—
1851	1,026,500	17.50	20.00	22.50	30.00	60.00	120	325	5,000
1851O	400,000	21.50	25.00	40.00	90.00	175	500	1,850	—
1852	1,535,500	15.00	16.00	18.50	23.50	50.00	120	290	2,550
1852O	430,000	22.50	30.00	45.00	125	235	550	1,800	—
1853	95,000	95.00	125	200	295	425	575	800	—

Seated Liberty Dime. Seated Liberty, stars around top 1/2 of border, arrows at date. Value within wreath.

KM# 77 **Designer:** Christian Gobrecht. **Weight:** 2.4900 g. **Composition:** 0.9000 Silver, 0.0720 oz. ASW.

Date	Mintage	G-4	VG-8	F-12	VF-20	XF-40	AU-50	MS-60	MS-65	Prf-65
1853	12,078,010	8.00	9.00	10.00	14.00	45.00	125	330	2,500	31,500
1853O	1,100,000	11.00	14.00	20.00	45.00	145	400	900	—	—
1854	4,470,000	8.75	9.25	10.00	15.00	45.00	125	330	2,500	31,500
1854O	1,770,000	10.00	11.00	14.00	25.00	75.00	175	600	—	—
1855	2,075,000	8.75	9.25	14.00	20.00	55.00	150	350	3,800	31,500

Seated Liberty Dime. Seated Liberty, stars around top 1/2 of border, date below. Value within wreath.

KM# A63.2 **Designer:** Christian Gobrecht. **Weight:** 2.4900 g. **Composition:** 0.9000 Silver, 0.0720 oz. ASW. **Notes:** The two 1856 varieties are distinguished by the size of the numerals in the date.

Date	Mintage	G-4	VG-8	F-12	VF-20	XF-40	AU-50	MS-60	MS-65	Prf-65
1856 small date	5,780,000	14.00	15.00	18.00	22.00	37.50	115	250	7,050	38,000
1856 large date	Inc. above	16.00	18.50	19.50	25.00	65.00	175	475	—	—
1856O	1,180,000	16.00	18.50	19.50	35.00	85.00	215	625	5,250	—
1856S	70,000	160	225	375	550	1,200	1,750	—	—	—
1857	5,580,000	14.00	15.50	16.50	22.50	37.50	110	260	2,600	3,400
1857O	1,540,000	14.00	16.00	18.50	27.50	70.00	200	375	2,600	—
1858	1,540,000	14.00	15.50	16.50	22.50	55.00	145	260	2,600	3,400
1858O	290,000	19.00	25.00	40.00	85.00	165	280	800	5,000	—
1858S	60,000	150	200	325	475	1,000	1,500	—	—	—
1859	430,000	16.00	20.00	25.00	45.00	70.00	140	350	—	3,400
1859O	480,000	16.00	20.00	25.00	45.00	80.00	225	550	—	—
1859S	60,000	160	225	375	550	1,350	3,000	—	—	—
1860S	140,000	40.00	55.00	75.00	145	325	800	—	—	—

Seated Liberty Dime. "United States of America" replaced stars. Value within wreath.

KM# 92   Obv. Designer: Christian Gobrecht.
Weight: 2.4900 g. **Composition:** 0.9000 Silver,
0.0720 oz. ASW. **Notes:** The 1873 "closed-3" and
"open-3" varieties are distinguished by the amount
of space between the upper left and lower left serifs
of the 3 in the date.

Date	Mintage	G-4	VG-8	F-12	VF-20	XF-40	AU-50	MS-60	MS-65	Prf-65
1860	607,000	15.00	22.00	29.00	31.00	55.00	125	275	1,350	1,400
1860O	40,000	450	600	1,000	1,950	3,500	5,500	8,500	—	—
1861	1,884,000	15.00	17.00	20.00	23.00	34.00	85.00	150	1,250	1,400
1861S	172,500	55.00	90.00	165	275	400	900	1,400	—	—
1862	847,550	16.00	17.50	19.50	25.00	45.00	77.50	165	1,250	1,400
1862S	180,750	45.00	65.00	95.00	185	375	775	1,000	—	—
1863	14,460	425	500	650	900	950	1,100	1,300	—	1,400
1863S	157,500	40.00	55.00	80.00	145	275	650	1,200	—	—
1864	11,470	425	500	650	750	900	1,000	1,200	—	1,400
1864S	230,000	35.00	45.00	75.00	110	225	425	1,200	—	—
1865	10,500	475	575	700	875	1,000	1,200	1,350	—	1,400
1865S	175,000	45.00	55.00	85.00	145	325	850	—	—	—
1866	8,725	500	600	775	950	1,100	1,200	1,800	—	1,750
1866S	135,000	50.00	65.00	100.00	150	325	700	1,900	—	—
1867	6,625	600	700	950	1,100	1,450	1,600	1,800	—	1,750
1867S	140,000	50.00	60.00	90.00	160	325	700	1,200	—	—
1868	464,000	18.00	22.00	29.00	39.00	85.00	175	300	—	1,400
1868S	260,000	30.00	35.00	50.00	85.00	165	300	600	—	—
1869	256,600	25.00	35.00	45.00	80.00	135	250	600	—	1,400
1869S	450,000	25.00	30.00	40.00	55.00	85.00	175	400	—	—
1870	471,000	18.00	22.00	30.00	40.00	50.00	80.00	150	—	1,400
1870S	50,000	300	375	500	650	850	1,200	2,000	—	—
1871	907,710	16.00	20.00	25.00	33.00	55.00	175	300	—	1,400
1871CC	20,100	2,500	3,500	4,500	6,500	10,000	—	—	—	—
1871S	320,000	35.00	55.00	75.00	130	195	350	900	—	—
1872	2,396,450	12.00	15.00	17.00	20.00	31.00	95.00	175	—	1,400
1872CC	35,480	950	1,250	1,850	3,000	6,500	—	—	—	—
1872S	190,000	40.00	65.00	85.00	150	250	450	1,100	—	—
1873 closed 3	1,568,600	12.50	15.00	18.00	22.00	50.00	100.00	200	—	1,400
1873 open 3	Inc. above	28.00	35.00	50.00	75.00	125	250	650	—	—
1873CC	12,400	—	—	—	—	—	—	—	—	—

Note: 1873-CC, Heritage Sale, April 1999, MS-64, $632,500.

Seated Liberty Dime. Seated Liberty, arrows at date. Value within wreath.

KM# 105   Designer: Christian Gobrecht. **Weight:**
2.5000 g. **Composition:** 0.9000 Silver, 0.0723 oz.
ASW.

Date	Mintage	G-4	VG-8	F-12	VF-20	XF-40	AU-50	MS-60	MS-65	Prf-65
1873	2,378,500	15.00	18.50	25.00	55.00	150	350	500	4,500	4,500
1873CC	18,791	2,350	3,250	4,250	6,500	10,000	—	—	—	—
1873S	455,000	20.00	30.00	40.00	70.00	190	400	1,500	—	—
1874	2,940,700	13.50	17.50	22.50	50.00	150	315	500	4,500	4,500
1874CC	10,817	5,000	6,500	8,000	12,500	25,000	—	—	—	—
1874S	240,000	60.00	75.00	100.00	160	250	450	1,500	—	—

Seated Liberty Dime. Seated Liberty, date below. Value within wreath.

KM# A92 Designer: Christian Gobrecht. **Weight:** 2.5000 g. **Composition:** 0.9000 Silver, 0.0723 oz. ASW. **Notes:** On the 1876-CC doubled-obverse variety, doubling appears in the words "of America" in the legend.

Date	Mintage	G-4	VG-8	F-12	VF-20	XF-40	AU-50	MS-60	MS-65	Prf-65
1875	10,350,700	14.00	16.00	17.50	20.00	30.00	75.00	125	2,250	4,600
1875CC mint mark in wreath	4,645,000	15.00	19.00	22.50	35.00	47.50	90.00	190	2,700	—
1875CC mint mark under wreath	Inc. above	15.00	19.00	27.50	45.00	75.00	165	235	3,000	—
1875S mint mark in wreath	9,070,000	20.00	25.00	30.00	43.00	65.00	125	225	3,100	—
1875S mint mark under wreath	Inc. above	12.50	15.50	17.50	20.00	27.50	72.50	125	1,100	—
1876 Type 1 rev	11,461,150	14.00	16.00	17.50	20.00	30.00	75.00	125	1,100	1,200
1876 Type 2 rev	Inc. above	20.00	25.00	30.00	40.00	60.00	120	200	—	—
1876CC Type 1 rev	8,270,000	20.00	25.00	30.00	40.00	65.00	125	225	—	—
1876CC Type 2 rev	Inc. above	25.00	35.00	48.00	65.00	90.00	175	300	—	—
1876CC doubled die obverse	Inc. above	20.00	26.00	44.00	100.00	185	340	600	—	—
1876S Type 1 rev	10,420,000	14.00	16.00	17.50	20.00	30.00	75.00	125	1,750	—
1876S Type 2 rev	Inc. above	18.00	20.00	24.00	30.00	40.00	90.00	150	—	—
1877 Type 1 rev	7,310,510	14.00	16.00	17.50	20.00	30.00	75.00	125	1,100	1,200
1877 Type 2 rev	Inc. above	18.00	20.00	24.00	30.00	40.00	90.00	150	—	—
1877CC Type 1 rev	7,700,000	25.00	35.00	48.00	65.00	90.00	175	300	1,100	—
1877CC Type 2 rev	Inc. above	20.00	25.00	30.00	40.00	65.00	125	225	—	—
1877S Type 1 rev	2,340,000	—	—	—	—	—	—	—	—	—
1877S Type 2 rev	Inc. above	14.00	18.00	20.00	30.00	50.00	105	225	—	—
1878 Type 1 rev	1,678,800	28.00	35.00	50.00	65.00	100.00	175	—	—	—
1878 Type 2 rev	Inc. above	14.00	16.00	20.00	30.00	36.00	72.50	125	1,500	1,200
1878CC Type 1 rev	200,000	100.00	135	175	285	450	700	—	—	—
1878CC Type 2 rev	Inc. above	65.00	90.00	125	225	370	500	900	3,500	—
1879	15,100	275	310	375	425	500	575	675	1,750	1,500
1880	37,335	250	275	315	350	400	450	550	1,750	1,500
1881	24,975	265	300	350	400	475	550	650	2,500	1,600
1882	3,911,100	14.00	16.00	17.50	20.00	30.00	75.00	125	1,100	1,200
1883	7,675,712	14.00	16.00	17.50	20.00	30.00	75.00	125	1,100	1,200
1884	3,366,380	14.00	16.00	17.50	20.00	30.00	75.00	125	1,100	1,200
1884S	564,969	30.00	35.00	45.00	55.00	125	280	650	—	—
1885	2,533,427	14.00	16.00	17.50	20.00	30.00	75.00	125	1,100	1,200
1885S	43,690	450	650	950	1,750	2,400	3,600	5,000	—	—
1886	6,377,250	12.50	15.00	17.00	20.00	27.50	72.50	125	1,100	1,200
1886S	206,524	50.00	70.00	80.00	125	175	280	600	—	—
1887	11,283,939	14.00	16.00	17.50	20.00	30.00	75.00	125	1,100	1,200
1887S	4,454,450	12.50	15.00	17.00	20.00	38.00	80.00	125	1,100	—
1888	5,496,487	14.00	16.00	17.50	20.00	30.00	75.00	125	1,100	1,200
1888S	1,720,000	12.50	15.00	17.00	25.00	40.00	95.00	200	—	—
1889	7,380,711	14.00	16.00	17.50	20.00	30.00	75.00	125	1,100	1,200
1889S	972,678	14.00	18.00	25.00	45.00	70.00	150	475	4,500	—
1890	9,911,541	14.00	16.00	17.50	20.00	30.00	75.00	125	1,100	1,200
1890S	1,423,076	14.00	15.00	22.50	50.00	85.00	155	400	4,900	—
1891	15,310,600	14.00	16.00	17.50	20.00	30.00	75.00	125	1,100	1,200
1891O	4,540,000	12.50	15.00	17.00	20.00	27.50	72.50	175	1,750	—
1891O /horizontal O	Inc. above	65.00	95.00	125	175	225	400	—	—	—
1891S	3,196,116	13.50	15.00	17.50	20.00	30.00	75.00	225	1,650	—
1891S/S	Inc. above	25.00	30.00	40.00	85.00	135	250	—	—	—

Barber Dime. Laureate head right, date at angle below. Value within wreath.

KM# 113 Designer: Charles E. Barber. **Diameter:** 17.9 **Weight:** 2.5000 g. **Composition:** 0.9000 Silver, 0.0723 oz. ASW.

Date	Mintage	G-4	VG-8	F-12	VF-20	XF-40	AU-50	MS-60	MS-65	Prf-65
1892	12,121,245	5.00	7.00	16.00	23.50	27.50	70.00	110	750	1,450
1892O	3,841,700	11.00	15.00	32.50	54.00	75.00	96.00	160	1,275	—
1892S	990,710	66.00	115	200	235	285	335	425	4,000	—
1893	3,340,792	8.25	12.50	20.00	30.00	46.00	82.50	160	1,000	1,450
1893O	1,760,000	31.00	45.00	115	150	190	250	330	3,250	—
1893S	2,491,401	14.00	25.00	37.50	45.00	85.00	155	300	4,350	—
1894	1,330,972	25.00	45.00	115	155	190	235	320	1,200	1,450

Date	Mintage	G-4	VG-8	F-12	VF-20	XF-40	AU-50	MS-60	MS-65	Prf-65
1894O	720,000	70.00	105	205	275	445	650	1,550	15,500	—
1894S	24	—	—	—	—	—	—	—1,300,000		—

Note: 1894S, Eliasberg Sale, May 1996, Prf-64, $451,000.

Date	Mintage	G-4	VG-8	F-12	VF-20	XF-40	AU-50	MS-60	MS-65	Prf-65
1895	690,880	85.00	180	345	480	575	650	775	2,800	2,000
1895O	440,000	385	575	880	1,250	2,500	3,800	6,000	19,500	—
1895S	1,120,000	43.50	60.00	130	185	240	320	500	7,800	—
1896	2,000,762	11.50	23.00	55.00	90.00	100.00	120	160	1,500	1,450
1896O	610,000	80.00	155	295	375	480	715	1,000	9,400	—
1896S	575,056	85.00	160	280	325	400	525	770	4,600	—
1897	10,869,264	2.50	3.45	8.00	15.00	32.50	76.00	130	700	1,450
1897O	666,000	69.50	115	280	375	480	615	975	4,700	—
1897S	1,342,844	21.00	45.00	96.00	125	185	275	450	4,250	—
1898	16,320,735	2.50	3.45	8.00	15.00	32.50	76.00	130	720	1,450
1898O	2,130,000	13.00	27.50	85.00	140	205	285	450	4,150	—
1898S	1,702,507	8.50	15.00	32.50	47.50	80.00	160	370	3,850	—
1899	19,580,846	2.50	2.80	7.50	11.50	26.00	70.00	115	700	1,450
1899O	2,650,000	9.75	19.50	70.00	100.00	150	230	415	4,850	—
1899S	1,867,493	8.50	16.00	26.00	34.00	47.50	110	300	4,600	—
1900	17,600,912	2.80	4.00	7.00	11.00	27.50	780	100.00	825	1,450
1900O	2,010,000	19.50	38.50	110	150	225	355	595	6,000	—
1900S	5,168,270	4.75	6.25	12.50	19.50	31.50	75.00	155	1,900	—
1901	18,860,478	2.50	3.75	6.50	10.00	27.50	65.00	110	850	1,450
1901O	5,620,000	3.75	5.25	16.00	27.50	67.50	180	450	4,500	—
1901S	593,022	80.00	150	360	450	520	675	1,000	5,500	—
1902	21,380,777	3.00	3.75	5.50	8.00	23.00	65.00	100.00	700	1,450
1902O	4,500,000	3.45	5.25	15.00	32.50	62.50	135	340	4,650	—
1902S	2,070,000	8.00	21.00	55.00	85.00	135	200	385	4,000	—
1903	19,500,755	2.50	3.75	4.40	8.00	25.00	65.00	110	1,150	1,450
1903O	8,180,000	3.50	5.00	13.50	23.50	50.00	110	250	5,100	—
1903S	613,300	84.00	130	340	490	770	845	1,150	3,750	—
1904	14,601,027	2.50	3.75	6.25	9.50	25.00	65.00	110	1,950	1,450
1904S	800,000	45.00	75.00	160	240	345	480	750	4,500	—
1905	14,552,350	2.80	3.45	5.60	8.00	25.00	65.00	110	700	1,450
1905O	3,400,000	4.00	10.00	34.00	57.50	96.00	155	285	1,900	—
1905S	6,855,199	3.50	3.85	9.00	18.50	45.00	100.00	220	800	—
1906	19,958,406	1.75	2.20	3.75	6.75	22.00	62.50	100.00	700	1,450
1906D	4,060,000	2.75	3.85	7.00	15.00	36.00	80.00	175	1,600	—
1906O	2,610,000	5.50	13.00	47.50	75.00	100.00	135	200	1,300	—
1906S	3,136,640	2.80	5.25	12.50	22.00	46.00	115	240	1,300	—
1907	22,220,575	1.75	2.20	3.40	6.75	22.00	62.50	110	700	1,450
1907D	4,080,000	2.50	4.00	8.50	17.50	45.00	115	280	4,600	—
1907O	5,058,000	3.45	6.75	31.50	47.50	62.50	110	210	1,350	—
1907S	3,178,470	3.45	5.50	16.00	27.50	67.50	150	420	2,500	—
1908	10,600,545	2.20	2.50	3.40	6.75	22.00	62.50	110	700	1,450
1908D	7,490,000	2.15	2.50	4.65	9.50	30.00	62.50	130	1,150	—
1908O	1,789,000	5.00	11.00	42.50	61.00	96.00	150	300	1,700	—
1908S	3,220,000	3.45	5.25	11.50	22.00	47.50	175	325	2,750	—
1909	10,240,650	2.20	2.50	3.40	6.75	22.00	62.50	110	700	1,700
1909D	954,000	7.50	19.50	60.00	96.00	135	230	500	3,600	—
1909O	2,287,000	4.00	7.50	12.50	22.00	50.00	96.00	190	2,000	—
1909S	1,000,000	9.00	20.00	85.00	125	190	330	535	3,200	—
1910	11,520,551	1.85	2.20	3.40	9.50	23.00	62.50	110	700	1,450
1910D	3,490,000	2.50	4.00	8.50	19.50	47.50	110	220	1,550	—
1910S	1,240,000	5.25	10.00	50.00	71.00	110	200	435	2,600	—
1911	18,870,543	1.75	2.10	3.40	6.75	22.00	62.50	110	700	1,700
1911D	11,209,000	1.75	2.10	3.40	6.75	25.00	62.50	110	750	—
1911S	3,520,000	2.80	3.75	8.50	19.00	41.50	110	200	1,300	—
1912	19,350,700	1.75	2.10	3.40	6.75	22.00	62.50	110	700	1,700
1912D	11,760,000	1.75	2.10	3.75	6.75	22.00	62.50	110	700	—
1912S	3,420,000	2.20	2.75	5.60	12.50	34.00	96.00	160	850	—
1913	19,760,622	1.75	2.10	3.00	6.50	22.00	62.50	110	700	1,450
1913S	510,000	22.00	32.00	85.00	135	240	330	480	1,350	—
1914	17,360,655	1.75	2.10	3.00	6.50	22.00	62.50	110	700	1,700
1914D	11,908,000	1.75	2.10	3.40	6.50	22.00	62.50	110	700	—
1914S	2,100,000	3.00	4.00	8.00	17.50	41.50	80.00	150	1,350	—
1915	5,620,450	2.20	2.50	3.00	7.00	22.00	62.50	110	700	2,000
1915S	960,000	7.00	12.00	32.50	47.50	70.00	135	250	1,600	—
1916	18,490,000	1.75	2.15	3.40	8.00	22.00	62.50	110	700	—
1916S	5,820,000	1.75	2.65	4.00	8.00	23.50	65.00	110	850	—

Mercury Dime.

KM# 140 Designer: Adolph A. Weinman.
Diameter: 17.9 **Weight:** 2.5000 g. **Composition:**
0.9000 Silver, 0.0723 oz. ASW. **Notes:** All
specimens listed as -65FSB are for fully struck
MS-65 coins with fully split and rounded
horizontal bands on the fasces.

Mint mark

Date	Mintage	G-4	VG-8	F-12	VF-20	XF-40	AU-50	MS-60	MS-63	MS-65	-65FSB
1916	22,180,080	3.45	4.70	6.25	7.00	12.00	22.50	30.00	43.00	110	120
1916D	264,000	1,000	1,600	2,700	3,850	6,200	9,250	13,750	18,400	26,500	44,500
1916S	10,450,000	4.00	5.50	9.75	15.00	25.00	30.00	46.00	60.00	210	600
1917	55,230,000	1.85	2.25	2.50	5.50	8.00	12.50	28.00	55.00	155	400
1917D	9,402,000	4.00	6.00	11.00	26.00	51.00	92.50	120	300	1,100	6,000
1917S	27,330,000	1.80	2.40	3.50	6.50	14.00	28.00	64.00	170	470	1,150
1918	26,680,000	2.50	3.20	5.75	12.00	34.00	42.00	70.00	95.00	420	1,150
1918D	22,674,800	2.65	3.25	5.00	12.00	32.00	46.00	105	210	600	33,500
1918S	19,300,000	2.40	3.00	3.85	10.00	24.00	38.50	96.00	230	660	6,600
1919	35,740,000	1.90	2.50	3.00	5.50	12.00	23.00	37.00	105	315	700
1919D	9,939,000	3.50	6.50	12.00	25.00	46.00	72.00	180	420	2,100	38,500
1919S	8,850,000	2.90	3.25	8.00	17.00	42.00	72.00	180	450	1,250	13,000
1920	59,030,000	1.50	1.75	2.25	4.00	8.50	14.00	28.00	67.00	235	515
1920D	19,171,000	2.50	2.85	4.50	8.00	24.00	46.00	110	310	750	4,000
1920S	13,820,000	2.40	2.75	4.00	8.50	21.00	42.00	110	300	1,300	8,000
1921	1,230,000	60.00	75.00	125	280	550	875	1,175	1,465	3,100	4,400
1921D	1,080,000	78.00	125	205	380	675	1,175	1,325	1,650	3,250	5,600
1923	50,130,000	1.50	2.00	2.25	4.00	7.00	15.00	28.00	42.00	115	295
1923S	6,440,000	2.60	3.00	7.50	18.00	75.00	100.00	160	375	1,150	6,900
1924	24,010,000	1.50	2.00	2.75	4.50	13.50	26.50	42.00	88.00	175	520
1924D	6,810,000	3.00	4.25	6.50	22.00	63.00	100.00	175	460	1,050	1,400
1924S	7,120,000	2.90	3.75	4.25	12.00	60.00	95.00	170	450	1,100	14,000
1925	25,610,000	1.50	1.75	2.35	4.00	9.00	16.00	28.00	75.00	210	1,000
1925D	5,117,000	4.00	4.25	12.00	44.00	135	190	350	725	1,750	3,500
1925S	5,850,000	2.50	2.75	7.00	14.00	85.00	100.00	185	475	1,400	4,400
1926	32,160,000	1.50	1.75	2.00	3.00	6.00	12.00	25.00	55.00	240	525
1926D	6,828,000	2.90	4.00	5.00	10.00	32.00	43.00	125	260	550	2,650
1926S	1,520,000	10.50	12.50	29.00	70.00	290	410	900	1,425	3,000	6,500
1927	28,080,000	1.50	1.75	2.00	3.50	6.00	11.00	26.00	48.00	138	400
1927D	4,812,000	2.90	5.00	7.50	21.00	88.00	92.50	175	360	1,285	8,500
1927S	4,770,000	2.25	3.75	5.00	9.00	32.00	48.00	285	550	1,400	7,700
1928	19,480,000	1.50	1.75	1.85	3.50	4.50	16.00	27.50	48.00	120	300
1928D	4,161,000	3.75	4.00	9.00	22.00	55.00	85.00	175	315	875	2,500
1928S Large S	740,000	2.75	3.25	4.50	10.00	30.00	60.00	200	385	640	—
1928S Small S	Inc. above	2.00	2.25	3.00	6.50	19.00	37.00	125	280	425	1,900
1929	25,970,000	1.50	1.75	2.10	3.00	4.50	10.00	21.00	28.00	60.00	265
1929D	5,034,000	2.00	3.00	4.00	8.00	15.00	22.00	27.00	30.00	75.00	225
1929S	4,730,000	1.50	1.85	2.25	5.00	7.00	20.00	32.50	42.00	90.00	525
1929S Doubled Die Obv	Inc. above	5.00	9.00	16.00	25.00	40.00	60.00	90.00	140	275	—
1930	6,770,000	1.50	1.75	2.10	3.75	7.00	13.00	26.00	48.00	120	525
1930S	1,843,000	2.50	3.50	4.80	6.50	19.00	45.00	82.00	122	200	565
1931	3,150,000	2.25	3.00	3.35	4.25	12.50	22.50	33.00	62.50	135	—
1931D	1,260,000	9.00	11.00	15.00	18.00	45.00	56.00	100.00	125	285	350
1931 Doubled Die Obv & Rev	Inc. above	—	—	—	50.00	70.00	90.00	135	200	485	—
1931S	1,800,000	4.00	5.00	5.50	11.00	22.00	45.00	96.00	135	275	2,100
1931S Doubled Die Obv	—	7.50	10.00	13.00	25.00	35.00	60.00	140	200	425	—
1934	24,080,000	—	1.45	1.75	3.00	6.50	10.00	29.00	33.00	42.00	150
1934D	6,772,000	1.60	2.10	3.25	7.50	14.00	27.50	50.00	60.00	78.00	360
1935	58,830,000	—	1.35	1.50	2.15	4.25	7.50	10.00	15.00	30.00	70.00
1935D	10,477,000	1.50	1.90	2.85	6.50	13.00	25.00	37.00	46.00	84.00	600
1935S	15,840,000	1.35	1.65	2.00	3.00	5.50	14.00	24.00	28.00	37.00	500
1936	87,504,130	—	—	1.50	2.50	3.50	6.50	9.00	15.00	26.50	90.00
1936 Doubled Die Obv	Inc. above	—	—	8.00	15.00	25.00	35.00	50.00	100.00	165	—
1936D	16,132,000	—	1.65	2.10	4.25	8.50	17.00	28.00	36.00	53.00	295
1936S	9,210,000	—	1.50	1.90	3.00	6.00	12.50	20.00	30.00	33.00	85.00
1937	56,865,756	—	—	1.50	2.00	3.75	6.00	8.00	12.00	24.00	42.00
1937 Doubled Die Obv	Inc. above	—	—	—	6.00	9.00	12.00	20.00	40.00	60.00	—
1937D	14,146,000	—	1.40	1.80	3.00	6.00	12.50	22.00	30.00	43.00	100.00
1937S	9,740,000	—	1.50	2.00	3.00	5.50	10.00	22.00	27.00	36.00	195
1937S Doubled Die Obv	Inc. above	—	—	—	5.00	7.00	9.00	24.00	40.00	80.00	—
1938	22,198,728	—	—	1.50	2.25	3.75	7.50	13.00	15.00	25.00	80.00
1938D	5,537,000	1.75	2.25	3.25	5.00	6.00	12.00	18.00	24.00	34.00	65.00
1938S	8,090,000	1.50	2.00	2.75	3.25	5.00	12.00	21.00	27.50	37.00	135
1939	67,749,321	—	—	1.50	2.00	3.25	4.50	9.00	11.00	25.00	170

Date	Mintage	G-4	VG-8	F-12	VF-20	XF-40	AU-50	MS-60	MS-63	MS-65	-65FSB
1939 Doubled Die Obv	Inc. above	—	—	—	4.00	6.00	8.00	14.00	20.00	35.00	—
1939D	24,394,000	—	1.25	1.50	2.00	3.50	5.50	7.50	10.00	26.00	45.00
1939S	10,540,000	1.50	1.75	2.25	3.50	6.75	14.00	25.00	32.00	50.00	750
1940	65,361,827	—	—	—	1.25	2.50	4.00	6.00	11.00	30.00	57.50
1940D	21,198,000	—	—	—	1.40	3.00	5.00	8.00	13.00	32.00	55.00
1940S	21,560,000	—	—	—	1.40	3.00	4.50	8.50	12.50	32.00	95.00
1941	175,106,557	—	—	—	1.25	1.60	2.75	6.00	10.00	30.00	42.00
1941 Doubled Die Obv	Inc. above	—	—	—	10.00	16.00	30.00	55.00	80.00	140	—
1941D	45,634,000	—	—	—	1.40	2.00	4.00	8.00	13.00	23.00	40.00
1941D Doubled Die Obv	Inc. above	—	—	—	9.00	14.00	20.00	30.00	60.00	90.00	—
1941S Small S	43,090,000	—	—	—	1.40	2.00	4.50	7.00	10.00	30.00	50.00
1941S Large S	Inc. above	2.50	4.00	8.00	15.00	25.00	60.00	110	145	250	—
1941S Doubled Die Rev	—	1.75	2.50	3.00	4.00	5.00	7.50	18.00	25.00	50.00	—
1942	205,432,329	—	—	—	1.25	1.60	2.00	6.00	11.00	24.00	52.50
1942/41	Inc. above	525	525	625	735	800	1,500	2,250	4,000	12,500	38,500
1942D	60,740,000	—	—	—	1.40	2.00	4.00	8.00	12.75	27.50	40.00
1942/41D	Inc. above	500	505	680	840	920	1,400	2,650	4,500	7,000	19,500
1942S	49,300,000	—	—	—	1.40	2.00	4.50	9.50	16.00	24.00	140
1943	191,710,000	—	—	—	1.25	1.60	2.25	6.00	10.00	31.00	50.00
1943D	71,949,000	—	—	—	1.40	2.00	3.00	7.75	12.00	30.00	40.00
1943S	60,400,000	—	—	—	1.40	2.00	4.50	9.00	13.00	26.50	66.00
1944	231,410,000	—	—	—	1.25	1.60	2.25	6.00	10.00	23.00	80.00
1944D	62,224,000	—	—	—	1.40	2.00	3.00	7.50	15.00	23.00	40.00
1944S	49,490,000	—	—	—	1.40	2.00	4.00	7.50	16.00	30.00	60.00
1945	159,130,000	—	—	—	1.25	1.00	2.25	6.00	10.00	23.00	8,000
1945D	40,245,000	—	—	—	1.40	2.00	2.75	6.50	10.00	24.00	40.00
1945S	41,920,000	—	—	—	1.40	2.00	4.00	7.00	10.00	24.00	135
1945S micro S	Inc. above	3.00	4.00	6.00	9.00	13.00	20.00	28.00	38.00	115	650

Roosevelt Dime.

KM# 195 Designer: John R. Sinnock.
Diameter: 17.9 **Weight:** 2.5000 g.
Composition: 0.9000 Silver, 0.0723 oz. ASW.

Mint mark
1946-69

Date	Mintage	G-4	VG-8	F-12	VF-20	XF-40	AU-50	MS-60	MS-65	Prf-65
1946	225,250,000	—	—	—	—	1.10	1.45	2.00	14.00	—
1946D	61,043,500	—	—	—	—	1.10	1.50	2.25	15.00	—
1946S	27,900,000	—	—	—	—	1.20	1.55	2.35	17.00	—
1947	121,520,000	—	—	—	—	1.30	2.00	4.00	15.00	—
1947D	46,835,000	—	—	—	—	1.50	2.25	5.00	17.00	—
1947S	34,840,000	—	—	—	—	1.30	2.00	5.00	16.00	—
1948	74,950,000	—	—	—	—	1.40	2.00	4.50	15.00	—
1948D	52,841,000	—	—	—	—	1.60	2.50	6.00	17.00	—
1948S	35,520,000	—	—	—	—	1.50	2.25	5.00	14.00	—
1949	30,940,000	—	—	1.50	2.00	3.00	8.00	16.00	50.00	—
1949D	26,034,000	—	—	1.35	1.50	2.25	5.00	9.00	22.00	—
1949S	13,510,000	—	1.60	2.00	3.50	7.50	14.00	40.00	65.00	—
1950	50,181,500	—	—	—	1.40	2.25	3.50	10.00	25.00	55.00
1950D	46,803,000	—	—	—	—	—	2.50	5.00	12.00	—
1950S	20,440,000	—	1.20	1.50	2.00	3.75	9.00	32.00	60.00	—
1951	102,937,602	—	—	—	—	—	1.60	2.50	10.00	60.00
1951D	56,529,000	—	—	—	—	—	1.45	2.50	8.00	—
1951S	31,630,000	—	—	—	1.20	2.00	4.00	10.00	26.00	—
1952	99,122,073	—	—	—	—	—	1.35	2.50	9.00	40.00
1952D	122,100,000	—	—	—	—	—	1.25	2.50	10.00	—
1952S	44,419,500	—	—	—	1.35	1.50	2.75	5.50	15.00	—
1953	53,618,920	—	—	—	—	—	1.35	2.25	8.00	45.00
1953D	136,433,000	—	—	—	—	—	1.35	2.00	8.00	—
1953S	39,180,000	—	—	—	—	—	1.75	3.00	15.00	—
1954	114,243,503	—	—	—	—	—	1.10	1.50	7.00	20.00
1954D	106,397,000	—	—	—	—	—	1.10	1.50	7.00	—
1954S	22,860,000	—	—	—	—	—	1.25	1.50	10.00	—
1955	12,828,381	—	—	—	1.25	1.40	1.70	2.75	10.00	18.00
1955D	13,959,000	—	—	—	1.35	1.50	1.85	2.75	10.00	—
1955S	18,510,000	—	—	—	1.30	1.45	1.75	2.25	9.00	—
1956	109,309,384	—	—	—	—	—	1.35	1.50	9.00	8.00
1956D	108,015,100	—	—	—	—	—	1.45	1.60	10.00	—
1957	161,407,952	—	—	—	—	—	1.35	1.50	8.00	6.00
1957D	113,354,330	—	—	—	—	—	1.35	1.50	8.00	—
1958	32,785,652	—	—	—	—	—	1.35	1.50	8.50	6.00
1958D	136,564,600	—	—	—	—	—	1.35	1.50	9.00	—
1959	86,929,291	—	—	—	—	—	1.35	1.50	8.00	5.00

Date	Mintage	G-4	VG-8	F-12	VF-20	XF-40	AU-50	MS-60	MS-65	Prf-65
1959D	164,919,790	—	—	—	—	—	1.35	1.50	8.00	—
1960	72,081,602	—	—	—	—	—	1.35	1.50	7.50	5.00
1960D	200,160,400	—	—	—	—	—	1.35	1.50	7.50	—
1961	96,758,244	—	—	—	—	—	1.35	1.50	6.50	4.50
1961D	209,146,550	—	—	—	—	—	1.35	1.50	6.50	—
1962	75,668,019	—	—	—	—	—	1.35	1.50	7.00	4.50
1962D	334,948,380	—	—	—	—	—	1.35	1.50	7.00	—
1963	126,725,645	—	—	—	—	—	1.35	1.50	6.50	4.00
1963D	421,476,530	—	—	—	—	—	1.35	1.50	6.50	—
1964	933,310,762	—	—	—	—	—	1.35	1.50	6.00	4.00
1964D	1,357,517,180	—	—	—	—	—	1.35	1.50	6.00	—

Roosevelt Dime.

KM# 195a   Designer: John R. Sinnock.   **Diameter:** 17.9 **Weight:** 2.2700 g. **Composition:** Copper-Nickel Clad Copper **Notes:** The 1979-S and 1981-S Type II proofs have clearer mint marks than the Type I proofs of those years. On the 1982 no-mint-mark variety, the mint mark was inadvertently left off.

1982 No mint mark

Mint mark 1968 - present

Date	Mintage	MS-65	Prf-65
1965	1,652,140,570	1.00	—
1966	1,382,734,540	1.00	—
1967	2,244,007,320	1.50	—
1968	424,470,000	1.00	—
1968D	480,748,280	1.00	—
1968S	(3,041,506)	—	1.00
1969	145,790,000	3.00	—
1969D	563,323,870	1.00	—
1969S	(2,934,631)	—	0.80
1970	345,570,000	1.00	—
1970S No S	—	—	1,300
1970D	754,942,100	1.00	—
1970S	(2,632,810)	—	1.00
1971	162,690,000	2.00	—
1971D	377,914,240	1.00	—
1971S	(3,220,733)	—	1.00
1972	431,540,000	1.00	—
1972D	330,290,000	1.00	—
1972S	(3,260,996)	—	1.00
1973	315,670,000	1.00	—
1973D	455,032,426	1.00	—
1973S	(2,760,339)	—	1.00
1974	470,248,000	1.00	—
1974D	571,083,000	1.00	—
1974S	(2,612,568)	—	1.00
1975	585,673,900	1.00	—
1975D	313,705,300	1.00	—
1975S	(2,845,450)	—	2.00
1976	568,760,000	1.50	—
1976D	695,222,774	1.00	—
1976S	(4,149,730)	—	1.00
1977	796,930,000	1.00	—
1977D	376,607,228	1.00	—
1977S	(3,251,152)	—	2.00
1978	663,980,000	1.00	—
1978D	282,847,540	1.00	—
1978S	(3,127,781)	—	1.00
1979	315,440,000	1.00	—
1979D	390,921,184	1.00	—
1979 type I	—	—	1.00
1979S type I	(3,677,175)	—	1.00
1979S type II	Inc. above	—	2.00
1980P	735,170,000	1.00	—
1980D	719,354,321	.70	—
1980S	(3,554,806)	—	1.00
1981P	676,650,000	1.00	—
1981D	712,284,143	1.00	—
1981S type I	—	—	1.00
1981S type II	—	—	2.00
1982P	519,475,000	8.50	—
1982 no mint mark	—	300	—

Date	Mintage	MS-65	Prf-65
1982D	542,713,584	3.00	—
1982S	(3,857,479)	—	2.00
1983P	647,025,000	7.00	—
1983D	730,129,224	2.50	—
1983S	(3,279,126)	—	2.00
1984P	856,669,000	1.00	—
1984D	704,803,976	2.00	—
1984S	(3,065,110)	—	2.00
1985P	705,200,962	1.00	—
1985D	587,979,970	1.00	—
1985S	(3,362,821)	—	1.00
1986P	682,649,693	2.00	—
1986D	473,326,970	2.00	—
1986S	(3,010,497)	—	2.75
1987P	762,709,481	1.00	—
1987D	653,203,402	1.00	—
1987S	(4,227,728)	—	1.00
1988P	1,030,550,000	1.00	—
1988D	962,385,488	1.00	—
1988S	(3,262,948)	—	3.00
1989P	1,298,400,000	1.00	—
1989D	896,535,597	1.00	—
1989S	(3,220,194)	—	4.00
1990P	1,034,340,000	1.00	—
1990D	839,995,824	1.00	—
1990S	(3,299,559)	—	2.00
1991P	927,220,000	1.00	—
1991D	601,241,114	1.00	—
1991S	(2,867,787)	—	3.00
1992P	593,500,000	1.00	—
1992D	616,273,932	1.00	—
1992S	(2,858,981)	—	4.00
1993P	766,180,000	1.00	—
1993D	750,110,166	1.50	—
1993S	(2,633,439)	—	7.00
1994P	1,189,000,000	1.00	—
1994D	1,303,268,110	1.00	—
1994S	(2,484,594)	—	5.00
1995P	1,125,500,000	1.50	—
1995D	1,274,890,000	2.00	—
1995S	(2,010,384)	—	20.00
1996P	1,421,163,000	1.00	—
1996D	1,400,300,000	1.00	—
1996W	1,457,949	25.00	—
1996S	(2,085,191)	—	2.50
1997P	991,640,000	2.00	—
1997D	979,810,000	1.00	—
1997S	(1,975,000)	—	11.00
1998P	1,163,000,000	1.00	—
1998D	1,172,250,000	1.25	—
1998S	(2,078,494)	—	4.00

Date	Mintage	MS-65	Prf-65
1999P	2,164,000,000	1.00	—
1999D	1,397,750,000	1.00	—
1999S	(2,557,897)	—	4.00
2000P	1,842,500,000	1.00	—
2000D	1,818,700,000	1.00	—
2000S	(3,097,440)	—	1.00
2001P	1,369,590,000	1.00	—
2001D	1,412,800,000	1.00	—
2001S	(2,249,496)	—	1.00
2002P	1,187,500,000	1.00	—
2002D	1,379,500,000	1.00	—
2002S	(2,268,913)	—	2.00
2003P	1,085,500,000	1.00	—
2003D	986,500,000	1.00	—
2003S	(2,076,165)	—	2.00
2004P	1,328,000,000	1.00	—
2004D	1,159,500,000	1.00	—
2004S	(1,804,396)	—	4.75
2005P	1,412,000,000	1.00	—
2005D	1,423,500,000	1.00	—
2005S	—	—	2.25
2006P	1,381,000,000	1.00	—
2006D	1,447,000,000	1.00	—
2006S	—	—	2.25

Date	Mintage	MS-65	Prf-65
2007P	—	1.00	—
2007D	—	1.00	—
2007S	—	—	2.25

Roosevelt Dime.

KM# A195   Composition: Silver ASW.

Date	Mintage	Prf-65
1992S	(1,317,579)	5.00
1993S	(761,353)	9.00
1994S	(785,329)	9.00
1995S	(838,953)	25.00
1996S	(830,021)	9.00
1997S	(821,678)	25.00
1998S	(878,792)	9.00
1999S	(804,565)	6.50
2000S	(965,921)	4.00
2001S	(849,600)	5.00
2002S	(888,826)	5.00
2003S	(1,090,425)	4.00
2004S	—	4.50
2005S	—	3.50
2006S	—	3.50
2007S	—	3.50

20 CENTS

Seated Liberty within circle of stars, date below. Eagle with arrows in talons, value below.

KM# 109   Designer: William Barber.   **Diameter:** 22 **Weight:** 5.0000 g. **Composition:** 0.9000 Silver, 0.1447 oz. ASW.

Date	Mintage	G 4	VG-8	F 12	VF-20	XF-40	AU-50	MS-60	MS-65	Prf-65
1875	39,700	165	210	270	025	415	550	835	5,500	9,500
1875S	1,155,000	100.00	110	120	175	210	320	500	4,900	—
Note: 1875-S exists as a branch mint proof										
1875 Clear S	—	110	120	135	200	235	350	600	5,500	—
1875 S over horizontal S also known as filled S	—	100.00	110	120	175	210	320	500	4,900	—
1875 $ Sign var.	—	—	120	130	150	225	260	375	1,300	—
1875CC	133,290	335	305	475	600	775	1,150	1,650	10,000	—
1876	15,900	185	225	285	350	410	535	800	5,600	9,400
1876CC	10,000	20,000	25,000	30,000	35,000	50,000	60,000	—	—	175,000
Note: 1876CC, Eliasberg Sale, April 1997, MS-65, $148,500. Heritage 1999 ANA, MS-63, $86,500.										
1877 proof only	510	—	—	2,700	2,900	3,300	3,500	—	—	10,000
1878 proof only	600	—	—	2,000	2,300	2,400	2,800	—	—	9,500

QUARTER

Draped Bust Quarter. Small eagle.

KM# 25   Designer: Robert Scot.   **Diameter:** 27.5 **Weight:** 6.7400 g. **Composition:** 0.8920 Silver, 0.1933 oz. ASW.

Date	Mintage	G-4	VG-8	F-12	VF-20	XF-40	AU-50	MS-60	MS-65
1796	6,146	9,250	16,500	28,000	36,500	42,500	68,000	82,500	235,000

Draped Bust Quarter. Draped bust right, flanked by stars, date at angle below. Heraldic eagle.

KM# 36 Designer: Robert Scot. **Diameter:** 27.5 **Weight:** 6.7400 g. **Composition:** 0.8920 Silver, 0.1933 oz. ASW.

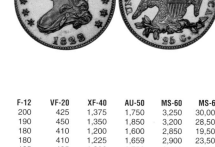

Date	Mintage	G-4	VG-8	F-12	VF-20	XF-40	AU-50	MS-60	MS-65
1804	6,738	3,250	5,400	7,500	10,500	18,500	31,000	52,500	225,000
1805	121,394	230	285	520	960	2,500	4,450	6,600	62,000
1806/5	206,124	250	375	650	1,400	2,850	5,000	7,150	72,000
1806	Inc. above	220	275	500	900	2,350	4,250	6,300	56,000
1807	220,643	220	275	500	925	2,350	4,250	6,300	58,000

Liberty Cap Quarter. Draped bust left, flanked by stars, date below. Eagle with arrows in talons, banner above, value below.

KM# 44 Designer: John Reich. **Diameter:** 27 **Weight:** 6.7400 g. **Composition:** 0.8920 Silver, 0.1933 oz. ASW. **Notes:** Varieties of the 1819 strikes are distinguished by the size of the 9 in the date. Varieties of the 1820 strikes are distinguished by the size of the 0 in the date. One 1822 variety and one 1828 variety have "25" engraved over "50" in the denomination. The 1827 restrikes were produced privately using dies sold as scrap by the U.S. Mint.

Date	Mintage	G-4	VG-8	F-12	VF-20	XF-40	AU-50	MS-60	MS-65
1815	89,235	100.00	135	200	425	1,375	1,750	3,250	30,000
1818/15	361,174	100.00	130	190	450	1,350	1,850	3,200	28,500
1818	Inc. above	95.00	125	180	410	1,200	1,600	2,850	19,500
1819 small 9	144,000	95.00	125	180	410	1,225	1,659	2,900	23,500
1819 large 9	Inc. above	95.00	130	185	435	1,300	1,750	3,100	25,000
1820 small O	127,444	95.00	125	180	420	1,300	1,700	3,100	34,500
1820 large O	Inc. above	95.00	125	180	415	1,225	1,600	2,900	32,500
1821	216,851	100.00	130	185	420	1,275	1,650	2,875	20,000
1822	64,080	110	135	200	440	1,225	2,750	4,200	—
1822 25/50C.	Inc. above	1,650	3,350	4,350	6,800	12,500	20,000	33,000	125,000
1823/22	17,800	30,000	35,000	48,500	58,500	68,000	100,000	175,000	—

Note: 1823/22, Superior, Aug. 1990, Proof, $62,500.

Date	Mintage	G-4	VG-8	F-12	VF-20	XF-40	AU-50	MS-60	MS-65
1824/2 mintage unrecorded	—	275	425	600	1,650	4,200	7,000	14,500	65,000
1825/22	168,000	125	175	260	500	1,550	2,100	3,000	22,500
1825/23	Inc. above	115	150	235	450	1,400	1,850	3,400	25,000
1825/24	Inc. above	100.00	135	210	420	1,325	1,700	3,150	22,000
1827 original curl base 2	4,000	—	—	—	70,000	75,000	80,000	—	—

Note: Eliasberg, April 1997, VF-20, $39,600.

Date	Mintage	G-4	VG-8	F-12	VF-20	XF-40	AU-50	MS-60	MS-65
1827 restrike, square base 2	Inc. above	—	—	—	—	—	—	—	—

Note: 1827 restrike, Eliasberg, April 1997, Prf-65, $77,000.

Date	Mintage	G-4	VG-8	F-12	VF-20	XF-40	AU-50	MS-60	MS-65
1828	102,000	90.00	110	180	400	1,100	1,650	3,000	26,000
1828 25/50C.	Inc. above	165	320	550	1,250	2,650	4,250	9,500	—

Liberty Cap Quarter. Draped bust left, flanked by stars, date below. Eagle with arrows in talons, value below.

KM# 55 Designer: William Kneass. **Diameter:** 24.3 **Composition:** 0.8920 Silver **Notes:** Varieties of the 1831 strikes are distinguished by the size of the lettering on the reverse.

Date	Mintage	G-4	VG-8	F-12	VF-20	XF-40	AU-50	MS-60	MS-65
1831 small letter	398,000	70.00	95.00	115	160	400	850	1,175	19,500
1831 large letter	Inc. above	70.00	90.00	110	150	385	775	1,100	17,000
1832	320,000	70.00	90.00	110	150	385	775	1,075	22,750
1833	156,000	75.00	100.00	115	170	420	855	1,400	20,500
1834	286,000	70.00	90.00	110	150	385	775	1,100	17,000
1834 0 over O	—	—	—	—	—	—	—	—	—
1835	1,952,000	70.00	90.00	110	150	385	775	1,100	23,750
1836	472,000	70.00	90.00	110	150	385	775	1,100	18,850

Date	Mintage	G-4	VG-8	F-12	VF-20	XF-40	AU-50	MS-60	MS-65
1837	252,400	70.00	90.00	110	150	385	775	1,100	17,000
1838	832,000	70.00	90.00	110	150	385	775	1,100	19,500

Seated Liberty Quarter. Seated Liberty, stars around top 1/2 of border, date below. Eagle with arrows in talons, value below.

KM# 64.1   Designer: Christian Gobrecht.
Diameter: 24.3 **Weight:** 6.6800 g.
Composition: 0.9000 Silver, 0.1933 oz. ASW.

Date	Mintage	G-4	VG-8	F-12	VF-20	XF-40	AU-50	MS-60	MS-65
1838	Inc. above	42.00	50.00	60.00	110	360	550	1,250	30,000
1839	491,146	36.00	44.00	52.00	85.00	350	550	1,250	34,000
1840O	425,200	46.00	54.00	75.00	135	375	575	1,350	38,500

Seated Liberty Quarter. Drapery added to Liberty's left elbow, stars around top 1/2 of border. Eagle with arrows in talons, value below.

KM# 64.2   Designer: Christian Gobrecht.
Diameter: 24.3 **Weight:** 6.6800 g. **Composition:**
0.9000 Silver, 0.1933 oz. ASW. **Notes:** Two varieties
for 1842 and 1842-O are distinguished by the size of
the numerals in the date. 1852 obverse dies were
used to strike the 1853 no-arrows variety, with the 2
being recut to form a 3.

Date	Mintage	G-4	VG-8	F-12	VF-20	XF-40	AU-50	MS-60	MS-65
1840	188,127	27.00	52.00	75.00	125	225	350	950	12,000
1840O	Inc. above	29.00	39.00	70.00	115	250	450	1,000	—
1841	120,000	65.00	90.00	125	170	275	385	750	11,000
1841O	452,000	21.50	27.50	50.00	85.00	165	350	700	10,000
1842 small date	88,000	—			—	—	—	—	—

Note: 1842 small date, Fliasherg, April 1997, Prf-63, $66,000.

Date	Mintage	G-4	VG-8	F-12	VF-20	XF-40	AU-50	MS-60	MS-65
1842 large date	Inc. above	100.00	125	190	275	375	850	1,850	—
1842O small date	769,000	425	650	1,200	1,950	4,000	—	—	—
1842O large date	Inc. above	28.00	42.00	55.00	70.00	135	300	900	—
1843	645,600	22.00	26.00	34.00	45.00	75.00	175	400	6,750
1843O	968,000	25.00	31.50	55.00	125	250	750	2,000	11,000
1844	421,200	20.00	25.00	31.50	50.00	80.00	160	450	5,500
1844O	740,000	25.00	28.50	40.00	75.00	140	280	1,000	6,000
1845	922,000	20.00	25.00	31.50	45.00	70.00	150	465	5,000
1846	510,000	20.00	25.00	36.50	55.00	85.00	175	475	6,000
1847	734,000	20.00	25.00	31.50	50.00	70.00	150	450	5,000
1847O	368,000	30.00	45.00	70.00	135	300	750	1,900	—
1848	146,000	40.00	60.00	110	185	225	375	1,000	10,000
1849	340,000	20.00	30.00	45.00	65.00	125	275	750	9,000
1849O	—	550	750	1,150	1,850	3,250	5,750	—	—
1850	190,800	40.00	50.00	80.00	125	175	275	800	—
1850O	412,000	20.00	30.00	60.00	110	175	450	1,300	—
1851	160,000	60.00	75.00	125	225	285	400	850	8,500
1851O	88,000	185	275	425	700	1,250	2,250	4,000	—
1852	177,060	50.00	60.00	100.00	185	225	350	500	4,800
1852O	96,000	195	275	475	800	1,350	3,500	8,000	—
1853 recut date	44,200	450	650	900	1,100	1,350	1,800	2,600	9,000

Seated Liberty Quarter. Seated Liberty, arrows at date. Rays around eagle.

KM# 78   Designer: Christian Gobrecht.
Diameter: 24.3 **Weight:** 6.2200 g. **Composition:**
0.9000 Silver, 0.1800 oz. ASW.

Date	Mintage	G-4	VG-8	F-12	VF-20	XF-40	AU-50	MS-60	MS-65	Prf-65
1853	15,210,020	20.00	23.00	32.00	46.00	150	275	950	16,500	100,000
1853/4	Inc. above	40.00	65.00	100.00	200	275	750	1,750	—	—
1853O	1,332,000	18.00	35.00	50.00	100.00	275	1,100	2,750	—	—

Seated Liberty Quarter. Seated Liberty, arrows at date. Eagle with arrows in talons, value below.

KM# 81 **Designer:** Christian Gobrecht.
Diameter: 24.3 **Weight:** 6.6800 g. **Composition:**
0.9000 Silver, 0.1933 oz. ASW. **Notes:** The 1854-O
"huge O" variety has an oversized mint mark.

Date	Mintage	G-4	VG-8	F-12	VF-20	XF-40	AU-50	MS-60	MS-65	Prf-65
1854	12,380,000	15.00	20.00	27.50	35.00	75.00	225	440	7,500	17,500
1854O	1,484,000	17.00	24.00	35.00	60.00	125	300	1,750	—	—
1854O huge O	Inc. above	800	1,350	2,850	4,750	7,500	12,500	17,000	—	—
1855	2,857,000	15.00	20.00	27.50	35.00	75.00	225	440	8,500	18,500
1855O	176,000	50.00	75.00	110	240	475	950	2,750	—	—
1855S	396,400	40.00	60.00	80.00	225	500	1,250	2,000	—	—

Seated Liberty Quarter. Seated Liberty, date below. Eagle with arrows in talons, value below.

KM# A64.2 **Designer:** Christian Gobrecht.
Diameter: 24.3 **Weight:** 6.2200 g. **Composition:**
0.9000 Silver, 0.1800 oz. ASW.

Date	Mintage	G-4	VG-8	F-12	VF-20	XF-40	AU-50	MS-60	MS-65	Prf-65
1856	7,264,000	15.00	20.00	27.50	35.00	60.00	145	290	4,250	15,000
1856O	968,000	20.00	30.00	40.00	60.00	110	250	1,000	8,500	—
1856S	286,000	45.00	65.00	110	250	450	900	2,200	—	—
1856S/S	Inc. above	150	275	500	1,250	2,000	—	—	—	—
1857	9,644,000	15.00	20.00	27.50	35.00	60.00	145	290	4,000	9,500
1857O	1,180,000	15.00	20.00	29.00	40.00	80.00	275	975	—	—
1857S	82,000	125	175	275	450	700	950	2,750	—	—
1858	7,368,000	15.00	20.00	27.50	35.00	60.00	160	300	4,000	6,500
1858O	520,000	25.00	30.00	45.00	70.00	135	360	1,350	—	—
1858S	121,000	70.00	110	175	300	750	1,250	—	—	—
1859	1,344,000	17.00	24.00	30.00	40.00	75.00	175	375	6,000	7,000
1859O	260,000	25.00	30.00	50.00	80.00	150	400	1,000	15,000	—
1859S	80,000	125	150	250	500	1,500	2,500	—	—	—
1860	805,400	18.00	22.00	28.00	33.00	60.00	160	500	—	5,250
1860O	388,000	20.00	30.00	40.00	55.00	100.00	275	1,200	—	—
1860S	56,000	200	350	600	975	4,000	6,000	—	—	—
1861	4,854,600	16.00	19.00	27.00	32.00	55.00	150	290	4,200	5,500
1861S	96,000	90.00	145	235	400	1,250	2,750	—	—	—
1862	932,550	18.00	22.00	33.00	40.00	65.00	165	300	4,350	5,350
1862S	67,000	80.00	125	200	325	700	1,600	2,750	—	—
1863	192,060	30.00	45.00	60.00	120	185	300	650	4,350	5,500
1864	94,070	90.00	120	160	245	345	400	650	5,000	5,500
1864S	20,000	400	600	900	1,350	2,350	3,750	7,000	—	—
1865	59,300	85.00	115	150	235	325	375	875	9,500	5,500
1865S	41,000	125	175	250	425	750	1,250	2,350	11,500	—
1866 unique	—	—	—	—	—	—	—	—	—	—

Seated Liberty Quarter. Seated Liberty, date below. "In God We Trust" above eagle.

KM# 98 **Designer:** Christian Gobrecht.
Diameter: 24.3 **Weight:** 6.2200 g. **Composition:**
0.9000 Silver, 0.1800 oz. ASW. **Notes:** The 1873
closed-3 and open-3 varieties are distinguished by
the amount of space between the upper left and
lower left serifs in the 3.

Date	Mintage	G-4	VG-8	F-12	VF-20	XF-40	AU-50	MS-60	MS-65	Prf-65
1866	17,525	475	600	750	1,000	1,200	1,500	2,250	7,500	3,000
1866S	28,000	325	375	675	1,050	1,450	2,000	3,000	—	—
1867	20,625	250	325	500	675	850	975	1,200	—	2,450
1867S	48,000	275	385	600	900	1,350	1,700	—	—	—
1868	30,000	200	250	325	400	500	650	900	7,000	3,450
1868S	96,000	95.00	110	195	300	625	1,350	2,000	—	—
1869	16,600	350	450	600	800	900	1,000	1,275	—	2,500
1869S	76,000	110	135	225	375	700	1,400	2,400	16,000	—

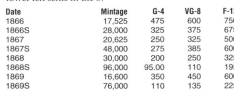

Date	Mintage	G-4	VG-8	F-12	VF-20	XF-40	AU-50	MS-60	MS-65	Prf-65
1870	87,400	55.00	80.00	145	245	295	425	850	6,000	2,750
1870CC	8,340	4,500	6,500	9,500	15,000	—	—	—	—	—
1871	119,160	40.00	65.00	75.00	150	195	350	650	6,000	2,500
1871CC	10,890	3,500	4,500	7,500	12,500	18,000	—	—	—	—
1871S	30,900	375	500	700	950	1,200	1,850	3,000	10,000	—
1872	182,950	30.00	40.00	80.00	110	155	300	600	6,500	2,500
1872CC	22,850	1,100	1,500	2,250	3,750	6,500	7,500	14,000	—	—
1872S	83,000	900	1,250	1,750	2,400	3,500	4,500	7,500	—	—
1873 closed 3	212,600	250	350	475	800	1,200	1,800	2,800	—	2,600
1873 open 3	Inc. above	30.00	42.50	80.00	120	175	250	450	5,000	—
1873CC 6 known	4,000	—	75,000	—	—	—	—	—	—	—

Note: 1873CC, Heritage, April 1999, MS-62, $106,375.

Seated Liberty Quarter. Seated Liberty, arrows at date. "In God We Trust" above eagle.

KM# 106 Designer: Christian Gobrecht.
Diameter: 24.3 **Weight:** 6.2500 g. **Composition:** 0.9000 Silver, 0.1808 oz. ASW.

Date	Mintage	G-4	VG-8	F-12	VF-20	XF-40	AU-50	MS-60	MS-65	Prf-65
1873	1,271,700	16.00	23.00	30.00	60.00	200	400	775	4,250	8,000
1873CC	12,462	3,500	4,500	8,000	11,000	17,000	—	—	—	—
1873S	156,000	25.00	40.00	85.00	140	275	550	1,200	8,000	—
1874	471,900	20.00	26.00	40.00	70.00	220	420	850	4,000	6,750
1874S	392,000	23.00	30.00	50.00	110	240	425	900	4,500	—

Seated Liberty Quarter. Seated Liberty, date below. "In God We Trust" above eagle.

KM# A98 Designer: Christian Gobrecht.
Diameter: 24.3 **Weight:** 6.2500 g. **Composition:** 0.9000 Silver, 0.1808 oz. ASW. **Notes:** The 1876-CC fine-reeding variety has a more finely reeded edge.

Date	Mintage	G-4	VG-8	F-12	VF-20	XF-40	AU-50	MS-60	MS-65	Prf-65
1875	4,293,500	14.00	17.00	25.00	30.00	50.00	135	225	1,600	2,300
1875CC	140,000	75.00	110	225	350	550	850	1,600	15,000	—
1875S	680,000	25.00	36.00	67.00	110	175	275	575	3,200	—
1876	17,817,150	14.00	17.00	25.00	30.00	50.00	135	225	1,600	2,250
1876CC	4,944,000	30.00	40.00	50.00	65.00	90.00	150	325	3,600	—
1876CC fine reeding	Inc. above	30.00	40.00	50.00	65.00	90.00	150	325	3,600	—
1876S	8,596,000	16.00	19.00	25.00	30.00	50.00	135	225	2,000	—
1877	10,911,710	14.00	17.00	25.00	30.00	50.00	135	225	1,600	2,250
1877CC	4,192,000	30.00	40.00	50.00	65.00	90.00	150	325	2,000	—
1877S	8,996,000	14.00	17.00	25.00	30.00	50.00	135	225	1,600	—
1877S /horizontal S	Inc. above	45.00	60.00	95.00	175	250	375	650	—	—
1878	2,260,800	16.00	18.00	28.00	34.00	55.00	145	250	2,750	2,300
1878CC	996,000	35.00	45.00	55.00	80.00	110	150	450	3,500	—
1878S	140,000	165	200	300	400	650	875	1,450	—	—
1879	14,700	190	235	285	325	400	485	575	1,700	2,250
1880	14,955	190	235	285	325	400	485	575	1,600	2,250
1881	12,975	200	250	300	350	425	500	600	1,650	2,200
1882	16,300	200	250	300	350	425	500	600	1,850	2,200
1883	15,439	210	265	315	365	435	525	625	2,450	2,200
1884	8,875	375	450	550	650	750	750	850	1,900	2,200
1885	14,530	210	265	315	365	435	525	625	2,600	2,200
1886	5,886	500	600	700	800	900	1,000	1,250	2,600	2,400
1887	10,710	300	350	450	550	650	750	850	2,350	2,200
1888	10,833	275	325	425	500	600	700	800	2,000	2,350
1888S	1,216,000	15.00	20.00	27.50	30.00	60.00	160	245	2,450	—
1889	12,711	250	300	375	425	500	575	675	1,750	2,350
1890	80,590	65.00	85.00	100.00	125	200	300	425	—	2,350
1891	3,920,600	15.00	20.00	27.50	30.00	60.00	160	245	1,750	2,350
1891O	68,000	150	225	325	550	950	1,250	3,000	14,500	—
1891S	2,216,000	16.00	22.00	29.00	65.00	52.50	185	275	2,400	—

Barber Quarter. Laureate head right, flanked by stars, date below. Heraldic eagle.

KM# 114 Designer: Charles E. Barber. **Diameter:** 24.3 **Weight:** 6.2500 g. **Composition:** 0.9000 Silver, 0.1808 oz. ASW.

Date	Mintage	G-4	VG-8	F-12	VF-20	XF-40	AU-50	MS-60	MS-65	Prf-65
1892	8,237,245	5.25	8.50	25.00	46.00	75.00	120	220	1,300	2,000
1892O	2,640,000	13.50	21.50	41.50	55.00	96.00	150	300	1,650	—
1892S	964,079	30.00	50.00	80.00	125	190	300	480	4,850	—
1893	5,484,838	6.25	8.50	27.50	41.50	75.00	120	210	1,750	2,000
1893O	3,396,000	8.00	13.50	30.00	55.00	100.00	160	275	1,900	—
1893S	1,454,535	18.00	34.00	62.50	110	160	300	480	8,400	—
1894	3,432,972	5.50	9.50	34.00	50.00	93.50	150	250	1,550	2,000
1894O	2,852,000	8.50	16.00	41.50	67.50	125	225	340	3,000	—
1894S	2,648,821	8.25	12.50	38.00	62.50	115	205	315	3,000	—
1895	4,440,880	6.00	9.00	31.50	41.50	80.00	135	230	1,900	2,000
1895O	2,816,000	11.00	18.00	46.00	75.00	135	225	400	2,750	—
1895S	1,764,681	18.00	27.50	60.00	100.00	150	285	445	4,150	—
1896	3,874,762	5.00	7.00	25.00	41.50	80.00	135	235	1,600	2,000
1896O	1,484,000	26.00	48.50	115	250	425	750	850	7,750	—
1896S	188,039	690	1,100	1,800	2,750	4,300	5,500	8,000	56,000	—
1897	8,140,731	5.00	6.25	21.50	33.50	75.00	120	220	1,300	2,000
1897O	1,414,800	18.00	38.50	115	235	395	640	1,000	4,150	—
1897S	542,229	85.00	120	275	300	440	700	1,000	7,000	—
1898	11,100,735	5.00	6.25	22.50	33.50	75.00	120	220	1,300	2,000
1898O	1,868,000	13.00	27.50	75.00	150	295	435	650	10,000	—
1898S	1,020,592	12.00	18.50	47.50	65.00	96.00	210	400	7,200	—
1899	12,624,846	5.00	6.25	22.50	33.50	75.00	120	215	1,300	2,000
1899O	2,644,000	11.00	19.00	35.00	60.00	130	275	415	3,400	—
1899S	708,000	17.00	28.50	70.00	85.00	135	275	440	3,800	—
1900	10,016,912	6.00	8.00	21.50	35.00	71.50	135	215	1,300	2,000
1900O	3,416,000	11.00	25.00	62.50	100.00	150	345	585	3,800	—
1900S	1,858,585	8.00	15.00	38.00	55.00	80.00	135	385	5,400	—
1901	8,892,813	11.00	13.00	25.00	41.50	80.00	135	215	2,250	2,200
1901O	1,612,000	40.00	60.00	135	275	470	685	900	5,750	—
1901S	72,664	7,000	11,000	16,500	21,000	28,500	38,000	42,000	100,000	—
1902	12,197,744	6.00	8.00	19.50	33.50	70.00	125	220	1,300	2,100
1902O	4,748,000	8.50	16.00	52.50	82.50	150	245	485	5,000	—
1902S	1,524,612	13.50	22.00	55.00	95.00	170	260	540	3,600	—
1903	9,670,064	6.75	8.00	19.00	33.50	66.00	115	215	2,600	2,000
1903O	3,500,000	8.00	12.50	41.50	65.00	125	260	450	5,800	—
1903S	1,036,000	15.50	25.00	46.00	80.00	145	285	450	2,900	—
1904	9,588,813	8.00	9.75	20.00	36.00	72.50	125	225	1,475	2,000
1904O	2,456,000	11.00	21.50	62.50	100.00	225	460	850	3,250	—
1905	4,968,250	11.00	13.00	27.50	41.50	75.00	125	215	1,650	2,000
1905O	1,230,000	18.50	32.50	82.50	160	260	375	515	6,600	—
1905S	1,884,000	11.00	15.00	43.50	66.00	115	225	350	3,650	—
1906	3,656,435	6.75	8.00	19.00	33.50	70.00	115	215	1,300	2,000
1906D	3,280,000	7.00	8.00	25.00	42.50	71.50	155	220	2,200	—
1906O	2,056,000	7.00	9.00	41.50	60.00	105	200	300	1,400	—
1907	7,192,575	5.25	8.00	17.50	33.50	66.00	115	215	1,300	2,000
1907D	2,484,000	6.00	9.00	29.00	52.50	80.00	180	250	2,750	—
1907O	4,560,000	5.25	8.00	19.00	38.50	70.00	135	220	2,600	—
1907S	1,360,000	10.00	18.50	47.50	75.00	135	275	480	3,500	—
1908	4,232,545	5.00	6.25	18.50	33.50	70.00	115	215	1,300	2,200
1908D	5,788,000	5.00	6.25	17.50	32.50	70.00	120	250	1,750	—
1908O	6,244,000	5.00	8.50	17.50	38.50	75.00	125	215	1,300	—
1908S	784,000	20.00	40.00	92.50	160	320	520	775	5,100	—
1909	9,268,650	5.00	6.25	17.50	33.50	66.00	115	215	1,300	2,000
1909D	5,114,000	6.25	8.00	22.00	41.50	90.00	160	215	2,350	—
1909O	712,000	25.00	60.00	175	400	900	1,250	1,700	9,000	—
1909S	1,348,000	8.00	11.00	37.50	57.50	96.00	200	300	2,400	—
1910	2,244,551	7.75	10.00	30.00	46.00	80.00	140	215	1,300	2,000
1910D	1,500,000	8.00	11.00	47.50	75.00	130	260	375	2,250	—
1911	3,720,543	5.25	8.00	17.50	33.50	72.50	125	215	1,300	2,000
1911D	933,600	8.00	19.00	95.00	215	330	500	700	6,250	—
1911S	988,000	7.00	12.00	51.50	80.00	160	300	400	1,500	—
1912	4,400,700	5.75	8.00	17.50	33.50	70.00	115	215	1,300	2,000
1912S	708,000	10.00	13.00	46.00	77.50	125	230	390	2,750	—
1913	484,613	15.00	25.00	75.00	185	415	535	960	5,000	2,200
1913D	1,450,800	12.50	13.50	38.50	58.50	94.00	185	275	1,400	—
1913S	40,000	1,500	2,350	3,800	5,750	6,500	7,250	9,000	25,000	—
1914	6,244,610	5.00	6.25	17.50	30.00	57.50	115	215	1,300	2,200
1914D	3,046,000	5.00	6.25	17.50	30.00	57.50	115	215	1,300	—

Date	Mintage	G-4	VG-8	F-12	VF-20	XF-40	AU-50	MS-60	MS-65	Prf-65
1914S	264,000	70.00	105	200	315	520	700	940	3,550	—
1915	3,480,450	5.00	6.25	17.50	30.00	66.00	115	215	1,300	2,200
1915D	3,694,000	5.00	6.25	17.50	30.00	66.00	115	215	1,300	—
1915S	704,000	9.00	13.00	35.00	57.50	110	220	285	1,300	—
1916	1,788,000	5.00	9.50	17.50	27.50	57.50	115	215	1,300	—
1916D	6,540,800	5.00	6.25	17.50	30.00	57.50	115	215	1,300	—
1916D/D	—	15.00	22.00	30.00	50.00	125	—	—	—	—

Standing Liberty Quarter.
Right breast exposed; Type 1.

KM# 141   Designer: Hermon A. MacNeil. **Diameter:** 24.3 **Weight:** 6.2500 g. **Composition:** 0.9000 Silver, 0.1808 oz. ASW.

Breast exposed

Date	Mintage	G-4	VG-8	F-12	VF-20	XF-40	AU-50	MS-60	MS-65	-65FH
1916	52,000	3,500	6,350	9,500	13,000	14,500	16,500	18,500	30,000	37,500
1917	8,792,000	24.00	40.00	52.00	70.00	95.00	175	200	750	1,500
1917D	1,509,200	28.00	42.00	55.00	85.00	125	195	235	950	2,550
1917S	1,952,000	30.00	44.00	60.00	90.00	160	210	240	1,200	4,100

Standing Liberty Quarter. Right breast covered; Type 2.
Three stars below eagle.

KM# 145   Designer: Hermon A. MacNeil. **Diameter:** 24.3 **Weight:** 6.2500 g. **Composition:** 0.9000 Silver, 0.1808 oz. ASW.

Mint mark   Breast covered

Date	Mintage	G-4	VG-8	F-12	VF-20	XF-40	AU-50	MS-60	MS-65	-65FH
1917	13,880,000	22.00	33.00	42.50	54.00	75.00	105	165	575	950
1917D	6,224,400	40.00	45.00	65.00	78.00	110	160	225	1,325	3,500
1917S	5,522,000	40.00	45.00	63.00	75.00	108	155	215	1,100	3,650
1918	14,240,000	17.00	21.00	29.00	35.00	46.00	80.00	135	560	1,750
1918D	7,380,000	26.00	36.00	66.00	78.00	122	195	250	1,485	4,850
1918S	11,072,000	17.00	21.00	32.00	35.00	48.00	95.00	185	1,250	13,500
1918/17S	Inc. above	1,550	2,250	3,850	5,200	7,500	13,500	17,850	110,000	320,000
1919	11,324,000	33.00	44.00	55.00	74.00	80.00	118	175	600	1,650
1919D	1,944,000	85.00	110	195	345	565	695	825	2,950	28,500
1919S	1,836,000	80.00	105	185	285	510	585	750	4,200	30,000
1920	27,860,000	15.00	18.00	25.00	37.00	51.00	90.00	165	600	2,100
1920D	3,586,400	48.00	65.00	88.00	120	160	215	325	2,250	7,200
1920S	6,380,000	19.00	25.00	30.00	37.00	57.00	110	235	2,650	24,000
1921	1,916,000	185	220	450	625	750	1,100	1,500	3,850	5,500
1923	9,716,000	15.00	18.00	35.00	37.00	55.00	95.00	155	620	4,000
1923S	1,360,000	300	425	675	985	1,250	1,650	2,300	4,750	6,500
1924	10,920,000	15.00	18.00	25.00	34.00	45.00	90.00	170	585	1,650
1924D	3,112,000	56.00	68.00	108	135	185	220	300	610	5,750
1924S	2,860,000	27.00	32.00	43.00	57.00	105	220	315	1,850	6,500
1925	12,280,000	4.00	4.75	7.00	18.50	44.00	90.00	150	575	950
1926	11,316,000	3.50	4.00	6.00	14.00	37.00	80.00	140	585	2,250
1926D	1,716,000	6.50	10.00	20.00	40.00	75.00	118	170	545	22,500
1926S	2,700,000	4.50	5.40	11.00	30.00	110	225	325	2,175	28,000
1927	11,912,000	3.50	4.00	6.00	12.00	32.00	70.00	105	550	1,300
1927D	976,400	14.00	19.00	32.00	70.00	140	210	250	600	2,650
1927S	396,000	35.00	48.00	110	285	1,000	2,650	4,750	12,000	165,000
1928	6,336,000	3.50	4.75	6.00	12.00	32.00	65.00	100.00	540	2,150
1928D	1,627,600	4.75	6.00	7.50	20.00	42.50	90.00	135	540	5,650
1928S Large S	2,644,000	6.00	7.50	10.00	25.00	65.00	115	200	—	—
1928S Small S	Inc. above	4.50	5.50	6.50	16.50	38.00	70.00	125	560	900

Date	Mintage	G-4	VG-8	F-12	VF-20	XF-40	AU-50	MS-60	MS-65	-65FH
1929	11,140,000	3.50	4.75	6.00	12.00	32.00	65.00	100.00	540	900
1929D	1,358,000	4.25	5.50	6.75	16.00	38.50	79.00	135	540	5,850
1929S	1,764,000	4.00	5.50	6.50	15.00	34.00	75.00	120	540	875
1930	5,632,000	3.50	4.00	6.00	12.00	32.00	65.00	100.00	540	875
1930S	1,556,000	4.00	5.50	6.50	15.00	34.00	70.00	115	550	925

Washington Quarter.

KM# 164 **Designer:** John Flanagan. **Diameter:** 24.3 **Weight:** 6.2000 g. **Composition:** Silver

Mint mark 1932-64

Date	Mintage	G-4	VG-8	F-12	VF-20	XF-40	AU-50	MS-60	MS-65	Prf-65
1932	5,404,000	4.00	5.20	6.00	7.50	9.75	15.00	26.00	435	—
1932D	436,800	165	180	205	240	345	500	1,000	24,500	—
1932S	408,000	195	200	205	240	285	300	500	7,000	—
1934 Medium Motto	31,912,052	3.50	3.90	4.50	5.40	6.90	10.00	27.50	110	—
1934 Heavy Motto	Inc. above	4.50	5.75	7.00	12.50	18.00	30.00	50.00	225	—
1934 Light motto	Inc. above	4.00	5.00	6.00	10.00	15.00	26.00	45.00	400	—
1934 Doubled Die Obverse	Inc. above	75.00	100.00	165	200	320	450	800	8,000	—
1934D Medium Motto	3,527,200	5.00	6.00	8.50	13.50	28.00	95.00	245	1,550	—
1934D Heavy Motto	Inc. above	6.00	8.00	11.00	16.00	37.00	110	295	1,900	—
1935	32,484,000	3.20	3.30	3.50	3.90	5.20	10.00	21.50	145	—
1935D	5,780,000	3.50	4.00	7.50	14.00	30.00	130	255	975	—
1935S	5,660,000	3.50	4.00	5.00	7.50	15.00	38.50	100.00	465	—
1936	41,303,837	3.20	3.30	3.50	3.90	4.90	9.50	22.50	115	1,950
1936D	5,374,000	5.00	6.50	8.50	22.00	55.00	275	625	1,850	—
1936S	3,828,000	3.50	4.00	4.40	6.25	13.50	52.50	115	420	—
1937	19,701,542	3.20	3.30	3.50	3.90	4.50	16.00	23.50	94.00	665
1937D	7,189,600	3.50	4.00	5.00	6.25	13.50	34.00	67.00	175	—
1937S	1,652,000	4.00	5.00	7.00	15.00	34.00	100.00	170	415	—
1938	9,480,045	4.00	4.75	5.25	6.25	16.00	46.00	94.00	250	405
1938S	2,832,000	4.75	5.25	6.00	9.75	22.50	57.50	112	300	—
1939	33,548,795	3.20	3.30	3.50	3.90	4.20	7.00	16.00	56.00	345
1939D	7,092,000	3.50	4.00	4.50	5.25	11.00	20.00	45.00	125	—
1939S	2,628,000	4.00	4.40	5.25	9.00	22.00	60.00	110	375	—
1940	35,715,246	3.20	3.30	3.50	3.90	4.20	5.50	18.50	57.50	250
1940D	2,797,600	3.50	4.25	7.00	12.50	27.50	70.00	135	350	—
1940S	8,244,000	3.50	4.00	5.00	6.50	9.00	18.00	28.00	62.50	—
1941	79,047,287	—	—	—	—	3.25	4.40	9.75	45.00	205
1941D	16,714,800	—	—	—	3.50	4.50	15.00	35.00	70.00	—
1941S	16,080,000	—	—	—	3.25	6.50	12.50	31.00	70.00	—
1942	102,117,123	—	—	—	—	3.25	3.50	5.50	37.50	190
1942D	17,487,200	—	—	—	3.25	6.00	11.00	19.00	45.00	—
1942S	19,384,000	—	—	—	3.75	9.00	24.00	80.00	180	—
1943	99,700,000	—	—	—	—	3.25	3.75	5.00	44.00	—
1943D	16,095,600	—	—	—	3.75	8.00	16.50	31.00	52.50	—
1943S	21,700,000	—	—	3.00	5.00	7.50	15.00	28.00	60.00	—
1943S Double Die Obv.	Inc. above	40.00	75.00	125	175	225	275	500	3,500	—
1944	104,956,000	—	—	—	—	3.25	3.50	5.00	37.50	—
1944D	14,600,800	—	—	—	3.25	4.25	10.00	20.00	37.50	—
1944S	12,560,000	—	—	—	3.25	4.00	9.00	15.00	37.50	—
1945	74,372,000	—	—	—	—	3.25	3.25	5.00	45.00	—
1945D	12,341,600	—	—	—	3.50	6.50	11.50	19.00	47.50	—
1945S	17,004,001	—	—	—	3.25	3.75	6.00	9.00	38.50	—
1946	53,436,000	—	—	—	—	3.25	3.50	5.00	47.50	—
1946D	9,072,800	—	—	—	3.25	4.25	5.50	10.00	47.50	—
1946S	4,204,000	—	—	—	3.25	4.00	5.00	9.00	50.00	—
1947	22,556,000	—	—	—	—	3.75	5.00	11.50	47.50	—
1947D	15,338,400	—	—	—	3.25	3.65	4.50	11.00	44.00	—
1947S	5,532,000	—	—	—	3.25	3.65	4.50	10.00	40.00	—
1948	35,196,000	—	—	—	3.25	3.40	4.00	5.50	45.00	—
1948D	16,766,800	—	—	—	3.25	3.65	7.00	13.50	62.50	—
1948S	15,960,000	—	—	—	3.25	3.50	5.00	8.00	50.00	—
1949	9,312,000	—	—	—	3.50	6.50	15.00	38.50	65.00	—
1949D	10,068,400	—	—	—	3.40	5.00	10.00	18.00	50.00	—
1950	24,971,512	—	—	—	—	3.25	3.50	5.50	30.00	65.00
1950D	21,075,600	—	—	—	—	3.25	3.50	5.00	32.00	—
1950D/S	Inc. above	30.00	33.00	40.00	60.00	140	215	275	3,400	—
1950S	10,284,004	—	—	—	—	3.50	4.50	9.00	40.00	—
1950S/D	Inc. above	32.00	36.00	44.00	70.00	180	315	400	850	—

Date	Mintage	G-4	VG-8	F-12	VF-20	XF-40	AU-50	MS-60	MS-65	Prf-65
1950S/S	Inc. above	—	—	—	—	—	—	—	—	—
1951	43,505,602	—	—	—	—	3.25	3.50	6.00	32.00	65.00
1951D	35,354,800	—	—	—	—	3.25	3.50	7.00	38.00	—
1951S	9,048,000	—	—	3.00	4.50	6.00	9.00	24.00	52.00	—
1952	38,862,073	—	—	—	—	3.25	3.50	5.50	35.00	46.00
1952D	49,795,200	—	—	—	—	3.25	3.50	5.00	32.00	—
1952S	13,707,800	—	—	—	4.00	6.00	9.00	21.00	42.00	—
1953	18,664,920	—	—	—	—	—	3.25	5.50	30.00	46.00
1953D	56,112,400	—	—	—	—	—	3.25	4.25	29.00	—
1953S	14,016,000	—	—	—	—	3.25	3.50	5.00	30.00	—
1954	54,645,503	—	—	—	—	—	3.25	5.00	30.00	21.00
1954D	42,305,500	—	—	—	—	—	3.25	4.75	30.00	—
1954S	11,834,722	—	—	—	—	—	3.25	4.00	25.00	—
1955	18,558,381	—	—	—	—	—	3.25	3.50	25.00	24.00
1955D	3,182,400	—	—	—	—	4.20	4.40	4.70	42.00	—
1956	44,813,384	—	—	—	—	—	3.25	4.00	24.00	23.00
1956 Double Bar 5	Inc. above	—	3.50	4.00	5.00	6.50	9.00	20.00	—	—
1956 Type B rev, proof rev die	Inc. above	—	—	8.00	12.00	20.00	30.00	40.00	100.00	—
1956D	32,334,500	—	—	—	—	3.25	3.35	3.50	26.00	—
1957	47,779,952	—	—	—	—	—	3.25	3.50	23.00	10.00
1957 Type B rev, proof rev die	Inc. above	—	—	—	6.50	10.00	16.00	30.00	110	—
1957D	77,924,160	—	—	—	—	—	3.25	3.40	26.00	—
1958	7,235,652	—	—	—	—	3.25	3.35	3.70	20.00	6.00
1958 Type B rev, proof rev die	Inc. above	—	—	—	6.50	10.00	16.00	24.00	90.00	—
1958D	78,124,900	—	—	—	—	—	3.50	3.70	20.00	—
1959	25,533,291	—	—	—	—	—	3.25	3.70	20.00	4.30
1959 Type B rev, proof rev die	Inc. above	—	—	4.00	5.00	10.00	14.00	20.00	70.00	—
1959D	62,054,232	—	—	—	—	—	3.25	3.70	25.00	—
1960	30,855,602	—	—	—	—	—	3.25	3.70	17.00	—
1960 Type B rev, proof rev die	Inc. above	—	—	—	6.50	10.00	16.00	24.00	90.00	—
1960D	63,000,324	—	—	—	—	—	3.25	3.70	17.00	—
1961	40,064,244	—	—	—	—	—	3.20	3.70	22.50	8.00
1961 Type B rev, proof rev die	Inc. above	—	—	—	5.00	10.00	14.00	20.00	70.00	—
1961D	83,656,928	—	—	—	—	—	3.20	3.70	16.00	—
1962	39,374,019	—	—	—	—	—	3.20	3.70	18.00	—
1962 Type B rev, proof rev die	Inc. above	—	—	—	10.00	15.00	25.00	60.00	175	—
1962D	127,554,756	—	—	—	—	—	3.20	3.70	16.00	—
1963	77,391,645	—	—	—	—	—	3.20	3.70	15.00	—
1963 Type B rev, proof rev die	Inc. above	—	—	—	5.00	10.00	14.00	20.00	70.00	—
1963D	135,288,184	—	—	—	—	—	3.20	3.70	15.00	—
1964	564,341,347	—	—	—	—	—	3.20	3.70	15.00	20.00
1964 Type B rev, proof rev die	Inc. above	—	—	—	5.00	10.00	14.00	20.00	70.00	—
1964D	704,135,528	—	—	—	1.50	—	3.20	3.70	15.00	—
1964D Type B rev, proof rev die	Inc. above	—	—	—	40.00	55.00	75.00	125	450	—

Washington Quarter.

KM# 164a   Designer: John Flanagan. **Diameter:** 24.3 **Weight:** 5.6700 g. **Composition:** Copper-Nickel Clad Copper

Date	Mintage	MS-65	Prf-65
1965	1,819,717,540	8.00	—
1965 SMS	—	7.50	—
1966	821,101,500	4.50	—
1966 SMS	—	9.00	—
1967 SMS	—	10.00	—
1967	1,524,031,848	6.50	—
1968	220,731,500	7.50	—
1968D	101,534,000	9.00	—
1968S	(3,041,506)	—	6.50
1969	176,212,000	14.00	—
1969D	114,372,000	12.00	—
1969S	(2,934,631)	—	7.00
1970	136,420,000	12.00	—
1970D	417,341,364	9.50	—
1970S	(2,632,810)	—	7.00

Date	Mintage	MS-65	Prf-65
1971	109,284,000	9.00	—
1971D	258,634,428	8.00	—
1971S	(3,220,733)	—	4.00
1972	215,048,000	7.50	—
1972D	311,067,732	10.00	—
1972S	(3,260,996)	—	3.50
1973	346,924,000	10.00	—
1973D	232,977,400	12.50	—
1973S	(2,760,339)	—	3.00
1974	801,456,000	12.00	—
1974D	353,160,300	18.00	—
1974S	(2,612,568)	—	6.50
1975 none minted	—	—	—
1975D none minted	—	—	—
1975S none minted	—	—	—

Washington Quarter. Bicentennial design, drummer boy.

KM# 204 Rev. Designer: Jack L. Ahr.
Diameter: 24.3 **Weight:** 5.6700 g.
Composition: Copper-Nickel Clad Copper

Mint mark 1968 - present

Date	Mintage	MS-60	MS-65	Prf-65
1976	809,784,016	.60	10.00	—
1976D	860,118,839	.60	10.00	—
1976S	(4,149,730)	—	—	3.25

Washington Quarter. Bicentennial design, drummer boy.

KM# 204a Rev. Designer: Jack L. Ahr.
Diameter: 24.3 **Weight:** 5.7500 g.
Composition: Silver Clad

Date	Mintage	MS-60	MS-65	Prf-65
1976S	4,908,319	2.00	4.00	3.00
1976S	(3,998,621)	—	—	5.00

Washington Quarter. Regular design resumed.

KM# A164a Diameter: 24.3 **Weight:** 5.6700 g.
Composition: Copper-Nickel Clad Copper **Notes:**
KM#164 design and composition resumed. The
1979-S and 1981 Type II proofs have clearer mint
marks than the Type I proofs for those years.

Date	Mintage	MS-65	Prf-65
1977	468,556,000	10.00	—
1977D	256,524,978	9.00	—
1977S	(3,251,152)	—	5.00
1978	521,452,000	10.00	—
1978D	287,373,152	11.00	—
1978S	(3,127,781)	—	5.00
1979	515,708,000	10.00	—
1979D	489,789,780	9.00	—
1979S T-I	—	—	4.00
1979S T-II	—	—	8.00
1980P	635,832,000	11.00	—
1980D	518,327,487	8.50	—
1980S	(3,554,806)	—	5.00
1981P	601,716,000	10.00	—
1981D	575,722,833	9.00	—
1981S T-I	—	—	5.00
1981S T-II	—	—	7.50
1982P	500,931,000	32.50	—
1982D	480,042,788	22.00	—
1982S	(3,857,479)	—	7.00
1983P	673,535,000	45.00	—
1983D	617,806,446	40.00	—
1983S	(3,279,126)	—	5.00

Date	Mintage	MS-65	Prf-65
1984P	676,545,000	16.00	—
1984D	546,483,064	12.50	—
1984S	(3,065,110)	—	4.50
1985P	775,818,962	32.00	—
1985D	519,962,888	10.00	—
1985S	(3,362,821)	5.00	6.00
1986P	551,199,333	12.00	—
1986D	504,298,660	15.00	—
1986S	(3,010,497)	—	5.00
1987P	582,499,481	10.50	—
1987D	655,594,696	10.00	—
1987S	(4,227,728)	—	5.00
1988P	562,052,000	16.00	—
1988D	596,810,688	14.00	—
1988S	(3,262,948)	—	6.50
1989P	512,868,000	18.00	—
1989D	896,535,597	5.50	—
1989S	(3,220,194)	—	5.00
1990P	613,792,000	17.00	—
1990D	927,638,181	7.00	—
1990S	(3,299,559)	—	6.00
1991P	570,968,000	15.00	—
1991D	630,966,693	14.00	—
1991S	(2,867,787)	—	5.00
1992P	384,764,000	20.00	—
1992D	389,777,107	27.50	—
1992S	(2,858,981)	—	4.50
1993P	639,276,000	11.00	—
1993D	645,476,128	14.00	—
1993S	(2,633,439)	—	5.00
1994P	825,600,000	18.00	—
1994D	880,034,110	8.00	—
1994S	(2,484,594)	—	13.50
1995P	1,004,336,000	22.00	—
1995D	1,103,216,000	20.00	—
1995S	(2,010,384)	—	12.50
1996P	925,040,000	15.00	—
1996D	906,868,000	14.00	—
1996S	—	—	4.50
1997P	595,740,000	12.50	—
1997D	599,680,000	16.00	—
1997S	(1,975,000)	—	10.00
1998P	896,268,000	13.50	—
1998D	821,000,000	13.50	—
1998S	—	—	10.00

Washington Quarter.

KM# A164b Composition: Silver **Notes:**
Resumption of silver.

Date	Mintage	Prf-65
1992S	(1,317,579)	5.00
1993S	(761,353)	6.50
1994S	(785,329)	13.50
1995S	(838,953)	18.00
1996S	—	16.00
1997S	—	17.00
1998S	—	10.00

50 State Quarters

Connecticut

KM# 297 **Composition:** Copper-Nickel Clad Copper

Date	Mintage	MS-63	MS-65	Prf-65
1999P	688,744,000	1.00	10.00	—
1999D	657,480,000	1.00	9.00	—
1999S	(3,713,359)	—	—	12.00

KM# 297a **Weight:** 6.2500 g. **Composition:** 0.9000 Silver, 0.1808 oz. ASW.

Date	Mintage	MS-63	MS-65	Prf-65
1999S	(804,565)	—	—	65.00

Delaware

KM# 293 **Diameter:** 24.3 **Weight:** 5.6700 g. **Composition:** Copper-Nickel Clad Copper

Date	Mintage	MS-63	MS-65	Prf-65
1999P	373,400,000	1.40	8.00	—
1999D	401,424,000	1.25	20.00	—
1999S	(3,713,359)	—	—	12.00

KM# 293a **Weight:** 6.2500 g. **Composition:** 0.9000 Silver, 0.1808 oz. ASW.

Date	Mintage	MS-63	MS-65	Prf-65
1999S	(804,565)	—	—	65.00

Georgia

KM# 296 **Composition:** Copper-Nickel Clad Copper

Date	Mintage	MS-63	MS-65	Prf-65
1999P	451,188,000	1.20	14.00	—
1999D	488,744,000	1.20	14.00	—
1999S	(3,713,359)	—	—	12.00

KM# 296a **Weight:** 6.2500 g. **Composition:** 0.9000 Silver, 0.1808 oz. ASW.

Date	Mintage	MS-63	MS-65	Prf-65
1999S	(804,565)	—	—	65.00

New Jersey

KM# 295 **Composition:** Copper-Nickel Clad Copper

Date	Mintage	MS-63	MS-65	Prf-65
1999P	363,200,000	1.00	10.00	—
1999D	299,028,000	1.00	9.00	—
1999S	(3,713,359)	—	—	12.00

KM# 295a **Weight:** 6.2500 g. **Composition:** 0.9000 Silver, 0.1808 oz. ASW.

Date	Mintage	MS-63	MS-65	Prf-65
1999S	(804,565)	—	—	65.00

Pennsylvania

KM# 294 **Diameter:** 24.3 **Weight:** 5.6700 g. **Composition:** Copper-Nickel Clad Copper

Date	Mintage	MS-63	MS-65	Prf-65
1999P	349,000,000	1.00	15.00	—
1999D	358,332,000	1.00	20.00	—
1999S	(3,713,359)	—	—	12.00

KM# 294a **Weight:** 6.2500 g. **Composition:** 0.9000 Silver, 0.1808 oz. ASW.

Date	Mintage	MS-63	MS-65	Prf-65
1999S	(804,565)	—	—	65.00

Maryland

KM# 306 **Composition:** Copper-Nickel Clad Copper

Date	Mintage	MS-63	MS-65	Prf-65
2000P	678,200,000	1.00	11.00	—
2000D	556,526,000	1.00	11.00	—
2000S	(4,078,747)	—	—	3.50

KM# 306a **Weight:** 6.2500 g. **Composition:** 0.9000 Silver, 0.1808 oz. ASW.

Date	Mintage	MS-63	MS-65	Prf-65
2000S	(965,921)	—	—	5.50

Massachusetts

KM# 305 **Composition:** Copper-Nickel Clad Copper

Date	Mintage	MS-63	MS-65	Prf-65
2000P	629,800,000	1.00	10.00	—
2000D	535,184,000	1.00	12.00	—
2000S	(4,078,747)	—	—	3.50

KM# 305a **Weight:** 6.2500 g. **Composition:** 0.9000 Silver, 0.1808 oz. ASW.

Date	Mintage	MS-63	MS-65	Prf-65
2000S	(965,921)	—	—	5.50

New Hampshire

KM# 308 **Composition:** Copper-Nickel Clad Copper

Date	Mintage	MS-63	MS-65	Prf-65
2000P	673,040,000	1.00	12.50	—
2000D	495,976,000	1.00	10.00	—
2000S	(4,078,747)	—	—	3.50

KM# 308a **Weight:** 6.2500 g. **Composition:** 0.9000 Silver, 0.1808 oz. ASW.

Date	Mintage	MS-63	MS-65	Prf-65
2000S	(965,921)	—	—	5.50

South Carolina

KM# 307 **Weight:** 5.6000 g. **Composition:** Copper-Nickel Clad Copper

Date	Mintage	MS-63	MS-65	Prf-65
2000P	742,756,000	1.40	9.00	—
2000P	742,756,000	1.40	9.00	—
2000D	566,208,000	1.40	12.00	—
2000D	566,208,000	1.40	12.00	—
2000S	(4,078,747)	—	—	3.50
2000S	(4,078,747)	—	—	3.50

KM# 307a **Weight:** 6.2500 g. **Composition:** 0.9000 Silver, 0.1808 oz. ASW.

Date	Mintage	MS-63	MS-65	Prf-65
2000S	(965,921)	—	—	5.50

Virginia

KM# 309 **Composition:** Copper-Nickel Clad Copper

Date	Mintage	MS-63	MS-65	Prf-65
2000P	943,000,000	1.00	8.00	—
2000D	651,616,000	1.00	8.00	—
2000S	(4,078,747)	—	—	3.35

KM# 309a **Weight:** 6.2500 g. **Composition:** 0.9000 Silver, 0.1808 oz. ASW.

Date	Mintage	MS-63	MS-65	Prf-65
2000S	(965,921)	—	—	5.50

Kentucky

KM# 322 **Composition:** Copper-Nickel Clad Copper

Date	Mintage	MS-63	MS-65	Prf-65
2001P	353,000,000	1.20	7.00	—
2001D	370,564,000	1.00	8.00	—
2001S	(3,009,800)	—	—	11.00

KM# 322a **Weight:** 6.2500 g. **Composition:** 0.9000 Silver, 0.1808 oz. ASW.

Date	Mintage	MS-63	MS-65	Prf-65
2001S	(849,500)	—	—	21.00

New York

KM# 318 **Composition:** Copper-Nickel Clad Copper

Date	Mintage	MS-63	MS-65	Prf-65
2001P	655,400,000	1.00	8.50	—
2001D	619,640,000	1.00	8.50	—
2001S	(3,009,800)	—	—	11.00

KM# 318a **Weight:** 6.2500 g. **Composition:** 0.9000 Silver, 0.1808 oz. ASW.

Date	Mintage	MS-63	MS-65	Prf-65
2001S	(849,600)	—	—	24.00

North Carolina

KM# 319   Composition: Copper-Nickel Clad Copper

Date	Mintage	MS-63	MS-65	Prf-65
2001P	627,600,000	1.00	7.50	—
2001D	427,876,000	1.00	8.50	—
2001S	(3,009,800)	—	—	11.00

KM# 319a   Weight: 6.2500 g. **Composition:** 0.9000 Silver, 0.1808 oz. ASW.

Date	Mintage	MS-63	MS-65	Prf-65
2001S	(849,600)	—	—	22.00

Rhode Island

KM# 320   Weight: 5 6000 g. **Composition:** Copper Nickel Clad Copper

Date	Mintage	MS-63	MS-65	Prf-65
2001P	423,000,000	1.00	6.50	—
2001D	447,100,000	1.00	8.00	—
2001S	(3,009,800)	—	—	11.00

KM# 320a   Weight: 6.2500 g. **Composition:** 0.9000 Silver, 0.1808 oz. ASW.

Date	Mintage	MS-63	MS-65	Prf-65
2001S	(849,600)	—	—	19.00

Vermont

KM# 321   Composition: Copper-Nickel Clad Copper

Date	Mintage	MS-63	MS-65	Prf-65
2001P	423,400,000	1.20	7.00	—
2001D	459,404,000	1.00	7.00	—
2001S	(3,009,800)	—	—	11.00

KM# 321a   Weight: 6.2500 g. **Composition:** 0.9000 Silver, 0.1808 oz. ASW.

Date	Mintage	MS-63	MS-65	Prf-65
2001S	(849,600)	—	—	19.00

Indiana

KM# 334   Weight: 5.6700 g. **Composition:** Copper-Nickel Clad Copper

Date	Mintage	MS-63	MS-65	Prf-65
2002P	362,600,000	1.00	6.00	—
2002D	327,200,000	1.00	6.50	—
2002S	(3,084,185)	—	—	4.00

KM# 334a   Weight: 6.2500 g. **Composition:** 0.9000 Silver, 0.1808 oz. ASW.

Date	Mintage	MS-63	MS-65	Prf-65
2002S	(892,229)	—	—	9.00

Louisiana

KM# 333   Composition: Copper-Nickel Clad Copper

Date	Mintage	M3-03	MS-65	Prf-65
2002P	362,000,000	1.00	6.50	—
2002D	402,204,000	1.00	7.00	—
2002S	(3,084,185)	—	—	4.00

KM# 333a   Weight: 6.2500 g. **Composition:** 0.9000 Silver, 0.1808 oz. ASW.

Date	Mintage	MS-63	MS-65	Prf-65
2002S	(892,229)	—	—	9.00

Mississippi

KM# 335   Weight: 5.6700 g. **Composition:** Copper-Nickel Clad Copper

Date	Mintage	MS-63	MS-65	Prf-65
2002P	290,000,000	1.00	5.00	—
2002D	289,600,000	1.00	6.00	—
2002S	(3,084,185)	—	—	4.00

KM# 335a   Weight: 6.2500 g. **Composition:** 0.9000 Silver, 0.1808 oz. ASW.

Date	Mintage	MS-63	MS-65	Prf-65
2002S	(892,229)	—	—	9.00

Ohio

KM# 332   Composition: Copper-Nickel Clad Copper

Date	Mintage	MS-63	MS-65	Prf-65
2002P	217,200,000	1.00	6.50	—
2002D	414,832,000	1.00	7.00	—
2002S	(3,084,185)	—	—	4.00

KM# 332a   Weight: 6.2500 g. **Composition:** 0.9000 Silver, 0.1808 oz. ASW.

Date	Mintage	MS-63	MS-65	Prf-65
2002S	(892,229)	—	—	9.00

Arkansas

KM# 347   Composition: Copper-Nickel Clad Copper

Date	Mintage	MS-63	MS-65	Prf-65
2003P	228,000,000	1.00	7.00	—
2003D	229,800,000	1.00	7.00	—
2003S	(3,270,603)	—	—	3.50

KM# 347a   Weight: 6.2500 g. **Composition:** 0.9000 Silver, 0.1808 oz. ASW.

Date	Mintage	MS-63	MS-65	Prf-65
2003S	—	—	—	5.25

Tennessee

KM# 331   Composition: Copper-Nickel Clad Copper

Date	Mintage	MS-63	MS-65	Prf-65
2002P	361,600,000	1.40	6.50	—
2002D	286,468,000	1.40	7.00	—
2002S	(3,084,185)	—	—	4.00

KM# 331a   Weight: 6.2500 g. **Composition:** 0.9000 Silver, 0.1808 oz. ASW.

Date	Mintage	MS-63	MS-65	Prf-65
2002S	(892,229)	—	—	9.00

Illinois

KM# 343   Weight: 5.6700 g. **Composition:** Copper-Nickel Clad Copper

Date	Mintage	MS-63	MS-65	Prf-65
2003P	225,800,000	1.10	7.00	—
2003D	237,400,000	1.10	6.00	—
2003S	(3,270,603)	—	—	3.50

KM# 343a   Weight: 6.2500 g. **Composition:** 0.9000 Silver, 0.1808 oz. ASW.

Date	Mintage	MS-63	MS-65	Prf-65
2003S	—	—	—	5.25

Alabama

KM# 344   Weight: 5.6700 g. **Composition:** Copper-Nickel Clad Copper

Date	Mintage	MS-63	MS-65	Prf-65
2003P	225,000,000	1.00	7.00	—
2003D	232,400,000	1.00	7.00	—
2003S	(3,270,603)	—	—	3.50

KM# 344a   Weight: 6.2500 g. **Composition:** 0.9000 Silver, 0.1808 oz. ASW.

Date	Mintage	MS-63	MS-65	Prf-65
2003S	—	—	—	5.25

Maine

KM# 345   Composition: Copper-Nickel Clad Copper

Date	Mintage	MS-63	MS-65	Prf-65
2003P	217,400,000	1.00	6.50	—
2003D	213,400,000	1.00	8.00	—
2003S	(3,270,603)	—	—	3.50

KM# 345a   Weight: 6.2500 g. **Composition:** 0.9000 Silver, 0.1808 oz. ASW.

Date	Mintage	MS-63	MS-65	Prf-65
2003S	—	—	—	5.25

Missouri

KM# 346 **Composition:** Copper-Nickel Clad Copper

Date	Mintage	MS-63	MS-65	Prf-65
2003P	225,000,000	1.00	7.00	—
2003D	228,200,000	1.00	7.00	—
2003S	(3,270,603)	—	—	3.50

KM# 346a **Weight:** 6.2500 g. **Composition:** 0.9000 Silver, 0.1808 oz. ASW.

Date	Mintage	MS-63	MS-65	Prf-65
2003S	—	—	—	5.25

Florida

KM# 356 **Weight:** 5.6700 g. **Composition:** Copper-Nickel Clad Copper

Date	Mintage	MS-63	MS-65	Prf-65
2004P	240,200,000	.75	6.50	—
2004D	241,600,000	.75	7.00	—
2004S	—	—	—	5.00

KM# 356a **Weight:** 6.2500 g. **Composition:** 0.9000 Silver, 0.1808 oz. ASW.

Date	Mintage	MS-63	MS-65	Prf-65
2004S	—	—	—	6.00

Iowa

KM# 358 **Weight:** 5.6700 g. **Composition:** Copper-Nickel Clad Copper

Date	Mintage	MS-63	MS-65	Prf-65
2004P	213,800,000	.75	6.50	—
2004D	251,800,000	.75	7.00	—
2004S	—	—	—	5.00

KM# 358a **Weight:** 6.2500 g. **Composition:** 0.9000 Silver, 0.1808 oz. ASW.

Date	Mintage	MS-63	MS-65	Prf-65
2004S	—	—	—	6.00

Michigan

KM# 355 **Weight:** 5.6700 g. **Composition:** Copper-Nickel Clad Copper

Date	Mintage	MS-63	MS-65	Prf-65
2004P	233,800,000	.75	6.50	—
2004D	225,800,000	.75	6.50	—
2004S	—	—	—	5.00

KM# 355a **Weight:** 6.2500 g. **Composition:** 0.9000 Silver, 0.1808 oz. ASW.

Date	Mintage	MS-63	MS-65	Prf-65
2004S	—	—	—	6.00

Texas

KM# 357 **Weight:** 5.6700 g. **Composition:** Copper-Nickel Clad Copper

Date	Mintage	MS-63	MS-65	Prf-65
2004P	278,800,000	.75	7.00	—
2004D	263,000,000	.75	7.00	—
2004S	—	—	—	5.00

KM# 357a **Weight:** 6.2500 g. **Composition:** 0.9000 Silver, 0.1808 oz. ASW.

Date	Mintage	MS-63	MS-65	Prf-65
2004S	—	—	—	6.00

Wisconsin

KM# 359 **Weight:** 5.6700 g. **Composition:** Copper-Nickel Clad Copper

Date	Mintage	MS-63	MS-65	Prf-65
2004P	226,400,000	1.00	8.00	—
2004D	226,800,000	1.00	10.00	—
2004D Extra Leaf Low	Est. 9,000	300	600	—
2004D Extra Leaf High	Est. 3,000	400	900	—
2004S	—	—	—	5.00

KM# 359a **Weight:** 6.2500 g. **Composition:** 0.9000 Silver, 0.1808 oz. ASW.

Date	Mintage	MS-63	MS-65	Prf-65
2004S	—	—	—	6.00

California

KM# 370   Weight: 5.7000 g. **Composition:** Copper-Nickel Clad Copper

Date	Mintage	MS-63	MS-65	Prf-65
2005P	257,200,000	.75	5.00	—
2005P Satin Finish	Inc. above	3.50	6.00	—
2005D	263,200,000	.75	5.00	—
2005D Satin Finish	Inc. above	3.50	6.00	—
2005S	—	—	—	3.00

KM# 370a   Weight: 6.2500 g. **Composition:** 0.9000 Silver, 0.1808 oz. ASW.

Date	Mintage	MS-63	MS-65	Prf-65
2005S	—	—	—	5.50

Oregon

KM# 372   Weight: 5.6700 g. **Composition:** Copper-Nickel Clad Copper

Date	Mintage	MS-63	MS-65	Prf-65
2005P	316,200,000	.75	5.00	—
2005P Satin Finish	Inc. above	3.50	6.00	—
2005D	404,000,000	.75	5.00	—
2005D Satin Finish	Inc. above	3.50	6.00	—
2005S	—	—	—	3.00

KM# 372a   Weight: 6.2500 g. **Composition:** 0.9000 Silver, 0.1808 oz. ASW.

Date	Mintage	MS-63	MS-65	Prf-65
2005S	—	—	—	5.50

Kansas

KM# 373   Composition: Copper-Nickel Clad Copper

Date	Mintage	MS-63	MS-65	Prf-65
2005P	263,400,000	.75	5.00	—
2005P Satin Finish	Inc. above	3.50	6.00	—
2005D	300,000,000	.75	5.00	—
2005D Satin Finish	Inc. above	3.50	6.00	—
2005S	—	—	—	3.00

KM# 373a   Weight: 6.2500 g. **Composition:** 0.9000 Silver, 0.1808 oz. ASW.

Date	Mintage	MS-63	MS-65	Prf-65
2005S	—	—	—	5.50

West Virginia

KM# 374   Weight: 5.6700 g. **Composition:** Copper-Nickel Clad Copper

Date	Mintage	MS-63	MS-65	Prf-65
2005P	365,400,000	.75	5.00	—
2005P Satin Finish	Inc. above	3.50	6.00	—
2005D	356,200,000	.75	5.00	—
2005D Satin Finish	Inc. above	3.50	6.00	—
2005S	—	—	—	3.00

KM# 374a   Weight: 6.2500 g. **Composition:** 0.9000 Silver, 0.1808 oz. ASW.

Date	Mintage	MS-63	MS-65	Prf-65
2005S	—	—	—	5.50

Minnesota

KM# 371   Weight: 5.7000 g. **Composition:** Copper-Nickel Clad Copper

Date	Mintage	MS-63	MS-65	Prf-65
2005P	226,400,000	.75	5.00	—
2005P Satin Finish	Inc. above	3.50	6.00	—
2005D	226,800,000	.75	5.00	—
2005D Satin Finish	Inc. above	3.50	6.00	—
2005S	—	—	—	3.00

KM# 371a   Weight: 6.2500 g. **Composition:** 0.9000 Silver, 0.1808 oz. ASW.

Date	Mintage	MS-63	MS-65	Prf-65
2005S	—	—	—	5.50

Colorado

KM# 384   Diameter: 24 **Weight:** 5.6400 g. **Composition:** Copper-Nickel Clad Copper

Date	Mintage	MS-63	MS-65	Prf-65
2006P	274,800,000	.75	5.00	—
2006P Satin Finish	Inc. above	3.00	5.00	—
2006D	294,200,000	.75	5.00	—
2006D Satin Finish	Inc. above	3.00	5.00	—
2006S	—	—	—	5.00

KM# 384a   Weight: 6.2500 g. **Composition:** 0.9000 Silver, 0.1808 oz. ASW.

Date	Mintage	MS-63	MS-65	Prf-65
2006S	—	—	—	5.75

Nebraska

KM# 383   Diameter: 24.16 **Weight:** 5.7300 g.
Composition: Copper-Nickel Clad Copper

Date	Mintage	MS-63	MS-65	Prf-65
2006P	318,000,000	.75	6.00	—
2006P Satin Finish	Inc. above	3.00	5.00	—
2006D	273,000,000	.75	6.00	—
2006D Satin Finish	Inc. above	3.00	5.00	—
2006S	—	—	—	5.00

KM# 383a   Weight: 6.2500 g. **Composition:**
0.9000 Silver, 0.1808 oz. ASW.

Date	Mintage	MS-63	MS-65	Prf-65
2006S	—	—	—	5.75

Nevada

KM# 382   Diameter: 24.21 **Weight:** 5.6800 g.
Composition: Copper-Nickel Clad Copper

Date	Mintage	MS-63	MS-65	Prf-65
2006P	277,000,000	.75	6.00	—
2006P Satin Finish	Inc. above	3.00	5.00	—
2006D	312,800,000	.75	6.00	—
2006D Satin Finish	Inc. above	3.00	5.00	—
2006S	—	—	—	5.00

KM# 382a   Weight: 6.2500 g. **Composition:**
0.9000 Silver, 0.1808 oz. ASW.

Date	Mintage	MS-63	MS-65	Prf-65
2006S	—	—	—	5.75

North Dakota

KM# 385   Diameter: 24.23 **Weight:** 5.6100 g.
Composition: Copper-Nickel Clad Copper

Date	Mintage	MS-63	MS-65	Prf-65
2006P	305,800,000	.75	5.00	—
2006P Satin Finish	Inc. above	3.00	5.00	—
2006D	359,000,000	.75	5.00	—
2006D Satin Finish	Inc. above	3.00	5.00	—
2006S	—	—	—	5.00

KM# 385a   Weight: 6.2500 g. **Composition:**
0.9000 Silver, 0.1808 oz. ASW.

Date	Mintage	MS-63	MS-65	Prf-65
2006S	—	—	—	5.75

South Dakota

KM# 386   Diameter: 24.18 **Weight:** 5.6400 g.
Composition: Copper-Nickel Clad Copper

Date	Mintage	MS-63	MS-65	Prf-65
2006P	245,000,000	.75	5.00	—
2006P Satin Finish	Inc. above	3.00	5.00	—
2006D	265,800,000	.75	5.00	—
2006D Satin Finish	Inc. above	3.00	5.00	—
2006S	—	—	—	5.00

KM# 386a   Weight: 6.2500 g. **Composition:**
0.9000 Silver, 0.1808 oz. ASW.

Date	Mintage	MS-63	MS-65	Prf-65
2006S	—	—	—	5.75

Idaho

KM# 398   Composition: Copper-Nickel Clad
Copper

Date	Mintage	MS-63	MS-65	Prf-65
2007P	294,600,000	.75	8.00	—
2007D	286,800,000	.75	8.00	—
2007S	—	—	—	4.00

KM# 398a   Weight: 6.2500 g. **Composition:**
0.9000 Silver, 0.1808 oz. ASW.

Date	Mintage	MS-63	MS-65	Prf-65
2007S	Inc. above	—	—	6.50

Montana

KM# 396   Composition: Copper-Nickel Clad
Copper

Date	Mintage	MS-63	MS-65	Prf-65
2007P	257,000,000	.75	8.00	—
2007D	256,240,000	.75	5.00	—
2007S	—	—	—	4.00

KM# 396a   Weight: 6.2500 g. **Composition:**
0.9000 Silver, 0.1808 oz. ASW.

Date	Mintage	MS-63	MS-65	Prf-65
2007S	Inc. above	—	—	6.50

Utah

KM# 400 **Composition:** Copper-Nickel Clad Copper

Date	Mintage	MS-63	MS-65	Prf-65
2007P	—	—	—	—
2007D	—	—	—	—
2007S	—	—	—	4.00

KM# 400a **Weight:** 6.2500 g. **Composition:** 0.9000 Silver, 0.1808 oz. ASW.

Date	Mintage	MS-63	MS-65	Prf-65
2007S	Inc. above	—	—	6.50

Wyoming

KM# 399 **Composition:** Copper-Nickel Clad Copper

Date	Mintage	MS-63	MS-65	Prf-65
2007P	—	—	—	—
2007D	—	—	—	—
2007S	—	—	—	4.00

KM# 399a **Weight:** 6.2500 g. **Composition:** 0.9000 Silver, 0.1808 oz. ASW.

Date	Mintage	MS-63	MS-65	Prf-65
2007S	Inc. above	—	—	6.50

Washington

KM# 397 **Composition:** Copper-Nickel Clad Copper

Date	Mintage	MS-63	MS-65	Prf-65
2007P	265,200,000	.75	8.00	—
2007D	280,000,000	.75	8.00	—
2007S	—	—	—	4.00

KM# 397a **Weight:** 6.2500 g. **Composition:** 0.9000 Silver, 0.1808 oz. ASW.

Date	Mintage	MS-63	MS-65	Prf-65
2007S	Inc. above	—	—	6.50

HALF DOLLAR

Flowing Hair Half Dollar.

KM# 16 **Designer:** Robert Scot. **Diameter:** 32.5 **Weight:** 13.4800 g. **Composition:** 0.8920 Silver, 0.3866 oz. ASW. **Notes:** The 1795 "recut date" variety had the date cut into the dies twice, so both sets of numbers are visible on the coin. The 1795 "3 leaves" variety has three leaves under each of the eagle's wings on the reverse.

Date	Mintage	G-4	VG-8	F-12	VF-20	XF-40	MS-60
1794	23,464	2,650	5,200	7,750	19,500	35,000	125,000
1795	299,680	650	900	1,600	2,750	8,500	25,000
1795 recut date	Inc. above	700	950	1,650	2,900	9,000	29,500
1795 3 leaves	Inc. above	2,600	3,000	4,400	6,850	13,500	50,000

Draped Bust Half Dollar. Small eagle.

KM# 26 **Designer:** Robert Scot. **Diameter:** 32.5 **Weight:** 13.4800 g. **Composition:** 0.8920 Silver, 0.3866 oz. ASW. **Notes:** The 1796 strikes have either 15 or 16 stars on the obverse.

Date	Mintage	G-4	VG-8	F-12	VF-20	XF-40	MS-60
1796 15 stars	3,918	29,000	36,500	60,000	87,500	108,000	175,000
1796 16 stars	Inc. above	30,500	38,500	67,500	92,000	115,000	205,000
1797	Inc. above	28,500	36,000	70,000	89,500	110,000	175,000

Draped Bust Half Dollar. Draped bust right, flanked by stars, date at angle below. Heraldic eagle.

KM# 35 **Designer:** Robert Scot. **Diameter:** 32.5 **Weight:** 13.4800 g. **Composition:** 0.8920 Silver, 0.3866 oz. ASW. **Notes:** The two varieties of the 1803 strikes are distinguished by the size of the 3 in the date. The several varieties of the 1806 strikes are distinguished by the style of 6 in the date, size of the stars on the obverse, and whether the stem of the olive branch held by the reverse eagle extends through the claw.

Date	Mintage	G-4	VG-8	F-12	VF-20	XF-40	MS-60
1801	30,289	850	1,100	2,350	3,600	8,100	36,500
1802	29,890	775	1,000	2,250	3,500	7,750	45,000
1803 small 3	188,234	160	185	325	600	1,850	10,750
1803 large 3	Inc. above	150	175	250	450	1,250	8,900
1805	211,722	150	175	250	425	1,200	7,900
1805/4	Inc. above	190	300	500	850	2,200	30,000
1806 knobbed 6, large stars	839,576	150	175	250	385	1,150	—
1806 knobbed 6, small stars	Inc. above	150	175	250	385	1,150	7,750
1806 knobbed 6, stem not through claw	Inc. above	20,000	35,000	42,000	57,500	90,000	—
1806 pointed-top 6, stem not through claw	Inc. above	170	210	285	465	1,325	7,950
1806 pointed-top 6, stem through claw	Inc. above	150	185	250	385	1,150	7,500
1806/5	Inc. above	165	200	285	450	1,650	10,500
1806 /inverted 6	Inc. above	185	350	550	1,000	2,850	25,000
1807	301,076	150	175	250	365	1,150	7,250

Capped Bust. Draped bust left, flanked by stars, date at angle below. "50 C." below eagle.

KM# 37 Designer: John Reich. **Diameter:** 32.5 **Weight:** 13.4800 g. **Composition:** 0.8920 Silver, 0.3866 oz. ASW. **Notes:** There are three varieties of the 1807 strikes. Two are distinguished by the size of the stars on the obverse. The third was struck from a reverse die that had a 5 cut over a 2 in the "50C" denomination. Two varieties of the 1811 are distinguished by the size of the 8 in the date. A third has a period between the 8 and second 1 in the date. One variety of the 1817 has a period between the 1 and 7 in the date. Two varieties of the 1819/18 overdate are distinguished by the size of the 9 in the date. Two varieties of the 1820 are distinguished by the size of the date. On the 1823 varieties, the "broken 3" appears to be almost separated in the middle of the 3 in the date; the "patched 3" has the error repaired; the "ugly 3" has portions of its detail missing. The 1827 "curled-2" and "square-2" varieties are distinguished by the numeral's base -- either curled or square. Among the 1828 varieties, "knobbed 2" and "no knob" refers to whether the upper left serif of the digit is rounded. The 1830 varieties are distinguished by the size of the 0 in the date. The four 1834 varieties are distinguished by the sizes of the stars, date and letters in the inscriptions. The 1836 "50/00" variety was struck from a reverse die that had "50" recut over "00" in the denomination.

Date	Mintage	G-4	VG-8	F-12	VF-20	XF-40	AU-50	MS-60	MS-65
1807 small stars	750,500	125	175	325	550	1,150	3,500	5,900	54,000
1807 large stars	Inc. above	100.00	165	275	475	800	2,500	4,800	—
1807 50/20 C.	Inc. above	85.00	115	185	300	575	2,850	4,600	30,000
1807 bearded goddess	—	350	550	900	1,800	3,450	7,500	—	—
1808	1,368,600	75.00	85.00	100.00	135	325	600	1,800	15,000
1808/7	Inc. above	90.00	110	135	240	425	1,150	2,400	—
1809 Normal edge	1,405,810	75.00	85.00	100.00	135	275	525	1,600	15,000
1809 XXXX edge	Inc. above	80.00	105	130	185	290	540	2,450	—
1809 IIIIIII edge	Inc. above	85.00	110	140	210	325	560	3,200	—
1810	1,276,276	72.00	83.00	95.00	130	245	475	1,550	14,000
1811 small 8	1,203,644	74.00	85.00	95.00	125	190	450	1,250	12,800
1811 large 8	Inc. above	74.00	85.00	95.00	130	200	500	1,300	13,500
1811 dated 18.11	Inc. above	85.00	95.00	110	180	375	700	1,900	—
1812	1,628,059	72.00	83.00	95.00	130	200	385	1,450	9,800
1812/1 small 8	Inc. above	85.00	95.00	125	200	300	700	2,400	16,000
1812/1 large 8	Inc. above	1,550	2,100	3,950	6,000	8,800	21,000	—	—
1812 Single leaf below wing	Inc. above	750	950	1,250	2,400	4,000	6,800	12,500	—
1813	1,241,903	72.00	83.00	95.00	130	200	460	1,575	11,000
1813 50/UNI reverse	1,241,903	85.00	95.00	125	175	350	900	1,900	—
1814	1,039,075	72.00	83.00	95.00	130	200	500	1,475	10,500
1814/3	Inc. above	100.00	135	190	285	475	1,100	2,350	16,500
1814 E/A in States	Inc. above	85.00	95.00	125	160	300	675	1,850	—
1814 Single leaf below wing	Inc. above	75.00	90.00	160	235	575	1,350	2,600	—
1815/2	47,150	1,100	1,450	1,850	2,850	4,200	6,000	11,500	85,000
1817	1,215,567	72.00	83.00	95.00	130	200	400	11,500	1,500
1817/3	Inc. above	125	185	280	450	800	1,800	3,750	43,500
1817/4	—	60,000	80,000	150,000	200,000	250,000	340,000	—	—
1817 dated 181.7	Inc. above	90.00	100.00	130	130	240	650	1,500	12,500
1817 Single leaf below wing	Inc. above	85.00	95.00	120	175	400	900	2,200	—
1818	1,960,322	60.00	68.00	85.00	105	185	420	1,300	10,500
1818/7 Large 8	Inc. above	90.00	100.00	115	140	240	760	1,600	15,500
1818/7 Small 8	Inc. above	90.00	100.00	115	140	240	760	1,600	15,500
1819	2,208,000	60.00	35.00	52.00	105	175	400	1,250	11,000
1819/8 small 9	Inc. above	57.50	62.50	75.00	100.00	200	550	1,300	1,150
1819/8 large 9	Inc. above	57.50	62.50	75.00	100.00	200	550	1,300	11,500
1820 Curl Base 2, small date	751,122	67.00	85.00	100.00	145	280	650	1,350	13,000
1820 Square Base 2 with knob, large date	Inc. above	67.00	85.00	100.00	145	280	650	1,350	13,000
1820 Square Base 2 without know, large date	Inc. above	67.00	85.00	100.00	145	280	650	1,350	13,000
1820 E's without Serifs	Inc. above	260	320	425	650	950	2,200	4,800	—
1820/19 Square Base 2	Inc. above	95.00	115	140	200	340	875	2,000	25,000
1820/19 Curled Base 2	Inc. above	95.00	115	140	200	350	900	2,100	30,000
1821	1,305,797	58.00	67.00	80.00	98.00	165	525	1,200	10,000
1822	1,559,573	58.00	67.00	80.00	98.00	165	385	1,150	9,000
1822/1	Inc. above	80.00	90.00	125	190	290	750	1,650	12,000

Date	Mintage	G-4	VG-8	F-12	VF-20	XF-40	AU-50	MS-60	MS-65
1823	1,694,200	55.00	64.00	75.00	90.00	150	350	1,050	8,600
1823 broken 3	Inc. above	74.00	88.00	115	165	400	1,050	2,800	—
1823 patched 3	Inc. above	70.00	80.00	105	145	250	600	1,500	15,000
1823 ugly 3	Inc. above	66.00	76.00	98.00	135	225	900	1,700	14,000
1824	3,504,954	55.00	64.00	75.00	90.00	150	350	1,050	8,600
1824/21	Inc. above	60.00	70.00	84.00	100.00	170	450	1,250	10,850
1824/4	Inc. above	60.00	70.00	88.00	110	190	500	1,350	11,250
1824 1824/various dates	Inc. above	70.00	85.00	100.00	145	240	875	1,850	15,000
1825	2,943,166	55.00	64.00	75.00	90.00	150	350	1,050	8,600
1826	4,004,180	55.00	64.00	75.00	90.00	150	350	1,050	8,600
1827 curled 2	5,493,400	70.00	80.00	95.00	130	190	500	1,350	12,500
1827 square 2	Inc. above	55.00	64.00	75.00	90.00	150	350	1,050	8,600
1827/6	Inc. above	85.00	95.00	120	155	235	450	1,250	11,500
1828 curled-base 2, no knob	3,075,200	55.00	64.00	75.00	90.00	150	350	1,050	8,600
1828 curled-base 2, knobbed 2	Inc. above	65.00	75.00	95.00	125	165	375	1,350	9,800
1828 small 8s, square-base 2, large letters	Inc. above	55.00	64.00	75.00	90.00	150	350	1,050	8,600
1828 small 8s, square-base 2, small letters	Inc. above	60.00	75.00	100.00	140	250	750	1,350	10,000
1828 large 8s, square-base 2	Inc. above	55.00	64.00	75.00	90.00	150	350	1,100	9,250
1829	3,712,156	52.00	60.00	65.00	75.00	140	340	1,050	9,000
1829 Large letters	Inc. above	56.00	67.00	75.00	85.00	160	420	1,250	10,500
1829/7	Inc. above	70.00	80.00	95.00	125	200	385	1,250	12,000
1830 Small O rev	4,764,800	52.00	60.00	65.00	75.00	140	340	1,000	8,500
1830 Large O	Inc. above	55.00	65.00	70.00	80.00	150	375	1,150	9,000
1830 Large letter rev	Inc. above	1,500	2,250	3,000	3,750	4,800	9,800	—	—
1831	5,873,660	52.00	60.00	65.00	75.00	140	340	1,000	8,500
1832 small letters	4,797,000	52.00	60.00	65.00	75.00	140	340	1,000	8,500
1832 large letters	Inc. above	52.00	60.00	70.00	95.00	165	360	1,150	8,850
1833	5,206,000	52.00	60.00	65.00	75.00	140	340	1,000	8,500
1834 small date, large stars, small letters	6,412,004	52.00	60.00	65.00	75.00	140	340	1,000	8,500
1834 small date, small stars, small letters	Inc. above	52.00	60.00	65.00	75.00	140	340	1,000	8,500
1834 large date, small letters	Inc. above	52.00	60.00	65.00	75.00	140	340	1,000	8,500
1834 large date, large letters	Inc. above	52.00	60.00	65.00	75.00	140	340	1,000	8,500
1835	5,352,006	52.00	60.00	65.00	75.00	140	340	1,000	9,000
1836	6,545,000	52.00	60.00	65.00	75.00	140	340	1,000	8,500
1836 50/00	Inc. above	80.00	85.00	110	185	300	800	1,750	15,000

Bust Half Dollar. Draped bust left, flanked by stars, date at angle below. "50 Cents" below eagle.

KM# 58 **Designer:** Christian Gobrecht. **Diameter:** 30 **Weight:** 13.3600 g. **Composition:** 0.9000 Silver, 0.3866 oz. ASW.

Date	Mintage	G-4	VG-8	F-12	VF-20	XF-40	AU-50	MS-60	MS-65
1836	1,200	850	1,075	1,550	1,950	2,800	3,900	7,250	58,000
1837	3,629,820	55.00	65.00	80.00	120	195	350	1,000	15,000

Bust Half Dollar. Draped bust left, flanked by stars, date below. "Half Dol." below eagle.

KM# 65   Designer: Christian Gobrecht. **Diameter:** 30 **Weight:** 13.3600 g. **Composition:** 0.9000 Silver, 0.3866 oz. ASW.

Date	Mintage	G-4	VG-8	F-12	VF-20	XF-40	AU-50	MS-60	MS-65
1838	3,546,000	55.00	65.00	80.00	120	195	350	1,000	18,500
1838O proof only	Est. 20	—	—	—	—	250,000	300,000	—	—
1839	1,392,976	60.00	70.00	100.00	145	225	390	1,100	30,000
1839O	178,976	240	320	425	650	900	1,350	2,850	40,000

Seated Liberty Half Dollar. Seated Liberty, date below. "Half Dol." below eagle.

KM# 68   Designer: Christian Gobrecht. **Diameter:** 30.6 **Weight:** 13.3600 g. **Composition:** 0.9000 Silver, 0.3866 oz. ASW. **Notes:** The 1839 varieties are distinguished by whether there's drapery extending from Liberty's left elbow. One variety of the 1840 strikes has smaller lettering; another used the old reverse of 1838. Varieties of 1842 and 1846 are distinguished by the size of the numerals in the date.

Date	Mintage	G-4	VG-8	F-12	VF-20	XF-40	AU-50	MS-60	MS-65
1839 no drapery from elbow	Inc. above	45.00	80.00	150	340	800	1,850	6,000	178,000
1839 drapery	Inc. above	38.00	50.00	59.00	86.00	165	265	1,000	25,000
1840 small letters	1,435,008	36.00	46.00	60.00	84.00	150	325	600	7,500
1840 reverse 1838	Inc. above	150	200	275	350	650	1,350	3,400	30,000
1840O	855,100	36.00	48.00	57.00	90.00	140	275	450	—
1841	310,000	50.00	65.00	100.00	150	235	325	1,200	6,850
1841O	401,000	30.00	44.00	56.00	82.00	180	230	600	7,000
1842 small date	2,012,764	38.00	55.00	75.00	120	175	325	1,300	13,500
1842 medium date	Inc. above	30.00	41.00	51.00	64.00	115	220	750	8,800
1842O small date	957,000	650	850	1,400	2,450	4,650	7,750	16,500	—
1842O medium date	Inc. above	35.00	42.00	55.00	90.00	185	500	1,250	10,500
1843	3,844,000	28.00	39.00	51.00	65.00	110	225	500	4,500
1843O	2,268,000	30.00	41.00	51.00	65.00	120	240	550	—
1844	1,766,000	30.00	41.00	51.00	65.00	110	210	440	4,500
1844O	2,005,000	30.00	41.00	51.00	70.00	110	225	550	—
1844/1844O	Inc. above	500	775	1,000	1,300	2,500	5,750	10,000	—
1845	589,000	35.00	45.00	65.00	125	210	325	850	12,000
1845O	2,094,000	30.00	41.00	51.00	70.00	135	240	550	9,400
1845O no drapery	Inc. above	35.00	47.00	70.00	115	185	375	750	—
1846 medium date	2,210,000	30.00	41.00	51.00	70.00	110	200	500	9,000
1846 tall date	Inc. above	35.00	47.00	70.00	85.00	145	250	650	12,000
1846 /horizontal 6	Inc. above	175	250	325	450	625	1,000	2,500	—
1846O medium date	2,304,000	30.00	41.00	51.00	65.00	110	225	550	12,000
1846O tall date	Inc. above	165	285	365	620	1,050	2,000	6,650	—
1847/1846	1,156,000	2,000	2,750	3,750	5,250	7,700	12,500	21,000	—
1847	Inc. above	35.00	45.00	54.00	67.00	105	250	480	9,000
1847O	2,584,000	30.00	41.00	51.00	65.00	120	275	640	7,000
1848	580,000	45.00	65.00	95.00	185	265	485	1,000	9,000
1848O	3,180,000	30.00	41.00	51.00	70.00	110	285	750	9,000
1849	1,252,000	35.00	45.00	54.00	67.00	108	365	1,250	15,000
1849O	2,310,000	30.00	41.00	51.00	70.00	110	250	650	9,000

Date	Mintage	G-4	VG-8	F-12	VF-20	XF-40	AU-50	MS-60	MS-65
1850	227,000	275	325	400	550	675	1,000	1,500	—
1850O	2,456,000	35.00	28.00	45.00	80.00	135	275	650	9,000
1851	200,750	335	450	550	850	950	1,200	2,250	—
1851O	402,000	40.00	55.00	95.00	120	185	300	700	9,000
1852	77,130	425	500	700	925	1,100	1,350	1,700	—
1852O	144,000	75.00	125	200	350	600	1,250	3,850	26,000
1853O mintage unrecorded	—	—	250,000	—	—	450,000	—	—	—

Note: 1853O, Eliasberg Sale, 1997, VG-8, $154,000.

Seated Liberty Half Dollar. Seated Liberty, arrows at date. Rays around eagle.

KM# 79   Designer: Christian Gobrecht. **Weight:** 12.4400 g. **Composition:** 0.9000 Silver, 0.3599 oz. ASW.

Date	Mintage	G-4	VG-8	F-12	VF-20	XF-40	AU-50	MS-60	MS-65	Prf-65
1853	3,532,708	28.00	10.00	47.00	90.00	250	590	1,650	21,500	175,000
1853O	1,328,000	38.00	48.00	57.00	125	310	750	2,350	27,500	—

Seated Liberty Half Dollar. Seated Liberty, arrows at date. "Half Dol." below eagle.

KM# 82   Designer: Christian Gobrecht. **Weight:** 12.4400 g. **Composition:** 0.9000 Silver, 0.3599 oz. ASW.

Date	Mintage	G-4	VG-8	F-12	VF-20	XF-40	AU-50	MS-60	MS-65	Prf-65
1854	2,982,000	28.00	38.00	47.00	60.00	100.00	270	675	8,000	37,500
1854O	5,240,000	28.00	38.00	47.00	60.00	100.00	270	600	8,000	—
1855	759,500	30.00	40.00	49.00	63.00	120	325	700	9,000	39,500
1855/4	Inc. above	65.00	84.00	160	250	375	600	2,000	17,500	37,000
1855O	3,688,000	28.00	38.00	47.00	60.00	100.00	270	650	8,000	—
1855S	129,950	350	475	800	1,500	3,150	6,850	19,500	—	—

Seated Liberty Half Dollar. Seated Liberty, date below. "Half Dol." below eagle.

KM# A68   Designer: Christian Gobrecht. **Weight:** 12.4400 g. **Composition:** 0.9000 Silver, 0.3599 oz. ASW.

Date	Mintage	G-4	VG-8	F-12	VF-20	XF-40	AU-50	MS-60	MS-65	Prf-65
1856	938,000	32.00	38.00	50.00	70.00	110	195	425	6,500	12,500

Date	Mintage	G-4	VG-8	F-12	VF-20	XF-40	AU-50	MS-60	MS-65	Prf-65
1856O	2,658,000	28.00	38.00	52.00	60.00	100.00	190	385	12,500	—
1856S	211,000	85.00	120	160	260	500	1,250	3,500	19,000	—
1857	1,988,000	28.00	38.00	50.00	60.00	100.00	190	385	5,150	12,500
1857O	818,000	33.00	40.00	52.00	85.00	135	275	885	12,500	—
1857S	158,000	100.00	120	145	285	575	975	3,500	19,000	—
1858	4,226,000	28.00	38.00	47.00	60.00	90.00	190	385	6,500	12,500
1858O	7,294,000	28.00	38.00	47.00	60.00	90.00	190	385	12,500	—
1858S	476,000	38.00	48.00	62.00	110	215	400	950	12,500	—
1859	748,000	30.00	41.00	51.00	70.00	120	200	650	6,600	5,500
1859O	2,834,000	28.00	38.00	47.00	60.00	100.00	190	450	6,500	—
1859S	566,000	38.00	44.00	59.00	100.00	215	375	750	12,500	—
1860	303,700	38.00	42.00	51.00	100.00	150	350	1,000	6,500	5,500
1860O	1,290,000	30.00	41.00	52.00	70.00	100.00	190	450	5,150	—
1860S	472,000	38.00	40.00	51.00	85.00	135	245	850	12,500	—
1861	2,888,400	30.00	40.00	49.00	65.00	100.00	190	440	5,150	5,500
1861O	2,532,633	30.00	41.00	53.00	86.00	125	235	450	5,150	—
1861S	939,500	35.00	44.00	53.00	70.00	120	195	975	9,500	—
1862	253,550	38.00	51.00	57.00	120	200	295	750	5,150	5,500
1862S	1,352,000	30.00	41.00	52.00	75.00	120	195	460	9,000	—
1863	503,660	35.00	48.00	57.00	85.00	135	250	750	5,150	5,500
1863S	916,000	33.00	45.00	52.00	70.00	120	195	460	9,000	—
1864	379,570	30.00	48.00	57.00	120	195	250	750	5,150	5,500
1864S	658,000	33.00	45.00	51.00	70.00	125	215	675	9,000	—
1865	511,900	28.00	47.00	55.00	90.00	150	275	750	5,150	5,500
1865S	675,000	35.00	45.00	52.00	70.00	120	235	500	9,000	—
1866 proof, unique	—	—	—	—	—	—	—	—	—	—
1866S	60,000	460	575	850	1,250	2,550	3,350	5,400	68,000	—

Seated Liberty Half Dollar. Seated Liberty, date below. "In God We Trust" above eagle.

KM# 99 Designer: Christian Gobrecht. **Weight:** 12.4400 g. **Composition:** 0.9000 Silver, 0.3599 oz. ASW.
Notes: In 1866 the motto "In God We Trust" was added to the reverse. The "closed-3" and "open-3" varieties are distinguished by the amount of space between the upper and lower left serifs of the 3.

Date	Mintage	G-4	VG-8	F-12	VF-20	XF-40	AU-50	MS-60	MS-65	Prf-65
1866	745,625	35.00	45.00	53.00	80.00	120	225	350	4,800	3,750
1866S	994,000	33.00	43.00	51.00	70.00	110	275	650	5,000	—
1867	449,925	38.00	48.00	59.00	110	165	250	350	4,800	3,750
1867S	1,196,000	32.00	42.00	51.00	70.00	110	250	350	7,000	—
1868	418,200	48.00	55.00	95.00	185	225	300	525	7,100	3,750
1868S	1,160,000	32.00	42.00	51.00	70.00	110	250	350	7,000	—
1869	795,900	35.00	45.00	49.00	70.00	110	190	385	4,600	3,750
1869S	656,000	35.00	47.00	51.00	70.00	120	265	600	7,000	—
1870	634,900	35.00	45.00	50.00	80.00	120	250	475	7,000	3,750
1870CC	54,617	900	1,500	1,900	3,900	12,500	30,000	100,000	—	—
1870S	1,004,000	31.00	43.00	53.00	85.00	150	275	575	7,000	—
1871	1,204,560	32.00	42.00	52.00	75.00	120	165	350	7,000	3,750
1871CC	153,950	225	325	600	1,200	1,950	10,000	15,000	—	—
1871S	2,178,000	30.00	41.00	49.00	70.00	110	215	400	7,000	—
1872	881,550	32.00	40.00	49.00	75.00	120	195	430	2,850	3,750
1872CC	272,000	85.00	125	275	400	1,500	4,000	8,000	50,000	—
1872S	580,000	31.00	47.00	67.00	135	225	375	975	7,000	—
1873 closed 3	801,800	35.00	46.00	64.00	98.00	135	250	545	4,500	3,750
1873 open 3	Inc. above	2,650	3,400	4,350	5,500	7,900	13,500	30,000	—	—
1873CC	122,500	225	320	425	950	1,900	6,500	12,000	80,000	—
1873S no arrows	5,000	—	—	—	—	—	—	—	—	—

Note: 1873S no arrows, no specimens known to survive.

Seated Liberty Half Dollar. Seated Liberty, arrows at date. "In God We Trust" above eagle.

KM# 107 **Designer:** Christian Gobrecht. **Weight:** 12.5000 g. **Composition:** 0.9000 Silver, 0.3617 oz. ASW.

Date	Mintage	G-4	VG-8	F-12	VF-20	XF-40	AU-50	MS-60	MS-65	Prf-65
1873	1,815,700	32.00	49.00	60.00	90.00	230	400	850	17,500	9,000
1873CC	214,560	150	275	375	850	2,000	2,400	5,700	42,000	—
1873S	233,000	55.00	78.00	130	245	425	675	2,200	40,000	—
1874	2,360,300	32.00	42.00	56.00	85.00	210	400	850	12,750	9,000
1874CC	59,000	400	575	1,000	1,750	3,600	5,600	10,500	—	—
1874S	394,000	43.00	65.00	85.00	185	365	685	1,850	20,000	—

Seated Liberty Half Dollar. Seated Liberty, date below. "In God We Trust" above eagle.

KM# A99 **Designer:** Christian Gobrecht. **Weight:** 12.5000 g. **Composition:** 0.9000 Silver, 0.3617 oz. ASW.

Date	Mintage	G-4	VG-8	F-12	VF-20	XF-40	AU-50	MS-60	MS-65	Prf-65
1875	6,027,500	28.00	38.00	47.00	56.00	88.00	180	420	3,500	3,375
1875CC	1,008,000	50.00	56.00	75.00	125	200	325	650	8,350	—
1875S	3,200,000	28.00	38.00	47.00	63.00	100.00	165	360	2,700	—
1876	8,419,150	28.00	38.00	47.00	56.00	88.00	165	360	5,300	3,775
1876CC	1,956,000	50.00	56.00	75.00	115	180	275	560	4,200	—
1876S	4,528,000	28.00	38.00	47.00	56.00	88.00	165	360	2,700	—
1877	8,304,510	28.00	38.00	47.00	56.00	88.00	165	360	2,700	3,825
1877CC	1,420,000	50.00	56.00	75.00	115	180	275	630	3,250	—
1877S	5,356,000	28.00	38.00	47.00	56.00	88.00	165	360	2,700	—
1878	1,378,400	35.00	46.00	67.00	80.00	120	165	425	3,650	3,900
1878CC	62,000	450	600	1,000	1,500	3,150	4,850	7,000	43,500	—
1878S	12,000	23,500	37,500	45,000	47,500	52,000	60,000	70,000	175,000	—
1879	5,900	275	310	360	400	465	575	700	3,650	3,150
1880	9,755	260	280	315	355	410	535	700	3,750	3,150
1881	10,975	270	300	335	385	455	565	700	4,000	3,150
1882	5,500	340	365	385	450	525	600	750	3,850	3,150
1883	9,039	325	340	365	435	500	575	775	3,950	3,150
1884	5,275	385	375	415	500	560	635	800	3,850	3,150
1885	6,130	390	425	475	550	625	700	825	3,850	3,150
1886	5,886	400	500	600	700	775	875	1,000	3,900	3,150
1887	5,710	500	525	650	775	875	950	1,100	3,900	3,150
1888	12,833	280	300	365	400	485	550	800	3,900	3,150
1889	12,711	275	315	350	400	485	550	800	3,900	3,150
1890	12,590	285	310	365	415	500	550	800	3,850	3,150
1891	200,600	55.00	60.00	94.00	122	155	260	480	3,850	3,150

Barber Half Dollar. Laureate head right, flanked by stars, date below. Heraldic eagle.

KM# 116 Designer: Charles E. Barber. **Diameter:** 30.6 **Weight:** 12.5000 g. **Composition:** 0.9000 Silver, 0.3617 oz. ASW.

Mint mark

Date	Mintage	G-4	VG-8	F-12	VF-20	XF-40	AU-50	MS-60	MS-65	Prf-65
1892	935,245	28.50	40.00	65.00	115	180	295	450	3,600	3,500
1892O	390,000	310	400	515	575	630	690	850	4,500	—
1892O micro O	—	2,000	3,750	4,500	7,000	10,000	17,500	24,000	64,000	—
1892S	1,029,028	250	325	425	530	600	700	940	5,350	—
1893	1,826,792	20.00	31.00	75.00	135	205	325	520	5,350	3,500
1893O	1,389,000	36.00	62.50	130	220	360	435	625	10,000	—
1893S	740,000	185	220	300	500	635	725	1,275	28,500	—
1894	1,148,972	32.50	50.00	118	200	290	375	500	3,850	3,500
1894O	2,138,000	22.00	34.00	95.00	170	290	365	525	7,250	—
1894S	4,048,690	19.00	28.00	70.00	125	230	335	490	11,500	—
1895	1,835,218	18.00	25.00	72.00	150	235	335	595	3,900	3,500
1895O	1,766,000	23.00	39.00	115	210	285	395	595	7,500	—
1895S	1,108,086	33.00	54.00	130	235	310	410	575	8,650	—
1896	950,762	21.50	28.00	90.00	160	265	365	565	6,000	3,500
1896O	924,000	42.00	56.00	185	290	475	750	1,500	15,500	—
1896S	1,140,948	105	145	210	350	495	750	1,400	11,250	—
1897	2,480,731	12.50	15.00	47.50	100.00	160	345	485	4,150	3,500
1897O	632,000	170	230	495	835	1,100	1,350	1,750	9,750	—
1897S	933,900	155	215	385	550	840	1,050	1,500	8,500	—
1898	2,956,735	12.50	15.00	38.50	96.00	165	345	485	3,850	3,500
1898O	874,000	37.50	75.00	225	355	525	625	1,250	10,500	—
1898S	2,358,550	27.50	52.50	87.50	175	335	440	950	10,250	—
1899	5,538,846	13.50	16.00	39.50	100.00	170	350	475	4,150	3,500
1899O	1,724,000	26.00	37.50	80.00	170	300	420	675	8,350	—
1899S	1,686,411	23.00	40.00	80.00	140	225	360	660	6,900	—
1900	4,762,912	13.50	15.50	37.50	94.00	155	310	485	4,000	3,500
1900O	2,744,000	17.50	22.50	62.00	165	285	375	860	16,500	—
1900S	2,560,322	15.00	18.50	46.50	100.00	200	310	640	10,500	—
1901	4,268,813	13.50	16.00	38.50	96.00	180	300	510	4,400	3,500
1901O	1,124,000	16.50	26.50	80.00	205	350	475	1,350	16,500	—
1901S	847,044	34.00	55.00	160	355	610	1,050	1,850	19,500	—
1902	4,922,777	12.50	13.50	32.50	86.00	175	295	475	4,850	3,500
1902O	2,526,000	13.50	17.00	52.50	105	225	360	725	12,500	—
1902S	1,460,670	16.00	19.00	62.50	150	260	420	750	8,400	—
1903	2,278,755	13.50	16.00	47.50	100.00	200	325	500	11,000	3,500
1903O	2,100,000	13.00	17.00	54.00	115	210	335	665	10,000	—
1903S	1,920,772	15.00	18.00	55.00	125	235	380	610	8,800	—
1904	2,992,670	12.00	13.50	34.00	85.00	155	300	475	6,000	3,500
1904O	1,117,600	20.00	32.50	80.00	220	385	590	1,100	12,500	—
1904S	553,038	38.50	70.00	260	565	1,075	1,775	6,250	38,500	—
1905	662,727	22.50	29.50	95.00	180	270	345	565	7,500	3,500
1905O	505,000	30.00	50.00	125	235	340	440	760	5,250	—
1905S	2,494,000	15.50	18.00	50.00	125	230	365	615	9,800	—
1906	2,638,675	11.75	13.25	31.00	85.00	165	290	475	3,800	3,500
1906D	4,028,000	11.75	13.25	32.50	93.50	160	300	485	4,500	—
1906O	2,446,000	11.75	13.25	44.00	100.00	185	310	600	6,500	—
1906S	1,740,154	13.00	16.50	57.50	110	215	310	610	6,500	—
1907	2,598,575	11.75	13.25	30.00	85.00	155	300	470	3,650	3,500
1907D	3,856,000	11.75	13.25	30.00	78.50	155	300	470	3,600	—
1907O	3,946,000	11.75	13.25	32.00	93.50	165	325	575	3,700	—
1907S	1,250,000	16.00	22.00	80.00	170	310	650	1,275	13,500	—
1908	1,354,545	11.75	13.25	30.00	83.00	155	285	470	4,350	3,500
1908D	3,280,000	11.75	13.25	30.00	83.00	155	295	485	3,700	—
1908O	5,360,000	11.75	13.25	30.00	93.50	155	315	540	3,600	—
1908S	1,644,828	18.50	27.00	75.00	160	285	435	850	6,600	—
1909	2,368,650	12.50	16.00	32.50	84.00	160	275	470	3,600	3,500
1909O	925,400	16.00	23.50	58.00	140	300	510	775	4,950	—
1909S	1,764,000	12.00	13.50	37.50	100.00	190	395	600	4,650	—
1910	418,551	20.00	28.50	90.00	170	330	415	610	3,900	3,500

Date	Mintage	G-4	VG-8	F-12	VF-20	XF-40	AU-50	MS-60	MS-65	Prf-65
1910S	1,948,000	13.50	16.50	37.50	100.00	190	350	650	6,850	—
1911	1,406,543	11.75	13.25	30.00	83.00	155	290	475	3,600	3,500
1911D	695,080	13.00	16.00	41.00	94.00	195	285	550	3,800	—
1911S	1,272,000	13.50	16.50	41.00	98.00	180	325	580	6,100	—
1912	1,550,700	11.75	13.25	30.00	83.00	160	295	480	4,350	3,500
1912D	2,300,800	13.00	13.50	30.00	83.00	155	310	470	3,600	—
1912S	1,370,000	15.00	20.00	41.50	100.00	195	330	535	6,250	—
1913	188,627	78.00	90.00	235	420	600	850	1,150	5,250	3,500
1913D	534,000	17.00	21.00	44.00	100.00	200	300	485	5,250	—
1913S	604,000	20.00	25.00	53.50	110	225	365	610	4,850	—
1914	124,610	155	175	325	550	775	1,025	1,400	8,500	3,500
1914S	992,000	15.00	19.00	41.00	98.00	190	315	575	5,000	—
1915	138,450	118	175	285	380	575	900	1,250	6,400	3,500
1915D	1,170,400	11.75	13.25	30.00	80.00	155	285	470	3,600	—
1915S	1,604,000	15.50	20.00	41.50	99.00	170	295	485	3,675	—

Walking Liberty Half Dollar.

KM# 142 Designer: Adolph A. Weinman. **Diameter:** 30.6 **Weight:** 12.5000 g. **Composition:** Silver ASW.
Notes: The mint mark appears on the obverse below the word "Trust" on 1916 and some 1917 issues. Starting with some 1917 issues and continuing through the remainder of the series, the mint mark was changed to the reverse, at about the 8 o'clock position near the rim.

Obverse mint mark   Reverse mint mark

Date	Mintage	G-4	VG-8	F-12	VF-20	XF-40	AU-50	MS-60	MS-65	Prf-65
1916	608,000	45.00	52.50	100.00	180	250	285	350	1,800	—
1916D	1,014,400	45.00	52.50	80.00	140	225	265	375	2,400	—
1916S	508,000	110	130	285	470	650	750	1,100	6,250	—
1917D obv.	765,400	22.00	31.50	80.00	160	235	350	640	8,000	—
1917S obv.	952,000	27.50	44.00	135	375	720	1,225	2,300	19,500	—
1917	12,292,000	7.00	7.25	9.00	20.00	44.00	75.00	135	1,000	—
1917D rev.	1,940,000	10.00	16.50	45.00	135	275	575	975	18,500	—
1917S rev.	5,554,000	7.00	8.00	16.50	33.00	65.00	160	345	13,000	—
1918	6,634,000	7.00	7.25	16.00	70.00	160	275	580	3,800	—
1918D	3,853,040	8.00	13.00	36.00	96.00	235	500	1,350	25,000	—
1918S	10,282,000	7.00	7.25	15.00	35.00	65.00	200	525	18,000	—
1919	962,000	19.00	32.50	78.50	275	550	920	1,350	7,500	—
1919D	1,165,000	18.00	38.50	100.00	325	765	1,550	6,250	130,000	—
1919S	1,552,000	17.50	30.00	75.00	325	850	1,800	3,450	20,500	—
1920	6,372,000	7.00	7.25	16.00	44.00	75.00	160	350	5,250	—
1920D	1,551,000	12.00	20.00	70.00	250	475	960	1,550	12,000	—
1920S	4,624,000	7.00	7.50	20.00	80.00	225	520	850	12,500	—
1921	246,000	185	225	350	780	1,550	2,750	4,350	18,000	—
1921D	208,000	315	390	550	940	2,200	3,400	5,300	27,500	—
1921S	548,000	46.00	70.00	220	750	4,800	8,600	14,000	105,000	—
1923S	2,178,000	8.50	11.50	27.50	115	315	700	1,400	15,000	—
1927S	2,392,000	7.00	7.50	13.50	47.50	160	415	1,050	10,000	—
1928S	1,940,000	10.00	12.50	24.00	110	300	600	1,650	10,500	—
1928S	Inc. above	6.75	7.25	15.00	70.00	195	450	1,000	10,750	—
1929D	1,001,200	8.00	12.00	19.00	60.00	110	210	415	3,500	—
1929S	1,902,000	7.00	7.50	12.50	28.50	115	230	425	3,550	—
1933S	1,786,000	8.50	11.00	12.50	20.00	60.00	260	625	4,500	—
1934	6,964,000	7.00	7.25	7.50	7.00	11.00	26.00	85.00	625	—
1934D	2,361,400	7.00	7.50	8.00	10.00	29.00	90.00	155	1,700	—
1934S	3,652,000	7.00	7.50	8.00	8.50	27.00	105	395	5,200	—
1935	9,162,000	7.00	7.25	7.50	8.00	8.50	22.50	45.00	585	—
1935D	3,003,800	7.00	7.50	8.00	10.00	32.50	70.00	140	3,150	—
1935S	3,854,000	7.00	7.50	8.00	8.50	29.00	100.00	295	3,700	—
1936	12,617,901	7.00	7.25	7.50	8.00	8.50	21.50	38.50	300	6,600
1936D	4,252,400	7.00	7.50	8.00	8.50	20.00	55.00	80.00	700	—
1936S	3,884,000	7.00	7.50	8.00	8.50	21.50	62.50	135	1,050	—
1937	9,527,728	7.00	7.00	7.50	8.00	8.50	22.50	40.00	335	1,700
1937D	1,676,000	7.00	7.75	8.50	14.00	33.50	110	225	850	—
1937S	2,090,000	7.00	7.50	8.00	8.50	25.50	65.00	175	850	—
1938	4,118,152	7.00	7.50	8.00	8.50	9.50	41.50	70.00	550	1,275
1938D	491,600	90.00	100.00	115	135	220	260	525	1,550	—

Date	Mintage	G-4	VG-8	F-12	VF-20	XF-40	AU-50	MS-60	MS-65	Prf-65
1939	6,820,808	6.00	6.25	6.50	7.00	8.50	22.50	42.50	230	1,150
1939D	4,267,800	7.00	7.25	7.50	8.00	8.50	26.00	47.50	275	—
1939S	2,552,000	7.00	7.50	8.00	9.00	25.00	80.00	150	370	—
1940	9,167,279	6.00	6.25	6.50	7.00	8.50	11.00	30.00	210	1,000
1940S	4,550,000	7.00	7.25	7.50	8.00	11.00	22.00	52.50	420	—
1941	24,207,412	6.00	6.25	6.50	7.00	8.50	11.00	32.50	160	850
1941D	11,248,400	7.00	7.25	7.50	8.00	8.50	18.00	38.50	200	—
1941S	8,098,000	7.00	7.25	7.50	8.00	8.50	27.50	75.00	1,175	—
1942	47,839,120	6.00	6.25	6.50	7.00	8.50	11.00	32.50	150	850
1942D	10,973,800	7.00	7.25	7.50	8.00	8.50	19.00	38.50	345	—
1942S	12,708,000	7.00	7.25	7.50	8.00	8.50	17.50	38.50	700	—
1943	53,190,000	6.00	6.25	6.50	7.00	8.50	11.00	33.50	150	—
1943D	11,346,000	7.00	7.25	7.50	8.00	8.50	25.00	43.50	330	—
1943S	13,450,000	7.00	7.25	7.50	8.00	8.50	18.50	43.50	485	—
1944	28,206,000	6.00	6.25	6.50	7.00	8.50	11.00	33.50	220	—
1944D	9,769,000	7.00	7.25	7.50	8.00	8.50	20.00	37.50	240	—
1944S	8,904,000	7.00	7.25	7.50	8.00	8.50	16.00	38.50	490	—
1945	31,502,000	6.00	6.25	6.50	7.00	8.50	11.00	32.50	160	—
1945D	9,966,800	7.00	7.25	7.50	8.00	8.50	19.00	34.00	160	—
1945S	10,156,000	7.00	7.25	7.50	8.00	8.50	17.50	35.00	220	—
1946	12,118,000	6.00	6.25	6.50	7.00	8.50	11.00	32.50	250	—
1946D	2,151,000	7.00	7.25	7.50	8.00	25.50	38.50	50.00	150	—
1946S	3,724,000	6.75	7.25	7.50	8.00	8.50	19.00	43.50	165	—
1947	4,094,000	6.75	7.25	7.50	8.00	9.50	22.00	52.50	230	—
1947D	3,900,600	7.00	7.25	7.50	8.00	12.50	31.50	52.50	150	—

Franklin Half Dollar.

KM# 199   Designer: John R. Sinnock. **Diameter:** 30.6 **Weight:** 12.5000 g. **Composition:** 0.9000 Silver, 0.3617 oz. ASW.

Mint mark

Date	Mintage	G-4	VG-8	F-12	VF-20	XF-40	AU-50	MS-60	MS-65	-65FBL	-65CAM
1948	3,006,814	—	5.00	6.00	7.00	8.50	11.50	15.50	75.00	190	—
1948D	4,028,600	—	5.00	6.00	7.00	8.00	11.00	15.00	125	260	—
1949	5,614,000	—	—	—	—	6.00	12.00	38.50	145	300	—
1949D	4,120,600	—	—	—	—	8.00	25.00	43.50	900	1,750	—
1949S	3,744,000	—	—	—	7.00	11.00	30.00	62.50	155	650	—
1950	7,793,509	—	—	—	—	6.00	10.00	26.00	110	250	3,700
1950D	8,031,600	—	—	—	—	7.50	11.50	22.00	425	1,150	—
1951	16,859,602	—	—	—	—	—	6.50	11.00	75.00	235	2,200
1951D	9,475,200	—	—	—	—	7.50	17.50	26.00	170	525	—
1951S	13,696,000	—	—	—	—	—	15.00	23.50	125	775	—
1952	21,274,073	—	—	—	—	—	6.50	8.50	80.00	200	1,100
1952D	25,395,600	—	—	—	—	—	6.50	7.75	135	450	—
1952S	5,526,000	—	—	6.00	12.00	20.00	32.00	50.00	100.00	1,500	—
1953	2,796,920	—	—	—	—	8.00	16.00	25.00	125	850	475
1953D	20,900,400	—	—	—	—	—	6.50	8.00	160	400	—
1953S	4,148,000	—	—	—	—	—	15.00	25.00	65.00	16,000	—
1954	13,421,503	—	—	—	—	—	6.50	7.00	80.00	250	250
1954D	25,445,580	—	—	—	—	—	6.50	7.00	110	200	—
1954S	4,993,400	—	—	—	—	—	8.50	13.50	105	425	—
1955	2,876,381	—	18.00	20.00	21.00	22.00	23.00	24.00	65.00	185	195
1955 Bugs Bunny	—	—	20.00	22.00	23.00	25.00	26.00	28.00	100.00	750	—
1956	4,701,384	—	7.00	7.50	8.00	8.50	9.00	13.50	50.00	95.00	75.00
1957	6,361,952	—	—	—	—	—	6.50	7.00	62.50	95.00	135
1957D	19,966,850	—	—	—	—	—	6.50	7.00	65.00	100.00	—
1958	4,917,652	—	—	—	—	—	6.50	7.00	60.00	100.00	250
1958D	23,962,412	—	—	—	—	—	6.50	7.00	62.50	75.00	—
1959	7,349,291	—	—	—	—	—	6.50	7.00	105	250	475
1959D	13,053,750	—	—	—	—	—	6.50	7.00	135	190	—
1960	7,715,602	—	—	—	—	—	6.50	7.00	135	350	75.00
1960D	18,215,812	—	—	—	—	—	6.50	7.00	475	1,250	—
1961	11,318,244	—	—	—	—	—	6.50	7.00	145	1,750	75.00
1961D	20,276,442	—	—	—	—	—	6.50	7.00	200	875	—
1962	12,932,019	—	—	—	—	—	6.50	7.00	160	1,850	50.00
1962D	35,473,281	—	—	—	—	—	6.50	7.00	225	775	—

Date	Mintage	G-4	VG-8	F-12	VF-20	XF-40	AU-50	MS-60	MS-65	-65FBL	-65CAM
1963	25,239,645	—	—	—	—	—	6.50	7.00	55.00	775	50.00
1963D	67,069,292	—	—	—	—	—	6.50	7.00	70.00	125	—

Kennedy Half Dollar.

KM# 202 Obv. Designer: Gilroy Roberts. **Rev. Designer:** Frank Gasparro. **Diameter:** 30.6 **Weight:** 12.5000 g. **Composition:** 0.9000 Silver, 0.3617 oz. ASW.

Mint mark 1964

Date	Mintage	G-4	VG-8	F-12	VF-20	XF-40	MS-60	MS-65	Prf-65
1964	277,254,766	—	—	—	—	—	5.00	20.00	12.00
1964 Accented Hair	Inc. above	—	—	—	—	—	—	—	40.00
1964D	156,205,446	—	—	—	—	—	5.25	24.00	—

Kennedy Half Dollar.

KM# 202a Obv. Designer: Gilroy Roberts. **Rev. Designer:** Frank Gasparro. **Diameter:** 30.6 **Weight:** 11.5000 g. **Composition:** Silver ASW.

Mint mark 1965 - present

Date	Mintage	G-4	VG-8	F-12	VF-20	XF-40	MS-60	MS-65	Prf-65
1965	65,879,366	—	—	—	—	—	2.00	18.00	—
1965 SMS	2,360,000	—	—	—	—	—	—	15.00	—
1966	108,984,932	—	—	—	—	—	2.00	14.00	—
1966 SMS	2,261,583	—	—	—	—	—	—	17.00	—
1967	295,046,978	—	—	—	—	—	2.00	22.00	—
1967 SMS	18,633,440	—	—	—	—	—	—	18.00	—
1968D	246,951,930	—	—	—	—	—	2.00	18.00	—
1968S	3,041,506	—	—	—	—	—	—	—	7.00
1969D	129,881,800	—	—	—	—	—	2.00	20.00	—
1969S	2,934,631	—	—	—	—	—	—	—	7.50
1970D	2,150,000	—	—	—	—	—	13.00	38.00	—
1970S	2,632,010	—	—	—	—	—	—	—	20.00

Kennedy Half Dollar.

KM# 202b Obv. Designer: Gilroy Roberts. **Rev. Designer:** Frank Gasparro. **Diameter:** 30.6 **Weight:** 11.3400 g. **Composition:** Copper-Nickel Clad Copper

Date	Mintage	G-4	VG-8	F-12	VF-20	XF-40	MS-60	MS-65	Prf-65
1971	155,640,000	—	—	—	—	—	1.00	15.00	—
1971D	302,097,424	—	—	—	—	—	1.00	15.00	—
1971S	3,244,183	—	—	—	—	—	—	—	8.00
1972	153,180,000	—	—	—	—	—	1.00	20.00	—
1972D	141,890,000	—	—	—	—	—	1.00	14.00	—
1972S	3,267,667	—	—	—	—	—	—	—	7.00
1973	64,964,000	—	—	—	—	—	1.00	14.00	—
1973D	83,171,400	—	—	—	—	—	—	12.00	—
1973S	(2,769,624)	—	—	—	—	—	—	—	7.00
1974	201,596,000	—	—	—	—	—	1.00	18.00	—
1974D	79,066,300	—	—	—	—	—	1.00	20.00	—
1974S	(2,617,350)	—	—	—	—	—	—	—	5.00
1975 none minted	—	—	—	—	—	—	—	—	—
1975D none minted	—	—	—	—	—	—	—	—	—
1975S none minted	—	—	—	—	—	—	—	—	—

Kennedy Half Dollar. Bicentennial design, Independence Hall.

KM# 205   Rev. Designer: Seth Huntington. **Weight:** 11.1000 g. **Composition:** Copper Nickel

Date	Mintage	G-4	VG-8	F-12	VF-20	XF-40	MS-60	MS-65	Prf-65
1976	234,308,000	—	—	—	—	—	1.00	22.00	—
1976D	287,565,248	—	—	—	—	—	1.00	9.00	—
1976S	(7,059,099)	—	—	—	—	—	—	—	4.00

Kennedy Half Dollar. Bicentennial design, Independence Hall.

KM# 205a   Rev. Designer: Seth Huntington. **Weight:** 11.5000 g. **Composition:** 0.4000 Silver, 0.1479 oz. ASW.

Date	Mintage	G-4	VG-8	F-12	VF-20	XF-40	MS-60	MS-65	Prf-65
1976S	4,908,319	—	—	—	—	—	—	13.00	—
1976S	(3,998,625)	—	—	—	—	—	—	12.00	6.00

Kennedy Half Dollar. Regular design resumed.

KM# A202b   Diameter: 30.6 **Weight:** 11.3400 g. **Composition:** Copper-Nickel Clad Copper **Notes:** KM#202b design and composition resumed. The 1979-S and 1981-S Type II proofs have clearer mint marks than the Type I proofs of those years.

Date	Mintage	MS-65	Prf-65
1977	43,598,000	18.00	—
1977D	31,449,106	20.00	—
1977S	(3,251,152)	—	4.50
1978	14,350,000	12.00	—
1978D	13,765,799	7.50	—
1978S	(3,127,788)	—	6.00
1979	68,312,000	11.00	—
1979D	15,815,422	9.00	—
1979S type I, proof	3,677,175	—	6.00
1979S type II, proof	Inc. above	—	20.00
1980P	44,134,000	9.00	—
1980D	33,456,449	6.50	—
1980S	(3,547,030)	—	6.00
1981P	29,544,000	8.00	—
1981D	27,839,533	8.50	—
1981S type I, proof	(4,063,083)	—	5.00
1981S type II, proof	Inc. above	—	17.50
1982P	10,819,000	10.00	—
1982P no initials FG	—	40.00	—
1982D	13,140,102	9.00	—
1982S	(38,957,479)	—	6.50
1983P	34,139,000	20.00	—
1983D	32,472,244	10.00	—
1983S	(3,279,126)	—	6.50
1984P	26,029,000	10.00	—
1984D	26,262,158	15.00	—
1984S	(3,065,110)	—	7.00
1985P	18,706,962	10.00	—
1985D	19,814,034	12.00	—
1985S	(3,962,138)	—	6.00
1986P	13,107,633	25.00	—
1986D	15,336,145	17.00	—
1986S	(2,411,180)	—	8.00
1987P	2,890,758	14.00	—
1987D	2,890,758	10.00	—
1987S	(4,407,728)	—	6.50
1988P	13,626,000	16.00	—
1988D	12,000,096	12.00	—
1988S	(3,262,948)	—	6.00
1989P	24,542,000	18.00	—
1989D	23,000,216	14.00	—
1989S	(3,220,194)	—	8.00
1990P	22,780,000	20.00	—
1990D	20,096,242	15.00	—
1990S	(3,299,559)	—	7.00
1991P	14,874,000	15.00	—
1991D	15,054,678	18.00	—
1991S	(2,867,787)	—	16.00
1992P	17,628,000	18.00	—
1992D	17,000,106	8.00	—
1992S	(2,858,981)	—	8.00
1993P	15,510,000	15.00	—
1993D	15,000,006	14.00	—
1993S	(2,633,439)	—	14.00
1994P	23,718,000	8.00	—
1994D	23,828,110	8.00	—
1994S	(2,484,594)	—	11.00
1995P	26,496,000	9.00	—
1995D	26,288,000	8.00	—
1995S	(2,010,384)	—	35.00
1996P	24,442,000	11.00	—
1996D	24,744,000	8.00	—
1996S	(2,085,191)	—	16.00
1997P	20,882,000	14.00	—
1997D	19,876,000	10.00	—
1997S	(1,975,000)	—	34.00
1998P	15,646,000	14.00	—
1998D	15,064,000	14.00	—
1998S	(2,078,494)	—	22.00
1999P	8,900,000	14.00	—
1999D	10,682,000	14.00	—
1999S	(2,557,897)	—	24.00
2000P	22,600,000	9.00	—
2000D	19,466,000	14.00	—
2000S	(3,082,944)	—	8.00
2001P	21,200,000	9.00	—

Date	Mintage	MS-65	Prf-65
2001D	19,504,000	9.00	—
2001S	(2,235,000)	—	10.00
2002P	3,100,000	10.00	—
2002D	2,500,000	10.00	—
2002S	(2,268,913)	—	8.00
2003P	2,500,000	14.00	—
2003D	2,500,000	14.00	—
2003S	2,076,165	—	6.00
2004P	2,900,000	14.00	—
2004D	2,900,000	14.00	—
2004S	1,789,488	—	13.00
2005P	3,800,000	9.00	—
2005P Satin finish	1,160,000	8.00	—
2005D	3,500,000	9.00	—
2005D Satin finish	1,160,000	10.00	—
2005S	2,275,000	—	7.00
2006P	2,400,000	12.00	—
2006P Satin finish	847,361	12.00	—
2006D	2,000,000	20.00	—
2006D Satin finish	847,361	14.00	—
2006S	1,934,965	—	10.00
2007P	—	7.00	—
2007P Satin finish	—	—	—
2007D	—	7.00	—
2007D Satin finish	—	—	—
2007S	—	—	10.00

Kennedy Half Dollar.

KM# B202b   **Composition:** Silver ASW.

Date	Mintage	Prf-65
1992S	(1,317,579)	12.00
1993S	(761,353)	32.00
1994S	(785,329)	36.00
1995S	(838,953)	92.00
1996S	(830,021)	40.00
1997S	(821,678)	75.00
1998S	(878,792)	25.00
1998S Matte Proof	(62,350)	325
1999S	(804,565)	38.00
2000S	(965,921)	0.00
2001S	(849,600)	20.00
2002S	(888,816)	14.00
2003S	(1,040,425)	14.50
2004S	1,175,935	14.00
2005S	1,069,679	9.00
2006S	988,140	11.00
2007S	—	12.00

DOLLAR

Flowing Hair Dollar.

KM# 17   **Designer:** Robert Scot.   **Diameter:** 39-40   **Weight:** 26.9600 g.   **Composition:** 0.8920 Silver, 0.7731 oz. ASW.   **Notes:** The two 1795 varieties have either two or three leaves under each of the eagle's wings on the reverse.

Date	Mintage	F-12	VF-20	XF-40	AU-50	MS-60	MS-63
1794	1,758	115,000	160,000	235,000	340,000	500,000	800,000
1795 2 leaves	203,033	3,350	5,500	12,850	22,500	54,000	110,000
1795 3 leaves	Inc. above	3,100	4,950	11,500	19,500	46,500	98,000
1795 Silver plug	—	10,500	14,500	30,000	—	—	—

Draped Bust Dollar. Small eagle.

KM# 18 Designer: Robert Scot. **Diameter:** 39-40 **Weight:** 26.9600 g. **Composition:** 0.8920 Silver, 0.7731 oz. ASW. **Notes:** The 1796 varieties are distinguished by the size of the numerals in the date and letters in "United States of America." The 1797 varieties are distinguished by the number of stars to the left and right of the word "Liberty" and by the size of the letters in "United States of America." The 1798 varieties have either 13 or 15 stars on the obverse.

Date	Mintage	F-12	VF-20	XF-40	AU-50	MS-60	MS-63
1795 Off-center bust	Inc. above	2,550	4,250	8,400	13,500	36,500	74,000
1795 Centered bust	—	2,600	4,300	8,600	13,750	37,000	—
1796 small date, small letters	72,920	2,900	4,800	9,650	14,950	44,000	90,000
1796 small date, large letters	Inc. above	2,700	4,800	9,850	15,400	48,500	—
1796 large date, small letters	Inc. above	2,950	5,100	10,250	15,500	27,000	65,000
1797 9 stars left, 7 stars right, small letters	7,776	4,000	8,250	16,500	36,500	85,000	125,000
1797 9 stars left, 7 stars right, large letters	Inc. above	2,950	5,250	10,000	16,500	42,500	90,000
1797 10 stars left, 6 stars right	Inc. above	2,750	4,700	9,800	16,000	45,000	98,000
1798 13 stars	327,536	2,850	4,700	10,000	17,000	60,000	—
1798 15 stars	Inc. above	3,400	5,850	12,000	21,500	75,000	—

Draped Bust Dollar. Draped bust right, flanked by stars, date below. Heraldic eagle.

KM# 32 Designer: Robert Scot. **Diameter:** 39-40 **Weight:** 26.9600 g. **Composition:** 0.8920 Silver, 0.7731 oz. ASW. **Notes:** The 1798 "knob 9" variety has a serif on the lower left of the 9 in the date. The 1798 varieties are distinguished by the number of arrows held by the eagle on the reverse and the number of berries on the olive branch. On the 1798 "high-8" variety, the 8 in the date is higher than the other numerals. The 1799 varieties are distinguished by the number and positioning of the stars on the obverse and by the size of the berries in the olive branch on the reverse. On the 1700 "irregular date" variety, the first 9 in the date is smaller than the other numerals. Some varieties of the 1800 strikes had letters in the legend cut twice into the dies; as the dies became worn, the letters were touched up. On the 1800 "very wide date, low 8" variety, the spacing between the numerals in the date are wider than other varieties and the 8 is lower than the other numerals. The 1800 "small berries" variety refers to the size of the berries in the olive branch on the reverse. The 1800 "12 arrows" and "10 arrows" varieties refer to the number of arrows held by the eagle. The 1800 "Americai" variety appears to have the faint outline of an "I" after "America" in the reverse legend. The "close" and "wide" varieties of 1802 refer to the amount of space between the numerals in the date. The 1800 large-3 and small-3 varieties are distinguished by the size of the 3 in the date.

Date	Mintage	F-12	VF-20	XF-40	AU-50	MS-60	MS-63
1798 knob 9	Inc. above	1,225	2,075	3,950	8,250	21,750	43,500
1798 10 arrows	Inc. above	1,225	2,075	3,950	8,250	21,750	43,500
1798 4 berries	Inc. above	1,225	2,075	3,950	8,250	21,750	43,500

Date	Mintage	F-12	VF-20	XF-40	AU-50	MS-60	MS-63
1798 5 berries, 12 arrows	Inc. above	1,225	2,075	3,950	8,250	21,750	43,500
1798 high 8	Inc. above	1,225	2,075	3,950	8,250	21,750	43,500
1798 13 arrows	Inc. above	1,225	2,075	3,950	8,250	21,750	45,000
1799/98 13-star reverse	423,515	1,450	2,350	4,300	8,600	23,500	45,000
1799/98 15-star reverse	Inc. above	1,325	2,125	4,000	8,300	24,500	47,500
1799 irregular date, 13-star reverse	Inc. above	1,300	2,150	3,900	8,200	23,500	45,000
1799 irregular date, 15-star reverse	Inc. above	1,275	2,125	3,950	8,250	21,500	42,500
1799 perfect date, 7- and 6-star obverse, no berries	Inc. above	1,200	2,050	3,850	8,150	18,500	42,500
1799 perfect date, 7- and 6-star obverse, small berries	Inc. above	1,200	2,050	3,850	8,150	18,500	42,500
1799 perfect date, 7- and 6-star obverse, medium large berries	Inc. above	1,225	2,050	3,850	8,150	18,500	42,500
1799 perfect date, 7- and 6-star obverse, extra large berries	Inc. above	1,225	2,050	3,850	8,150	18,500	51,500
1799 8 stars left, 5 stars right on obverse	Inc. above	1,300	2,150	3,900	8,200	24,000	45,000
1800 "R" in "Liberty" double cut	220,920	1,275	2,125	3,950	8,250	21,500	45,000
1800 first "T" in "States" double cut	Inc. above	1,275	2,125	3,950	8,250	21,500	45,000
1800 both letters double cut	Inc. above	1,275	2,125	3,950	8,250	21,500	45,000
1800 "T" in "United" double cut	Inc. above	1,275	2,125	3,950	8,250	21,500	45,000
1800 very wide date, low 8	Inc. above	1,275	2,125	3,950	8,250	21,500	—
1800 small berries	Inc. above	1,300	2,150	3,900	8,200	22,000	48,500
1800 dot date	Inc. above	150	2,350	4,300	8,600	21,500	45,000
1800 12 arrows	Inc. above	1,275	2,125	3,950	8,250	21,500	45,000
1800 10 arrows	Inc. above	1,275	2,125	3,950	8,250	21,500	48,500
1800 "Americai"	Inc. above	1,450	2,350	4,300	8,600	21,500	49,000
1801	54,454	1,400	2,400	4,000	8,300	25,000	—
1801 proof restrike	—	—	—	—	—	—	—
1802/1 close	Inc. above	1,450	2,350	4,300	8,600	20,500	—
1802/1 wide	Inc. above	1,450	2,350	4,300	8,600	20,500	—
1802 close, perfect date	Inc. above	1,300	2,150	3,900	8,200	20,500	—
1802 wide, perfect date	Inc. above	1,275	2,125	3,950	8,250	21,500	—
1802 proof restrike, mintage unrecorded	—	—	—	—	—	—	—
1803 large 3	85,634	1,325	2,225	4,000	8,300	20,500	47,500
1803 small 3	Inc. above	1,450	2,350	4,300	8,600	21,500	48,500
1803 proof restrike, mintage unrecorded	—	—	—	—	—	—	—
1804 15 known	—	—	—	—	3,000,000	—	—

Note: 1804, Childs Sale, Aug. 1999, Prf-68, $4,140,000.

Gobrecht Dollar. "C Gobrecht F." in base. Eagle flying left amid stars.

KM# 59.1   Obv. Designer: Christian Gobrecht. **Diameter:** 38.1 **Weight:** 26.7300 g. **Composition:** 0.9000 Silver, 0.7734 oz. ASW.

Date	Mintage	VF-20	XF-40	AU-50	Prf-60
1836	1,000	11,500	14,850	—	25,500

"C. Gobrecht F." in base. Eagle flying in plain field.

KM# 59.2   Obv. Designer: Christian Gobrecht.. **Diameter:** 38.1 **Weight:** 26.7300 g. **Composition:** 0.9000 Silver, 0.7734 oz. ASW.

Date	Mintage	VF-20	XF-40	AU-50	Prf-60
1836 Restrike	—	—	—	—	24,000

"C. Gobrecht F." in base.

KM# 59a.1   Diameter: 38.1 **Weight:** 26.7300 g. **Composition:** 0.9000 Silver, 0.7734 oz. ASW.

Date	Mintage	VF-20	XF-40	AU-50	Prf-60
1836	600	—	—	—	—

"C. Gobrecht F." in base. Eagle flying left amid stars.

KM# 59a.2 **Diameter:** 38.1 **Weight:** 26.7300 g. **Composition:** 0.9000 Silver, 0.7734 oz. ASW.

Date	Mintage	VF-20	XF-40	AU-50	Prf-60
1836 Restrike	—	—	—	—	—

Designer's name omitted in base. Eagle in plain field.

KM# 59a.3 **Diameter:** 38.1 **Weight:** 26.7300 g. **Composition:** 0.9000 Silver, 0.7734 oz. ASW.

Date	Mintage	VF-20	XF-40	AU-50	Prf-60
1839	300	—	—	—	38,000

Designer's name omitted in base. Eagle in plain field.

KM# 59a.4 **Diameter:** 38.1 **Weight:** 26.7300 g. **Composition:** 0.9000 Silver, 0.7734 oz. ASW.

Date	Mintage	VF-20	XF-40	AU-50	Prf-60
1839 Restrike	—	—	—	—	36,500

Note: All other combinations are restrikes of the late 1850's.

Seated Liberty Dollar. Seated Liberty, date below. No motto above eagle.

KM# 71 **Designer:** Christian Gobrecht. **Diameter:** 38.1 **Weight:** 26.7300 g. **Composition:** 0.9000 Silver, 0.7734 oz. ASW.

Date	Mintage	G-4	VG-8	F-12	VF-20	XF-40	AU-50	MS-60	MS-63	MS-65	Prf-65
1840	61,005	240	275	325	385	600	900	5,500	16,500	—	62,500
1841	173,000	190	210	240	320	400	625	2,200	4,950	44,000	—
1842	184,618	190	210	240	320	400	600	2,150	4,650	—	90,000
1843	165,100	190	210	240	320	400	625	2,350	8,500	—	—
1844	20,000	220	240	300	395	535	840	4,200	12,500	47,000	—
1845	24,500	275	305	360	420	575	840	9,000	23,500	—	70,000
1846	110,600	205	230	275	350	480	600	2,600	5,900	—	85,000
1846O	59,000	215	250	315	400	560	1,000	17,500	17,500	37,500	—
1847	140,750	190	210	245	320	395	625	2,350	5,400	27,500	44,000
1848	15,000	285	350	480	590	800	1,250	3,750	8,250	40,000	96,000
1849	62,600	205	220	260	340	460	675	2,350	6,900	32,500	120,000
1850	7,500	360	475	650	800	1,100	1,800	6,250	13,000	50,000	47,500
1850O	40,000	295	450	450	670	1,125	3,550	12,500	22,500	60,000	—
1851	1,300	4,000	4,850	5,750	7,750	14,500	24,500	37,500	64,000	90,000	62,500
1851 Restrike	—	—	—	—	—	—	—	—	—	—	54,500
1852	1,100	3,500	4,150	5,200	7,000	13,750	24,000	35,000	60,000	71,500	62,500
1852 Restrike	—	—	—	—	—	—	—	—	—	—	56,500
1853	46,110	335	400	550	650	875	1,275	3,300	7,350	34,500	79,500
1854	33,140	1,000	1,300	1,850	2,600	3,750	4,950	8,000	11,000	2,800	47,500
1855	26,000	900	1,150	1,350	2,000	2,950	3,850	7,000	16,500	—	38,000
1856	63,500	345	425	600	650	1,050	1,900	4,000	8,250	—	27,000
1857	94,000	385	475	550	700	1,100	1,300	2,750	8,000	28,500	29,500

Date	Mintage	G-4	VG-8	F-12	VF-20	XF-40	AU-50	MS-60	MS-63	MS-65	Prf-65
1858 proof only	Est. 800	3,200	3,600	4,000	4,800	5,500	7,300	—	—	—	27,000
Note: Proof Only restruck in later years.											
1859	256,500	275	320	390	575	650	900	2,000	6,000	—	13,000
1859O	360,000	250	270	295	365	440	685	1,950	5,000	32,500	—
1859S	20,000	310	390	485	600	1,250	3,000	14,500	35,000	62,500	—
1860	218,930	250	290	375	460	550	600	1,850	3,900	27,500	13,500
1860O	515,000	240	270	295	365	440	675	1,750	4,600	16,500	—
1861	78,500	600	750	975	950	1,200	1,550	2,750	5,500	25,000	13,500
1862	12,090	440	600	875	925	1,100	1,450	2,700	5,600	37,500	13,500
1863	27,660	375	525	575	600	700	1,100	2,700	5,500	23,500	20,000
1864	31,170	350	410	500	530	640	1,050	2,700	6,000	22,000	13,000
1865	47,000	300	350	400	600	750	1,350	2,700	4,750	35,000	13,000
1866 2 known without motto	—	—	—	—	—	—	—	—	—	—	—

Seated Liberty Dollar. Seated Liberty, date below. "In God We Trust" above eagle.

KM# 100 Designer: Christian Gobrecht. Diameter: 38.1 Weight: 26.7300 g. Composition: 0.9000 Silver, 0.7734 oz. ASW. Notes: In 1866 the motto "In God We Trust" was added to the reverse above the eagle.

Date	Mintage	G-4	VG-8	F-12	VF-20	XF-40	AU-50	MS-60	MS-63	MS-65	Prf-65
1866	49,625	250	280	345	485	560	900	1,650	3,150	25,500	12,500
1867	47,525	230	260	325	430	525	875	1,500	3,250	27,500	11,000
1868	162,700	225	250	315	405	475	850	1,600	6,600	35,000	12,500
1869	424,300	230	240	295	395	450	650	1,450	3,550	32,500	11,000
1870	416,000	200	215	245	320	440	600	1,400	3,250	25,500	12,500
1870CC	12,462	420	500	720	1,050	1,700	3,000	10,250	20,500	42,500	—
1870S 12-15 known	—	50,000	44,000	65,000	125,000	250,000	500,000	750,000	1,250,000	—	—
Note: 1870S, Eliasberg Sale, April 1997, EF-45 to AU-50, $264,000.											
1871	1,074,760	190	205	240	340	425	600	1,100	3,000	25,500	11,000
1871CC	1,376	2,000	2,750	4,000	6,000	9,750	18,500	50,000	175,000	300,000	—
1872	1,106,450	190	205	250	340	425	600	1,100	2,950	25,500	11,000
1872CC	3,150	900	1,300	2,200	3,250	5,300	10,000	19,000	47,500	—	—
1872S	9,000	250	325	450	650	1,100	2,750	8,500	23,500	62,500	—
1873	293,600	220	240	285	360	475	700	1,250	3,150	31,500	11,500
1873CC	2,300	3,450	4,750	6,500	10,000	17,000	35,000	80,000	135,000	—	—
1873S none known	700	—	—	—	—	—	—	—	—	—	—

Trade Dollar. Seated Liberty, "In God We Trust" in base above date. Trade Dollar below eagle.

KM# 108 Designer: William Barber. Diameter: 38.1 Weight: 27.2200 g. Composition: 0.9000 Silver, 0.7876 oz. ASW.

Date	Mintage	G-4	VG-8	F-12	VF-20	XF-40	AU-50	MS-60	MS-65	Prf-65
1873	397,500	100.00	125	144	200	250	300	1,050	12,000	12,000

Date	Mintage	G-4	VG-8	F-12	VF-20	XF-40	AU-50	MS-60	MS-65	Prf-65
1873CC	124,500	220	265	320	435	950	1,350	8,500	122,000	—
1873S	703,000	115	135	155	210	265	385	1,450	15,500	—
1874	987,800	100.00	145	330	160	180	270	925	13,850	10,800
1874CC	1,373,200	200	245	290	335	450	600	3,000	26,500	—
1874S	2,549,000	90.00	135	140	150	175	270	925	11,000	—
1875	218,900	160	185	375	460	590	850	2,450	13,000	10,700
1875CC	1,573,700	175	215	250	290	385	490	2,150	40,000	—
1875S	4,487,000	80.00	125	130	140	165	260	900	11,000	—
1875S/CC	Inc. above	175	275	365	525	850	1,350	4,250	65,000	—
1876	456,150	90.00	135	140	150	175	270	925	7,500	10,500
1876CC	509,000	200	245	285	325	425	650	6,000	78,500	—
1876S	5,227,000	80.00	125	130	140	165	260	900	11,000	—
1877	3,039,710	90.00	135	140	150	175	270	925	16,000	10,500
1877CC	534,000	195	245	300	385	575	700	2,450	60,000	—
1877S	9,519,000	80.00	125	130	140	165	260	900	11,000	—
1878 proof only	900	—	—	—	1,200	1,300	1,500	—	—	13,500
1878CC	97,000	425	525	675	1,000	2,250	4,200	12,000	112,000	—
1878S	4,162,000	80.00	125	130	140	165	260	900	11,000	—
1879 proof only	1,541	—	—	—	1,175	1,275	1,400	—	—	10,500
1880 proof only	1,987	—	—	—	1,150	1,250	1,350	—	—	10,500
1881 proof only	960	—	—	—	1,200	1,300	1,400	—	—	10,500
1882 proof only	1,097	—	—	—	1,175	1,275	1,375	—	—	10,500
1883 proof only	979	—	—	—	1,200	1,300	1,400	—	—	10,500
1884 proof only	10	—	—	—	—	—	100,000	—	—	—

Note: 1884, Eliasberg Sale, April 1997, Prf-66, $396,000.

1885 proof only	5	—	—	—	—	—	—	—	—	—

Note: 1885, Eliasberg Sale, April 1997, Prf-65, $907,500.

Morgan Dollar. Laureate head left, date below flanked by stars. Eagle within 1/2 wreath.

KM# 110 Designer: George T. Morgan. **Diameter:** 38.1 **Weight:** 26.7300 g. **Composition:** 0.9000 Silver, 0.7734 oz. ASW. **Notes:** "65DMPL" values are for coins grading MS-65 deep-mirror prooflike. The 1878 "8 tail feathers" and "7 tail feathers" varieties are distinguished by the number of feathers in the eagle's tail. On the "reverse of 1878" varieties, the top of the top feather in the arrows held by the eagle is straight across and the eagle's breast is concave. On the "reverse of 1879 varieties," the top feather in the arrows held by the eagle is slanted and the eagle's breast is convex. The 1890-CC "tail-bar variety has a bar extending from the arrow feathers to the wreath on the reverse, the result of a die gouge.

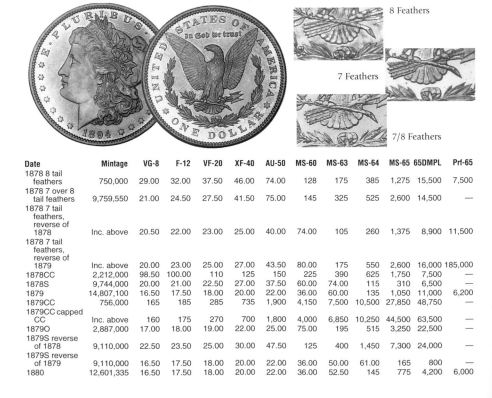

8 Feathers

7 Feathers

7/8 Feathers

Date	Mintage	VG-8	F-12	VF-20	XF-40	AU-50	MS-60	MS-63	MS-64	MS-65	65DMPL	Prf-65
1878 8 tail feathers	750,000	29.00	32.00	37.50	46.00	74.00	128	175	385	1,275	15,500	7,500
1878 7 over 8 tail feathers	9,759,550	21.00	24.50	27.50	41.50	75.00	145	325	525	2,600	14,500	—
1878 7 tail feathers, reverse of 1878	Inc. above	20.50	22.00	23.00	25.00	40.00	74.00	105	260	1,375	8,900	11,500
1878 7 tail feathers, reverse of 1879	Inc. above	20.00	23.00	25.00	27.00	43.50	80.00	175	550	2,600	16,000	185,000
1878CC	2,212,000	98.50	100.00	110	125	150	225	390	625	1,750	7,500	—
1878S	9,744,000	20.00	21.00	22.50	27.00	37.50	60.00	74.00	115	310	6,500	—
1879	14,807,100	16.50	17.50	18.00	20.00	22.00	36.00	60.00	135	1,050	11,000	6,200
1879CC	756,000	165	185	285	735	1,900	4,150	7,500	10,500	27,850	48,750	—
1879CC capped CC	Inc. above	160	175	270	700	1,800	4,000	6,850	10,250	44,500	63,500	—
1879O	2,887,000	17.00	18.00	19.00	22.00	25.00	75.00	195	515	3,250	22,500	—
1879S reverse of 1878	9,110,000	22.50	23.50	25.00	30.00	47.50	125	400	1,450	7,300	24,000	—
1879S reverse of 1879	9,110,000	16.50	17.50	18.00	20.00	22.00	36.00	50.00	61.00	165	800	—
1880	12,601,335	16.50	17.50	18.00	20.00	22.00	36.00	52.50	145	775	4,200	6,000

Date	Mintage	VG-8	F-12	VF-20	XF-40	AU-50	MS-60	MS-63	MS-64	MS-65	65DMPL	Prf-65
1880CC reverse of 1878	591,000	175	210	245	300	355	575	600	1,265	2,775	11,000	—
1880CC 80/79 reverse of 1878	Inc. above	190	230	270	335	410	640	850	1,700	4,000	—	—
1880CC 8/7 reverse of 1878	Inc. above	170	200	235	290	360	600	700	1,300	2,900	—	—
1880CC reverse of 1879	Inc. above	170	200	240	285	345	550	580	725	1,650	7,000	—
1880CC 8/7 high 7 reverse of 1879	Inc. above	175	205	245	290	355	575	620	800	1,850	—	—
1880CC 8/7 low 7 reverse of 1879	Inc. above	175	205	245	290	355	575	620	800	1,850	—	—
1880O	5,305,000	17.00	18.00	19.00	22.00	25.00	62.50	385	1,750	24,500	70,000	—
1880S	8,900,000	16.50	17.50	18.00	20.00	22.00	36.00	45.00	58.00	165	650	—
1881	9,163,975	16.50	17.50	18.00	20.00	22.00	36.00	63.00	150	830	17,750	6,300
1881CC	296,000	375	385	410	425	460	555	575	625	975	2,850	—
1881O	5,708,000	16.50	17.50	18.00	20.00	22.00	36.00	51.00	210	1,675	19,250	—
1881S	12,760,000	16.50	17.50	18.00	20.00	22.00	36.00	45.00	58.00	165	785	—
1882	11,101,100	16.50	17.50	18.00	20.00	22.00	36.00	47.00	65.00	425	5,200	6,000
1882CC	1,133,000	92.00	100.00	110	130	155	220	235	265	530	1,900	—
1882O	6,090,000	17.00	18.00	19.00	22.00	25.00	39.00	52.00	110	960	4,850	—
1882O/S	Inc. above	25.00	32.00	39.00	52.00	88.00	255	1,150	3,250	32,500	34,000	—
1882S	9,250,000	16.50	17.50	18.00	20.00	22.00	36.00	47.00	58.00	165	2,950	—
1883	12,291,039	16.50	17.50	18.00	20.00	22.00	36.00	47.00	64.00	195	1,625	6,150
1883CC	1,204,000	92.00	100.00	110	130	155	215	230	265	435	1,500	—
1883O	8,725,000	16.50	17.60	18.00	20.00	22.00	36.00	45.00	58.00	165	975	—
1883S	6,250,000	16.50	18.00	19.50	33.50	145	635	2,750	4,250	22,500	94,500	—
1884	14,070,875	16.50	17.50	18.00	20.00	22.00	36.00	47.00	62.00	245	3,350	6,000
1884CC	1,136,000	125	135	160	175	195	215	225	260	415	1,550	—
1884O	9,730,000	16.50	17.50	18.00	20.00	22.00	36.00	45.00	58.00	165	675	—
1884S	3,200,000	16.50	18.00	19.50	42.50	255	5,750	31,500	110,000	198,000	220,000	—
1885	17,787,767	16.50	17.50	18.00	20.00	22.00	36.00	47.00	58.00	165	700	6,000
1885CC	228,000	550	585	600	630	635	650	675	720	1,450	3,000	—
1885O	9,185,000	16.50	17.50	18.00	20.00	22.00	36.00	45.00	58.00	165	685	—
1885S	1,497,000	21.00	28.00	40.00	64.00	125	240	310	720	1,675	27,500	—
1886	19,963,886	16.50	18.00	19.00	20.00	22.00	36.00	45.00	58.00	165	850	6,000
1886O	10,710,000	16.50	17.50	21.00	23.00	78.00	685	3,750	10,500	220,000	300,000	—
1886S	750,000	47.50	62.50	85.00	90.00	180	320	465	775	3,150	16,500	—
1887	20,290,710	16.50	17.50	18.00	20.00	22.00	36.00	45.00	58.00	165	685	6,000
1887/6	Inc. above	23.00	26.00	34.00	55.00	165	425	725	1,300	4,900	36,500	—
1887O	11,550,000	16.50	17.50	21.00	23.00	25.00	52.00	110	460	3,200	10,350	—
1887S	1,771,000	18.00	19.00	22.00	24.00	44.00	110	285	700	3,250	29,500	—
1888	19,183,833	16.50	17.50	18.00	20.00	22.00	36.00	45.00	58.00	182	2,950	6,150
1888O	12,150,000	16.50	17.50	18.00	20.00	22.00	36.00	49.00	90.00	460	2,450	—
1888O Hot Lips	Inc. above	55.00	125	250	600	3,000	—	—	—	—	—	—
1888S	657,000	115	190	210	225	235	300	465	875	3,150	12,850	—
1889	21,726,811	16.50	17.50	18.00	20.00	22.00	36.00	45.00	63.00	310	2,950	6,000
1889CC	350,000	675	1,050	1,750	3,650	7,250	22,500	43,500	53,000	290,000	—	—
1889O	11,875,000	17.00	18.00	20.50	24.00	31.50	135	410	760	4,650	14,500	—
1889S	700,000	37.50	60.00	65.00	82.00	125	210	400	585	1,950	25,500	—
1890	16,802,590	16.50	17.50	18.00	20.00	22.00	36.00	48.00	160	2,050	17,500	6,000
1890CC	2,309,041	96.00	100.00	110	160	245	450	950	2,650	6,750	14,750	—
1890CC tail bar	Inc. above	155	175	225	400	700	1,450	3,600	5,500	—	9,800	—
1890O	10,701,000	19.00	20.00	21.00	23.00	25.00	56.00	115	365	1,475	8,850	—
1890S	8,230,373	17.00	18.00	19.00	22.00	25.00	56.00	110	270	875	9,850	—
1891	8,694,206	17.50	18.50	19.50	22.00	26.00	52.50	185	685	7,000	27,500	6,000
1891CC	1,618,000	96.00	98.50	110	150	220	360	800	1,450	5,000	24,500	—
1891CC Spitting Eagle	Inc. above	105	115	135	185	260	425	900	1,600	6,000	—	—
1891O	7,954,529	17.00	18.00	19.00	22.00	35.00	135	350	850	7,500	25,500	—
1891S	5,296,000	17.00	18.00	19.00	22.00	25.00	56.00	135	315	1,250	9,500	—
1892	1,037,245	20.00	20.00	25.00	34.00	75.00	155	420	1,100	3,600	19,000	6,250
1892CC	1,352,000	195	220	315	535	800	1,650	2,450	3,750	10,000	33,500	—
1892O	2,744,000	20.00	21.00	22.00	32.00	62.50	160	325	775	5,000	38,500	—
1892S	1,200,000	26.00	32.00	135	365	1,950	34,500	63,500	100,000	175,000	195,000	—
1893	378,792	245	250	260	300	400	750	1,350	2,650	7,350	66,000	6,150
1893CC	677,000	265	345	725	1,850	2,350	3,700	6,800	14,000	56,000	85,000	—
1893O	300,000	205	250	380	620	975	2,250	7,500	19,750	210,000	215,000	—
1893S	100,000	3,750	5,450	7,500	11,500	27,500	85,000	150,000	250,000	415,000	435,000	—
1894	110,972	1,400	1,700	1,850	2,350	2,950	4,950	6,750	11,800	46,000	44,000	7,250
1894O	1,723,000	60.00	65.00	70.00	105	310	580	4,000	10,500	53,000	59,500	—
1894S	1,260,000	62.00	65.00	110	150	510	695	1,150	1,940	6,850	19,800	—
1895 proof only	12,880	21,500	27,500	29,000	33,500	37,500	—	—	—	—	—	79,000
1895O	450,000	335	415	595	725	1,450	17,000	57,500	94,000	225,000	—	—
1895S	400,000	450	510	600	990	1,850	4,150	7,000	9,100	21,500	42,500	—
1896	9,967,762	16.50	17.50	18.00	20.00	22.00	36.00	45.00	68.00	190	1,350	6,000
1896O	4,900,000	17.00	18.00	20.00	24.00	185	1,450	8,350	46,000	190,000	180,000	—

Date	Mintage	VG-8	F-12	VF-20	XF-40	AU-50	MS-60	MS-63	MS-64	MS-65	65DMPL	Prf-65
1896S	5,000,000	22.00	35.00	60.00	235	895	1,775	4,100	5,400	19,500	110,000	—
1897	2,822,731	16.50	17.50	18.00	20.00	22.00	36.00	49.00	68.00	275	3,750	6,000
1897O	4,004,000	17.50	19.50	21.00	25.00	110	735	4,850	15,000	50,000	58,500	—
1897S	5,825,000	17.50	18.50	19.00	21.00	24.00	58.00	115	175	600	2,200	—
1898	5,884,735	16.50	17.50	18.00	20.00	22.00	36.00	45.00	62.00	275	1,375	6,000
1898O	4,440,000	16.50	17.50	18.00	20.00	22.00	36.00	45.00	58.00	165	850	—
1898S	4,102,000	20.00	25.00	35.00	55.00	105	260	475	875	2,300	16,000	—
1899	330,846	170	185	215	240	275	320	370	535	975	2,775	6,000
1899O	12,290,000	16.50	17.50	18.00	20.00	22.00	36.00	47.00	58.00	165	1,225	—
1899S	2,562,000	21.00	26.00	37.50	62.50	125	320	480	800	1,850	16,500	—
1900	8,880,938	16.50	17.50	18.00	20.00	22.00	36.00	49.00	63.00	185	26,500	6,000
1900O	12,590,000	16.50	17.50	18.00	20.00	22.00	36.00	49.00	69.00	190	4,300	—
1900O/CC	Inc. above	37.50	47.50	62.50	100.00	190	350	925	1,400	3,250	19,000	—
1900S	3,540,000	18.00	21.00	25.00	37.50	85.00	325	420	600	1,450	22,000	—
1901	6,962,813	27.50	36.00	57.50	110	395	2,150	17,000	56,000	220,000	—	6,500
1901 doubled die reverse	Inc. above	275	450	900	2,000	3,850	—	—	—	—	—	—
1901O	13,320,000	16.50	17.50	18.00	20.00	22.00	36.00	45.00	65.00	190	8,800	6,500
1901S	2,284,000	19.50	21.00	31.50	46.00	220	470	700	1,075	3,750	13,500	—
1902	7,994,777	17.50	18.00	19.00	22.00	25.00	44.00	100.00	138	435	38,500	6,000
1902O	8,636,000	16.50	17.50	18.00	20.00	22.00	36.00	45.00	58.00	185	9,400	—
1902S	1,530,000	60.00	82.00	160	220	315	425	625	1,135	2,850	15,000	—
1903	4,652,755	48.00	50.00	52.00	58.00	60.00	75.00	92.00	125	280	12,600	6,000
1903O	4,450,000	325	350	375	400	415	425	450	475	675	5,350	5,350
1903S	1,241,000	95.00	130	215	425	2,100	4,400	7,000	8,500	10,500	40,000	—
1903S Micro S	Inc. above	135	225	450	1,150	3,000	—	—	—	—	—	—
1904	2,788,650	21.00	23.00	25.00	27.00	32.00	78.00	280	715	3,650	38,000	6,000
1904O	3,720,000	21.00	23.00	25.00	27.00	29.00	37.00	48.00	60.00	165	950	—
1904S	2,304,000	35.00	47.50	87.00	230	560	1,150	4,350	6,250	8,750	19,000	—
1921	44,690,000	15.50	16.00	16.50	17.00	18.50	25.00	35.00	44.00	175	11,000	—
1921D	20,345,000	15.50	16.00	16.50	18.50	21.00	45.00	56.00	155	330	10,000	—
1921S	21,695,000	15.50	16.00	16.50	18.00	20.00	34.00	69.00	165	875	31,000	—

Peace Dollar. Liberty Head left. Eagle facing right pearched on rock.

KM# 150 **Designer:** Anthony DeFrancisci. **Diameter:** 38.1 **Weight:** 26.7300 g. **Composition:** 0.9000 Silver, 0.7734 oz. ASW. **Notes:** Commonly called Peace dollars.

Mint mark

Date	Mintage	G-4	VG-8	F-12	VF-20	XF-40	AU-50	MS-60	MS-63	MS-64	MS-65
1921	1,006,473	100.00	125	135	140	150	170	245	535	850	2,400
1922	51,737,000	13.00	14.00	14.50	15.00	16.00	17.00	21.00	30.00	50.00	180
1922D	15,063,000	13.00	14.30	14.90	15.60	16.60	18.50	26.50	49.00	92.50	440
1922S	17,475,000	13.00	14.30	14.90	15.60	16.60	18.50	26.50	69.00	300	2,500
1923	30,800,000	13.00	14.00	14.50	15.00	16.00	17.00	21.00	30.00	50.00	180
1923D	6,811,000	13.00	16.00	16.50	17.00	18.00	22.00	52.00	125	285	1,225
1923S	19,020,000	13.00	14.30	14.90	15.60	16.60	18.50	28.50	74.00	375	6,750
1924	11,811,000	13.00	14.00	14.50	15.00	16.00	17.00	21.00	30.00	50.00	180
1924S	1,728,000	25.00	30.00	31.00	33.00	44.00	66.50	200	600	1,675	9,500
1925	10,198,000	13.00	14.00	14.50	15.00	16.00	17.00	21.00	30.00	50.00	180
1925S	1,610,000	16.50	19.50	21.00	25.00	29.00	46.00	75.00	195	1,050	21,000
1926	1,939,000	15.00	17.00	18.00	18.50	19.00	22.50	40.00	77.00	120	380
1926D	2,348,700	15.50	17.00	17.50	18.00	22.00	32.50	66.00	150	300	600
1926S	6,980,000	15.00	16.00	16.50	17.50	18.50	19.50	40.00	96.00	300	1,100
1927	848,000	23.50	27.50	30.00	31.50	33.50	50.00	70.00	175	440	3,350
1927D	1,268,900	22.50	26.00	28.00	30.00	32.00	80.00	145	355	1,000	5,000
1927S	866,000	22.50	27.00	29.00	31.00	34.00	80.00	135	425	1,575	11,350
1928	360,649	355	435	445	455	465	475	525	925	1,450	4,400
1928S Lg S	1,632,000	29.00	35.00	39.00	44.00	50.00	80.00	210	765	1,850	25,000
1928S Sm S	Inc. above	28.00	33.00	34.00	38.00	43.50	66.00	155	595	1,575	19,500
1934	954,057	16.00	19.50	20.00	21.00	22.50	46.00	120	245	465	930
1934D Lg D	1,569,500	17.00	20.00	21.00	23.00	26.00	60.00	165	600	900	2,850
1934D Sm D	Inc. above	16.00	17.80	19.50	21.00	22.00	46.00	135	500	725	1,900
1934S	1,011,000	26.00	31.00	48.00	85.00	200	500	1,750	3,850	6,250	8,500

Date	Mintage	G-4	VG-8	F-12	VF-20	XF-40	AU-50	MS-60	MS-63	MS-64	MS-65
1935	1,576,000	15.00	18.00	20.00	21.50	22.00	30.00	60.00	105	210	680
1935S	1,964,000	15.00	18.00	19.00	20.00	23.00	92.00	235	370	625	1,325

Eisenhower Dollar.

KM# 203 **Designer:** Frank Gasparro. **Diameter:** 38.1 **Weight:** 22.6800 g. **Composition:** Copper-Nickel Clad Copper

Date	Mintage	Proof	MS-63	Prf-65
1971	47,799,000	—	10.00	—
1971D	68,587,424	—	8.00	—
1972 Low Relief	75,890,000	—	7.00	—
1972 High Relief	Inc. above	—	175	—
1972 Modified High Relief	Inc. above	—	40.00	—
1972D	92,548,511	—	5.50	—
1973	2,000,056	—	14.00	—
1973D	2,000,000	—	15.00	—
1973S	—	2,769,624	—	12.00
1974	27,366,000	—	5.50	—
1974D	35,466,000	—	7.00	—
1974S	—	2,617,350	—	11.00

Eisenhower Dollar.

KM# 203a **Designer:** Frank Gasparro. **Diameter:** 38.1 **Weight:** 24.5900 g. **Composition:** 0.4000 Silver, 0.3162 oz. ASW.

Date	Mintage	Proof	MS-63	Prf-65
1971S	6,868,530	—	7.50	—
1971S	—	4,265,234	—	11.00
1971S Peg Leg "R" Variety	Inc. above	—	—	17.00
1971S Partial Peg Leg "R" Variety	Inc. above	—	—	18.00
1972S	2,193,056	—	7.50	—
1972S	—	1,811,631	—	14.00
1973S	1,833,140	—	8.50	—
1973S	—	1,005,617	—	35.00
1974S	1,720,000	—	7.50	—
1974S	—	1,306,579	—	14.00

Eisenhower Dollar. Bicentennial design, moon behind Liberty Bell.

KM# 206 **Rev. Designer:** Dennis R. Williams. **Diameter:** 38.1 **Weight:** 22.6800 g. **Composition:** Copper-Nickel Clad Copper **Notes:** In 1976 the lettering on the reverse was changed to thinner letters, resulting in the Type II variety for that year. The Type I variety was minted 1975 and dated 1976.

Type I

Type II

Date	Mintage	Proof	MS-63	Prf-65
1976 type I	117,337,000	—	10.00	—

Date	Mintage	Proof	MS-63	Prf-65
1976 type II	Inc. above	—	5.00	—
1976D type I	103,228,274	—	6.00	—
1976D type II	Inc. above	—	5.00	—
1976S type I	—	2,909,369	—	13.00
1976S type II	—	4,149,730	—	9.00

Eisenhower Dollar. Bicentennial design, moon behind Liberty Bell.

KM# 206a **Rev. Designer:** Dennis R. Williams. **Weight:** 24.5900 g. **Composition:** 0.4000 Silver, 0.3162 oz. ASW.

Date	Mintage	Proof	MS-63	Prf-65
1976S	4,908,319	—	12.50	—
1976S	—	3,998,621	—	20.00

Eisenhower Dollar. Regular design resumed.

KM# A203 **Diameter:** 38.1 **Composition:** Copper-Nickel Clad Copper

Date	Mintage	Proof	MS-63	Prf-65
1977	12,596,000	—	9.00	—
1977D	32,983,006	—	9.00	—
1977S	—	3,251,152	—	10.00
1978	25,702,000	—	5.00	—
1978D	33,012,890	—	5.00	—
1978S	—	3,127,788	—	12.00

Susan B. Anthony Dollar. Susan B. Anthony bust right.
Eagle landing on moon, symbolic of Apollo manned moon landing.

KM# 207 **Designer:** Frank Gasparro. **Diameter:** 26.5 **Weight:** 8.1000 g. **Composition:** Copper-Nickel Clad Copper **Notes:** The 1979-S and 1981-S Type II coins have a clearer mint mark than the Type I varieties for those years.

Date	Mintage	MS-63	Prf-65
1979S Proof, Type II	Inc. above	—	110
1979S	109,576,000	3.00	—
1980P	27,610,000	3.00	—
1980D	41,628,708	2.00	—
1980S	20,422,000	3.50	—
1980S Proof	3,547,030	—	8.00
1981P	3,000,000	7.50	—
1981D	3,250,000	7.50	—
1981S	3,492,000	7.50	—
1981S Proof, Type I	4,063,083	—	8.00
1981S Proof, Type II	Inc. above	—	230
1999P	29,592,000	4.00	—
1999P Proof; *maximum mintage	(750,000)	—	25.00
1999D	11,776,000	4.00	—

Date	Mintage	MS-63	Prf-65
1979P Near date	360,222,000	60.00	—
1979P	Inc. above	2.50	—
1979D	288,015,744	3.00	—
1979S Proof, Type I	(3,677,175)	—	8.00

Sacagawea Dollar. Sacagawea bust right, with baby on back.
Eagle in flight left.

KM# 310 **Diameter:** 26.4 **Weight:** 8.0700 g. **Composition:** Copper-Zinc-Manganese-Nickel Clad Copper

Date	Mintage	MS-63	Prf-65
2003D	3,090,000	2.50	—
2003S	(3,116,590)	—	20.00
2004P	2,660,000	2.50	—
2004D	2,660,000	2.50	—
2004S	—	—	22.50
2005P	2,520,000	2.50	—
2005D	2,520,000	2.50	—
2005S	—	—	22.50
2006P	4,900,000	2.50	—
2006D	2,800,000	2.50	—
2006S	—	—	22.50
2007P	—	2.50	—
2007D	—	2.50	—
2007S	—	—	22.50

Date	Mintage	MS-63	Prf-65
2000P	767,140,000	2.00	—
2000D	518,916,000	2.00	—
2000S	(4,048,865)	—	10.00
2001P	62,468,000	4.00	—
2001D	70,909,500	4.00	—
2001S	(3,084,600)	—	100.00
2002P	3,865,610	2.00	—
2002D	3,732,000	2.00	—
2002S	(3,157,739)	—	28.50
2003P	3,090,000	2.50	—

Presidents

George Washington

KM# 401   **Diameter:** 26.4 **Weight:** 8.0700 g.
Composition: Copper-Zinc-Manganese-Nickel Clad
Copper **Notes:** Date and mint mark incuse on edge.

Date	Mintage	MS-63	MS-65	Prf-65
2007P	176,680,000	2.00	—	—
ND (2007) Plain edge error	Inc. above	75.00	—	—
2007D	163,680,000	2.00	—	—
2007S	—	—	—	—

James Madison

KM# 404   **Diameter:** 26.4 **Weight:** 8.0700 g.
Composition: Copper-Zinc-Manganese-Nickel Clad
Copper **Notes:** Date and mint mark incuse on edge.

Date	Mintage	MS-63	MS-65	Prf-65
2007P	—	2.00	—	—
2007D	—	2.00	—	—
2007S	—	—	—	—

John Adams

KM# 402   **Diameter:** 26.4 **Weight:** 8.0700 g.
Composition: Copper-Zinc-Manganese-Nickel Clad
Copper **Notes:** Date and mint mark incuse on edge.

Date	Mintage	MS-63	MS-65	Prf-65
2007P	112,420,000	2.00	—	—
2007P Double edge lettering	Inc. above	250	—	—
2007D	102,810,000	2.00	—	—
2007S	—	—	—	—

Thomas Jefferson

KM# 403   **Diameter:** 26.4 **Weight:** 8.0700 g.
Composition: Copper-Zinc-Manganese-Nickel Clad
Copper **Notes:** Date and mint mark incuse on edge.

Date	Mintage	MS-63	MS-65	Prf-65
2007P	—	2.00	—	—
2007D	—	2.00	—	—
2007S	—	—	—	—

GOLD

Liberty Head - Type 1. Liberty head left within circle of stars. Value, date within 3/4 wreath.

KM# 73   **Designer:** James B. Longacre. **Diameter:**
13 **Weight:** 1.6720 g. **Composition:** 0.9000 Gold,
0.0484 oz. AGW. **Notes:** On the "closed wreath"
varieties of 1849, the wreath on the reverse extends
closer to the numeral 1.

Date	Mintage	F-12	VF-20	XF-40	AU-50	MS-60
1849 open wreath	688,567	120	175	220	300	650
1849 small head, no L	—	—	—	—	—	—
1849 closed wreath	Inc. above	120	160	200	215	260
1849C closed wreath	11,634	800	950	1,450	2,400	8,850
1849C open wreath	Inc. above	135,000	240,000	320,000	475,000	600,000
1849D open wreath	21,588	1,050	1,300	1,875	2,600	6,000
1849O open wreath	215,000	140	185	265	335	800
1850	481,953	120	160	200	295	260
1850C	6,966	900	1,150	1,600	2,350	9,000
1850D	8,382	1,050	1,250	1,725	2,950	12,500
1850O	14,000	200	275	390	775	3,300
1851	3,317,671	120	160	200	215	260
1851C	41,267	840	1,150	1,500	1,700	3,150
1851D	9,882	1,000	1,250	1,675	2,500	5,650
1851O	290,000	160	195	240	265	775
1852	2,045,351	120	160	200	215	260
1852C	9,434	845	1,040	1,400	1,700	5,100

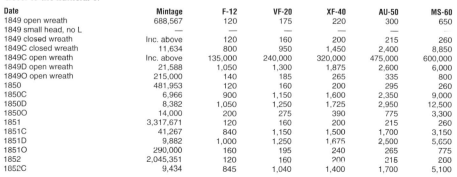

Date	Mintage	F-12	VF-20	XF-40	AU-50	MS-60
1852D	6,360	1,025	1,250	1,675	2,300	10,000
1852O	140,000	130	175	260	385	1,400
1853	4,076,051	120	160	200	215	260
1853C	11,515	900	1,100	1,400	2,000	5,600
1853D	6,583	1,040	1,250	1,700	2,650	9,700
1853O	290,000	135	160	235	270	665
1854	736,709	120	160	200	215	260
1854D	2,935	1,050	1,400	2,350	6,000	13,000
1854S	14,632	260	360	525	775	2,450

Indian Head - Type 2. Indian head with headdress left. Value, date within wreath.

KM# 83 **Designer:** James B. Longacre. **Diameter:** 15 **Weight:** 1.6720 g. **Composition:** 0.9000 Gold, 0.0484 oz. AGW.

Date	Mintage	F-12	VF-20	XF-40	AU-50	MS-60
1854	902,736	225	310	440	575	2,350
1855	758,269	225	310	440	575	2,350
1855C	9,803	975	1,450	3,750	11,500	33,000
1855D	1,811	3,250	4,750	9,800	22,000	48,000
1855O	55,000	345	440	600	1,500	7,800
1856S	24,600	525	820	1,325	2,500	8,650

Indian Head - Type 3. Indian head with headdress left. Value, date within wreath.

KM# 86 **Designer:** James B. Longacre. **Diameter:** 15 **Weight:** 1.6720 g. **Composition:** 0.9000 Gold, 0.0484 oz. AGW. **Notes:** The 1856 varieties are distinguished by whether the 5 in the date is slanted or upright. The 1873 varieties are distinguished by the amount of space between the upper left and lower left serifs in the 3.

Date	Mintage	F-12	VF-20	XF-40	AU-50	MS-60	Prf-65
1856 upright 5	1,762,936	140	170	225	250	460	—
1856 slanted 5	Inc. above	135	160	200	215	310	55,000
1856D	1,460	2,350	3,650	5,800	8,000	32,000	—
1857	774,789	125	155	200	215	310	32,000
1857C	13,280	900	1,150	1,750	3,750	13,250	—
1857D	3,533	1,000	1,300	2,300	4,400	11,000	—
1857S	10,000	260	520	650	1,300	6,200	—
1858	117,995	125	155	200	215	310	28,500
1858D	3,477	1,025	1,250	1,600	2,850	10,000	—
1858S	10,000	300	400	575	1,450	5,350	—
1859	168,244	125	155	200	215	310	17,000
1859C	5,235	885	1,050	1,700	4,250	9,850	—
1859D	4,952	1,050	1,500	2,100	3,250	10,500	—
1859S	15,000	210	265	525	1,250	5,500	—
1860	36,668	125	155	200	215	310	16,500
1860D	1,566	2,150	2,500	4,200	7,000	13,500	—
1860S	13,000	300	380	500	750	1,650	—
1861	527,499	125	155	200	215	310	14,850
1861D mintage unrecorded	—	4,950	7,000	11,000	21,000	41,500	—
1862	1,361,390	125	155	200	215	310	15,000
1863	6,250	370	500	925	2,100	3,900	18,000
1864	5,950	290	370	475	825	1,050	18,000
1865	3,725	290	370	590	750	1,600	18,000
1866	7,130	300	385	470	685	1,025	18,000
1867	5,250	325	420	525	675	1,160	17,500
1868	10,525	265	290	415	500	1,025	19,000
1869	5,925	315	460	530	725	1,150	17,000
1870	6,335	255	290	410	500	875	16,000
1870S	3,000	300	475	785	1,250	2,650	—
1871	3,930	260	290	390	480	750	18,000
1872	3,530	260	295	400	480	975	18,500
1873 closed 3	125,125	325	425	825	950	1,650	—
1873 open 3	Inc. above	125	155	200	215	310	—
1874	198,820	125	155	200	215	310	30,000
1875	420	1,650	2,350	4,650	5,200	10,000	32,500
1876	3,245	240	300	360	475	725	16,750
1877	3,920	150	210	340	460	725	18,000
1878	3,020	195	250	365	480	675	15,500
1879	3,030	170	225	285	3,300	525	14,000

Date	Mintage	F-12	VF-20	XF-40	AU-50	MS-60	Prf-65
1880	1,636	150	180	215	245	425	14,000
1881	7,707	150	180	215	245	410	11,500
1882	5,125	160	185	215	245	410	10,500
1883	11,007	150	175	215	245	410	11,000
1884	6,236	150	175	215	245	410	10,000
1885	12,261	150	175	215	245	410	10,000
1886	6,016	150	175	215	245	410	10,000
1887	8,543	150	175	215	245	410	10,000
1888	16,580	150	175	215	245	410	10,000
1889	30,729	150	175	215	245	340	10,000

$2.50 (QUARTER EAGLE)

GOLD

Liberty Cap. Liberty cap on head, right, flanked by stars. Heraldic eagle.

KM# 27 Designer: Robert Scot. **Diameter:** 20 **Weight:** 4.3700 g. **Composition:** 0.9160 Gold, 0.1287 oz. AGW. **Notes:** The 1796 "no stars" variety does not have stars on the obverse. The 1804 varieties are distinguished by the number of stars on the obverse.

Date	Mintage	F-12	VF-20	XF-40	MS-60
1796 no stars	963	30,000	42,000	70,000	165,000
1796 stars	432	28,000	40,000	63,000	140,000
1797	427	17,000	23,000	27,500	120,000
1798	1,094	4,750	10,000	12,500	55,000
1802/1	3,035	4,400	8,000	9,500	32,000
1804 13-star reverse	3,327	23,500	36,500	72,000	200,000
1804 14-star reverse	Inc. above	4,800	7,400	9,000	27,500
1805	1,781	6,000	7,500	9,000	21,000
1806/4	1,616	5,750	8,000	9,500	23,000
1806/5	Inc. above	6,000	8,000	18,000	77,000
1807	6,812	5,500	7,000	9.00	21,000

Turban Head. Turban on head left flanked by stars. Banner above eagle.

KM# 40 Designer: John Reich. **Diameter:** 20 **Weight:** 4.3700 g. **Composition:** 0.9160 Gold, 0.1287 oz. AGW.

Date	Mintage	F-12	VF-20	XF-40	MS-60
1808	2,710	22,500	31,000	45,000	125,000

Turban Head. Turban on head left within circle of stars. Banner above eagle.

KM# 46 Designer: John Reich. **Diameter:** 18.5 **Weight:** 4.3700 g. **Composition:** 0.9160 Gold, 0.1287 oz. AGW.

Date	Mintage	F-12	VF-20	XF-40	MS-60
1821	6,448	5,500	6,250	7,500	23,000
1824/21	2,600	5,500	6,250	7,250	22,000
1825	4,434	5,500	6,500	7,800	21,000
1826/25	760	6,000	7,000	8,500	36,000
1827	2,800	5,500	7,500	9,000	22,500

Turban Head. Turban on head left within circle of stars. Banner above eagle.

KM# 49 Designer: John Reich. **Diameter:** 18.2 **Weight:** 4.3700 g. **Composition:** 0.9160 Gold, 0.1287 oz. AGW.

Date	Mintage	F-12	VF-20	XF-40	MS-60
1829	3,403	4,900	5,850	6,700	12,500

Date	Mintage	F-12	VF-20	XF-40	MS-60
1830	4,540	4,950	5,850	6,700	12,500
1831	4,520	4,950	5,850	6,700	12,500
1832	4,400	4,950	5,850	6,700	12,500
1833	4,160	4,950	5,850	6,800	12,750
1834	4,000	8,800	12,000	16,000	36,000

Classic Head. Classic head left within circle of stars. No motto above eagle.

KM# 56   Designer: William Kneass. **Diameter:** 18.2 **Weight:** 4.1800 g. **Composition:** 0.8990 Gold, 0.1208 oz. AGW.

Date	Mintage	VF-20	XF-40	AU-50	MS-60	MS-65
1834	112,234	475	675	965	3,300	27,000
1835	131,402	475	675	950	3,200	32,000
1836	547,986	475	675	940	3,100	29,000
1837	45,080	500	800	1,500	4,000	35,000
1838	47,030	500	625	1,100	3,200	30,000
1838C	7,880	1,700	3,000	8,000	27,000	55,000
1839	27,021	500	900	1,900	5,500	—
1839C	18,140	1,500	2,650	4,500	26,500	—
1839/8	Inc. above	—	—	—	—	—
1839D	13,674	1,750	3,450	8,000	24,000	—
1839O	17,781	700	1,100	2,500	7,250	—

Coronet Head. Coronet head left within circle of stars. No motto above eagle.

KM# 72   Designer: Christian Gobrecht. **Diameter:** 18 **Weight:** 4.1800 g. **Composition:** 0.9000 Gold, 0.1209 oz. AGW. **Notes:** Varieties for 1843 are distinguished by the size of the numerals in the date. One 1848 variety has "Cal." inscribed on the reverse, indicating it was made from California gold. The 1873 "closed-3" and "open-3" varieties are distinguished by the amount of space between the upper left and lower left serifs in the 3 in the date.

1948 "Cal."

Date	Mintage	F-12	VF-20	XF-40	AU-50	MS-60	Prf-65
1840	18,859	160	190	900	2,950	6,000	—
1840C	12,822	975	1,400	1,600	6,000	13,000	—
1840D	3,532	2,000	3,200	8,700	15,500	35,000	—
1840O	33,580	250	400	825	2,100	11,000	—
1841	—	—	48,000	85,000	96,000	—	—
1841C	10,281	750	1,500	2,000	3,500	18,500	—
1841D	4,164	950	2,100	4,750	11,000	25,000	—
1842	2,823	500	900	2,600	6,500	20,000	140,000
1842C	6,729	700	1,700	3,500	8,000	27,000	—
1842D	4,643	900	2,100	4,000	11,750	38,000	—
1842O	19,800	240	370	1,200	2,500	14,000	—
1843	100,546	160	180	450	915	3,000	140,000
1843C small date, Crosslet 4	26,064	1,500	2,400	5,500	9,000	29,000	—
1843C large date, Plain 4	Inc. above	800	1,600	2,200	3,500	8,800	—
1843D small date, Crosslet 4	36,209	920	1,800	2,350	3,250	10,500	—
1843O small date, Crosslet 4	288,002	165	190	250	350	1,700	—
1843O large date, Plain 4	76,000	210	260	465	1,600	8,000	—
1844	6,784	225	365	850	2,000	7,500	140,000
1844C	11,622	700	1,600	2,600	7,000	20,000	—
1844D	17,332	785	1,650	2,200	3,200	7,800	—
1845	91,051	190	250	350	600	1,275	140,000
1845D	19,460	950	1,900	2,600	3,900	15,000	—
1845O	4,000	550	1,050	2,300	9,000	20,000	—
1846	21,598	200	275	500	950	6,000	140,000
1846C	4,808	725	1,575	3,500	8,950	18,750	—
1846D	19,303	800	1,400	2,000	3,000	12,000	—
1846O	66,000	170	280	400	1,150	6,500	—
1847	29,814	140	220	360	825	3,800	—
1847C	23,226	900	1,800	2,300	3,500	7,250	—
1847D	15,784	800	1,650	2,250	3,250	10,500	—
1847O	124,000	160	240	400	1,000	4,000	—
1848	7,497	315	500	850	2,400	7,000	125,000
1848 "Cal."	1,389	8,000	15,000	26,000	36,000	50,000	—
1848C	16,788	800	1,600	2,100	3,800	13,750	—
1848D	13,771	1,000	2,000	2,500	4,500	12,000	—

Date	Mintage	F-12	VF-20	XF-40	AU-50	MS-60	Prf-65
1849	23,294	180	275	475	1,000	2,600	—
1849C	10,220	800	1,475	2,150	5,150	23,500	—
1849D	10,945	950	2,000	2,500	4,500	18,000	—
1850	252,923	160	180	275	350	1,100	—
1850C	9,148	800	1,500	2,100	3,400	17,500	—
1850D	12,148	950	1,800	2,500	4,000	15,000	—
1850O	84,000	170	225	450	1,200	4,900	—
1851	1,372,748	145	180	200	225	325	—
1851C	14,923	900	1,750	2,300	4,800	13,000	—
1851D	11,264	950	1,700	2,600	4,200	13,000	—
1851O	148,000	160	200	220	1,000	4,650	—
1852	1,159,681	150	175	200	250	325	—
1852C	9,772	675	1,500	2,100	4,250	18,000	—
1852D	4,078	840	1,600	2,800	7,250	17,000	—
1852O	140,000	160	190	300	950	5,000	—
1853	1,404,668	150	180	200	225	350	—
1853D	3,178	950	2,100	3,400	4,900	18,000	—
1854	596,258	150	180	215	240	350	—
1854C	7,295	800	1,500	2,400	5,000	14,750	—
1854D	1,760	1,750	2,900	6,950	12,000	27,500	—
1854O	153,000	150	185	240	425	1,600	—
1854S	246	32,500	70,000	115,000	215,000	300,000	—
1855	235,480	145	180	225	250	360	—
1855C	3,677	800	1,675	3,300	6,500	25,000	—
1855D	1,123	1,750	3,250	7,500	24,000	46,000	—
1856	384,240	145	175	210	250	390	75,000
1856C	7,913	650	1,150	2,200	4,400	15,500	—
1856D	874	3,500	6,700	12,500	30,000	72,500	
1856O	21,100	180	240	750	1,500	8,000	—
1856S	71,120	160	250	375	950	4,500	—
1857	214,130	150	190	205	230	380	75,000
1857D	2,364	875	1,750	2,900	3,850	13,000	—
1857O	34,000	155	210	350	1,100	4,600	—
1857S	69,200	160	210	340	900	6,500	—
1858	47,377	150	200	250	360	1,350	59,000
1858C	9,056	825	1,500	2,100	3,350	9,250	—
1859	39,444	150	185	265	400	1,250	61,000
1859D	2,244	1,000	1,900	3,300	4,900	20,000	—
1859S	15,200	200	350	1,000	2,800	7,000	—
1860	22,675	150	200	265	470	1,300	58,000
1860C	7,469	815	1,550	2,200	3,950	21,000	—
1860S	35,600	170	250	675	1,200	4,000	—
1861	1,283,878	150	180	210	230	325	31,500
1861S	24,000	200	400	1,000	3,700	7,400	—
1862	98,543	160	200	300	520	1,375	32,500
1862/1	Inc. above	450	950	2,000	4,000	8,000	—
1862S	8,000	500	1,000	2,100	4,500	17,000	—
1863	30	—	—	—	—	—	95,000
1863S	10,800	250	500	1,500	3,200	13,500	—
1864	2,874	2,500	5,500	8,800	21,500	37,500	27,000
1865	1,545	2,400	6,000	8,000	19,000	38,000	30,000
1865S	23,376	160	225	650	1,650	5,000	—
1866	3,110	650	1,300	3,500	6,000	11,500	25,000
1866S	38,960	180	300	650	1,600	6,250	—
1867	3,250	190	385	900	1,250	4,800	27,000
1867S	28,000	170	250	625	1,750	4,000	—
1868	3,625	170	235	400	675	1,600	27,000
1868S	34,000	150	200	300	1,100	4,000	—
1869	4,345	170	250	450	715	3,000	24,500
1869S	29,500	160	240	440	775	5,000	—
1870	4,555	165	225	425	740	3,800	22,750
1870S	16,000	155	215	400	800	4,900	—
1871	5,350	160	230	325	600	2,200	24,000
1871S	22,000	150	185	280	530	2,200	—
1872	3,030	200	400	750	1,100	4,650	22,000
1872S	18,000	155	225	415	900	4,500	—
1873 closed 3	178,025	155	170	210	260	535	22,500
1873 open 3	Inc. above	155	165	195	250	300	—
1873S	27,000	160	225	425	900	2,800	—
1874	3,940	170	240	380	720	2,100	32,000
1875	420	1,750	3,500	5,000	11,000	21,500	32,500
1875S	11,600	150	200	300	850	4,500	—
1876	4,221	170	275	675	925	3,200	22,000
1876S	5,000	170	225	525	980	3,300	—
1877	1,652	275	400	800	1,100	3,250	22,000
1877S	35,400	150	160	200	230	635	—
1878	286,260	150	160	200	225	275	26,000
1878S	178,000	150	160	200	235	340	—
1879	88,990	150	160	195	235	300	26,000

Date	Mintage	F-12	VF-20	XF-40	AU-50	MS-60	Prf-65
1879S	43,500	155	200	300	550	2,150	—
1880	2,996	170	210	335	600	1,300	20,250
1881	691	900	2,200	3,400	5,000	10,000	19,000
1882	4,067	160	210	290	400	700	15,000
1883	2,002	175	220	440	1,000	2,600	15,500
1884	2,023	175	225	420	600	1,600	16,000
1885	887	400	715	1,800	2,500	4,400	15,000
1886	4,088	170	190	270	425	1,100	16,500
1887	6,282	175	200	245	325	700	16,500
1888	16,098	160	180	240	285	340	15,000
1889	17,648	155	180	230	250	325	17,000
1890	8,813	170	190	240	280	500	13,750
1891	11,040	165	175	215	230	400	14,000
1892	2,545	170	180	250	325	765	15,000
1893	30,106	165	175	200	240	300	14,000
1894	4,122	170	180	225	325	800	13,500
1895	6,199	150	175	225	275	395	12,500
1896	19,202	150	175	225	235	285	12,500
1897	29,904	150	175	210	235	285	12,500
1898	24,165	150	175	210	235	285	12,500
1899	27,350	150	175	210	235	300	12,500
1900	67,205	150	175	240	320	415	12,500
1901	91,322	150	175	200	235	275	12,500
1902	133,733	150	170	200	235	275	12,500
1903	201,257	150	170	200	235	275	13,000
1904	160,960	150	170	200	240	275	12,500
1905	217,944	150	170	200	240	275	12,500
1906	176,490	150	170	200	240	275	12,500
1907	336,448	150	170	200	240	275	12,500

Indian Head.

KM# 128 **Designer:** Bela Lyon Pratt. **Diameter:** 18 **Weight:** 4.1800 g. **Composition:** 0.9000 Gold, 0.1209 oz. AGW.

Date	Mintage	VF-20	XF-40	AU-50	MS-60	MS-63	MS-65	Prf-65
1908	565,057	165	220	230	275	1,800	8,500	16,000
1909	441,899	175	220	230	275	2,600	11,000	30,000
1910	492,682	175	220	230	275	2,600	12,500	18,000
1911	704,191	175	220	230	280	1,600	12,500	16,000
1911D	55,680	2,500	3,650	5,000	9,850	24,500	90,000	16,000
1912	616,197	175	220	230	275	2,800	16,000	16,000
1913	722,165	175	220	230	280	1,725	14,000	16,500
1914	240,117	175	220	235	260	480	8,500	34,000	16,500
1914D	448,000	175	220	230	300	2,650	40,000	23,000
1915	606,100	175	220	230	275	1,650	13,500	15,250
1925D	578,000	175	220	230	275	1,450	7,000	—
1926	446,000	175	220	230	275	1,450	7,000	—
1927	388,000	175	220	230	275	1,450	7,000	—
1928	416,000	175	220	230	275	1,450	7,000	—
1929	532,000	180	230	250	340	1,600	10,000	—

$3

GOLD

Indian head with headdress, left. Value, date within wreath.

KM# 84 **Designer:** James B. Longacre. **Diameter:** 20.5 **Weight:** 5.0150 g. **Composition:** 0.9000 Gold, 0.1451 oz. AGW. **Notes:** The 1873 "closed-3" and "open-3" varieties are distinguished by the amount of space between the upper left and lower left serifs of the 3 in the date.

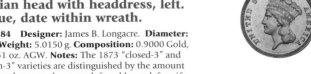

Date	Mintage	VF-20	XF-40	AU-50	MS-60	MS-65	Prf-65
1854	138,618	850	1,100	2,000	3,400	18,000	125,000
1854D	1,120	8,300	15,000	29,000	65,000	—	—
1854O	24,000	1,000	2,000	4,000	20,000	—	—
1855	50,555	900	1,100	2,000	3,300	32,000	120,000
1855S	6,600	1,025	2,150	5,700	25,000	—	—
1856	26,010	880	1,100	2,150	3,500	27,000	—

Date	Mintage	VF-20	XF-40	AU-50	MS-60	MS-65	Prf-65
1856S	34,500	900	1,500	2,350	10,000	—	—
1857	20,891	900	1,100	2,100	3,500	—	62,500
1857S	14,000	950	2,200	5,500	18,000	—	—
1858	2,133	950	1,800	3,000	9,000	—	62,500
1859	15,638	900	1,800	1,800	3,000	—	60,000
1860	7,155	900	1,600	2,000	3,600	21,000	46,000
1860S	7,000	950	2,000	7,000	17,000	—	—
1861	6,072	925	1,500	2,200	3,600	27,000	46,000
1862	5,785	925	1,850	2,200	3,600	28,000	46,500
1863	5,039	900	1,450	2,200	3,600	20,000	43,000
1864	2,680	950	1,500	2,300	3,600	29,000	42,000
1865	1,165	1,350	2,500	6,000	10,000	39,000	40,000
1866	4,030	970	1,100	2,000	3,600	27,500	42,000
1867	2,650	950	1,100	2,400	4,000	28,000	41,500
1868	4,875	740	1,100	2,100	3,000	22,000	42,000
1869	2,525	1,150	2,200	2,600	4,000	—	46,000
1870	3,535	1,000	1,500	2,400	5,000	—	47,000
1870S unique	—	—	—	—	—	—	—
Note: H. W. Bass Collection. AU50, cleaned. Est. value, $1,250,000.							
1871	1,330	1,000	1,500	2,000	4,000	27,500	47,000
1872	2,030	900	1,800	2,250	3,600	—	33,000
1873 open 3, proof only	25	3,300	5,000	8,700	—	—	—
1873 closed 3, mintage unknown	—	4,000	6,000	10,000	—	—	42,000
1874	41,820	800	1,300	1,900	3,000	16,000	42,000
1875 proof only	20	20,000	28,000	47,500	—	—	175,000
1876	45	6,000	10,000	16,500	—	—	60,000
1877	1,488	1,200	2,900	5,200	12,000	60,000	43,500
1878	82,324	800	1,300	1,900	3,000	16,000	43,000
1879	3,030	850	1,300	2,000	2,650	19,000	32,000
1880	1,036	850	1,700	3,000	4,000	20,000	29,500
1881	554	1,400	2,750	5,500	8,000	24,000	25,000
1882	1,576	925	1,400	2,000	3,500	22,000	25,000
1883	989	1,000	1,600	3,500	3,600	24,000	25,000
1884	1,106	1,250	1,700	2,200	3,600	24,000	24,000
1885	910	1,300	1,800	2,850	3,900	24,000	25,000
1886	1,142	1,250	1,800	3,000	4,000	20,000	24,000
1887	6,160	900	1,300	2,000	3,000	18,000	21,000
1888	5,291	950	1,500	2,000	3,300	20,000	23,000
1889	2,429	925	1,300	1,700	3,100	18,000	22,000

$5 (HALF EAGLE)

GOLD

Liberty Cap. Liberty cap on head, right, flanked by stars. Heraldic eagle.

KM# 19 Designer: Robert Scot. **Diameter:** 25 **Weight:** 8.7500 g. **Composition:** 0.9160 Gold, 0.2577 oz. AGW. **Notes:** From 1795 through 1798, varieties exist with either a "small eagle" or a "large (heraldic) eagle" on the reverse. After 1798, only the heraldic eagle was used. Two 1797 varieties are distinguished by the size of the 8 in the date. 1806 varieties are distinguished by whether the top of the 6 has a serif.

Date	Mintage	F-12	VF-20	XF-40	MS-60
1795 small eagle	8,707	11,500	17,000	19,000	47,000
1795 large eagle	Inc. above	8,800	14,000	20,000	75,000
1796/95 small eagle	6,196	12,000	17,500	24,000	75,000
1797/95 large eagle	3,609	8,600	14,000	22,000	150,000
1797 15 stars, small eagle	Inc. above	14,000	21,000	35,000	150,000
1797 16 stars, small eagle	Inc. above	13,000	17,500	34,000	145,000
1798 small eagle	—	90,000	155,000	275,000	—
1798 large eagle, small 8	24,867	3,300	4,500	6,000	21,000
1798 large eagle, large 8, 13-star reverse	Inc. above	3,000	3,700	4,500	17,500
1798 large eagle, large 8, 14-star reverse	Inc. above	3,000	4,200	7,000	35,000
1799	7,451	3,000	3,800	5,300	16,500
1800	37,628	3,000	3,800	5,000	8,800
1802/1	53,176	3,000	4,000	4,300	8,900
1803/2	33,506	3,000	3,800	4,300	8,700
1804 small 8	30,475	3,000	3,800	4,300	8,700
1804 large 8	Inc. above	3,000	3,800	4,300	9,600

Date	Mintage	F-12	VF-20	XF-40	MS-60
1805	33,183	3,000	3,800	4,300	8,600
1806 pointed 6	64,093	3,200	3,700	4,300	9,000
1806 round 6	Inc. above	3,000	3,700	4,300	8,600
1807	32,488	3,000	3,800	4,300	8,700

Turban Head. Capped draped bust, left, flanked by stars. Healdic eagle.

KM# 38 Designer: John Reich. **Diameter:** 25 **Weight:** 8.7500 g. **Composition:** 0.9160 Gold, 0.2577 oz. AGW. **Notes:** The 1810 varieties are distinguished by the size of the numerals in the date and the size of the 5 in the "5D." on the reverse. The 1811 varieties are distinguished by the size of the 5 in the "5D." on the reverse.

Date	Mintage	F-12	VF-20	XF-40	MS-60
1807	51,605	2,400	3,000	4,300	8,400
1808	55,578	2,400	3,000	4,300	8,250
1808/7	Inc. above	3,000	3,800	4,500	13,000
1809/8	33,875	2,500	3,000	3,750	8,500
1810 small date, small 5	100,287	9,600	22,500	32,000	95,000
1810 small date, large 5	Inc. above	2,300	3,000	3,800	8,500
1810 large date, small 5	Inc. above	13,500	24,000	32,000	115
1810 large date, large 5	Inc. above	2,600	3,000	3,750	8,500
1811 small 5	99,581	2,600	3,000	3,750	8,500
1811 large 5	Inc. above	2,500	2,900	38,000	9,000
1812	58,087	2,400	2,850	4,000	8,000

Turban Head. Capped head, left, within circle of stars. Healdic eagle.

KM# 43 Designer: John Reich. **Diameter:** 25 **Weight:** 8.7500 g. **Composition:** 0.9160 Gold, 0.2577 oz. AGW. **Notes:** 1820 varieties are distinguished by whether the 2 in the date has a curved base or square base and by the size of the letters in the reverse inscriptions. 1832 varieties are distinguished by whether the 2 in the date has a curved base or square base and by the number of stars on the reverse. 1834 varieties are distinguished by whether the 4 has a serif at its far right.

Date	Mintage	F-12	VF-20	XF-40	MS-60
1813	95,428	2,400	2,750	3,800	7,800
1814/13	15,454	2,500	2,800	3,500	10,000
1815	635	27,000	33,000	70,000	—
Note: 1815, private sale, Jan. 1994, MS-61, $150,000					
1818	48,588	2,475	3,100	4,000	8,250
1819	51,723	9,600	16,500	275,000	62,000
1820 curved-base 2, small letters	263,806	2,600	3,000	4,500	11,000
1820 curved-base 2, large letters	Inc. above	2,600	3,000	4,150	20,000
1820 square-base 2	Inc. above	2,600	3,000	3,800	14,000
1821	34,641	7,000	15,000	23,000	70,000
1822 3 known	—	—	—	—	1,000,000
Note: 1822, private sale, 1993, VF-30, $1,000,000.					
1823	14,485	2,500	3,400	5,000	16,000
1824	17,340	5,000	10,000	16,000	38,000
1825/21	29,060	5,150	9,500	12,000	38,000
1825/24	Inc. above	—	—	250,000	350,000
Note: 1825/4, Bowers & Merena, March 1989, XF, $148,500.					
1826	18,069	4,000	7,500	9,300	32,000
1827	24,913	6,000	10,000	12,250	34,000
1828/7	28,029	15,000	27,500	41,000	125,000
Note: 1828/7, Bowers & Merena, June 1989, XF, $20,900.					
1828	Inc. above	6,000	13,000	21,000	7,000
1829 large planchet	57,442	15,000	27,500	50,000	135,000
Note: 1829 large planchet, Superior, July 1985, MS-65, $104,500.					
1829 small planchet	Inc. above	37,500	50,000	82,500	140,000
Note: 1829 small planchet, private sale, 1992 (XF-45), $89,000.					
1830 small "5D."	126,351	14,500	17,500	21,000	40,000
1830 large "5D."	Inc. above	14,500	17,500	21,000	40,000
1831	140,594	14,500	17,500	21,000	42,500
1832 curved-base 2, 12 stars	157,487	50,000	80,000	135,000	—
1832 square-base 2, 13 stars	Inc. above	14,500	17,500	21,000	40,000

Date	Mintage	F-12	VF-20	XF-40	MS-60
1833	193,630	14,500	17,500	21,000	40,000
1834 plain 4	50,141	14,500	17,500	21,000	40,000
1834 crosslet 4	Inc. above	14,500	17,500	21,000	40,000

Classic Head. Classic head, left, within circle of stars. No motto above eagle.

KM# 57 Designer: William Kneass. **Diameter:** 22.5 **Weight:** 8.3600 g. **Composition:** 0.8990 Gold, 0.2416 oz. AGW. **Notes:** 1834 varieties are distinguished by whether the 4 has a serif at its far right.

Date	Mintage	VF-20	XF-40	AU-50	MS-60	MS-65
1834 plain 4	658,028	390	550	950	3,000	48,000
1834 crosslet 4	Inc. above	1,650	2,900	6,000	20,000	—
1835	371,534	390	560	1,000	3,150	70,000
1836	553,147	390	550	1,000	2,950	70,000
1837	207,121	390	585	1,200	3,500	75,000
1838	286,588	390	5,500	1,000	3,700	58,000
1838C	17,179	2,200	4,000	13,000	38,500	—
1838D	20,583	2,000	3,850	9,000	25,000	—

Coronet Head. Coronet head, left, within circle of stars. No motto above eagle.

KM# 69 Designer: Christian Gobrecht. **Diameter:** 21.6 **Weight:** 8.3590 g. **Composition:** 0.9000 Gold, 0.2419 oz. AGW. **Notes:** Varieties for the 1842 Philadelphia strikes are distinguished by the size of the letters in the reverse inscriptions. Varieties for the 1842-C and -D strikes are distinguished by the size of the numerals in the date. Varieties for the 1843-O strikes are distinguished by the size of the letters in the reverse inscriptions.

Date	Mintage	F-12	VF-20	XF-40	MS-60	Prf-65
1839	118,143	250	275	480	4,000	—
1839/8 curved date	Inc. above	275	325	700	2,250	—
1839C	17,205	1,250	2,300	2,900	24,000	—
1839D	18,939	1,125	2,200	3,200	22,000	—
1840	137,382	200	230	360	3,700	—
1840C	18,992	1,200	2,200	3,000	26,000	—
1840D	22,896	1,200	2,200	3,000	16,000	— —
1840O	40,120	200	365	875	11,000	—
1841	15,833	200	400	875	5,500	—
1841C	21,467	1,200	1,850	2,400	20,000	—
1841D	30,495	1,400	1,800	2,350	15,000	—
1841O 2 known	50	—	—	—	—	—
1842 small letters	27,578	200	345	1,100	—	—
1842 large letters	Inc. above	350	750	2,000	11,000	—
1842C small date	28,184	4,500	10,000	23,000	110,000	—
1842C large date	Inc. above	900	1,800	2,200	18,000	—
1842D small date	59,608	1,000	2,000	2,300	15,000	—
1842D large date	Inc. above	1,400	2,350	6,500	48,000	—
1842O	16,400	550	1,000	3,400	22,000	—
1843	611,205	200	230	330	1,850	—
1843C	44,201	1,250	1,850	2,500	14,000	—
1843D	98,452	1,250	1,950	2,600	13,000	—
1843O small letters	19,075	300	660	1,700	26,000	—
1843O large letters	82,000	200	265	1,175	12,000	—
1844	340,330	200	230	330	2,000	—
1844C	23,631	1,300	1,900	3,000	24,000	—
1844D	88,982	1,500	1,950	2,400	12,000	—
1844O	364,600	220	250	375	4,700	—
1845	417,099	200	235	260	2,000	—
1845D	90,629	1,300	1,900	2,400	12,500	—
1845O	41,000	235	415	800	9,900	—
1846	395,942	200	230	330	2,400	—
1846C	12,995	1,350	1,900	3,000	24,000	—
1846D	80,294	1,250	1,800	2,400	13,000	—
1846O	58,000	215	375	1,000	11,500	—
1847	915,981	200	230	250	1,650	—
1847C	84,151	1,350	1,800	2,400	13,000	—
1847D	64,405	1,400	2,000	4,000	10,000	—

Date	Mintage	F-12	VF-20	XF-40	MS-60	Prf-65
1847O	12,000	550	2,200	6,750	28,000	—
1848	260,775	200	230	275	1,500	—
1848C	64,472	1,400	1,900	2,250	19,250	—
1848D	47,465	1,450	2,000	2,350	14,500	—
1849	133,070	200	230	280	2,800	—
1849C	64,823	1,500	1,900	2,400	14,000	—
1849D	39,036	1,550	2,000	2,600	16,500	—
1850	64,491	200	300	625	4,250	—
1850C	63,591	1,350	1,850	2,300	14,000	—
1850D	43,984	1,450	1,950	2,500	33,000	—
1851	377,505	200	230	250	2,800	—
1851C	49,176	1,300	1,900	2,350	17,500	—
1851D	62,710	1,400	1,950	2,400	15,000	—
1851O	41,000	280	590	1,500	13,000	—
1852	573,901	200	230	260	1,400	—
1852C	72,574	1,350	1,900	2,450	7,750	—
1852D	91,584	1,450	2,000	2,450	13,000	—
1853	305,770	200	230	250	1,400	—
1853C	65,571	1,500	1,950	2,350	8,500	—
1853D	89,678	1,550	2,000	2,500	11,000	—
1854	160,675	200	230	260	2,000	—
1854C	39,283	1,400	1,900	2,300	14,000	—
1854D	56,413	1,400	1,875	2,200	11,500	—
1854O	46,000	225	300	525	8,250	—
1854S	268	—	—	—	—	—

Note: 1854S, Bowers & Merena, Oct. 1982, AU-55, $170,000.

Date	Mintage	F-12	VF-20	XF-40	MS-60	Prf-65
1855	117,098	200	230	250	1,800	—
1855C	39,788	1,400	1,900	2,300	16,000	—
1855D	22,432	1,500	1,950	2,400	19,000	—
1855O	11,100	315	675	2,100	20,000	—
1855S	61,000	200	390	1,000	15,500	—
1856	197,990	200	230	240	2,300	—
1856C	28,457	1,450	1,875	2,400	20,000	—
1856D	19,786	1,475	1,950	2,600	15,000	—
1856O	10,000	370	650	1,600	14,000	—
1856S	105,100	200	300	700	6,750	—
1857	98,188	200	230	260	1,600	123,500
1857C	31,360	1,400	1,900	2,500	9,500	—
1857D	17,046	1,500	2,000	2,650	14,500	—
1857O	13,000	340	640	1,400	15,000	—
1857S	87,000	200	300	700	11,000	—
1858	15,136	200	240	550	3,850	190,000
1858C	38,856	1,400	1,900	2,350	11,000	—
1858D	15,362	1,500	2,000	2,450	12,500	—
1858S	18,600	400	825	2,350	31,000	—
1859	16,814	200	325	625	7,000	—
1859C	31,847	1,400	1,900	2,450	16,000	—
1859D	10,366	1,600	2,150	2,600	16,000	—
1859S	13,220	615	1,800	4,150	30,000	—
1860	19,825	200	280	575	3,500	100,000
1860C	14,813	1,500	2,100	3,000	15,000	—
1860D	14,635	1,500	1,900	2,600	15,000	—
1860S	21,200	500	1,100	2,100	27,000	—
1861	688,150	200	230	245	1,450	100,000
1861C	6,879	1,500	2,400	3,900	25,000	—
1861D	1,597	3,000	4,700	7,000	50,000	—
1861S	18,000	500	1,100	4,500	36,500	—
1862	4,465	400	800	1,850	20,000	96,000
1862S	9,500	1,500	3,000	6,000	62,000	—
1863	2,472	450	1,200	3,750	27,500	90,000
1863S	17,000	600	1,450	4,100	35,500	—
1864	4,220	350	650	1,850	15,000	72,000
1864S	3,888	2,300	4,750	16,000	55,000	—
1865	1,295	500	1,450	4,100	20,000	82,500
1865S	27,612	475	1,400	2,400	20,000	—
1866S	9,000	750	1,750	4,000	40,000	—

Coronet Head. Coronet head, left, within circle of stars. "In God We Trust" above eagle.

KM# 101 Designer: Christian Gobrecht. **Diameter:** 21.6 **Weight:** 8.3590 g. **Composition:** 0.9000 Gold, 0.2419 oz. AGW. **Notes:** The 1873 "closed-3" and "open-3" varieties are known and are distinguished by the amount of space between the upper left and lower left serifs of the 3 in the date.

Date	Mintage	VF-20	XF-40	AU-50	MS-60	MS-63	MS-65	Prf-65
1866	6,730	800	1,650	3,500	16,500	—	—	70,000
1866S	34,920	900	2,600	8,800	25,000	—	—	—
1867	6,920	500	1,500	3,300	11,500	—	—	70,000
1867S	29,000	1,400	2,900	8,000	34,500	—	—	—
1868	5,725	650	1,000	3,500	11,500	—	—	70,000
1868S	52,000	400	1,550	4,000	20,000	—	—	—
1869	1,785	925	2,400	3,500	17,500	34,000	—	65,000
1869S	31,000	500	1,750	4,000	26,000	—	—	—
1870	4,035	800	2,000	2,850	18,000	—	—	75,000
1870CC	7,675	5,250	15,000	30,000	110,000	137,500	200,000	—
1870S	17,000	950	2,600	8,250	29,000	—	—	—
1871	3,230	900	1,700	3,300	12,500	—	—	70,000
1871CC	20,770	1,250	3,000	12,000	60,000	—	—	—
1871S	25,000	500	950	2,950	13,000	—	—	—
1872	1,690	850	1,925	3,000	15,000	18,000	—	60,000
1872CC	16,980	1,250	5,000	20,000	60,000	—	—	—
1872S	36,400	460	800	3,400	13,500	—	—	—
1873 closed 3	49,305	215	225	140	1,200	6,500	24,000	70,000
1873 open 3	63,200	215	220	350	850	3,650	—	—
1873CC	7,410	2,600	12,500	27,500	60,000	—	—	—
1873S	31,000	525	1,400	3,250	21,000	—	—	—
1874	3,508	660	1,675	2,500	13,000	26,000	—	66,000
1874CC	21,198	850	1,700	9,500	36,000	—	—	—
1874S	16,000	640	2,100	4,800	22,500	—	—	—
1875	220	34,000	45,000	60,000	190,000	—	—	185,000
1875CC	11,828	1,400	4,500	11,500	52,000	—	—	—
1875S	9,000	715	2,250	5,000	16,500	32,500	—	—
1876	1,477	1,100	2,500	4,125	11,000	14,500	55,000	60,000
1876CC	6,887	1,450	5,000	14,000	46,500	82,500	165,000	—
1876S	4,000	2,000	3,600	9,500	30,000	—	—	—
1877	1,152	900	2,750	4,000	13,750	29,000	—	75,000
1877CC	8,680	1,000	3,300	11,000	52,500	—	—	—
1877S	26,700	400	650	1,400	9,200	—	—	—
1878	131,740	215	220	240	425	2,000	—	50,000
1878CC	9,054	3,100	7,200	20,000	60,000	—	—	—
1878S	144,700	215	220	3,000	675	4,250	—	—
1879	301,950	215	220	225	400	2,000	12,000	55,000
1879CC	17,281	575	1,500	3,150	22,000	—	—	—
1879S	426,200	215	225	240	950	3,300	—	—
1880	3,166,436	215	225	225	235	840	7,500	54,000
1880CC	51,017	425	815	1,375	9,900	—	—	—
1880S	1,348,900	215	220	225	235	800	5,750	—
1881	5,708,802	215	220	225	235	775	4,800	54,000
1881/80	Inc. above	330	600	750	1,500	4,500	—	—
1881CC	13,886	550	1,500	7,000	22,500	60,000	—	—
1881S	969,000	215	220	225	235	775	7,150	—
1882	2,514,568	215	220	225	235	800	6,150	54,000
1882CC	82,817	415	625	900	7,500	40,000	—	—
1882S	969,000	215	220	225	235	800	4,500	—
1883	233,461	215	220	225	260	1,200	—	40,000
1883CC	12,958	460	1,100	3,200	18,000	—	—	—
1883S	83,200	215	240	315	1,000	2,950	—	—
1884	191,078	215	220	225	650	2,250	—	35,000
1884CC	16,402	550	975	3,000	17,000	—	—	—
1884S	177,000	215	220	225	345	2,000	—	—
1885	601,506	215	220	225	260	825	4,800	35,000
1885S	1,211,500	215	220	225	235	790	4,000	—
1886	388,432	215	220	225	235	1,125	5,600	44,000
1886S	3,268,000	215	220	225	235	815	4,500	—
1887	87	—	14,500	20,000	—	—	—	120,000
1887S	1,912,000	215	220	225	235	800	4,800	—
1888	18,296	215	230	300	550	1,500	—	29,000
1888S	293,900	215	220	320	1,200	4,000	—	—
1889	7,565	350	440	515	1,150	2,400	—	30,000
1890	4,328	400	475	550	2,200	6,500	—	27,000
1890CC	53,800	330	460	615	1,600	8,000	55,000	—
1891	61,413	215	220	230	450	1,900	5,400	20,000

Date	Mintage	VF-20	XF-40	AU-50	MS-60	MS-63	MS-65	Prf-65
1891CC	208,000	315	415	525	750	3,150	31,500	—
1892	753,572	215	220	225	235	880	7,000	30,000
1892CC	82,968	315	400	575	1,500	6,000	33,500	—
1892O	10,000	515	1,000	1,375	3,300	—	—	—
1892S	298,400	215	220	225	525	3,300	—	—
1893	1,528,197	215	220	225	235	800	3,900	34,000
1893CC	60,000	345	465	770	1,400	6,350	—	—
1893O	110,000	225	315	480	950	6,500	—	—
1893S	224,000	215	220	225	245	825	9,000	—
1894	957,955	215	220	225	235	800	2,600	35,000
1894O	16,600	200	360	570	1,300	5,500	—	—
1894S	55,900	240	375	575	2,900	10,000	—	—
1895	1,345,936	215	220	225	235	800	4,500	29,000
1895S	112,000	215	275	400	3,150	6,500	26,000	—
1896	59,063	215	220	225	235	9,750	4,500	30,000
1896S	155,400	215	240	300	1,150	6,000	24,500	—
1897	867,883	215	220	225	235	825	4,500	35,000
1897S	354,000	215	220	235	865	5,150	—	—
1898	633,495	215	220	225	235	885	6,000	30,000
1898S	1,397,400	215	220	225	230	950	—	—
1899	1,710,729	215	220	225	235	730	3,600	30,000
1899S	1,545,000	215	220	225	235	1,000	9,600	—
1900	1,405,730	215	220	225	235	790	3,600	30,000
1900S	329,000	215	220	230	245	900	14,000	—
1901	616,040	215	220	225	235	750	3,650	27,000
1901S	3,648,000	215	220	225	235	730	3,600	—
1902	172,562	215	220	225	235	730	4,400	27,000
1902S	939,000	215	220	225	235	730	3,600	—
1903	227,024	215	220	225	235	730	4,000	27,000
1903S	1,855,000	215	220	225	235	730	3,600	—
1904	392,136	215	220	225	235	730	3,600	27,000
1904S	97,000	215	240	285	900	3,850	9,600	—
1905	302,308	215	220	225	235	740	4,000	27,000
1905S	880,700	215	225	250	235	1,500	9,600	—
1906	348,820	215	220	225	235	745	3,600	26,000
1906D	320,000	215	220	225	235	930	3,200	—
1906S	598,000	215	220	230	240	900	4,400	—
1907	626,192	215	220	225	235	730	3,400	23,000
1907D	888,000	215	220	225	235	730	3,400	—
1908	421,874	215	220	225	235	730	3,400	—

Indian Head.

KM# 129 Designer: Bela Lyon Pratt. **Diameter:**
21.6 **Weight:** 8.3590 g. **Composition:** 0.9000 Gold,
0.2419 oz. AGW.

Date	Mintage	VF-20	XF-40	AU-50	MS-60	MS-63	MS-65	Prf-65
1908	578,012	330	355	385	460	4,350	25,000	25,500
1908D	148,000	330	355	385	460	4,350	27,500	—
1908S	82,000	330	415	430	1,275	4,350	24,000	—
1909	627,138	330	355	385	460	4,350	25,000	36,000
1909D	3,423,560	330	355	385	460	4,350	25,000	—
1909O	34,200	2,000	3,400	6,000	21,000	66,000	260,000	—
1909S	297,200	330	355	385	1,400	11,000	45,000	—
1910	604,250	330	355	385	460	4,350	25,000	37,000
1910D	193,600	330	355	385	460	4,350	42,500	—
1910S	770,200	330	355	385	1,000	6,000	44,000	—
1911	915,139	330	355	385	460	4,350	25,000	28,500
1911D	72,500	475	535	515	4,500	37,000	241,500	—
1911S	1,416,000	340	355	385	560	4,350	41,500	—
1912	790,144	330	355	385	460	4,350	25,000	28,500
1912S	392,000	330	365	400	1,700	13,500	93,500	—
1913	916,099	330	355	385	460	4,350	25,000	28,000
1913S	408,000	340	350	385	1,400	11,500	120,000	—
1914	247,125	330	355	385	460	4,350	25,000	28,500
1914D	247,000	335	355	385	460	4,350	26,000	—
1914S	263,000	340	365	400	1,375	13,500	100,000	—
1915	588,075	330	355	385	460	4,350	25,000	39,000
1915S	164,000	340	400	385	2,000	17,000	110,000	—
1916S	240,000	330	355	385	560	4,350	25,000	—
1929	662,000	4,200	9,600	10,500	13,250	17,500	45,000	—

$10 (EAGLE)

GOLD

Liberty Cap. Small eagle.

KM# 21 **Designer:** Robert Scot. **Diameter:** 33 **Weight:** 17.5000 g. **Composition:** 0.9160 Gold, 0.5154 oz. AGW.

Date	Mintage	F-12	VF-20	XF-40	MS-60
1795 13 leaves	5,583	18,000	24,000	33,000	70,000
1795 9 leaves	Inc. above	26,000	40,000	60,000	230,000
1796	4,146	23,000	27,500	38,000	80,000
1797 small eagle	3,615	30,000	38,000	45,000	185,000

Liberty Cap. Liberty cap on head, right, flanked by stars. Heraldic eagle.

KM# 30 **Designer:** Robert Scot. **Diameter:** 33 **Weight:** 17.5000 g. **Composition:** 0.9160 Gold, 0.5154 oz. AGW. **Notes:** The 1798/97 varieties are distinguished by the positioning of the stars on the obverse.

Date	Mintage	F-12	VF-20	XF-40	MS-60
1797 large eagle	10,940	9,000	11,000	14,000	40,000
1798/97 9 stars left, 4 right	900	11,000	19,000	29,000	100,000
1798/97 7 stars left, 6 right	842	23,000	30,000	65,000	
1799	37,449	8,000	10,000	12,500	31,000
1800	5,999	8,200	11,000	12,000	33,000
1801	44,344	8,200	11,000	12,000	29,000
1803	15,017	8,200	11,000	12,000	32,000
1804	3,757	9,500	11,500	14,000	38,000

Coronet Head. Old-style head, left, within circle of stars. No motto above eagle.

KM# 66.1 **Designer:** Christian Gobrecht. **Diameter:** 27 **Weight:** 16.7180 g. **Composition:** 0.9000 Gold, 0.4837 oz. AGW.

Date	Mintage	F-12	VF-20	XF-40	MS-60	Prf-65
1838	7,200	800	1,200	2,900	35,500	—
1839 large letters	38,248	800	1,150	1,950	32,000	—

Coronet Head. New-style head, left, within circle of stars. No motto above eagle.

KM# 66.2 **Designer:** Christian Gobrecht. **Diameter:** 27 **Weight:** 16.7180 g. **Composition:** 0.9000 Gold, 0.4837 oz. AGW. **Notes:** The 1842 varieties are distinguished by the size of the numerals in the date.

Date	Mintage	F-12	VF-20	XF-40	MS-60	Prf-65
1839 small letters	Inc. above	825	1,600	3,500	30,000	—
1840	47,338	410	435	650	10,500	—

Date	Mintage	F-12	VF-20	XF-40	MS-60	Prf-65
1841	63,131	410	435	500	9,500	—
1841O	2,500	1,400	2,400	5,000	30,000	—
1842 small date	81,507	410	435	650	16,500	—
1842 large date	Inc. above	410	435	475	9,500	—
1842O	27,400	410	450	500	22,500	—
1843	75,462	410	435	500	19,000	—
1843O	175,162	410	435	475	12,000	—
1844	6,361	800	1,350	2,900	16,750	—
1844O	118,700	410	435	475	15,000	—
1845	26,153	410	600	775	14,000	—
1845O	47,500	410	435	700	16,500	—
1846	20,095	435	625	900	20,000	—
1846O	81,780	410	435	770	14,750	—
1847	862,258	410	435	380	3,000	—
1847O	571,500	410	435	450	4,850	—
1848	145,484	410	435	450	4,300	—
1848O	38,850	410	525	1,050	14,000	—
1849	653,618	410	435	450	3,400	—
1849O	23,900	425	710	2,100	25,000	—
1850	291,451	410	435	450	3,600	—
1850O	57,500	410	440	880	—	—
1851	176,328	410	435	500	5,150	—
1851O	263,000	410	435	450	5,750	—
1852	263,106	410	435	370	5,000	—
1852O	18,000	425	650	1,100	19,000	—
1853	201,253	410	435	450	3,500	—
1853O	51,000	410	435	500	13,000	—
1854	54,250	410	435	450	6,000	—
1854O small date	52,500	410	435	675	11,000	—
1854O large date	Inc. above	420	475	875	—	—
1854S	123,826	410	435	450	5,500	—
1855	121,701	410	435	450	4,150	—
1855O	18,000	415	435	1,250	20,000	—
1855S	9,000	800	1,500	2,500	29,500	—
1856	60,490	410	435	450	4,500	—
1856O	14,500	425	725	1,250	10,000	—
1856S	68,000	410	435	515	8,500	—
1857	16,606	410	515	850	12,000	—
1857O	5,500	600	1,000	1,850	20,000	—
1857S	26,000	410	450	1,000	10,000	—
1858	2,521	3,000	5,200	8,200	35,000	—
1858O	20,000	410	460	750	10,000	—
1858S	11,800	900	1,600	3,100	34,000	—
1859	16,093	410	435	800	10,500	—
1859O	2,300	2,000	4,000	8,200	47,500	—
1859S	7,000	1,200	1,800	4,500	40,000	—
1860	15,105	410	475	800	8,000	—
1860O	11,100	425	600	1,300	8,250	—
1860S	5,000	1,400	3,250	6,100	40,500	—
1861	113,233	410	435	450	4,000	—
1861S	15,500	690	1,600	2,950	32,500	—
1862	10,995	410	550	1,200	13,500	—
1862S	12,500	700	2,000	3,000	37,000	—
1863	1,248	2,400	3,650	10,000	42,500	—
1863S	10,000	700	1,600	3,350	24,000	—
1864	3,580	775	1,600	4,500	18,000	—
1864S	2,500	2,600	5,100	13,000	50,000	—
1865	4,005	900	1,950	3,500	32,000	—
1865S	16,700	1,700	5,500	12,000	45,000	—
1865S /inverted 186	—	1,300	3,000	6,100	50,000	—
1866S	8,500	1,000	2,800	3,800	44,000	—

Coronet Head. New-style head, left, within circle of stars. "In God We Trust" above eagle.

KM# 102 Designer: Christian Gobrecht.
Diameter: 27 **Weight:** 16.7180 g. **Composition:**
0.9000 Gold, 0.4837 oz. AGW. **Notes:** The 1873
"closed-3" and "open-3" varieties are distinguished
by the amount of space between the upper left and
lower left serifs of the 3 in the date.

Date	Mintage	VF-20	XF-40	AU-50	MS-60	MS-63	MS-65	Prf-65
1866	3,780	850	1,800	5,000	17,000	—	—	75,000
1866S	11,500	1,550	4,000	8,000	26,000	—	—	—
1867	3,140	1,500	2,600	5,000	26,000	—	—	75,000
1867S	9,000	2,000	6,000	12,000	40,000	—	—	—

Date	Mintage	VF-20	XF-40	AU-50	MS-60	MS-63	MS-65	Prf-65
1868	10,655	550	800	2,000	18,000	—	—	60,000
1868S	13,500	1,300	2,600	4,000	24,000	—	—	—
1869	1,855	1,600	3,000	6,000	36,000	—	—	—
1869S	6,430	1,600	2,700	6,250	25,000	—	—	—
1870	4,025	850	1,500	2,500	18,000	—	—	60,000
1870CC	5,908	10,000	22,000	42,000	90,000	—	—	—
1870S	8,000	1,300	3,000	7,000	34,000	—	—	—
1871	1,820	1,600	3,000	5,000	25,000	—	—	75,000
1871CC	8,085	2,600	6,000	21,000	60,000	—	—	—
1871S	16,500	1,300	1,700	6,000	30,000	—	—	—
1872	1,650	2,400	3,600	11,000	18,000	33,000	—	60,000
1872CC	4,600	3,150	11,000	24,000	60,000	—	—	—
1872S	17,300	550	950	1,800	22,000	—	—	—
1873 closed 3	825	5,000	10,000	17,500	55,000	—	—	60,000
1873CC	4,543	6,000	12,500	28,000	58,000	—	—	—
1873S	12,000	950	2,350	5,100	25,000	—	—	—
1874	53,160	290	425	450	2,100	8,750	—	60,000
1874CC	16,767	950	3,100	10,500	40,000	—	—	—
1874S	10,000	1,150	3,250	7,250	4,000	—	—	—
1875	120	40,000	59,000	80,000	95,000	—	—	185,000

Note: 1875, Akers, Aug. 1990, Proof, $115,000.

Date	Mintage	VF-20	XF-40	AU-50	MS-60	MS-63	MS-65	Prf-65
1875CC	7,715	4,250	11,000	25,000	65,000	—	—	—
1876	732	3,500	6,250	17,000	55,000	—	—	60,000
1876CC	4,696	2,400	7,950	23,000	50,000	—	—	—
1876S	5,000	1,475	2,000	6,500	40,000	—	—	—
1877	817	2,650	5,750	9,250	—	—	—	—
1877CC	3,332	2,600	6,400	15,000	48,000	—	—	—
1877S	17,000	500	850	2,200	23,000	—	—	—
1878	73,800	420	425	450	1,000	5,000	—	60,000
1878CC	3,244	4,000	10,000	16,000	47,000	—	—	—
1878S	26,100	475	615	2,150	16,000	—	—	—
1879	384,770	420	425	450	665	2,850	—	50,000
1879/78	Inc. above	420	450	800	1,250	2,000	—	—
1879CC	1,762	9,500	15,000	26,000	60,000	—	—	—
1879O	1,500	2,300	3,750	10,000	28,750	—	—	—
1879S	224,000	420	425	450	1,100	7,750	—	—
1880	1,644,876	420	425	450	465	2,250	—	45,000
1880CC	11,190	590	900	1,800	14,500	—	—	—
1880O	9,200	450	800	1,400	13,000	—	—	—
1880S	506,250	420	425	450	465	3,300	—	—
1881	3,877,260	420	425	450	465	1,200	—	45,000
1881CC	24,015	515	800	950	7,000	20,000	—	—
1881O	8,350	550	820	1,600	6,750	—	—	—
1881S	970,000	420	425	450	485	—	—	—
1882	2,324,400	420	425	450	465	1,200	—	42,000
1882CC	6,764	950	1,300	3,000	13,000	35,000	—	—
1882O	10,820	420	575	1,200	7,700	16,750	—	—
1882S	132,000	420	425	450	465	4,200	—	—
1883	208,740	420	425	450	465	2,400	—	42,000
1883CC	12,000	575	915	2,600	14,000	35,000	—	—
1883O	800	3,300	7,200	10,500	33,500	—	—	—
1883S	38,000	420	425	450	1,350	13,000	—	—
1884	76,005	420	425	450	750	4,000	—	46,000
1884CC	9,925	600	1,100	2,250	13,000	35,000	—	—
1884S	124,250	420	425	450	575	6,500	—	—
1885	253,527	420	425	450	465	4,200	—	43,000
1885S	228,000	420	425	450	465	4,300	22,000	—
1886	236,160	420	425	450	465	1,800	—	41,000
1886S	826,000	420	425	450	465	1,500	—	—
1887	53,680	420	425	450	800	4,750	—	37,000
1887S	817,000	420	425	450	465	1,950	—	—
1888	132,996	420	425	450	850	5,700	—	38,500
1888O	21,335	420	425	450	675	4,500	—	—
1888S	648,700	420	425	450	465	2,700	—	—
1889	4,485	600	700	1,100	2,700	7,200	—	43,000
1889S	425,400	420	425	450	465	1,500	22,000	—
1890	58,043	420	425	450	825	5,200	22,000	37,500
1890CC	17,500	420	450	650	2,000	13,500	—	—
1891	91,868	420	425	450	465	1,900	—	32,500
1891CC	103,732	515	575	770	1,350	6,000	—	—
1892	797,552	420	425	450	465	1,300	13,000	38,000
1892CC	40,000	475	600	825	3,800	9,000	22,000	—
1892O	28,688	420	425	450	465	6,000	—	—
1892S	115,500	420	425	450	465	4,500	—	—
1893	1,840,895	420	425	450	465	850	—	36,000
1893CC	14,000	550	900	1,800	8,500	18,000	—	—
1893O	17,000	420	425	450	625	5,300	—	—
1893S	141,350	420	425	450	500	4,400	—	—
1894	2,470,778	420	425	450	465	1,400	22,000	35,000

Date	Mintage	VF-20	XF-40	AU-50	MS-60	MS-63	MS-65	Prf-65
1894O	107,500	420	425	475	1,200	5,250	—	—
1894S	25,000	420	450	900	3,500	8,800	—	—
1895	567,826	420	425	450	465	1,400	22,000	33,000
1895O	98,000	420	425	475	525	4,800	—	—
1895S	49,000	420	425	700	2,250	9,500	—	—
1896	76,348	420	425	450	465	2,100	—	31,500
1896S	123,750	420	425	485	2,500	11,000	—	—
1897	1,000,159	420	425	450	465	1,400	22,000	35,000
1897O	42,500	420	425	450	750	4,200	—	—
1897S	234,750	420	425	450	870	5,000	—	—
1898	812,197	420	425	450	465	1,450	22,000	35,000
1898S	473,600	420	425	450	465	4,250	—	—
1899	1,262,305	420	425	450	465	1,400	22,000	31,000
1899O	37,047	420	425	450	550	4,750	—	—
1899S	841,000	420	425	450	465	3,250	—	—
1900	293,960	420	425	450	465	1,400	22,000	30,500
1900S	81,000	420	425	450	850	5,200	—	—
1901	1,718,825	420	425	450	465	1,400	22,000	30,500
1901O	72,041	420	425	450	465	3,700	—	—
1901S	2,812,750	420	425	450	465	1,400	22,000	—
1902	82,513	420	425	450	465	2,450	—	30,500
1902S	469,500	420	425	450	465	1,400	22,000	—
1903	125,926	420	425	450	465	2,500	—	30,000
1903O	112,771	420	425	450	465	3,250	—	—
1903S	538,000	420	425	450	465	1,400	22,000	—
1904	162,038	420	425	450	465	2,400	—	31,500
1904O	108,950	420	425	450	465	3,700	—	—
1905	201,078	420	425	450	465	1,450	22,000	30,000
1905S	369,250	420	425	450	1,100	4,500	—	—
1906	165,497	420	425	450	465	2,275	22,000	30,000
1906D	981,000	420	425	450	465	1,450	22,000	—
1906O	86,895	420	425	450	470	3,400	—	—
1906S	457,000	420	425	450	515	4,400	22,000	—
1907	1,203,973	420	425	450	465	1,400	—	30,000
1907D	1,030,000	420	425	450	465	1,400	—	—
1907S	210,500	420	425	450	600	4,650	—	—

Indian Head. No motto next to eagle.

KM# 125 **Designer:** Augustus Saint-Gaudens. **Diameter:** 27 **Weight:** 16.7180 g. **Composition:** 0.9000 Gold, 0.4837 oz. AGW. **Notes:** 1907 varieties are distinguished by whether the edge is rolled or wired, and whether the legend "E Pluribus Unum" has periods between each word.

Date	Mintage	VF-20	XF-40	AU-50	MS-60	MS-63	MS-65	Prf-65
1907 wire edge, periods before and after legend	500	9,500	14,900	16,900	22,000	36,500	65,000	—
1907 same, without stars on edge, unique	—	—	—	—	—	—	—	—
1907 rolled edge, periods	42	26,000	38,500	49,000	66,500	98,500	250,000	—
1907 without periods	239,406	470	480	530	625	2,950	9,800	—
1908 without motto	33,500	470	480	530	735	4,650	14,500	—
1908D without motto	210,000	475	485	535	635	6,250	38,500	—

Indian Head. "In God We Trust" left of eagle.

KM# 130 **Designer:** Augustus Saint-Gaudens. **Diameter:** 27 **Weight:** 16.7180 g. **Composition:** 0.9000 Gold, 0.4837 oz. AGW.

Date	Mintage	VF-20	XF-40	AU-50	MS-60	MS-63	MS-65	Prf-65
1908	341,486	470	480	530	595	4,450	14,500	52,500
1908D	836,500	475	485	540	625	6,850	29,000	—
1908S	59,850	485	495	620	2,950	8,500	25,500	—
1909	184,863	470	480	530	595	2,450	10,000	54,500
1909D	121,540	475	485	535	675	4,150	34,500	—
1909S	292,350	475	485	535	675	4,350	13,900	—
1910	318,704	470	480	530	595	2,350	8,500	54,500

Date	Mintage	VF-20	XF-40	AU-50	MS-60	MS-63	MS-65	Prf-65
1910D	2,356,640	465	475	525	595	2,185	8,600	—
1910S	811,000	475	485	535	675	7,250	55,000	—
1911	505,595	465	475	525	590	2,185	8,600	52,500
1911D	30,100	595	675	950	4,200	21,500	120,000	—
1911S	51,000	530	555	645	1,050	7,750	14,500	—
1912	405,083	470	480	530	595	2,350	9,350	52,500
1912S	300,000	475	485	535	675	5,300	48,500	—
1913	442,071	470	480	530	595	2,350	8,400	52,500
1913S	66,000	525	600	775	3,900	27,500	100,000	—
1914	151,050	470	480	530	595	2,400	9,000	52,500
1914D	343,500	470	480	530	595	2,450	15,500	—
1914S	208,000	480	490	540	715	6,350	32,500	—
1915	351,075	470	480	530	595	2,350	8,500	55,000
1915S	59,000	600	725	775	3,150	14,500	65,000	—
1916S	138,500	495	510	570	675	4,850	18,500	—
1920S	126,500	7,800	11,000	14,500	28,500	69,000	275,000	—
1926	1,014,000	465	475	525	575	1,485	5,500	—
1930S	96,000	5,500	7,000	8,500	14,500	31,500	67,500	—
1932	4,463,000	465	475	525	575	1,485	5,500	—
1933	312,500	110,000	140,000	150,000	185,000	245,000	650,000	—

$20 (DOUBLE EAGLE)

GOLD

Liberty. Coronet head, left, within circle of stars. "Twenty D." below eagle, no motto above eagle.

KM# 74.1 **Designer:** James B. Longacre. **Diameter:** 34 **Weight:** 33.4360 g. **Composition:** 0.9000 Gold, 0.9675 oz. AGW.

Date	Mintage	VF-20	XF-40	AU-50	MS-60	MS-63	MS-65	Prf-65
1849 unique, in Smithsonian collection	1	—	—	—	—	—	—	—
1850	1,170,261	905	1,450	3,000	8,500	43,500	175,000	—
1850O	141,000	1,250	3,500	9,800	45,000	—	—	—
1851	2,087,155	895	985	1,185	3,850	19,500	—	—
1851O	315,000	1,100	2,250	3,650	23,000	58,500	—	—
1852	2,053,026	895	985	1,000	3,950	17,500	—	—
1852O	190,000	1,250	2,650	3,800	22,500	—	—	—
1853	1,261,326	895	985	1,000	5,000	27,500	—	—
1853/2	Inc. above	975	2,250	6,850	33,500	—	—	—
1853O	71,000	1,150	3,650	4,850	32,500	65,000	—	—
1854	757,899	895	985	1,050	6,000	26,500	—	—
1854	Inc. above	1,250	2,350	6,000	—	—	—	—
1854O	3,250	95,000	225,000	365,000	425,000	—	—	—
1854S	141,468	975	1,325	3,000	6,000	15,500	52,500	—
1855	364,666	895	985	1,450	8,250	65,000	—	—
1855O	8,000	3,650	19,500	24,500	110,000	—	—	—
1855S	879,675	875	985	1,400	7,200	19,500	—	—
1856	329,878	895	985	1,450	8,400	24,500	—	—
1856O	2,250	97,500	165,000	300,000	525,000	750,000	—	—
1856S	1,189,750	875	985	1,300	5,900	15,000	30,000	—
1857	439,375	895	985	1,085	3,400	26,500	—	—
1857O	30,000	1,300	2,950	6,400	31,000	115,000	—	—
1857S	970,500	875	985	1,200	4,500	7,750	14,000	—
1858	211,714	950	1,100	1,450	5,500	34,500	—	—
1858O	35,250	1,950	3,850	7,500	42,000	—	—	—
1858S	846,710	875	1,000	1,700	8,500	—	—	—
1859	43,597	950	2,450	4,400	28,000	—	—	280,000
1859O	9,100	6,400	16,500	44,000	110,000	—	—	—
1859S	636,445	875	985	1,650	5,000	35,000	—	—

Date	Mintage	VF-20	XF-40	AU-50	MS-60	MS-63	MS-65	Prf-65
1860	577,670	875	985	1,085	4,650	18,000	63,500	275,000
1860O	6,600	3,650	14,500	24,000	100,000	—	—	—
1860S	544,950	895	1,075	1,600	7,350	18,500	48,000	—
1861	2,976,453	875	985	1,060	2,750	12,850	41,500	275,000
1861O	17,741	5,650	17,500	24,000	88,000	—	—	—
1861S	768,000	895	1,125	2,250	10,500	31,500	—	—

Liberty. Coronet head, left, within circle of stars. Paquet design, "Twenty D." below eagle.

KM# 93   Weight: 33.4360 g. **Composition:** 0.9000 Gold, 0.9675 oz. AGW. **Notes:** In 1861 the reverse was redesigned by Anthony C. Paquet, but it was withdrawn soon after its release. The letters in the inscriptions on the Paquet-reverse variety are taller than on the regular reverse.

Date	Mintage	VF-20	XF-40	AU-50	MS-60	MS-63	MS-65	Prf-65
1861 2 Known	—	—	—	—	—	—	—	—

Note: 1861 Paquet reverse, Bowers & Merena, Nov. 1988, MS-67, $660,000.

Date	Mintage	VF-20	XF-40	AU-50	MS-60	MS-63	MS-65	Prf-65
1861S	—	19,500	52,500	92,500	275,000	—	—	—

Note: Included in mintage of 1861S, KM#74.1

Liberty. Longacre design resumed.

KM# A74.1   Weight: 33.4360 g. **Composition:** 0.9000 Gold, 0.9675 oz. AGW.

Date	Mintage	VF-20	XF-40	AU-50	MS-60	MS-63	MS-65	Prf-65
1862	92,133	1,000	2,250	4,900	16,500	34,000	—	300,000
1862S	854,173	860	1,350	2,100	12,400	36,000	—	—
1863	142,790	875	1,900	3,950	19,500	39,500	—	300,000
1863S	966,570	860	1,050	1,950	7,350	32,500	—	—
1864	204,285	875	1,150	2,450	14,500	40,000	—	300,000
1864S	793,660	860	1,050	1,950	8,600	32,000	—	—
1865	351,200	875	975	1,350	6,200	26,000	—	300,000
1865S	1,042,500	860	950	1,150	4,200	9,000	19,500	—
1866S	Inc. below	3,400	13,500	44,500	60,000	—	—	—

Liberty. Coronet head, left, within circle of stars. "Twenty D." below eagle. "In God We Trust" above eagle.

KM# 74.2 **Designer:** James B. Longacre. **Diameter:** 34 **Weight:** 33.4360 g. **Composition:** 0.9000 Gold, 0.9675 oz. AGW. **Notes:** The 1873 "closed-3" and "open-3" varieties are known and are distinguished by the amount of space between the upper left and lower left serif in the 3 in the date.

Date	Mintage	VF-20	XF-40	AU-50	MS-60	MS-63	MS-65	Prf-65
1866	698,775	845	950	1,750	6,950	28,500	—	—
1866S	842,250	845	985	2,100	15,500	—	—	—
1867	251,065	845	975	1,200	3,250	30,000	—	—
1867S	920,750	845	985	1,900	15,000	—	—	—
1868	98,600	885	1,250	2,250	11,500	50,000	—	—
1868S	837,500	845	1,000	1,650	10,000	—	—	—
1869	175,155	855	1,075	1,600	6,800	22,750	—	—
1869S	686,750	845	985	1,350	7,000	45,000	—	—
1870	155,185	865	1,110	1,925	9,250	50,000	—	—
1870CC	3,789	125,000	195,000	360,000	700,000	—	—	—
1870S	982,000	845	975	1,225	5,450	34,000	—	—
1871	80,150	855	1,075	1,800	4,500	24,500	—	—
1871CC	17,387	9,500	19,500	40,000	97,500	300,000	650,000	—
1871S	928,000	845	910	935	4,750	22,000	—	—
1872	251,880	845	940	860	3,000	25,000	—	—
1872CC	26,900	2,375	5,450	7,000	33,000	—	—	—
1872S	780,000	845	940	860	3,000	21,000	—	—
1873 closed 3	Est. 208,925	845	1,000	1,100	2,600	—	—	—
1873 open 3	Est. 1,500,900	845	940	860	990	12,000	—	—
1873CC	22,410	2,900	4,750	8,000	36,000	100,000	—	—
1873S closed 3	1,040,600	845	910	860	1,800	23,000	—	—
1873S open 3	Inc. above	845	940	—	—	—	—	—
1874	366,800	845	940	860	1,400	22,000	—	—
1874CC	115,085	1,400	1,950	2,650	9,200	—	—	—
1874S	1,214,000	845	910	860	1,700	28,000	—	—
1875	295,740	845	940	860	1,000	13,000	—	—
1875CC	111,151	1,300	1,550	1,850	3,000	19,000	—	—
1875S	1,230,000	845	910	860	1,100	18,000	—	—
1876	583,905	845	940	810	975	11,500	70,500	185,000
1876CC	138,441	1,300	1,500	1,900	5,750	37,000	—	—
1876S	1,597,000	845	910	860	990	12,000	—	—

Liberty. Coronet head, left, within circle of stars. "Twenty Dollars" below eagle.

KM# 74.3 **Weight:** 33.4360 g. **Composition:** 0.9000 Gold, 0.9675 oz. AGW.

Date	Mintage	VF-20	XF-40	AU-50	MS-60	MS-63	MS-65	Prf-65
1877	397,670	805	905	940	850	5,250	—	—
1877CC	42,565	1,500	1,900	2,600	17,500	—	—	—
1877S	1,735,000	795	840	890	875	12,500	—	—

Date	Mintage	VF-20	XF-40	AU-50	MS-60	MS-63	MS-65	Prf-65
1878	543,645	815	905	940	850	5,600	—	—
1878CC	13,180	2,450	3,950	8,400	30,000	—	—	—
1878S	1,739,000	795	815	825	850	22,000	—	—
1879	207,630	825	905	890	1,000	14,000	—	—
1879CC	10,708	3,000	4,850	8,850	34,000	—	—	—
1879O	2,325	12,500	21,500	32,000	75,000	120,000	—	—
1879S	1,223,800	795	815	825	1,200	—	—	—
1880	51,456	825	905	955	3,000	16,500	—	—
1880S	836,000	795	815	825	950	16,000	—	—
1881	2,260	6,800	12,500	21,500	79,000	—	—	105,000
1881S	727,000	795	815	825	900	17,500	—	—
1882	630	11,500	29,500	50,000	110,000	135,000	—	—
1882CC	39,140	1,350	1,750	2,200	7,000	—	—	—
1882S	1,125,000	795	815	825	850	16,000	—	—
1883 proof only	92	—	—	14,000	—	—	—	—
1883CC	59,962	1,350	1,600	2,000	4,800	21,500	—	—
1883S	1,189,000	795	815	825	850	9,000	—	—
1884 proof only	71	—	—	15,000	—	—	—	150,000
1884CC	81,139	1,250	1,550	1,900	3,100	—	—	—
1884S	916,000	795	815	825	850	7,000	—	—
1885	828	8,800	13,850	12,000	35,000	—	—	—
1885CC	9,450	2,500	3,850	6,000	13,000	—	—	—
1885S	683,500	795	815	825	850	7,000	—	—
1886	1,106	12,500	29,500	42,500	73,500	140,000	—	96,000
1887	121	—	—	16,500	—	—	—	142,500
1887S	283,000	795	815	825	850	14,000	—	—
1888	226,266	795	815	825	850	4,500	32,000	—
1888S	859,600	795	815	825	850	5,500	—	—
1889	44,111	935	1,035	1,130	990	12,800	—	93,500
1889CC	30,945	1,500	1,750	2,200	4,700	17,500	—	—
1889S	774,700	795	815	825	850	12,500	—	—
1890	75,995	795	840	840	850	6,500	—	27,000
1890CC	91,209	1,250	1,450	2,000	4,750	22,000	—	—
1890S	802,750	795	815	840	850	8,800	—	—
1891	1,442	3,500	5,750	9,500	40,000	—	—	62,500
1891CC	5,000	4,800	9,000	9,500	20,000	45,000	—	—
1891S	1,288,125	795	815	840	850	3,500	—	—
1892	4,523	1,350	2,250	2,600	6,000	20,000	—	55,000
1892CC	27,265	1,350	1,750	2,200	5,000	31,000	—	—
1892S	930,150	795	815	840	850	4,000	—	—
1893	344,339	795	830	840	850	2,600	—	60,000
1893CC	18,402	1,550	1,900	2,500	5,000	18,000	—	—
1893S	996,175	760	770	785	815	3,000	11,500	—
1894	1,368,990	760	770	785	815	1,700	—	55,000
1894S	1,048,550	760	770	785	815	2,600	—	—
1895	1,114,656	760	770	785	815	1,300	13,000	54,000
1895S	1,143,500	760	770	785	815	2,500	15,000	—
1896	792,663	760	770	785	815	2,000	13,000	49,000
1896S	1,403,925	760	770	785	815	2,400	—	—
1897	1,383,261	760	770	785	815	1,350	—	55,000
1897S	1,470,250	760	770	785	815	1,400	14,000	—
1898	170,470	765	800	835	1,325	4,500	—	96,000
1898S	2,575,175	760	770	785	815	1,300	11,000	—
1899	1,669,384	760	770	785	815	1,100	8,500	49,000
1899S	2,010,300	760	770	785	815	1,900	12,500	—
1900	1,874,584	760	770	785	815	1,150	6,000	49,000
1900S	2,459,500	760	770	785	815	2,300	—	—
1901	111,526	760	770	785	815	1,100	6,500	—
1901S	1,596,000	760	770	785	815	3,850	—	—
1902	31,254	860	970	1,050	1,400	10,750	—	94,000
1902S	1,753,625	760	770	785	815	4,000	—	—
1903	287,428	760	770	785	815	1,100	6,000	51,500
1903S	954,000	760	770	785	815	1,800	12,000	—
1904	6,256,797	760	770	785	815	1,135	4,650	94,000
1904S	5,134,175	760	770	785	815	1,100	6,600	—
1905	59,011	765	790	825	1,250	15,500	—	110,000
1905S	1,813,000	760	770	785	815	3,850	16,500	—
1906	69,690	765	775	790	915	7,400	22,500	90,000
1906D	620,250	760	770	785	815	2,350	15,000	—
1906S	2,065,750	760	770	785	815	2,300	19,000	—
1907	1,451,864	760	770	785	815	1,100	7,500	—
1907D	842,250	760	770	785	815	2,350	7,000	—
1907S	2,165,800	760	770	785	815	2,400	17,000	—

Saint-Gaudens. Roman numerals in date. No motto below eagle.

KM# 126 **Designer:** Augustus Saint-Gaudens. **Diameter:** 34 **Weight:** 33.4360 g. **Composition:** 0.9000 Gold, 0.9675 oz. AGW.

Date	Mintage	VF-20	XF-40	AU-50	MS-60	MS-63	MS-65	Prf-65
MCMVII (1907) high relief, unique, AU-55, $150,000	—	—	—	—	—	—	—	—
MCMVII (1907) high relief, wire rim	11,250	7,500	8,500	10,800	13,500	21,700	46,500	—
MCMVII (1907) high relief, flat rim	Inc. above	7,750	8,850	11,250	15,000	24,650	49,500	—

Saint-Gaudens. Arabic numerals in date. No motto below eagle.

KM# 127 **Designer:** Augustus Saint-Gaudens. **Diameter:** 34 **Weight:** 33.4360 g. **Composition:** 0.9000 Gold, 0.9675 oz. AGW.

Date	Mintage	VF-20	XF-40	AU-50	MS-60	MS-63	MS-65	Prf-65
1907 large letters on edge, unique	—	—	—	—	—	—	—	—
1907 small letters on edge	361,667	805	815	840	875	1,075	3,350	—
1908	4,271,551	795	805	820	835	965	1,450	—
1908D	663,750	805	815	830	860	1,075	9,000	—

Saint-Gaudens. "In God We Trust" below eagle.

KM# 131 **Designer:** Augustus Saint-Gaudens. **Diameter:** 34 **Weight:** 33.4360 g. **Composition:** 0.9000 Gold, 0.9675 oz. AGW.

Date	Mintage	VF-20	XF-40	AU-50	MS-60	MS-63	MS-65	Prf-65
1908	156,359	800	810	830	885	1,750	21,500	49,500
1908 Roman finish; Prf64 Rare	—	—	—	—	—	—	—	—
1908D	349,500	805	815	840	875	1,095	5,350	—
1908S	22,000	1,450	2,050	4,650	8,250	20,000	43,000	—
1909/8	161,282	805	815	880	1,375	5,400	32,500	—

Date	Mintage	VF-20	XF-40	AU-50	MS-60	MS-63	MS-65	Prf-65
1909	Inc. above	815	835	850	935	3,350	42,500	49,000
1909D	52,500	845	855	975	1,950	8,250	37,500	—
1909S	2,774,925	805	815	840	855	1,050	5,250	—
1910	482,167	800	810	830	885	1,065	7,350	49,000
1910D	429,000	800	810	830	860	1,035	2,600	—
1910S	2,128,250	805	815	845	865	1,100	8,000	—
1911	197,350	805	815	850	875	1,875	15,500	39,500
1911D	846,500	800	810	830	860	1,035	1,500	—
1911S	775,750	800	810	830	865	1,035	6,200	—
1912	149,824	805	815	845	900	1,675	19,500	44,000
1913	168,838	805	815	845	905	2,850	33,000	44,000
1913D	393,500	800	810	830	860	1,075	6,500	—
1913S	34,000	855	865	880	1,450	4,200	42,500	—
1914	95,320	815	825	880	1,275	3,900	25,000	41,500
1914D	453,000	800	810	830	860	1,045	3,250	—
1914S	1,498,000	800	810	830	860	1,035	2,000	—
1915	152,050	805	815	840	865	2,150	28,500	47,500
1915S	567,500	800	810	830	860	1,035	2,000	—
1916S	796,000	805	815	840	900	1,065	2,450	—
1920	228,250	795	805	820	860	1,095	62,500	—
1920S	558,000	12,500	15,500	22,500	44,500	88,000	210,000	—
1921	528,500	17,500	29,500	43,500	100,000	240,000	950,000	—
1922	1,375,500	795	805	820	835	985	2,450	—
1922S	2,658,000	835	925	1,250	2,150	4,200	39,500	—
1923	566,000	795	805	820	835	985	4,750	—
1923D	1,702,250	805	815	830	845	985	1,550	—
1924	4,323,500	795	805	820	835	965	1,450	—
1924D	3,049,500	950	1,550	1,800	310	8,450	75,000	—
1924S	2,927,500	935	1,550	1,850	3,000	8,000	44,500	—
1925	2,831,750	795	805	820	835	965	1,450	—
1925D	2,938,500	1,550	2,100	2,375	4,450	11,500	96,000	—
1925S	3,776,500	1,350	1,950	3,450	9,000	24,500	105,000	—
1926	816,750	795	805	820	835	965	1,450	—
1926D	481,000	8,500	12,500	16,000	28,500	43,500	115,000	—
1926S	2,041,500	1,050	1,550	1,725	2,600	4,950	29,500	—
1927	2,946,750	795	805	820	835	965	1,450	—
1927D	180,000	155,000	220,000	265,000	340,000	1,500,000	2,100,000	—
1927S	3,107,000	5,850	8,250	12,750	26,500	57,500	130,000	—
1928	8,816,000	795	805	820	835	965	1,450	—
1929	1,779,750	5,750	9,000	12,500	18,500	39,500	105,000	—
1930S	74,000	15,500	26,500	30,000	39,000	125,000	235,000	—
1931	2,938,250	9,800	14,500	18,850	30,000	68,500	110,000	—
1931D	106,500	9,000	11,850	21,500	32,500	95,000	130,000	—
1932	1,101,750	8,000	14,500	16,850	26,500	72,500	110,000	—
1933	445,500	—	—	—	—	—	9,000,000	—

Note: Sotheby/Stack's Sale, July 2002. Thirteen known, only one currently available.

COMMEMORATIVE COINAGE
1892-1954

All commemorative half dollars of 1892-1954 have the following specifications: diameter -- 30.6 millimeters; weight -- 12.5000 grams; composition -- 0.9000 silver, 0.3617 ounces actual silver weight. Values for PDS sets contain one example each from the Philadelphia, Denver and San Francisco mints. Type coin prices are the most inexpensive single coin available from the date and mint-mark combinations listed.

QUARTER

COLUMBIAN EXPOSITION. KM# 115
Obverse: Queen Isabella **Diameter:** 24.3 **Weight:** 6.2500 g. **Composition:** 0.9000 Silver, 0.1808 oz. ASW.

Date	Mintage	AU-50	MS-60	MS-63	MS-64	MS-65
1893	24,214	590	665	875	1,400	4,200

HALF DOLLAR

COLUMBIAN EXPOSITION. KM# 117 Obv.
Designer: Charles E. Barber **Rev. Designer:** George T. Morgan

Date	Mintage	AU-50	MS-60	MS-63	MS-64	MS-65
1892	950,000	18.50	28.00	85.00	180	650
1893	1,550,405	15.50	28.00	80.00	195	875

LINCOLN-ILLINOIS. KM# 143 Obv.
Designer: George T. Morgan **Rev. Designer:** John R. Sinnock

Date	Mintage	AU-50	MS-60	MS-63	MS-64	MS-65
1918	100,058	135	155	170	250	525

PANAMA-PACIFIC EXPOSITION. KM# 135
Designer: Charles E. Barber.

Date	Mintage	AU-50	MS-60	MS-63	MS-64	MS-65
1915S	27,134	465	550	825	1,550	2,650

MAINE CENTENNIAL. KM# 146 **Designer:** Anthony de Francisci.

Date	Mintage	AU-50	MS-60	MS-63	MS-64	MS-65
1920	50,028	135	165	195	310	585

U.S. COMMEMORATIVES

PILGRIM TERCENTENARY. KM# 147.1
Designer: Cyrus E. Dallin.

Date	Mintage	AU-50	MS-60	MS-63	MS-64	MS-65
1920	152,112	85.00	110	122	160	465

PILGRIM TERCENTENARY. KM# 147.2
Designer: Cyrus E. Dallin. **Obverse:** 1921 date next to Pilgrim

Date	Mintage	AU-50	MS-60	MS-63	MS-64	MS-65
1921	20,053	175	200	225	285	600

2x2

ALABAMA CENTENNIAL. KM# 148.1
Designer: Laura G. Fraser. **Obverse:** "2x2" at right above stars **Notes:** "Fake 2x2" counterstamps exist.

Date	Mintage	AU-50	MS-60	MS-63	MS-64	MS-65
1921	6,006	315	330	600	950	1,975

ALABAMA CENTENNIAL. KM# 148.2 Obv.
Designer: Laura G. Fraser

Date	Mintage	AU-50	MS-60	MS-63	MS-64	MS-65
1921	59,038	190	215	525	685	1,800

MISSOURI CENTENNIAL. KM# 149.1
Designer: Robert Aitken.

Date	Mintage	AU-50	MS-60	MS-63	MS-64	MS-65
1921	15,428	410	725	925	1,775	5,000

MISSOURI CENTENNIAL. KM# 149.2
Designer: Robert Aitken. **Obverse:** 2 star 4 in field at left **Notes:** "Fake "2*4" counterstamps exist.

Date	Mintage	AU-50	MS-60	MS-63	MS-64	MS-65
1921	5,000	650	800	1,100	1,900	5,000

GRANT MEMORIAL. KM# 151.1 Designer:
Laura G. Fraser.

Date	Mintage	AU-50	MS-60	MS-63	MS-64	MS-65
1922	67,405	115	125	160	290	800

GRANT MEMORIAL. KM# 151.2 Designer:
Laura G. Fraser. **Obverse:** Star above the word "Grant" **Notes:** "Fake star" counterstamps exist.

Date	Mintage	AU-50	MS-60	MS-63	MS-64	MS-65
1922	4,256	950	1,300	2,100	2,850	7,250

MONROE DOCTRINE CENTENNIAL.
KM# 153 Designer: Chester Beach.

Date	Mintage	AU-50	MS-60	MS-63	MS-64	MS-65
1923S	274,077	58.00	75.00	145	525	2,950

HUGUENOT-WALLOON TERCENTENARY.
KM# 154 Designer: George T. Morgan. **Obverse:** Huguenot leader Gaspard de Coligny and William I of Orange

Date	Mintage	AU-50	MS-60	MS-63	MS-64	MS-65
1924	142,080	135	155	175	250	550

CALIFORNIA DIAMOND JUBILEE. KM# 155
Designer: Jo Mora.

Date	Mintage	AU-50	MS-60	MS-63	MS-64	MS-65
1925S	86,594	215	240	280	520	1,125

FORT VANCOUVER CENTENNIAL.
KM# 158 Designer: Laura G. Fraser.

Date	Mintage	AU-50	MS 60	MS-63	MS-64	MS-65
1925	14,994	335	415	475	600	1,450

LEXINGTON-CONCORD SESQUICENTENNIAL. KM# 156 Designer:
Chester Beach.

Date	Mintage	AU-50	MS-60	MS-63	MS-64	MS-65
1925	162,013	96.00	110	120	185	485

STONE MOUNTAIN MEMORIAL.
KM# 157.1 Designer: Gutzon Borglum.

Date	Mintage	AU-50	MS-60	MS-63	MS-64	MS-65
1925	1,314,709	70.00	77.00	85.00	90.00	285

OREGON TRAIL MEMORIAL. KM# 159
Designer: James E. and Laura G. Fraser.

Date	Mintage	AU-50	MS-60	MS-63	MS-64	MS-65
1926	47,955	140	170	190	210	335
1926S	83,055	140	170	185	205	335
Type coin	—	150	180	190	210	320
1928	6,028	220	245	280	290	390
1933D	5,008	375	400	410	420	540
1934D	7,006	205	220	230	240	365
1936	10,006	150	190	200	210	325
1936S	5,006	170	190	210	220	360
1937D	12,008	180	205	210	215	325
1938	6,006	160	175	210	215	335
1938D	6,005	160	175	215	235	335
1938S	6,006	160	175	210	220	335
1939	3,004	525	620	630	655	720
1939D	3,004	525	620	640	675	735
1939S	3,005	525	620	630	655	725

U.S. SESQUICENTENNIAL. KM# 160

Designer: John R. Sinnock.

Date	Mintage	AU-50	MS-60	MS-63	MS-64	MS-65
1926	141,120	88.00	115	150	600	4,400

VERMONT SESQUICENTENNIAL. KM# 162

Obv. Designer: Charles Keck

Date	Mintage	AU-50	MS-60	MS-63	MS-64	MS-65
1927	28,142	255	290	305	350	990

HAWAIIAN SESQUICENTENNIAL. KM# 163

Designer: Juliette M. Fraser. **Notes:** Counterfeits exist.

Date	Mintage	AU-50	MS-60	MS-63	MS-64	MS-65
1928	10,008	1,750	2,650	3,500	4,500	6,850

DANIEL BOONE BICENTENNIAL.

KM# 165.1 Designer: Augustus Lukeman.

Date	Mintage	AU-50	MS-60	MS-63	MS-64	MS-65
1934	10,007	125	135	140	150	275
1935	10,010	118	120	125	130	275
1935D	5,005	133	140	145	152	325
1935S	5,005	133	140	145	152	325

DANIEL BOONE BICENTENNIAL.

KM# 165.2 Designer: Augustus Lukeman.
Reverse: "1934" added above the word "Pioneer."

Date	Mintage	AU-50	MS-60	MS-63	MS-64	MS-65
1935	10,008	118	120	125	130	275
Type coin	—	130	135	145	150	240
1935D	2,003	375	415	430	485	860
1935S	2,004	375	415	430	450	890
1936	12,012	118	120	125	130	275
Type coin	—	—	110	—	—	—
1936D	5,005	133	140	145	152	325
1936S	5,006	133	140	145	152	325
1937	9,810	125	130	135	980	285
1937D	2,506	285	385	390	385	560
1937S	2,506	285	385	390	415	590
1938	2,100	360	395	410	415	555
1938D	2,100	360	395	410	430	545
1938S	2,100	360	395	410	415	595

MARYLAND TERCENTENARY. KM# 166

Designer: Hans Schuler.

Date	Mintage	AU-50	MS-60	MS-63	MS-64	MS-65
1934	25,015	160	180	195	215	350

TEXAS CENTENNIAL. KM# 167

Designer: Pompeo Coppini.

Date	Mintage	AU-50	MS-60	MS-63	MS-64	MS-65
1934	61,463	140	145	155	160	290
Type coin	—	145	158	163	165	260
1935	9,994	140	145	155	160	290
1935D	10,007	140	145	155	160	290
1935S	10,008	140	145	155	160	290
1936	8,911	140	145	155	160	290
1936D	9,039	140	145	155	160	290
1936S	9,055	140	145	155	160	290
1937	6,571	142	148	160	165	295
1937D	6,605	142	148	160	165	295
1937S	6,637	142	148	160	165	295
1938	3,780	240	265	275	300	500
1938D	3,775	240	265	275	300	485
1938S	3,814	240	265	275	300	485

ARKANSAS CENTENNIAL. KM# 168

Designer: Edward E. Burr.

Date	Mintage	AU-50	MS-60	MS-63	MS-64	MS-65
Type coin	—	110	115	125	130	210
1935	13,012	100.00	110	120	125	215
1935D	5,505	105	115	125	130	300
1935S	5,506	105	115	125	130	300
1936	9,660	100.00	110	120	125	230
1936D	9,660	100.00	110	120	125	230
1936S	9,662	100.00	110	120	125	230
1937	5,505	105	115	128	135	340
1937D	5,505	105	115	128	135	330
1937S	5,506	105	115	128	135	380
1938	3,156	165	190	210	210	620
1938D	3,155	165	190	195	210	610
1938S	3,156	165	190	195	210	675
1939	2,104	330	390	400	410	1,000
1939D	2,104	330	390	400	410	980
1939S	2,105	330	390	400	410	965

CONNECTICUT TERCENTENARY. KM# 169

Designer: Henry Kreiss.

Date	Mintage	AU-50	MS-60	MS-63	MS-64	MS-65
1935	25,018	255	290	310	380	540

HUDSON, N.Y., SESQUICENTENNIAL.

KM# 170 Designer: Chester Beach.

Date	Mintage	AU-50	MS-60	MS-63	MS-64	MS-65
1935	10,008	750	925	1,250	1,675	2,250

OLD SPANISH TRAIL. KM# 172 Designer:

L.W. Hoffecker. **Notes:** Counterfeits exist.

Date	Mintage	AU-50	MS-60	MS-63	MS-64	MS-65
1935	10,008	1,250	1,375	1,700	1,900	2,250

SAN DIEGO, CALIFORNIA - PACIFIC
EXPOSITION. KM# 171 Designer: Robert

Aitken.

Date	Mintage	AU-50	MS-60	MS-63	MS-64	MS-65
1935S	70,132	105	130	145	150	170
1936D	30,092	105	135	150	160	170

ALBANY, N.Y., CHARTER ANNIVERSARY.

KM# 173 Designer: Gertrude K. Lathrop.

Date	Mintage	AU-50	MS-60	MS-63	MS-64	MS-65
1936	17,671	320	330	380	385	470

ARKANSAS CENTENNIAL. KM# 187 Obv.

Designer: Henry Kreiss **Rev. Designer:** Edward E.
Burr **Obverse:** Sen. Joseph T. Robinson

Date	Mintage	AU-50	MS-60	MS-63	MS-64	MS-65
1936	25,265	145	150	165	100	420

U.S. COMMEMORATIVES

BATTLE OF GETTYSBURG 75TH
ANNIVERSARY. KM# 181 Designer: Frank Vittor.

Date	Mintage	AU-50	MS-60	MS-63	MS-64	MS-65
1936	26,928	435	475	500	525	765

COLUMBIA, S.C., SESQUICENTENNIAL.
KM# 178 Designer: A. Wolfe Davidson.

Date	Mintage	AU-50	MS-60	MS-63	MS-64	MS-65
1936	9,007	275	280	300	310	415
Type coin	—	280	290	330	335	385
1936D	8,009	275	280	300	310	415
1936S	8,007	275	280	300	310	415

BRIDGEPORT, CONN., CENTENNIAL.
KM# 175 Designer: Henry Kreiss.

Date	Mintage	AU-50	MS-60	MS-63	MS-64	MS-65
1936	25,015	140	150	190	200	315

DELAWARE TERCENTENARY. KM# 179
Designer: Carl L. Schmitz.

Date	Mintage	AU-50	MS-60	MS-63	MS-64	MS-65
1936	20,993	310	325	365	385	490

CINCINNATI MUSIC CENTER. KM# 176
Designer: Constance Ortmayer.

Date	Mintage	AU-50	MS-60	MS-63	MS-64	MS-65
Type coin	—	335	345	375	560	700
1936	5,005	315	330	360	540	925
1936D	5,005	315	330	360	540	750
1936S	5,006	315	330	360	540	750

ELGIN, ILL., CENTENNIAL. KM# 180
Designer: Trygve Rovelstad.

Date	Mintage	AU-50	MS-60	MS-63	MS-64	MS-65
1936	20,015	245	265	280	295	355

CLEVELAND-GREAT LAKES EXPOSITION.
KM# 177 Designer: Brenda Putnam.

Date	Mintage	AU-50	MS-60	MS-63	MS-64	MS-65
1936	50,030	135	140	150	160	245

LONG ISLAND TERCENTENARY. KM# 182
Designer: Howard K. Weinman.

Date	Mintage	AU-50	MS-60	MS-63	MS-64	MS-65
1936	81,826	88.00	98.00	110	130	420

LYNCHBURG, VA., SESQUICENTENNIAL.
KM# 183 Designer: Charles Keck.

Date	Mintage	AU-50	MS-60	MS-63	MS-64	MS-65
1936	20,013	235	265	280	295	365

WISCONSIN TERRITORIAL CENTENNIAL.
KM# 188 Designer: David Parsons.

Date	Mintage	AU-50	MS-60	MS-63	MS-64	MS-65
1936	25,015	230	255	275	315	400

NORFOLK, VA., BICENTENNIAL. KM# 184
Designer: William M. and Marjorie E. Simpson.

Date	Mintage	AU-50	MS-60	MS-63	MS-64	MS-65
1936	16,936	535	565	590	610	650

YORK COUNTY, MAINE, TERCENTENARY.
KM# 189 Designer: Walter H. Rich.

Date	Mintage	AU-50	MS-60	MS-63	MS-64	MS-65
1936	25,015	135	170	195	300	590

RHODE ISLAND TERCENTENARY.
KM# 185 Designer: Arthur G. Carey and John H. Benson.

Date	Mintage	AU-50	MS-60	MS-63	MS-64	MS-65
1936	20,013	100.00	110	120	130	260
Type coin	—	105	110	125	128	290
1936D	15,010	100.00	110	120	130	275
1936S	15,011	100.00	110	120	130	290

BATTLE OF ANTIETAM 75TH
ANNIVERSARY. KM# 190 Designer: William M. Simpson.

Date	Mintage	AU-50	MS-60	MS-63	MS-64	MS-65
1937	18,028	725	760	790	850	985

SAN FRANCISCO-OAKLAND BAY BRIDGE.
KM# 174 Designer: Jacques Schnier.

Date	Mintage	AU-50	MS-60	MS-63	MS-64	MS-65
1936	71,424	170	180	220	225	375

ROANOKE ISLAND, N.C.. KM# 186
Designer: William M. Simpson.

Date	Mintage	AU-50	MS-60	MS-63	MS-64	MS-65
1937	29,030	255	285	310	330	340

U.S. COMMEMORATIVES

NEW ROCHELLE, N.Y.. KM# 191 Designer:
Gertrude K. Lathrop.

Date	Mintage	AU-50	MS-60	MS-63	MS-64	MS-65
1938	15,266	420	445	460	470	610

IOWA STATEHOOD CENTENNIAL.
KM# 197 Designer: Adam Pietz.

Date	Mintage	AU-50	MS-60	MS-63	MS-64	MS-65
1946	100,057	115	120	125	130	260

BOOKER T. WASHINGTON. KM# 198
Designer: Isaac S. Hathaway. **Notes:** Actual mintages are higher, but unsold issues were melted to produce Washington Carver issues.

Date	Mintage	AU-50	MS-60	MS-63	MS-64	MS-65
1946	1,000,546	14.00	18.00	19.50	21.00	50.00
Type coin	—	15.00	16.00	17.50	18.50	56.00
1946D	200,113	16.00	20.00	21.00	30.00	64.00
1946S	500,729	14.00	18.00	19.50	21.00	50.00
1947	100,017	25.00	35.00	55.00	65.00	95.00
1947D	100,017	25.00	35.00	55.00	70.00	115
1947S	100,017	25.00	35.00	55.00	65.00	90.00
1948	8,005	38.00	58.00	85.00	86.00	100.00
1948D	8,005	38.00	58.00	85.00	86.00	94.00
1948S	8,005	38.00	58.00	85.00	95.00	98.00
1949	6,004	67.00	83.00	92.00	98.00	120
1949D	6,004	67.00	83.00	92.00	98.00	120
1949S	6,004	67.00	83.00	95.00	104	110
1950	6,004	45.00	65.00	78.00	88.00	98.00
1950D	6,004	45.00	65.00	75.00	88.00	96.00
1950S	512,091	15.00	20.00	24.00	28.00	52.00
1951	51,082	15.00	20.00	24.00	28.00	50.00
1951D	7,004	45.00	65.00	78.00	90.00	95.00
1951S	7,004	45.00	65.00	78.00	90.00	95.00

BOOKER T. WASHINGTON AND GEORGE WASHINGTON CARVER. KM# 200
Designer: Isaac S. Hathaway.

Date	Mintage	AU-50	MS-60	MS-63	MS-64	MS-65
1951	110,018	26.00	34.00	53.00	54.00	290
Type coin	—	14.00	16.00	18.50	20.00	52.50
1951D	10,004	35.00	43.00	60.00	58.00	140
1951S	10,004	35.00	43.00	60.00	58.00	140
1952	2,006,292	15.00	18.00	26.50	44.00	48.00
1952D	8,006	40.00	50.00	70.00	70.00	200
1952S	8,006	40.00	50.00	80.00	70.00	160
1953	8,003	35.00	47.00	75.00	85.00	260
1953D	8,003	35.00	47.00	75.00	85.00	175
1953S	108,020	26.00	33.00	50.00	55.00	120
1954	12,006	36.00	42.00	60.00	65.00	150
1954D	12,006	36.00	42.00	60.00	65.00	200
1954S	122,024	24.00	32.00	38.00	48.00	65.00

DOLLAR

LAFAYETTE. KM# 118 Designer: Charles E. Barber. **Diameter:** 38.1 **Weight:** 26.7300 g. **Composition:** 0.9000 Silver, 0.7734 oz. ASW.

Date	Mintage	AU-50	MS-60	MS-63	MS-64	MS-65
1900	36,026	675	1,025	2,150	3,700	10,850

LOUISIANA PURCHASE EXPOSITION.
KM# 120 Obv. Designer: Charles E. Barber
Obverse: William McKinley **Diameter:** 15 **Weight:** 1.6720 g. **Comp.:** 0.9000 Gold, 0.0484 oz. AGW.

Date	Mintage	AU-50	MS-60	MS-63	MS-64	MS-65
1903	17,500	715	765	1,080	2,150	3,300

LOUISIANA PURCHASE EXPOSITION.
KM# 119 Designer: Charles E. Barber. **Obverse:** Jefferson **Diameter:** 15 **Weight:** 1.6720 g. **Composition:** 0.9000 Gold, 0.0484 oz. AGW.

Date	Mintage	AU-50	MS-60	MS-63	MS-64	MS-65
1903	17,500	700	765	1,160	1,900	3,100

LEWIS AND CLARK EXPOSITION.
KM# 121 Obv. Designer: Charles E. Barber
Diameter: 15 **Weight:** 1.6720 g. **Composition:** 0.9000 Gold, 0.0484 oz. AGW.

Date	Mintage	AU-50	MS-60	MS-63	MS-64	MS-65
1904	10,025	1,050	1,350	2,550	5,900	12,250
1905	10,041	1,300	1,625	3,300	7,000	18,500

PANAMA-PACIFIC EXPOSITION. KM# 136
Obv. Designer: Charles Keck **Diameter:** 15
Weight: 1.6720 g. **Composition:** 0.9000 Gold, 0.0484 oz. AGW.

Date	Mintage	AU-50	MS-60	MS-63	MS-64	MS-65
1915S	15,000	650	750	950	1,500	2,450

MCKINLEY MEMORIAL. KM# 144 Obv.
Designer: Charles E. Barber **Rev. Designer:** George T. Morgan **Diameter:** 15 **Weight:** 1.6720 g.
Composition: 0.9000 Gold, 0.0484 oz. AGW.

Date	Mintage	AU-50	MS-60	MS-63	MS-64	MS-65
1916	9,977	625	685	800	1,550	2,350
1917	10,000	785	800	1,325	2,200	3,800

GRANT MEMORIAL. KM# 152.1 Obv.
Designer: Laura G. Fraser **Diameter:** 15 **Weight:** 1.6720 g. **Composition:** 0.9000 Gold, 0.0484 oz. AGW. **Notes:** Without an incuse "star" above the word GRANT on the obverse.

Date	Mintage	AU-50	MS-60	MS-63	MS-64	MS-65
1922	5,000	1,875	1,900	2,350	3,650	4,900

GRANT MEMORIAL. KM# 152.2 Obv.
Designer: Laura G. Fraser **Diameter:** 15 **Weight:** 1.6720 g. **Composition:** 0.9000 Gold, 0.0484 oz. AGW. **Notes:** Variety with an incuse "star" above the word GRANT on the obverse.

Date	Mintage	AU-50	MS-60	MS-63	MS-64	MS-65
1922	5,016	1,800	1,950	2,400	3,700	4,400

$2.50 (QUARTER EAGLE)

PANAMA-PACIFIC EXPOSITION. KM# 137
Obv. Designer: Charles E. Barber **Rev. Designer:**
George T. Morgan **Diameter:** 18 **Weight:** 4.1800 g.
Composition: 0.9000 Gold, 0.1209 oz. AGW.

Date	Mintage	AU-50	MS-60	MS-63	MS-64	MS-65
1915S	6,749	1,750	2,100	4,350	6,300	8,000

PHILADELPHIA SESQUICENTENNIAL.
KM# 161 **Obv. Designer:** John R. Sinnock
Diameter: 18 **Weight:** 4.1800 g. **Composition:**
0.9000 Gold, 0.1209 oz. AGW.

Date	Mintage	AU-50	MS-60	MS-63	MS-64	MS-65
1926	46,019	525	565	850	1,700	4,200

$50

**PANAMA-PACIFIC EXPOSITION
OCTAGONAL.** KM# 139 **Obv. Designer:**
Robert Aitken **Diameter:** 44 **Weight:** 83.5900 g.
Composition: 0.9000 Gold, 2.4186 oz. AGW.

Date	Mintage	AU-50	MS-60	MS-63	MS-64	MS-65
1915S	645	52,500	55,000	80,000	99,500	148,000

PANAMA-PACIFIC EXPOSITION ROUND.
KM# 138 **Obv. Designer:** Robert Aitken **Diameter:**
44 **Weight:** 83.5900 g. **Composition:** 0.9000 Gold,
2.4186 oz. AGW.

Date	Mintage	AU-50	MS-60	MS-63	MS-64	MS-65
1915S	483	54,000	60,000	82,500	105,000	145,000

COMMEMORATIVE COINAGE
1982-PRESENT

All commemorative silver dollar coins of 1982-present have the following specifications: diameter -- 38.1 millimeters; weight -- 26.7300 grams; composition -- 0.9000 silver, 0.7736 ounces actual silver weight. All commemorative $5 coins of 1982-present have the following specificiations: diameter -- 21.6 millimeters; weight -- 8.3590 grams; composition: 0.9000 gold, 0.242 ounces actual gold weight.

Note: In 1982, after a hiatus of nearly 20 years, coinage of commemorative half dollars resumed. Those designated with a 'W' were struck at the West Point Mint. Some issues were struck in copper--nickel. Those struck in silver have the same size, weight and composition as the prior commemorative half--dollar series.

HALF DOLLAR

GEORGE WASHINGTON, 250TH BIRTH ANNIVERSARY.
KM# 208 Obv. Designer: Elizabeth Jones **Diameter:** 30.6 **Weight:** 12.5000 g. **Composition:** 0.9000 Silver, 0.3617 oz. ASW.

Date	Mintage	Proof	MS-65	Prf-65
1982D	2,210,458	—	6.50	—
1982S	—	4,894,044	—	6.50

BICENTENNIAL OF THE CONGRESS.
KM# 224 Obv. Designer: Patricia L. Verani **Rev. Designer:** William Woodward and Edgar Z. Steever **Weight:** 11.3400 g. **Composition:** Copper-Nickel Clad Copper

Date	Mintage	Proof	MS-65	Prf-65
1989D	163,753	—	8.00	—
1989S	—	—	—	8.00

STATUE OF LIBERTY CENTENNIAL.
KM# 212 Obv. Designer: Edgar Z. Steever **Rev. Designer:** Sherl Joseph Winter **Weight:** 11.3400 g. **Composition:** Copper-Nickel Clad Copper

Date	Mintage	Proof	MS-65	Prf-65
1986D	928,008	—	5.50	—
1986S	—	6,925,627	—	5.50

MOUNT RUSHMORE 50TH ANNIVERSARY.
KM# 228 Obv. Designer: Marcel Jovine **Rev. Designer:** T. James Ferrell **Weight:** 11.3400 g. **Composition:** Copper-Nickel Clad Copper

Date	Mintage	Proof	MS-65	Prf-65
1991D	172,754	—	21.50	—
1991S	—	—	—	20.00

U.S. COMMEMORATIVES

1992 OLYMPICS. KM# 233 Obv. Designer:
William Cousins **Rev. Designer:** Steven M. Bieda **Weight:** 11.3400 g. **Composition:** Copper-Nickel Clad Copper

Date	Mintage	Proof	MS-65	Prf-65
1992P	161,607	—	8.50	—
1992S	—	519,645	—	8.50

WORLD WAR II 50TH ANNIVERSARY.
KM# 243 Obv. Designer: George Klauba **Rev. Designer:** William J. Leftwich **Weight:** 11.3400 g. **Composition:** Copper-Nickel Clad Copper

Date	Mintage	Proof	MS-65	Prf-65
(1993)P	192,968	—	29.00	—
(1993)P	—	290,343	—	26.50

500TH ANNIVERSARY OF COLUMBUS DISCOVERY. KM# 237 Designer: T. James
Ferrell. **Weight:** 11.3400 g. **Composition:** Copper-Nickel Clad Copper

Date	Mintage	Proof	MS-65	Prf-65
1992D	135,702	—	11.50	—
1992S	—	390,154	—	11.50

1994 WORLD CUP SOCCER. KM# 246 Obv.
Designer: Richard T. LaRoche **Rev. Designer:** Dean McMullen **Weight:** 11.3400 g. **Composition:** Copper-Nickel Clad Copper

Date	Mintage	Proof	MS-65	Prf-65
1994D	168,208	—	9.75	—
1994P	122,412	—	10.25	—
1994P	—	609,354	—	8.50

JAMES MADISON AND BILL OF RIGHTS.
KM# 240 Obv. Designer: T. James Ferrell **Rev. Designer:** Dean McMullen **Weight:** 12.5000 g. **Composition:** 0.9000 Silver, 0.3617 oz. ASW.

Date	Mintage	Proof	MS-65	Prf-65
1993W	173,224	—	20.00	—
1993S	—	559,758	—	16.50

ATLANTA OLYMPICS. KM# 257 Obverse:
Basketball **Weight:** 11.3400 g. **Composition:** Copper-Nickel Clad Copper

Date	Mintage	Proof	MS-65	Prf-65
1995S	—	169,655	—	18.00
1995S	171,001	—	22.50	—

ATLANTA OLYMPICS. KM# 262 Obv.
Designer: Edgar Z. Steever **Obverse:** Baseball
Weight: 11.3400 g. **Composition:** Copper-Nickel
Clad Copper

Date	Mintage	Proof	MS-65	Prf-65
1995S	164,605	—	22.50	—
1995S	—	118,087	—	19.00

ATLANTA OLYMPICS. KM# 267 **Obverse:**
Swimming **Weight:** 11.3400 g. **Composition:**
Copper-Nickel Clad Copper

Date	Mintage	Proof	MS-65	Prf-65
1996S	49,533	—	165	—
1996S	—	114,315	—	36 00

CIVIL WAR. KM# 254 Obv. **Designer:** Don
Troiani **Rev. Designer:** T. James Ferrell **Weight:**
11.3400 g. **Composition:** Copper-Nickel Clad
Copper

Date	Mintage	Proof	MS-65	Prf-65
1995S	119,510	—	42.50	—
1995S	—	330,099	—	41.50

U. S. CAPITOL VISITOR CENTER. KM# 323
Obv. Designer: Dean McMullen **Rev. Designer:**
Alex Shagin and Marcel Jovine **Weight:** 11.3400 g.
Composition: Copper-Nickel Clad Copper

Date	Mintage	Proof	MS-65	Prf-65
2001P	99,157	—	13.50	—
2001P	—	77,962	—	17.50

FIRST FLIGHT CENTENNIAL. KM# 348
Obv. Designer: John Mercanti **Rev. Designer:**
Donna Weaver **Weight:** 11.3400 g. **Composition:**
Copper-Nickel Clad Copper

Date	Mintage	Proof	MS-65	Prf-65
2003P	57,726	—	15.50	—
2003P	—	111,569	—	15.50

ATLANTA OLYMPICS. KM# 271 **Obverse:**
Soccer **Weight:** 11.3400 g. **Composition:** Copper-
Nickel Clad Copper

Date	Mintage	Proof	MS-65	Prf-65
1996S	52,836	—	110	—
1996S	—	122,412	—	105

AMERICAN BALD EAGLE. KM# 438
Weight: 11.3400 g. **Composition:** Copper Nickel
Clad Copper

Date	Mintage	Proof	MS-65	Prf-65
2008P	—	—	—	—

DOLLAR

LOS ANGELES XXIII OLYMPIAD. KM# 209

Obv. Designer: Elizabeth Jones

Date	Mintage	Proof	MS-65	Prf-65
1983P	294,543	—	13.50	—
1983D	174,014	—	13.50	—
1983S	174,014	—	13.50	—
1983S	—	1,577,025	—	13.50

STATUE OF LIBERTY CENTENNIAL.

KM# 214 Obv. Designer: John Mercanti **Rev. Designer:** John Mercanti and Matthew Peloso

Date	Mintage	Proof	MS-65	Prf-65
1986P	723,635	—	13.50	—
1986S	—	6,414,638	—	13.50

LOS ANGELES XXIII OLYMPIAD. KM# 210

Obv. Designer: Robert Graham

Date	Mintage	Proof	MS-65	Prf-65
1984P	217,954	—	13.50	—
1984D	116,675	—	14.50	—
1984S	116,675	—	14.50	—
1984S	—	1,801,210	—	13.50

CONSTITUTION BICENTENNIAL. KM# 220

Obv. Designer: Patricia L. Verani

Date	Mintage	Proof	MS-65	Prf-65
1987P	451,629	—	13.50	—
1987S	—	2,747,116	—	13.50

U.S. COMMEMORATIVES

OLYMPICS. KM# 222 Obv. Designer: Patricia L. Verani **Rev. Designer:** Sherl Joseph Winter

Date	Mintage	Proof	MS-65	Prf-65
1988D	191,368	—	13.50	—
1988S	—	1,359,366	—	13.50

EISENHOWER CENTENNIAL. KM# 227 Obv. Designer: John Mercanti **Rev. Designer:** Marcel Jovine and John Mercanti

Date	Mintage	Proof	MS-65	Prf-65
1990W	241,669	—	15.50	—
1990P	—	638,335	—	17.00

BICENTENNIAL OF THE CONGRESS.
KM# 225 Designer: William Woodward and Chester Y. Martin.

Date	Mintage	Proof	MS-65	Prf-65
1989D	135,203	—	16.50	—
1989S	—	762,198	—	18.50

KOREAN WAR. KM# 231 Obv. Designer: John Mercanti **Rev. Designer:** T. James Ferrell

Date	Mintage	Proof	MS-65	Prf-65
1991D	213,049	—	16.50	—
1991P	—	618,488	—	20.50

MOUNT RUSHMORE GOLDEN ANNIVERSARY. KM# 229 Obv. Designer:
Marika Somogyi **Rev. Designer:** Frank Gasparro

Date	Mintage	Proof	MS-65	Prf-65
1991P	133,139	—	32.50	—
1991S	—	738,419	—	30.00

COLUMBUS QUINCENTENARY. KM# 238
Obv. Designer: John Mercanti **Rev. Designer:** Thomas D. Rogers, Sr.

Date	Mintage	Proof	MS-65	Prf-65
1992D	106,949	—	29.00	—
1992P	—	385,241	—	39.00

USO 50TH ANNIVERSARY. KM# 232 Obv.
Designer: Robert Lamb **Rev. Designer:** John Mercanti

Date	Mintage	Proof	MS-65	Prf-65
1991D	124,958	—	14.00	—
1991S	—	321,275	—	19.50

OLYMPICS. KM# 234 Obv. Designer: John R.
Deecken and Chester Y. Martin **Rev. Designer:** Marcel Jovine

Date	Mintage	Proof	MS-65	Prf-65
1992D	187,552	—	24.50	—
1992S	—	504,505	—	26.00

WHITE HOUSE BICENTENNIAL. KM# 236

Obv. Designer: Edgar Z. Steever **Rev. Designer:** Chester Y. Martin

Date	Mintage	Proof	MS-65	Prf-65
1992D	123,803	—	31.50	—
1992W	—	375,851	—	31.50

THOMAS JEFFERSON 250TH BIRTH ANNIVERSARY. KM# 249 **Designer:** T. James Ferrell.

Date	Mintage	Proof	MS-65	Prf-65
1993P	266,927	—	23.00	—
1993S	—	332,891	—	28.00

JAMES MADISON AND BILL OF RIGHTS.

KM# 241 Obv. Designer: William Krawczewicz and Thomas D. Rogers, Sr. **Rev. Designer:** Dean McMullen and Thomas D. Rogers, Sr.

Date	Mintage	Proof	MS-65	Prf-65
1993D	98,383	—	19.50	—
1993S	—	534,001	—	20.00

WORLD WAR II 50TH ANNIVERSARY.

KM# 244 Designer: Thomas D. Rogers, Sr..

Date	Mintage	Proof	MS-65	Prf-65
1993D	94,708	—	31.50	—
1993W	—	322,422	—	40.00

NATIONAL PRISONER OF WAR MUSEUM.
KM# 251 Obv. Designer: Thomas Nielson and Alfred Maletsky **Rev. Designer:** Edgar Z. Steever

Date	Mintage	Proof	MS-65	Prf-65
1994W	54,790	—	96.00	—
1994P	—	220,100	—	46.50

VIETNAM VETERANS MEMORIAL. KM#
250 Obv. Designer: John Mercanti **Rev. Designer:** Thomas D. Rogers, Sr.

Date	Mintage	Proof	MS-65	Prf-65
1994W	57,317	—	85.00	—
1994P	—	226,262	—	69.00

U.S. CAPITOL BICENTENNIAL. KM# 253

Date	Mintage	Proof	MS-65	Prf-65
1994D	68,352	—	23.00	—
1994S	—	279,416	—	25.00

WOMEN IN MILITARY SERVICE MEMORIAL. KM# 252 Obv. Designer: T. James Ferrell Rev. Designer: Thomas D. Rogers, Sr.

Date	Mintage	Proof	MS-65	Prf-65
1994W	53,054	—	39.50	—
1994P	—	213,201	—	36.00

WORLD CUP SOCCER. KM# 247 Obv.

Designer: Dean McMullen and T. James Ferrell

Date	Mintage	Proof	MS-65	Prf-65
1994D	81,698	—	26.00	—
1994S	—	576,978	—	29.00

ATLANTA OLYMPICS. KM# 264 Obv.

Designer: John Mercanti **Obverse:** Track and field

Date	Mintage	Proof	MS-65	Prf-65
1995D	24,796	—	98.00	—
1995P	—	136,935	—	53.00

ATLANTA OLYMPICS. KM# 260 Obverse:

Gymnastics

Date	Mintage	Proof	MS-65	Prf-65
1995D	42,497	—	75.00	—
1995P	—	182,676	—	58.00

ATLANTA OLYMPICS. KM# 263 Obv.

Designer: John Mercanti **Obverse:** Cycling

Date	Mintage	Proof	MS-65	Prf-65
1995D	19,662	—	150	—
1995P	—	118,795	—	47.50

ATLANTA OLYMPICS, PARALYMPICS.

KM# 259 Obverse: Blind runner

Date	Mintage	Proof	MS-65	Prf-65
1995D	28,649	—	93.00	—
1995P	—	138,337	—	64.00

SPECIAL OLYMPICS WORLD GAMES.

KM# 266 Obv. Designer: Jamie Wyeth and T. James Ferrell **Rev. Designer:** Thomas D. Rogers, Sr.

Date	Mintage	Proof	MS-65	Prf-65
1995W	89,301	—	31.00	—
1995P	—	351,764	—	26.50

CIVIL WAR. KM# 255 Obv. Designer: Don Troiani and Edgar Z. Steever Rev. Designer: John Mercanti

Date	Mintage	Proof	MS-65	Prf-65
1995P	45,866	—	74.00	—
1995S	—	437,114	—	78.00

ATLANTA OLYMPICS. KM# 269 Rev. Designer: Thomas D. Rogers, Sr. Obverse: Tennis

Date	Mintage	Proof	MS-65	Prf-65
1996D	15,983	—	330	—
1996P	—	92,016	—	92.00

U.S. COMMEMORATIVES

ATLANTA OLYMPICS. **KM# 272** Rev.
Designer: Thomas D. Rogers, Sr. **Obverse:** Rowing

Date	Mintage	Proof	MS-65	Prf-65
1996D	16,258	—	345	—
1996P	—	151,890	—	75.00

ATLANTA OLYMPICS, PARALYMPICS.
KM# 268 **Rev. Designer:** Thomas D. Rogers, Sr.
Obverse: Wheelchair racer

Date	Mintage	Proof	MS-65	Prf-65
1996D	14,497	—	385	—
1996P	—	84,280	—	90.00

ATLANTA OLYMPICS. **KM# 272A** Rev.
Designer: Thomas D. Rogers, Sr. **Obverse:** High jumper

Date	Mintage	Proof	MS-65	Prf-65
1996D	15,697	—	400	—
1996P	—	124,502	—	60.00

NATIONAL COMMUNITY SERVICE. **KM#**
275 Obv. Designer: Thomas D. Rogers, Sr. **Rev. Designer:** William C. Cousins

Date	Mintage	Proof	MS-65	Prf-65
1996S	23,500	—	235	—
1996S	—	101,543	—	82.00

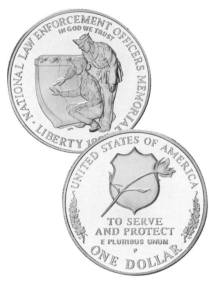

SMITHSONIAN INSTITUTION 150TH ANNIVERSARY. KM# 276 Obv. Designer:
Thomas D. Rogers, Sr. **Rev. Designer:** John Mercanti

Date	Mintage	Proof	MS-65	Prf-65
1996D	31,230	—	150	—
1996P	—	129,152	—	69.00

NATIONAL LAW ENFORCEMENT OFFICERS MEMORIAL. KM# 281 Designer:
Alfred Maletsky.

Date	Mintage	Proof	MS-65	Prf-65
1997P	—	110,428	—	170
1997P	28,575	—	165	—

JACKIE ROBINSON 50TH ANNIVERSARY.
KM# 279 **Obv. Designer:** Alfred Maletsky **Rev. Designer:** T. James Ferrell

Date	Mintage	Proof	MS-65	Prf-65
1997S	30,007	—	103	—
1997S	—	110,495	—	85.00

U.S. BOTANIC GARDENS 175TH ANNIVERSARY. KM# 278 Designer: Edgar Z.
Steever.

Date	Mintage	Proof	MS-65	Prf-65
1997P	57,272	—	45.00	—
1997P	—	264,528	—	44.00

BLACK REVOLUTIONARY WAR PATRIOTS.
KM# 288 Obv. Designer: John Mercanti **Rev. Designer:** Ed Dwight **Obverse:** Crispus Attucks

Date	Mintage	Proof	MS-65	Prf-65
1998S	37,210	–	175	—
1998S	—	75,070	—	123

DOLLEY MADISON. KM# 298 Designer:
Tiffany & Co..

Date	Mintage	Proof	MS-65	Prf-65
1999P	22,948	—	50.00	—
1999P	—	158,247	—	48.00

ROBERT F. KENNEDY. KM# 287 Obv.
Designer: Thomas D. Rogers, Sr. **Rev. Designer:** James M. Peed and Thomas D. Rogers, Sr.

Date	Mintage	Proof	MS-65	Prf-65
1998S	106,422	—	32.50	—
1998S	—	99,020	—	43.00

YELLOWSTONE. KM# 299 Obv. Designer:
Edgar Z. Steever **Rev. Designer:** William C. Cousins

Date	Mintage	Proof	MS-65	Prf-65
1999P	23,614	—	56.00	—
1999P	—	128,646	—	58.00

LEIF ERICSON. **KM# 313 Obv. Designer:**
John Mercanti **Rev. Designer:** T. James Ferrell

Date	Mintage	Proof	MS-65	Prf-65
2000P	28,150	—	92.50	—
2000 Iceland	—	15,947	—	25.00
2000P	—	58,612	—	70.00

AMERICAN INDIAN - BISON. **KM# 325**
Designer: James E. Fraser.

Date	Mintage	Proof	MS-65	Prf-65
2001D	197,131	—	260	—
2001P	—	272,869	—	290

LIBRARY OF CONGRESS BICENTENNIAL.
KM# 311 Obv. Designer: Thomas D. Rogers, Sr.
Rev. Designer: John Mercanti

Date	Mintage	Proof	MS-65	Prf-65
2000P	52,771	—	43.00	—
2000P	—	196,900	—	41.00

CAPITOL VISITOR CENTER. **KM# 324 Obv.**
Designer: Marika Somogyi **Rev. Designer:** John
Mercanti

Date	Mintage	Proof	MS-65	Prf-65
2001P	66,636	—	35.00	—
2001P	—	143,793	—	45.00

WEST POINT MILITARY ACADEMY BICENTENNIAL. KM# 338 Obv. Designer: T. James Ferrell Rev. Designer: John Mercanti

Date	Mintage	Proof	MS-65	Prf-65
2002W	103,201	—	23.50	—
2002W	—	288,293	—	24.50

FIRST FLIGHT CENTENNIAL. KM# 349

Obv. Designer: T. James Ferrell **Rev. Designer:** Norman E. Nemeth **Obverse:** Orville and Wilbur Wright **Reverse:** Wright Brothers airplane

Date	Mintage	Proof	MS-65	Prf-65
2003P	53,761	—	37.00	—
2003P	—	193,086	—	32.00

WINTER OLYMPICS - SALT LAKE CITY.

KM# 336 **Obv. Designer:** John Mercanti **Rev. Designer:** Donna Weaver

Date	Mintage	Proof	MS-65	Prf-65
2002P	35,388	—	35.00	—
2002P	—	142,873	—	42.00

125TH ANNIVERSARY OF EDISON'S ELECTRIC LIGHT. KM# 362 Obv. Designer: Donna Weaver Rev. Designer: John Mercanti

Date	Mintage	Proof	MS-65	Prf-65
2004P	68,031	—	40.00	—
2004P	—	213,409	—	41.00

U.S. COMMEMORATIVES

LEWIS AND CLARK CORPS OF DISCOVERY BICENTENNIAL. KM# 363

Date	Mintage	Proof	MS-65	Prf-65
2004P	90,323	—	35.00	—
2004P	—	288,492	—	33.00

U.S. MARINE CORPS, 230TH ANNIVERSARY. KM# 376

Date	Mintage	Proof	MS-65	Prf-65
2005P	130,000	—	47.00	—
2005P	—	370,000	—	54.00

CHIEF JUSTICE JOHN MARSHALL, 250TH BIRTH ANNIVERSARY. KM# 375 Obv.
Designer: John Mercanti **Rev. Designer:** Donna Weaver

Date	Mintage	Proof	MS-65	Prf-65
2005P	48,953	—	37.50	—
2005P	—	141,993	—	40.00

BENJAMIN FRANKLIN, 300TH ANNIVERSARY OF BIRTH. KM# 387
Obv. Designer: Norman E. Nemeth **Obverse:** Youthful Franklin flying kite **Reverse:** Revolutionary era "Join or Die" snake cartoon illustration

Date	Mintage	Proof	MS-65	Prf-65
2006P	58,000	—	53.00	—
2006P	—	142,000	—	57.00

CENTRAL HIGH SCHOOL DESEGREGATION. KM# 418 Obverse:
Childrens feet walking left with adult feet in military boots **Reverse:** Little Rock's Central High School

Date	Mintage	Proof	MS-65	Prf-65
2007P	—	—	—	—
2007P	—	—	—	—

BENJAMIN FRANKLIN, 300TH ANNIVERSARY OF BIRTH. KM# 388
Obverse: Bust 3/4 right, signature in oval below **Reverse:** Continental Dollar of 1776 in center

Date	Mintage	Proof	MS-65	Prf-65
2006P	58,000	—	52.00	—
2006P	—	142,000	—	54.00

SAN FRANCISCO MINT MUSEUM.
KM# 394 Obverse: 3/4 view of building **Reverse:** Reverse of 1880s Morgan silver dollar

Date	Mintage	Proof	MS-65	Prf-65
2006S	—	—	44.00	—
2006S	—	—	—	46.00

JAMESTOWN - 400TH ANNIVERSARY.
KM# 405 Obverse: Two settlers and Native American **Reverse:** Three ships

Date	Mintage	Proof	MS-65	Prf-65
2007P	—	—	—	—
2007P	—	—	—	—

$5 (HALF EAGLE)

STATUE OF LIBERTY CENTENNIAL.
KM# 215 Designer: Elizabeth Jones.

Date	Mintage	Proof	MS-65	Prf-65
1986W	95,248	—	190	—
1986W	—	404,013	—	190

OLYMPICS. KM# 223 Obv. Designer:
Elizabeth Jones **Rev. Designer:** Marcel Jovine

Date	Mintage	Proof	MS-65	Prf-65
1988W	62,913	—	190	—
1988W	—	281,456	—	190

CONSTITUTION BICENTENNIAL.
KM# 221 Designer: Marcel Jovine.

Date	Mintage	Proof	MS-65	Prf-65
1987W	214,225	—	190	—
1987W	—	651,659	—	190

BICENTENNIAL OF THE CONGRESS.
KM# 226 Obv. Designer: John Mercanti

Date	Mintage	Proof	MS-65	Prf-65
1989W	46,899	—	190	—
1989W	—	164,690	—	190

MOUNT RUSHMORE 50TH ANNIVERSARY.
KM# 230 Obv. Designer: John Mercanti **Rev.
Designer:** Robert Lamb and William C. Cousins

Date	Mintage	Proof	MS-65	Prf-65
1991W	31,959	—	285	—
1991W	—	111,991	—	225

WORLD WAR II 50TH ANNIVERSARY.
KM# 245 Obv. Designer: Charles J. Madsen **Rev.
Designer:** Edward S. Fisher

Date	Mintage	Proof	MS-65	Prf-65
1993W	—	65,461	—	330
1993W	23,089	—	360	—

COLUMBUS QUINCENTENARY. KM# 239
Obv. Designer: T. James Ferrell **Rev. Designer:**
Thomas D. Rogers, Sr.

Date	Mintage	Proof	MS-65	Prf-65
1992W	—	79,730	—	285
1992W	24,329	—	320	—

WORLD CUP SOCCER. KM# 248 Obv.
Designer: William J. Krawczewicz **Rev. Designer:**
Dean McMullen

Date	Mintage	Proof	MS-65	Prf-65
1994W	22,464	—	325	—
1994W	—	89,619	—	265

OLYMPICS. KM# 235 Obv. Designer:** James C.
Sharpe and T. James Ferrell **Rev. Designer:** James
M. Peed

Date	Mintage	Proof	MS-65	Prf-65
1992W	27,732	—	310	—
1992W	—	77,313	—	240

CIVIL WAR. KM# 256 Obv. Designer:** Don
Troiani **Rev. Designer:** Alfred Maletsky

Date	Mintage	Proof	MS-65	Prf-65
1995W	12,735	—	900	—
1995W	—	55,246	—	535

JAMES MADISON AND BILL OF RIGHTS.
KM# 242 Obv. Designer: Scott R. Blazek **Rev.
Designer:** Joseph D. Peña

Date	Mintage	Proof	MS-65	Prf-65
1993W	—	78,651	—	265
1993W	22,266	—	325	—

OLYMPICS. KM# 261 Obverse:** Torch runner

Date	Mintage	Proof	MS-65	Prf-65
1995W	—	57,442	—	410
1995W	14,675	—	775	—

OLYMPICS. KM# 265 Obverse:** Stadium

Date	Mintage	Proof	MS-65	Prf-65
1995W	—	43,124	—	535
1995W	10,579	—	1,200	—

Date	Mintage	Proof	MS-65	Prf-65
1997W	—	24,546	—	900

1996 ATLANTA OLYMPICS. KM# 270
Obverse: Cauldron

Date	Mintage	Proof	MS-65	Prf-65
1996W	—	38,555	—	650
1996W	9,210	—	1,000	—

OLYMPICS. KM# 274 Obverse: Flag bearer

Date	Mintage	Proof	MS-65	Prf-65
1996W	—	32,886	—	015
1996W	9,174	—	1,050	—

SMITHSONIAN INSTITUTION 150TH ANNIVERSARY. KM# 277 Obv. Designer:
Alfred Maletsky **Rev. Designer:** T. James Ferrell

Date	Mintage	Proof	MS-65	Prf-65
1996W	9,068	—	1,500	—
1996W	—	29,474	—	720

FRANKLIN DELANO ROOSEVELT.
KM# 282 Obv. Designer: T. James Ferrell **Rev. Designer:** James M. Peed and Thomas D. Rogers, Sr.

Date	Mintage	Proof	MS-65	Prf-65
1997W	11,894	—	1,100	—
1997W	—	29,474	—	565

JACKIE ROBINSON 50TH ANNIVERSARY.
KM# 280 Obv. Designer: William C. Cousins **Rev. Designer:** James M. Peed

Date	Mintage	Proof	MS-65	Prf-65
1997W	5,202	—	5,750	—

GEORGE WASHINGTON DEATH BICENTENNIAL. KM# 300 Designer: Laura G. Fraser.

Date	Mintage	Proof	MS-65	Prf-65
1999W	22,511	—	475	—
1999W	—	41,693	—	475

CAPITOL VISITOR CENTER. KM# 326
Designer: Elizabeth Jones.

Date	Mintage	Proof	MS-65	Prf-65
2001W	6,761	—	2,150	—
2001W	—	27,652	—	465

2002 SALT LAKE CITY WINTER OLYMPICS.
KM# 337 Designer: Donna Weaver.

Date	Mintage	Proof	MS-65	Prf-65
2002W	10,585	—	555	—
2002W	—	32,877	—	510

SAN FRANCISCO MINT MUSEUM.
KM# 395 Obverse: Frontal view of entrance **Reverse:** Eagle as on 1860's $5. Gold.

Date	Mintage	Proof	MS-65	Prf-65
2006	—	—	—	510

JAMESTOWN - 400TH ANNIVERSARY.
KM# 406 Obverse: Settler and Native American **Reverse:** Jamestown Memorial Church ruins

Date	Mintage	Proof	MS-65	Prf-65
2007W	—	—	—	510

AMERICAN BALD EAGLE. KM# 440

Date	Mintage	Proof	MS-65	Prf-65
2007W	—	—	—	510

$10 (EAGLE)

LOS ANGELES XXIII OLYMPIAD. KM# 211
Obv. Designer: James M. Peed and John Mercanti
Rev. Designer: John Mercanti **Diameter:** 27
Weight: 16.7180 g. **Composition:** 0.9000 Gold,
0.4837 oz. AGW.

Date	Mintage	Proof	MS-65	Prf-65
1984W	75,886	—	365	—
1984P	—	33,309	—	365
1984D	—	34,533	—	365
1984S	—	48,551	—	365
1984W	—	381,085	—	355

FIRST FLIGHT CENTENNIAL. KM# 350
Designer: Donna Weaver. **Weight:** 16.7180 g.
Composition: 0.9000 Gold, 0.4837 oz. AGW.

Date	Mintage	Proof	MS-65	Prf-65
2003P	10,129	—	625	—
2003P	—	21,846	—	560

LIBRARY OF CONGRESS. KM# 312 Obv.
Designer: John Mercanti **Rev. Designer:** Thomas
D. Rogers, Sr. **Weight:** 16.2590 g. **Composition:**
Platinum-Gold-Alloy **Notes:** Composition is 48
percent platinum, 48 percent gold, and 4 percent
alloy.

Date	Mintage	Proof	MS-65	Prf-65
2000W	6,683	—	3,600	—
2000W	—	27,167	—	1,350

AMERICAN EAGLE BULLION COINS

GOLD $5

KM# 216 Obv. Designer: Augustus Saint-Gaudens. **Rev. Designer:** Miley Busiek. **Diameter:** 16.5 **Weight:** 3.3930 g. **Composition:** 0.9167 Gold, 0.1000 oz. AGW.

Date	Mintage	Unc	Prf.
MCMLXXXVI (1986)	912,609	85.00	—
MCMLXXXVII (1987)	580,266	80.00	—
MCMLXXXVIII (1988)	159,500	200	—
MCMLXXXVIII (1988)P	143,881	—	80.00
MCMLXXXIX (1989)	264,790	85.00	—
MCMLXXXIX (1989)P	82,924	—	80.00
MCMXC (1990)	210,210	90.00	—
MCMXC (1990)P	99,349	—	80.00
MCMXCI (1991)	165,200	110	—
MCMXCI (1991)P	70,344	—	80.00
1992	209,300	95.00	—
1992P	64,902	—	80.00
1993	210,709	90.00	—
1993P	58,649	—	80.00
1994	206,380	90.00	—
1994W	62,100	—	80.00
1995	223,025	80.00	—
1995W	62,650	—	80.00

Date	Mintage	Unc	Prf.
1996	401,964	80.00	—
1996W	58,440	—	80.00
1997	528,515	80.00	—
1997W	35,000	—	91.00
1998	1,344,520	70.00	—
1998W	39,653	—	80.00
1999	2,750,338	70.00	—
1999W	48,426	—	80.00
2000	569,153	85.00	—
2000W	50,000	—	90.00
2001	269,147	85.00	—
2001W	37,547	—	80.00
2002	230,027	85.00	—
2002W	40,864	—	80.00
2003	245,029	85.00	—
2003W	40,634	—	85.00
2004	250,016	85.00	—
2004W	35,481	—	90.00
2005	300,043	80.00	—
2005W	48,455	—	95.00
2006	285,006	75.00	—
2006W	—	—	80.00

GOLD $10

KM# 217 Obv. Designer: Augustus Saint-Gaudens. **Rev. Designer:** Miley Busiek. **Diameter:** 22 **Weight:** 8.4830 g. **Composition:** 0.9167 Gold, 0.2500 oz. AGW.

Date	Mintage	Unc	Prf.
MCMLXXXVI (1986)	726,031	175	—
MCMLXXXVII (1987)	269,255	175	—
MCMLXXXVIII (1988)	49,000	175	—
MCMLXXXVIII (1988)P	98,028	—	200
MCMLXXXIX (1989)	81,789	175	—
MCMLXXXIX (1989P)	53,593	—	200
MCMXC (1990)	41,000	175	—
MCMXC (1990)P	62,674	—	200
MCMXCI (1991)	36,100	425	—
MCMXCI (1991)P	50,839	—	200
1992	59,546	175	—
1992P	46,290	—	200
1993	71,864	175	—
1993P	46,271	—	200
1994	72,650	175	—
1994W	47,600	—	200
1995	83,752	175	—
1995W	47,545	—	200
1996	60,318	175	—
1996W	39,190	—	200

Date	Mintage	Unc	Prf.
1997	108,805	175	—
1997W	29,800	—	200
1998	309,829	175	—
1998W	29,733	—	200
1999	564,232	175	—
1999W	34,416	—	200
2000	128,964	175	—
2000W	36,000	—	200
2001	71,280	175	—
2001W	25,630	—	200
2002	62,027	175	—
2002W	29,242	—	200
2003	74,029	175	—
2003W	31,000	—	200
2004	72,014	175	—
2004W	29,127	—	200
2005	72,015	175	—
2005W	34,637	—	200
2006	60,004	175	—
2006W	—	—	200

BULLION COINAGE

GOLD $25

KM# 218 Obv. Designer: Augustus Saint-Gaudens. **Rev. Designer:** Miley Busiek. **Diameter:** 27 **Weight:** 16.9660 g. **Composition:** 0.9167 Gold, 0.5000 oz. AGW.

Date	Mintage	Unc	Prf.
MCMLXXXVI (1986)	599,566	500	—
MCMLXXXVII (1987)	131,255	350	—
MCMLXXXVII (1987)P	143,398	—	400
MCMLXXXVIII (1988)	45,000	550	—
MCMLXXXVIII (1988)P	76,528	—	400
MCMLXXXIX (1989)	44,829	650	—
MCMLXXXIX (1989)P	44,264	—	400
MCMXC (1990)	31,000	800	—
MCMXC (1990)P	51,636	—	400
MCMXCI (1991)	24,100	1,300	—
MCMXCI (1991)P	53,125	—	400
1992	54,404	500	—
1992P	40,982	—	400
1993	73,324	350	—
1993P	43,319	—	400
1994	62,400	350	—
1994W	44,100	—	400
1995	53,474	385	—
1995W	45,511	—	400
1996	39,287	525	—
1996W	35,937	—	400
1997	79,605	350	—
1997W	26,350	—	400
1998	169,029	350	—
1998W	25,896	—	400
1999	263,013	350	—
1999W	30,452	—	400
2000	79,287	350	—
2000W	32,000	—	400
2001	48,047	500	—
2001W	23,261	—	400
2002	70,027	350	—
2002W	26,646	—	400
2003	79,029	350	—
2003W	29,000	—	400
2004	98,040	350	—
2004W	27,731	—	400
2005	80,023	350	—
2005W	33,598	—	400
2006	66,005	345	—
2006W	—	—	400

GOLD $50

KM# 219 Obv. Designer: Augustus Saint-Gaudens. **Rev. Designer:** Miley Busiek. **Diameter:** 32.7 **Weight:** 33.9310 g. **Composition:** 0.9167 Gold, 100000 oz. AGW.

Date	Mintage	Unc	Prf.
MCMLXXXVI (1986)	1,362,650	715	—
MCMLXXXVI (1986)W	446,290	—	725
MCMLXXXVII (1987)	1,045,500	715	—
MCMLXXXVII (1987)W	147,498	—	725
MCMLXXXVIII (1988)	465,000	715	—
MCMLXXXVIII (1988)W	87,133	—	725
MCMLXXXIX (1989)	415,790	715	—
MCMLXXXIX (1989)W	53,960	—	725
MCMXC (1990)	373,210	715	—
MCMXC (1990)W	62,401	—	725
MCMXCI (1991)	243,100	715	—
MCMXCI (1991)W	50,411	—	725
1992	275,000	715	—
1992W	44,835	—	725
1993	480,192	715	—
1993W	34,389	—	725
1994	221,633	715	—
1994W	36,300	—	725
1995	200,636	715	—
1995W	46,553	—	725
1996	189,148	715	—
1996W	37,302	—	725
1997	664,508	715	—
1997W	28,000	—	725
1998	1,468,530	710	—
1998W	26,060	—	725
1999	1,505,026	710	—
1999W	31,446	—	725
2000	433,319	715	—
2000W	33,000	—	725
2001	143,605	715	—
2001W	24,580	—	725
2002	222,029	715	—

Date	Mintage	Unc	Prf.	Date	Mintage	Unc	Prf.
2002W	24,242	—	725	2005	356,555	715	—
2003	416,032	715	—	2005W	34,695	—	725
2003W	29,000	—	725	2006	237,510	710	—
2004	417,019	715	—	2006W	—	—	725
2004W	28,731	—	725	2006W Reverse Proof	10,000	—	3,250

SILVER DOLLAR

KM# 273 Obv. Designer: Adolph A. Weinman.
Rev. Designer: John Mercanti. **Diameter:** 40.6
Weight: 31.1010 g. **Composition:** 0.9993 Silver,
0.9992 oz. ASW.

Date	Mintage	Unc	Prf.
1986	5,393,005	20.00	—
1986S	1,446,778	—	32.00
1987	11,442,335	14.50	—
1987S	904,732	—	32.00
1988	5,004,646	16.50	—
1988S	557,370	—	60.00
1989	5,203,327	14.50	—
1989S	617,694	—	37.50
1990	5,840,210	16.50	—
1990S	695,510	—	35.00
1991	7,191,066	14.50	—
1991S	511,924	—	55.00
1992	5,540,068	15.50	—
1992S	498,552	—	50.00
1993	6,763,762	14.50	—
1993P	403,625	—	195
1994	4,227,319	16.50	—
1994P	372,168	—	250
1995	4,672,051	15.50	—
1995P	395,400	—	225

Date	Mintage	Unc	Prf.
1995W 10th Anniversary	30,125	—	5,500
1996	3,603,386	47.50	—
1996P	473,021	—	70.00
1997	4,295,004	21.00	—
1997P	429,682	—	100.00
1998	4,847,549	14.50	—
1998P	452,319	—	60.00
1999	7,408,640	14.50	—
1999P	549,769	—	65.00
2000P	600,000	—	32.00
2000	9,239,132	14.50	—
2001	9,001,711	14.50	—
2001W	746,154	—	32.00
2002	10,539,026	14.50	—
2002W	647,342	—	35.00
2003	8,495,008	14.50	—
2003W	—	—	32.50
2004	8,882,754	14.50	—
2004W	783,219	—	32.50
2005	8,891,025	14.50	—
2005W	823,000	—	33.00
2006	10,676,522	14.50	—
2006W	—	—	33.00
2006P Reverse Proof	250,000	—	250
2006W	470,000	85.00	—

PLATINUM $10

Date	Mintage	Unc	Prf.
2004	15,010	165	—
2005	14,013	170	—
2006	11,001	170	—

KM# 283 Obv. Designer: John Mercanti. **Rev.
Designer:** Thomas D. Rogers Sr. **Weight:** 3.1100 g.
Composition: 0.9995 Platinum, 0.0999 oz.

Date	Mintage	Unc	Prf.
1997	70,250	150	—
1997W	36,996	—	150
1998	39,525	150	—
1999	55,955	145	—
2000	34,027	145	—
2001	52,017	145	—
2002	23,005	145	—
2003	22,007	145	—

KM# 289 Obv. Designer: John Mercanti.
Weight: 3.1100 g. **Composition:** 0.9995 Platinum,
0.0999 oz.

Date	Mintage	Unc	Prf.
1998W	19,832	—	150

KM# 301 Obv. Designer: John Mercanti.
Weight: 3.1100 g. **Composition:** 0.9995 Platinum,
0.0999 oz.

Date	Mintage	Unc	Prf.
1999W	19,123	—	145

KM# 314 Obv. Designer: John Mercanti.
Weight: 3.1100 g. **Composition:** 0.9995 Platinum,
0.0999 oz.

Date	Mintage	Unc	Prf.
2000W	15,651	—	145

KM# 327 Obv. Designer: John Mercanti.
Weight: 3.1100 g. **Composition:** 0.9995 Platinum,
0.0999 oz.

Date	Mintage	Unc	Prf.
2001W	12,193	—	145

KM# 339 Obv. Designer: John Mercanti.
Weight: 3.1100 g. **Composition:** 0.9995 Platinum,
0.0999 oz.

Date	Mintage	Unc	Prf.
2002W	12,365	—	145

KM# 351 Obv. Designer: John Mercanti. **Rev.
Designer:** Al Maletsky. **Weight:** 3.1100 g.
Composition: 0.9995 Platinum, 0.0999 oz.

Date	Mintage	Unc	Prf.
2003W	8,161	—	175

KM# 364 Obv. Designer: John Mercanti.
Weight: 3.1100 g. **Composition:** 0.9995 Platinum,
0.0999 oz.

Date	Mintage	Unc	Prf.
2004W	6,846	—	350

KM# 377 Obv. Designer: John Mercanti. **Rev.
Designer:** Donna Weaver. **Weight:** 3.1100 g.
Composition: 0.9995 Platinum, 0.0999 oz.

Date	Mintage	Unc	Prf.
2005W	8,000	—	210

KM# 389 Diameter: 17 **Weight:** 3.1100 g.
Composition: 0.9995 Platinum, 0.0999 oz.

Date	Mintage	Unc	Prf.
2006W	—	—	210

KM# 414 Weight: 3.1100 g. **Composition:**
0.9995 Platinum, 0.0999 oz.

Date	Mintage	Unc	Prf.
2007W	—	—	210

PLATINUM $25

KM# 284 Obv. Designer: John Mercanti. **Rev.
Designer:** Thomas D. Rogers Sr. **Weight:** 7.7857 g.
Composition: 0.9995 Platinum, 0.2502 oz.

Date	Mintage	Unc	Prf.
1997	27,100	365	—
1997W	18,628	—	365
1998	38,887	350	—
1999	39,734	350	—
2000	20,054	350	—
2001	21,815	365	—
2002	27,405	350	—
2003	25,207	365	—
2004	18,010	365	—
2005	12,013	365	—
2006	12,001	—	—

KM# 290   Obv. Designer: John Mercanti.
Weight: 7.7857 g. **Composition:** 0.9995 Platinum,
0.2502 oz.

Date	Mintage	Unc	Prf.
1998W	14,860	—	350

KM# 302   Obv. Designer: John Mercanti.
Weight: 7.7857 g. **Composition:** 0.9995 Platinum,
0.2502 oz.

Date	Mintage	Unc	Prf.
1999W	13,514	—	350

KM# 315   Obv. Designer: John Mercanti.
Weight: 7.7857 g. **Composition:** 0.9995 Platinum,
0.2502 oz.

Date	Mintage	Unc	Prf.
2000W	11,995	—	350

KM# 328   Obv. Designer: John Mercanti.
Weight: 7.7857 g. **Composition:** 0.9995 Platinum,
0.2502 oz.

Date	Mintage	Unc	Prf.
2001W	8,858	—	320

KM# 340   Obv. Designer: John Mercanti.
Weight: 7.7857 g. **Composition:** 0.9995 Platinum,
0.2502 oz.

Date	Mintage	Unc	Prf.
2002W	9,282	—	320

KM# 352   Obv. Designer: John Mercanti. **Rev.
Designer:** Al Maletsky. **Weight:** 7.7857 g.
Composition: 0.9995 Platinum, 0.2502 oz.

Date	Mintage	Unc	Prf.
2003W	6,045	—	385

KM# 365   Obv. Designer: John Mercanti.
Weight: 7.7857 g. **Composition:** 0.9995 Platinum,
0.2502 oz.

Date	Mintage	Unc	Prf.
2004W	5,035	—	950

KM# 378   Obv. Designer: John Mercanti. **Rev.
Designer:** Donna Weaver. **Weight:** 7.7857 g.
Composition: 0.9995 Platinum, 0.2502 oz.

Date	Mintage	Unc	Prf.
2005W	6,424	—	410

KM# 390   Diameter: 22 **Weight:** 7.7857 g.
Composition: 0.9995 Platinum, 0.2502 oz.

Date	Mintage	Unc	Prf.
2006W	—	—	410

KM# 415   Weight: 7.7857 g. **Composition:**
0.9995 Platinum, 0.2502 oz.

Date	Mintage	Unc	Prf.
2007W	—	—	410

PLATINUM $50

KM# 285   Obv. Designer: John Mercanti. **Rev. Designer:** Thomas D. Rogers Sr. **Weight:** 15.5520 g. **Composition:** 0.9995 Platinum, 0.4997 oz.

Date	Mintage	Unc	Prf.
1997	20,500	660	—
1997W	15,432	—	660
1998	32,415	660	—
1999	32,309	660	—
2000	18,892	660	—
2001	12,815	660	—
2002	24,005	660	—
2003	17,409	660	—
2004	98,040	660	—
2005	9,013	660	—
2006	9,602	—	—

KM# 316   Obv. Designer: John Mercanti. **Weight:** 15.5520 g. **Composition:** 0.9995 Platinum, 0.4997 oz.

Date	Mintage	Unc	Prf.
2000W	11,049	—	660

KM# 329   Obv. Designer: John Mercanti. **Weight:** 15.5520 g. **Composition:** 0.9995 Platinum, 0.4997 oz.

Date	Mintage	Unc	Prf.
2001W	8,268	—	660

KM# 291   Obv. Designer: John Mercanti. **Weight:** 15.5520 g. **Composition:** 0.9995 Platinum, 0.4997 oz.

Date	Mintage	Unc	Prf.
1998W	13,821	—	660

KM# 341   Obv. Designer: John Mercanti. **Weight:** 15.5520 g. **Composition:** 0.9995 Platinum, 0.4997 oz.

Date	Mintage	Unc	Prf.
2002W	8,772	—	660

KM# 303   Obv. Designer: John Mercanti. **Weight:** 15.5520 g. **Composition:** 0.9995 Platinum, 0.4997 oz.

Date	Mintage	Unc	Prf.
1999W	11,098	—	660

KM# 353   Obv. Designer: John Mercanti. **Rev. Designer:** Al Maletsky. **Weight:** 15.5520 g. **Composition:** 0.9995 Platinum, 0.4997 oz.

Date	Mintage	Unc	Prf.
2003W	6,181	—	660

KM# 366   Obv. Designer: John Mercanti. **Weight:** 15.5520 g. **Composition:** 0.9995 Platinum, 0.4997 oz.

Date	Mintage	Unc	Prf.
2004W	4,886	—	2,600

KM# 379   Obv. Designer: John Mercanti. **Rev. Designer:** Donna Weaver. **Weight:** 15.5520 g. **Composition:** 0.9995 Platinum, 0.4997 oz.

Date	Mintage	Unc	Prf.
2005W Proof	5,720	—	735

KM# 391   Diameter: 27 **Weight:** 15.5520 g. **Composition:** 0.9995 Platinum, 0.4997 oz.

Date	Mintage	Unc	Prf.
2006W	—	—	735

KM# 416   Weight: 15.5520 g. **Composition:** 0.9995 Platinum, 0.4997 oz.

Date	Mintage	Unc	Prf.
2007W	—	—	735

PLATINUM $100

KM# 286   Obv. Designer: John Mercanti. **Rev. Designer:** Thomas D. Rogers Sr. **Weight:** 31.1050 g. **Composition:** 0.9995 Platinum, 0.9995 oz.

Date	Mintage	Unc	Prf.
1997	56,000	1,350	—
1997W	15,885	—	1,400
1998	133,002	1,350	—
1999	56,707	1,350	—
2000	18,892	1,350	—
2001	14,070	1,350	—
2002	11,502	1,350	—
2003	8,007	1,350	—
2004	7,009	1,350	—
2005	6,310	1,350	—
2006	6,000	1,350	—

KM# 292   Obv. Designer: John Mercanti. **Weight:** 31.1050 g. **Composition:** 0.9995 Platinum, 0.9995 oz.

Date	Mintage	Unc	Prf.
1998W	14,203	—	1,275

KM# 304   Obv. Designer: John Mercanti. **Weight:** 31.1050 g. **Composition:** 0.9995 Platinum, 0.9995 oz.

Date	Mintage	Unc	Prf.
1999W	—	—	1,275

KM# 317   Obv. Designer: John Mercanti. **Weight:** 31.1050 g. **Composition:** 0.9995 Platinum, 0.9995 oz.

Date	Mintage	Unc	Prf.
2000W	—	—	1,275

BULLION COINAGE

KM# 330 **Obv. Designer:** John Mercanti.
Weight: 31.1050 g. **Composition:** 0.9995
Platinum, 0.9995 oz.

Date	Mintage	Unc	Prf.
2001W	8,990	—	1,275

KM# 367 **Obv. Designer:** John Mercanti. **Rev.**
Designer: Donna Weaver. **Weight:** 31.1050 g.
Composition: 0.9995 Platinum, 0.9995 oz.

Date	Mintage	Unc	Prf.
2004W	5,833	—	4,500

KM# 342 **Obv. Designer:** John Mercanti.
Weight: 31.1050 g. **Composition:** 0.9995
Platinum, 0.9995 oz.

Date	Mintage	Unc	Prf.
2002W	9,834	—	1,275

KM# 380 **Obv. Designer:** John Mercanti. **Rev.**
Designer: Donna Weaver. **Weight:** 31.1050 g.
Composition: 0.9995 Platinum, 0.9995 oz.

Date	Mintage	Unc	Prf.
2005W	6,700	—	1,345

KM# 354 **Obv. Designer:** John Mercanti. **Rev.**
Designer: Al Maletsky. **Weight:** 31.1050 g.
Composition: 0.9995 Platinum, 0.9995 oz.

Date	Mintage	Unc	Prf.
2003W	6,991	—	1,275

KM# 392 **Diameter:** 33 **Weight:** 31.1050 g.
Composition: 0.9995 Platinum, 0.9995 oz.

Date	Mintage	Unc	Prf.
2006W	—	—	1,345

KM# 417 **Weight:** 31.1050 g. **Composition:**
0.9995 Platinum, 0.9995 oz.

Date	Mintage	Unc	Prf.
2007W	—	—	1,345

MINT SETS

Mint, or uncirculated, sets contain one uncirculated coin of each denomination from each mint produced for circulation that year. Values listed here are only for those sets sold by the U.S. Mint. Sets were not offered in years not listed. In years when the Mint did not offer the sets, some private companies compiled and marketed uncirculated sets. Mint sets from 1947 through 1958 contained two examples of each coin mounted in cardboard holders, which caused the coins to tarnish. Beginning in 1959, the sets have been packaged in sealed Pliofilm packets and include only one specimen of each coin struck for that year (both P & D mints). Listings for 1965, 1966 and 1967 are for "special mint sets," which were of higher quality than regular mint sets and were prooflike. They were packaged in plastic cases. The 1970 large-date and small-date varieties are distinguished by the size of the date on the coin. The 1976 three-piece set contains the quarter, half dollar and dollar with the Bicentennial design. The 1971 and 1972 sets do not include a dollar coin; the 1979 set does not include an S-mint-marked dollar. Mint sets issued prior to 1959 were double sets (containing two of each coin) packaged in cardboard with a paper overlay. Original sets will always be toned and can bring large premiums if nicely preserved with good color.

Date	Sets Sold	Issue Price	Value	Date	Sets Sold	Issue Price	Value
1947 Est. 5,000	—	4.87	1,325	1976	1,892,513	6.00	8.50
1948 Est. 6,000	—	4.92	625	1977	2,006,869	7.00	8.75
1949 Est. 5,200	—	5.45	875	1978	2,162,609	7.00	8.00
1950 None issued	—	—	—	1979	2,526,000	8.00	7.50
1951	8,654	6.75	950	1980	2,815,066	9.00	7.75
1952	11,499	6.14	860	1981	2,908,145	11.00	15.00
1953	15,538	6.14	535	1982 & 1983 None issued	—	—	—
1954	25,599	6.19	285	1984	1,832,857	7.00	7.00
1955	49,656	3.57	170	1985	1,710,571	7.00	7.50
1956	45,475	3.34	165	1986	1,153,536	7.00	14.50
1957	32,324	4.40	285	1987	2,800,758	7.00	8.00
1958	50,314	4.43	155	1988	1,646,204	7.00	7.50
1959	187,000	2.40	58.00	1989	1,987,915	7.00	7.00
1960	260,485	2.40	32.00	1990	1,809,184	7.00	7.75
1961	223,704	2.40	50.00	1991	1,352,101	7.00	8.75
1962	385,285	2.40	20.00	1992	1,500,143	7.00	7.50
1963	606,612	2.40	20.00	1993	1,297,094	8.00	8.50
1964	1,008,100	2.40	20.00	1994	1,234,813	8.00	9.00
1965 Special Mint Set	2,360,000	4.00	10.00	1995	1,038,787	8.00	16.50
1966 Special Mint Set	2,261,583	4.00	9.75	1996	1,457,949	8.00	24.50
1967 Special Mint Set	1,863,344	4.00	18.50	1997	950,473	8.00	21.50
1968	2,105,128	2.50	6.50	1998	1,187,325	8.00	8.50
1969	1,817,392	2.50	9.25	1999	1,421,625	14.95	26.00
1970 large date	2,038,134	2.50	16.00	2000	1,490,160	14.95	10.00
1970 small date	Inc. above	2.50	65.00	2001	1,066,900	14.95	17.00
1971	2,193,306	3.50	8.00	2002	1,139,388	14.95	13.75
1972	2,750,000	3.50	7.50	2003	1,002,555	14.95	23.50
1973	1,767,691	6.00	18.00	2004	844,484	16.95	75.00
1974	1,975,981	6.00	8.00	2005	—	16.95	20.00
1975	1,921,488	6.00	10.50	2006	—	16.95	20.00
1976 3 coins	4,908,319	9.00	13.50	2007 (28 coins)	—	22.95	—

SETS & ROLLS

MODERN COMMEMORATIVE COIN SETS

Olympic, 1983-1984

Date	Price
1983 & 1984 3 coin set: 1983 and one 1984 uncirculated dollar and 1984W uncirculated gold $10; KM209, 210, 211.	455
1983S & 1984S 3 coin set: proof 1983 and 1984 dollar and 1984W gold $10; KM209, 210, 211.	455
1983 & 1984 6 coin set: 1983S and 1984S uncirculated and proof dollars, 1984W uncirculated and proof gold $10; KM209, 210, 211.	910
1983S & 1984S 2 coin set: proof dollars.	22.50
1983 collectors 3 coin set: 1983 PDS uncirculated dollars; KM209.	37.50
1984 collectors 3 coin set: 1984 PDS uncirculated dollars; KM210.	38.50

Statue of Liberty

Date	Price
1986 2 coin set: uncirculated silver dollar and clad half dollar; KM212, 214.	17.00
1986 2 coin set: proof silver dollar and clad half dollar; KM212, 214.	17.00
1986 3 coin set: uncirculated silver dollar, clad half dollar and gold $5; KM212, 214, 215.	225
1986 3 coin set: proof silver dollar, clad half dollar and gold $5; KM212, 214, 215.	225
1986 6 coin set: 1 each of the proof and uncirculated issues; KM212, 214, 215.	450

Constitution

Date	Price
1987 2 coin set: uncirculated silver dollar and gold $5; KM220, 221.	220
1987 2 coin set: proof silver dollar and gold $5; KM220, 221.	220
1987 4 coin set: silver dollar and $5 gold proof and uncirculated issues; KM220, 221.	445

Olympic, 1988

Date	Price
1988 2 coin set: uncirculated silver dollar and gold $5; KM222, 223.	220
1988 2 coin set: proof silver dollar and gold $5; KM222, 223.	220
1988 4 coin set: silver dollar and $5 gold proof and uncirculated issues; KM222, 223.	440

Congress

Date	Price
1989 2 coin set: uncirculated silver dollar and clad half dollar; KM224, 225.	20.00
1989 2 coin set: proof silver dollar and clad half dollar; KM224, 225.	21.00
1989 3 coin set: uncirculated silver dollar, clad half and gold $5; KM224, 225, 226.	220
1989 3 coin set: proof silver dollar, clad half and gold $5; KM224, 225, 226.	220
1989 6 coin set: 1 each of the proof and uncirculated issues; KM224, 225, 226.	440

Mt. Rushmore

Date	Price
1991 2 coin set: uncirculated half dollar and silver dollar; KM228, 229.	45.00
1991 2 coin set: proof half dollar and silver dollar; KM228, 229.	45.00
1991 3 coin set: uncirculated half dollar, silver dollar and gold $5; KM228, 229, 230.	300
1991 3 coin set: proof half dollar, silver dollar and gold $5; KM228, 229, 230.	225
1991 6 coin set: 1 each of proof and uncirculated issues; KM228, 229, 230.	495

Olympic, 1992

Date	Price
1992 2 coin set: uncirculated half dollar and silver dollar; KM233, 234.	28.00
1992 2 coin set: proof half dollar and silver dollar; KM233, 234.	28.00
1992 3 coin set: uncirculated half dollar, silver dollar and gold $5; KM233, 234, 235.	275
1992 3 coin set: proof half dollar, silver dollar and gold $5; KM233, 234, 235.	240
1992 6 coin set: 1 each of proof and uncirculated issues; KM233, 234, 235.	520

Columbus Quincentenary

Date	Price
1992 2 coin set: uncirculated half dollar and silver dollar; KM237, 238.	35.00
1992 2 coin set: proof half dollar and silver dollar; KM237, 238.	39.00
1992 3 coin set: uncirculated half dollar, silver dollar and gold $5; KM237, 238, 239.	320
1992 3 coin set: proof half dollar, silver dollar and gold $5; KM237, 238, 239.	265
1992 6 coin set: 1 each of proof and uncirculated issues; KM237, 238, 239.	780

Jefferson

Date	Price
1993 Jefferson: dollar, 1994 matte proof nickel and $2 note; KM249, 192.	100.00

Madison / Bill of Rights

Date	Price
1993 2 coin set: uncirculated half dollar and silver dollar; KM240, 241.	28.00
1993 2 coin set: proof half dollar and silver dollar; KM240, 241.	29.00
1993 3 coin set: uncirculated half dollar, silver dollar and gold $5; KM240, 241, 242.	320
1993 3 coin set: proof half dollar, silver dollar and gold $5; KM240, 241, 242.	250
1993 6 coin set: 1 each of proof and uncirculated issues; KM240, 241, 242.	550

World War II

Date	Price
1993 2 coin set: uncirculated half dollar and silver dollar; KM243, 244.	49.00
1993 2 coin set: proof half dollar and silver dollar; KM243, 244.	55.00

Date	Price
1993 3 coin set: uncirculated half dollar, silver dollar and gold $5; KM243, 244, 245.	345
1993 3 coin set: proof half dollar, silver dollar and gold $5; KM243, 244, 245.	335
1993 6 coin set: 1 each of proof and uncirculated issues; KM243, 244, 245.	665

World Cup

Date	Price
1994 2 coin set: uncirculated half dollar and silver dollar; KM246, 247.	32.00
1994 2 coin set: proof half dollar and silver dollar; KM246, 247.	37.00
1994 3 coin set: uncirculated half dollar, silver dollar and gold $5; KM246, 247, 248.	290
1994 3 coin set: proof half dollar, silver dollar and gold $5; KM246, 247, 248.	250
1994 6 coin set: 1 each of proof and uncirculated issues; KM246, 247, 248.	525

U.S. Veterans

Date	Price
1994 3 coin set: uncirculated POW, Vietnam, Women dollars; KM250, 251, 252.	170
1994 3 coin set: proof POW, Vietnam, Women dollars; KM250, 251, 252.	120

Olympic, 1995-96

Date	Price
1995 4 coin set: uncirculated basketball half, $1 gymnast & blind runner, $5 torch runner; KM257, 259, 260, 261.	715
1995 4 coin set: proof basketball half, $1 gymnast & blind runner, $5 torch runner; KM257, 259, 260, 261.	415
1995P 2 coin set: proof $1 gymnast & blind runner; KM259, 260.	105
1995P 2 coin set: proof $1 track & field, cycling; KM263, 264.	95.00
1995-96 4 coin set: proof halves, basketball, baseball, swimming, soccer; KM257, 262, 267, 271.	140
1995 & 96 8 coins in cherry wood case: proof silver dollars: blind runner, gymnast, cycling, track & field, wheelchair, tennis, rowing, high jump; KM259, 260, 263, 264, 268, 269, 272, 272A.	2,150
1995 & 96 16 coins in cherry wood case: bu and proof silver dollars: blind runner, gymnast, cycling, track & field, wheelchair, tennis, rowing, high jump; KM259, 260, 263, 264, 268, 269, 272, 272A.	2,350
1995 & 96 16 coins in cherry wood case: proof half dollars: basketball, baseball, swimming, soccer, KM257, 202, 267, 271. Proof silver dollars: blind runner, gymnast, cycling, track & field, wheelchair, tennis, rowing, high jump, KM259, 260, 263, 264, 268, 269, 272, 272A. Proof $5 gold: torch runner, stadium, cauldron, flag bearer, KM 261, 265, 270, 274.	2,400
1995 & 96 32 coins in cherry wood case: bu & proof half dollars: basketball, baseball, swimming, soccer, KM257, 262, 267, 271. BU & proof silver dollars: blind runner, gymnast, cycling, track & field, wheelchair, tennis, rowing, high jump, KM259, 260, 263, 264, 268, 269, 272, 272A. BU & proof $5 gold: torch runner, stadium, cauldron, flag bearer, KM261, 265, 270, 274.	6,600
1996P 2 coin set: proof $1 wheelchair & tennis; KM268, 269.	160
1996P 2 coin set: proof $1 rowing & high jump; KM272, 272A.	130

Civil War

Date	Price
1995 2 coin set: uncirculated half and dollar; KM254, 255.	90.00
1995 2 coin set: proof half and dollar; KM254, 255.	100.00

Date	Price
1995 3 coin set: uncirculated half, dollar and gold $5; KM254, 255, 256.	800
1995 3 coin set: proof half, dollar and gold $5; KM254, 255, 256.	500
1995 6 coin set: 1 each of proof and uncirculated issues; KM254, 255, 256.	1,275

Smithsonian

Date	Price
1996 2 coin set: proof dollar and $5 gold; KM276, 277.	615
1996 4 coin set: proof and B.U. ; KM276, 277.	2,100

Jackie Robinson

Date	Price
1997 2 coin set: proof dollar & $5 gold; KM279, 280.	800
1997 4 coin set: proof & BU; KM279, 280.	5,750
1997 legacy set.	850

Botanic Garden

Date	Price
1997 2 coin set: dollar, Jefferson nickel and $1 note; KM278, 192.	230

Franklin Delano Roosevelt

Date	Price
1997W 2 coin set: uncirculated and proof; KM282.	1,350

Kennedy

Date	Price
1998 2 coin set: proof; KM287.	70.00
1998 2 coin collectors set: Robert Kennedy dollar and John Kennedy half dollar; KM287, 202b. Matte finished.	325

Black Patriots

Date	Price
1998S 2 coin set: uncirculated and proof; KM288.	200

George Washington

Date	Price
1999 2 coin set: proof and uncirculated gold $5; KM300.	800

Dolley Madison

Date	Price
1999 2 coin set: proof and uncirculated silver dollars; KM298.	77.00

Yellowstone National Park

Date	Price
1999 2 coin set: proof and uncirculated silver dollars; KM299.	88.00

Millennium Coin & Currency

Date	Price
2000 2 coin set: uncirculated Sacagewea $1, silver Eagle & $1 note.	72.00

Leif Ericson

Date	Price
2000 2 coin set: proof and uncirculated silver dollars; KM313.	84.00

Capitol Visitor Center

Date	Price
2001 3 coin set: proof half, silver dollar, gold $5; KM323, 324, 326.	445

American Buffalo

Date	Price
2001 2 coin set: 90% silver unc. & proof $1.; KM325.	460
2001 coin & currency set 90% unc. dollar & replicas of 1899 $5 silver cert.; KM325.	240

Winter Olympics - Salt Lake City

Date	Price
2002 2 coin set: proof 90% silver dollar KM336 & $5.00 Gold KM337.	420
2002 4 coin set: 90% silver unc. & proof $1, KM336 & unc. & proof gold $5, KM337.	940

First Flight Centennial

Date	Price
2003 3 coin set: proof gold ten dollar KM350, proof silver dollar KM349 & proof clad half dollar KM348.	575

Lewis and Clark Bicentennial

Date	Price
2004 Coin and pouch set.	100.00
2004 coin and currency set: Uncirculated silver dollar, two 2005 nickels, replica 1901 $10 Bison note, silver plated peace medal, three stamps & two booklets.	85.00

Date	Price
2004 Westward Journey Nickel series coin and medal set: Proof Sacagawea dollar, two 2005 proof nickels and silver plated peace medal.	35.00

Thomas Alva Edison

Date	Price
2004 Uncirculated silver dollar and light bulb.	60.00

U.S. Marine Corps.

Date	Price
2005 Uncirculated silver dollar and stamp set.	75.00
2005 American Legacy: Proof Marine Corps dollar, Proof John Marshall dollar and 10 piece proof set.	180

Chief Justice John Marshall

Date	Price
2005 Coin and Chronicles set: Uncirculated silver dollar, booklet and BEP intaglio portrait.	60.00
2005 American Legacy: Proof Marine Corps dollar, Proof John Marshall dollar and 10 piece proof set.	180

Benjamin Franklin Tercentennary

Date	Price
2006 Coin and Chronicles set: Uncirculated "Scientist" silver dollar, four stamps, Poor Richards Almanac and intaglio print.	65.00

PROOF SETS

Proof coins are produced through a special process involving specially selected, highly polished planchets and dies. They usually receive two strikings from the coin press at increased pressure. The result is a coin with mirrorlike surfaces and, in recent years, a cameo effect on its raised design surfaces. Proof sets have been sold off and on by the U.S. Mint since 1858. Listings here are for sets from what is commonly called the modern era, since 1936. Values for earlier proofs are included in regular date listings. Sets were not offered in years not listed. Since 1968, proof coins have been produced at the San Francisco Mint; before that they were produced at the Philadelphia Mint. In 1942 the five-cent coin was struck in two compositions. Some proof sets for that year contain only one type (five-coin set); others contain both types. Two types of packaging were used in 1955 -- a box and a flat, plastic holder. The 1960 large-date and small-date sets are distinguished by the size of the date on the cent. Some 1968 sets are missing the mint mark on the dime, the result of an error in the preparation of an obverse die. The 1970 large-date and small-date sets are distinguished by the size of the date on the cent. Some 1970 sets are missing the mint mark on the dime, the result of an error in the preparation of an obverse die. Some 1971 sets are missing the mint mark on the five-cent piece, the result of an error in the preparation of an obverse die. The 1976 three-piece set contains the quarter, half dollar and dollar with the Bicentennial designs. The 1979 and 1981 Type II sets have clearer mint marks than the Type I sets for those years. Some 1983 sets are missing the mint mark on the dime, the result of an error in the preparation of an obverse die. Prestige sets contain the five regular-issue coins plus a commemorative silver dollar from that year. Sets issued prior to 1956 came in transparent envelopes stapled together in a small square box. In mid 1955 sets were changed to a flat clear cellophane envelope. In 1968 sets were changed to a clear hard plastic case as they still are currently issued.

Date	Sets Sold	Issue Price	Value	Date	Sets Sold	Issue Price	Value
1795 (2006) XPn1-XPn3	—	—	—	1879 (2006) XPn21-23	—	—	—
1836 (2006) XPn4, 10-11	—	—	—	1936	3,837	1.89	7,500
1863 (2006) XPn12-14	—	—	—	1937	5,542	1.89	4,350
1871 (2006) XPn15-17	—	—	—	1938	8,045	1.89	1,900
1879 (2006) XPn18-20	—	—	—	1939	8,795	1.89	1,800

Date	Sets Sold	Issue Price	Value	Date	Sets Sold	Issue Price	Value
1940	11,246	1.89	1,450	1991S	2,610,833	11.00	14.00
1941	15,287	1.89	1,425	1991S Prestige Set	256,954	59.00	65.00
1942 6 coins	21,120	1.89	1,450	1992S	2,675,618	12.00	7.50
1942 5 coins	Inc. above	1.89	1,350	1992S Prestige Set	183,285	59.00	84.00
1950	51,386	2.10	775	1992S Silver	1,009,585	21.00	15.00
1951	57,500	2.10	675	1992S Silver premier	308,055	37.00	15.00
1952	81,980	2.10	345	1993S	2,337,819	12.50	13.75
1953	128,800	2.10	310	1993S Prestige Set	224,045	57.00	35.00
1954	233,300	2.10	135	1993S Silver	570,213	21.00	35.00
1955 box	378,200	2.10	130	1993S Silver premier	191,140	37.00	35.00
1955 flat pack	Inc. above	2.10	145	1994S	2,308,701	13.00	14.00
1956	669,384	2.10	62.00	1994S Prestige Set	175,893	57.00	57.00
1957	1,247,952	2.10	24.00	1994S Silver	636,009	21.00	42.50
1958	875,652	2.10	50.00	1994S Silver premier	149,320	37.50	42.50
1959	1,149,291	2.10	24.50	1995S	2,010,384	12.50	42.50
1960 large date	1,691,602	2.10	21.00	1995S Prestige Set	107,112	57.00	135
1960 small date	Inc. above	2.10	32.50	1995S Silver	549,878	21.00	90.00
1961	3,028,244	2.10	13.75	1995S Silver premier	130,107	37.50	90.00
1962	3,218,019	2.10	13.75	1996S	2,085,191	16.00	18.50
1963	3,075,645	2.10	15.50	1996S Prestige Set	55,000	57.00	525
1964	3,950,762	2.10	12.50	1996S Silver	623,655	21.00	42.50
1968S	3,041,509	5.00	7.75	1996S Silver premier	151,366	37.50	42.50
1968S no mint mark dime	Inc. above	5.00	18,500	1997S	1,975,000	12.50	37.00
1969S	2,934,631	5.00	7.50	1997S Prestige Set	80,000	57.00	175
1970S large date	2,632,810	5.00	11.00	1997S Silver	605,473	21.00	66.00
1970S small date	Inc. above	5.00	95.00	1997S Silver premier	136,205	37.50	66.00
1970S no mint mark dime	Inc. above	5.00	1,350	1998S	2,078,494	12.50	24.00
1971S	3,224,138	5.00	6.00	1998S Silver	638,134	21.00	30.00
1971S no mint mark nickel				1998S Silver premier	240,658	37.50	30.00
Est. 1,655	1,655	5.00	1,475	1999S	2,557,899	19.95	67.00
1972S	3,267,667	5.50	5.50	1999S 5 quarter set	1,169,958	13.95	60.00
1973S	2,769,624	7.00	9.00	1999S Silver	804,565	31.95	365
1974S	2,617,350	7.00	11.75	2000S	3,097,442	19.95	20.00
1975S	2,909,369	7.00	11.00	2000S 5 quarter set	995,803	13.95	11.50
1975S no mint mark dime	Inc. above	7.00	50,000	2000S Silver	965,421	31.95	28.50
1976S 3 coins	3,998,621	12.00	18.50	2001S	2,249,498	19.95	100.00
1976S	4,149,730	7.00	10.75	2001S 5 quarter set	774,800	13.95	56.00
1977S	3,251,152	9.00	8.00	2001S Silver	849,600	31.95	175
1978S	3,127,788	9.00	9.00	2002S	2,319,766	19.95	35.00
1979S Type I	3,677,175	9.00	8.50	2002S 5 quarter set	764,419	13.95	21.50
1979S Type II	Inc. above	9.00	125	2002S Silver	892,229	31.95	60.00
1980S	3,547,030	10.00	8.25	2003 X#207, 208, 209.2	—	44.00	28.75
1981S Type I	4,063,083	11.00	8.00	2003S	2,175,684	19.95	22.50
1981S Type II	Inc. above	11.00	440	2003S 5 quarter set	1,225,507	13.95	17.50
1982S	3,857,479	11.00	5.25	2003S Silver	1,142,858	31.95	31.00
1983S	3,138,765	11.00	7.50	2004S 11 pieces	1,804,396	22.95	48.00
1983S Prestige Set	140,361	59.00	95.00	2004S 5 quarter set	987,960	15.95	25.00
1983S no mint mark dime	Inc. above	11.00	1,175	2004S Silver 11 pieces	1,187,673	37.95	39.50
1984S	2,748,430	11.00	7.00	2004S Silver 5 quarter set	594,137	23.95	25.00
1984S Prestige Set	316,600	59.00	26.00	2005S American Legacy	—	—	185
1985S	3,362,821	11.00	6.00	2005S 11 pieces	—	22.95	23.00
1986S	2,411,180	11.00	16.00	2005S 5 quarter set	—	15.95	16.00
1986S Prestige Set	599,317	48.50	33.00	2005S Silver 11 pieces	—	37.95	41.50
1987S	3,972,233	11.00	7.00	2005S Silver 5 quarter set	—	23.95	22.00
1987S Prestige Set	435,495	45.00	22.00	2005S American Legacy	—	—	185
1988S	3,031,287	11.00	7.50	2006S 10 pieces clad	—	22.95	25.50
1988S Prestige Set	231,661	45.00	31.50	2006S 5 quarter set	—	15.95	17.50
1989S	3,009,107	11.00	7.50	2006S Silver 10 Pieces	—	37.95	39.50
1989S Prestige Set	211,087	45.00	40.00	2006S Silver 5 quarter set	—	23.95	27.50
1990S	2,793,433	11.00	8.50	2007S 5 quarter set	—	13.95	15.50
1990S no S 1¢	3,555	11.00	7,500	2007S Silver 5 quarter set	—	22.95	25.50
1990S Prestige Set	506,126	45.00	25.00	2007S 14 pieces clad	—	—	—
1990S Prestige Set, no S 1¢	Inc. above	45.00	8,000	2007S Silver 14 pieces	—	—	—

COLONIAL COINAGE

MARYLAND

LORD BALTIMORE

PENNY (DENARIUM)

KM#1 **Composition:** Copper.

Date	AG	Good	VG	Fine	VF	XF	Unc
ND(1659) 4 known	—	—	—	—	—	—	—

4 PENCE (GROAT)

KM#2 **Composition:** Silver. **Obverse:** Large bust. **Reverse:** Large shield.

Date	AG	Good	VG	Fine	VF	XF	Unc
ND(1659)	750	1,250	2,500	4,500	8,500	15,000	—

KM#3 **Composition:** Silver. **Obverse:** Small bust. **Reverse:** Small shield.

Date	AG	Good	VG	Fine	VF	XF	Unc
ND(1659) unique	—	—	—	—	—	—	—

Note: Norweb $26,400

6 PENCE

KM#4 **Composition:** Silver. **Obverse:** Small bust. **Note:** Known in two other rare small-bust varieties and two rare large-bust varieties.

Date	AG	Good	VG	Fine	VF	XF	Unc
ND(1659)	450	950	1,750	3,500	6,750	12,500	—

SHILLING

KM#6 **Composition:** Silver. **Note:** Varieties exist; one is very rare.

Date	AG	Good	VG	Fine	VF	XF	Unc
ND(1659)	500	1,000	2,000	4,000	8,000	14,500	—

MASSACHUSETTS

NEW ENGLAND

3 PENCE

KM#1 **Composition:** Silver. **Obverse:** NE. **Reverse:** III.

Date	AG	Good	VG	Fine	VF	XF	Unc
ND(1652) 2 known	—	—	—	—	—	—	—

6 PENCE

KM#2 **Composition:** Silver. **Obverse:** NE. **Reverse:** VI.

Date	AG	Good	VG	Fine	VF	XF	Unc
ND(1652) 8 known	—	—	—	—	—	—	—

Note: Garrett $75,000

SHILLING

KM#3 **Composition:** Silver. **Obverse:** NE. **Reverse:** XII.

Date	AG	Good	VG	Fine	VF	XF	Unc
ND(1652)	2,000	4,500	7,500	15,000	35,000	—	—

OAK TREE

2 PENCE

KM#7   Composition: Silver.

Date	AG	Good	VG	Fine	VF	XF	Unc
1662	150	300	550	850	2,150	—	—

3 PENCE

KM#8   Composition: Silver **Note:** Two types of legends.

Date	AG	Good	VG	Fine	VF	XF	Unc
1652	200	400	650	1,000	2,600	—	—

6 PENCE

KM#9   Composition: Silver. **Note:** Three types of legends.

Date	AG	Good	VG	Fine	VF	XF	Unc
1652	250	450	750	1,250	3,000	—	—

SHILLING

KM#10   Composition: Silver. **Note:** Two types of legends.

Date	AG	Good	VG	Fine	VF	XF	Unc
1652	175	300	650	1,150	2,850	—	—

PINE TREE

3 PENCE

KM#11   Composition: Silver. **Obverse:** Tree without berries.

Date	AG	Good	VG	Fine	VF	XF	Unc
1652	150	300	450	750	1,600	—	—

KM#12   Composition: Silver. **Obverse:** Tree with berries.

Date	AG	Good	VG	Fine	VF	XF	Unc
1652	165	325	500	850	1,850	—	—

6 PENCE

KM#13   Composition: Silver. **Obverse:** Tree without berries; "spiney tree".

Date	AG	Good	VG	Fine	VF	XF	Unc
1652	525	950	1,650	2,000	3,000	—	—

KM#14   Composition: Silver. **Obverse:** Tree with berries.

Date	AG	Good	VG	Fine	VF	XF	Unc
1652	150	300	575	1,150	2,100	—	—

SHILLING

KM#15   Composition: Silver. **Note:** Large planchet. Many varieties exist; some are very rare.

Date	AG	Good	VG	Fine	VF	XF	Unc
1652	200	425	775	1,350	2,650	—	—

KM#16   Composition: Silver. **Note:** Small planchet; large dies. All examples are thought to be contemporary fabrications.

Date	AG	Good	VG	Fine	VF	XF	Unc
1652	—	—	—	—	—	—	—

KM#17   Composition: Silver. **Note:** Small planchet; small dies. Many varieties exist; some are very rare.

Date	AG	Good	VG	Fine	VF	XF	Unc
1652	150	300	575	1,250	2,300	—	—

WILLOW TREE

3 PENCE

KM#4 Composition: Silver.

Date	AG	Good	VG	Fine	VF	XF	Unc
1652 3 known	—	—	—	—	—	—	—

6 PENCE

KM#5 Composition: Silver.

Date	AG	Good	VG	Fine	VF	XF	Unc
1652	3,500	7,500	10,000	18,000	35,000	—	—

SHILLING

KM#6 Composition: Silver.

Date	AG	Good	VG	Fine	VF	XF	Unc
1652	4,000	10,000	12,500	20,000	36,500	—	—

NEW JERSEY

ST. PATRICK OR MARK NEWBY

FARTHING

KM#1 Composition: Copper.

Date	AG	Good	VG	Fine	VF	XF	Unc
ND(1682)	20.00	40.00	80.00	200	425	—	—

KM#1a Composition: Silver.

Date	AG	Good	VG	Fine	VF	XF	Unc
ND(1682)	350	550	1,150	1,650	2,750	—	—

HALFPENNY

KM#2 Composition: Copper.

Date	AG	Good	VG	Fine	VF	XF	Unc
ND(1682)	50.00	100.00	200	400	900	—	—

EARLY AMERICAN TOKENS

AMERICAN PLANTATIONS

1/24 REAL

KM#Tn5.1 Composition: Tin.**Obverse Legend:** ET HIB REX.

Date	AG	Good	VG	Fine	VF	XF	Unc
ND(1688)	65.00	125	165	210	285	450	—

KM#Tn5.3 Composition: Tin.**Reverse:** Horizontal 4.

Date	AG	Good	VG	Fine	VF	XF	Unc
ND(1688)	175	300	400	500	650	1,350	—

KM#Tn5.4 Composition: Tin.**Obverse Legend:** ET HIB REX.

Date	AG	Good	VG	Fine	VF	XF	Unc
ND(1688)	—	—	—	—	—	—	6,000

KM#Tn6 Composition: Tin.**Reverse:** Arms of Scotland left, Ireland right.

Date	AG	Good	VG	Fine	VF	XF	Unc
ND(1688)	450	750	1,250	2,000	2,500	—	—

COLONIAL COINAGE

KM#Tn5.2 **Composition:** Tin. **Obverse:** Rider's head left of "B" in legend. **Note:** Restrikes made in 1828 from two obverse dies.

Date	AG	Good	VG	Fine	VF	XF	Unc
ND(1828)	35.00	65.00	100.00	150	225	325	—

ELEPHANT

KM#Tn1.1 **Weight:** 15.5500 g. **Composition:** Copper. **Note:** Thick planchet.

Date	AG	Good	VG	Fine	VF	XF	Unc
ND(1664)	60.00	100.00	150	250	450	850	—

KM#Tn1.2 **Composition:** Copper. **Note:** Thin planchet.

Date	AG	Good	VG	Fine	VF	XF	Unc
ND(1664)	80.00	150	200	350	600	1,250	—

KM#Tn2 **Composition:** Copper. **Reverse:** Diagonals tie shield.

Date	AG	Good	VG	Fine	VF	XF	Unc
ND(1664)	120	185	225	400	700	1,450	—

KM#Tn3 **Composition:** Copper. **Reverse:** Sword right side of shield.

Date	AG	Good	VG	Fine	VF	XF	Unc
ND(1664) 3 known	—	—	—	—	—	—	—

Note: Norweb $1,320

KM#Tn4 **Composition:** Copper. **Reverse Legend:** LON DON.

Date	AG	Good	VG	Fine	VF	XF	Unc
ND(1684)	175	300	500	1,000	1,850	3,750	—

KM#Tn7 **Composition:** Copper. **Reverse Legend:** NEW ENGLAND.

Date	AG	Good	VG	Fine	VF	XF	Unc
ND(1694) 2 known	—	—	—	—	—	—	—

Note: Norweb $25,300

KM#Tn8.1 **Composition:** Copper. **Reverse Legend:** CAROLINA (PROPRIETORS).

Date	AG	Good	VG	Fine	VF	XF	Unc
ND(1694) 5 known	—	—	—	—	—	—	—

Note: Norweb $35,200

KM#Tn8.2 **Composition:** Copper. **Reverse Legend:** CAROLINA (PROPRIETORS, O over E).

Date	AG	Good	VG	Fine	VF	XF	Unc
1694	700	1,100	1,700	2,750	5,750	11,000	—

Note: Norweb $17,600

GLOUCESTER

KM#Tn15 **Composition:** Copper.

Date	AG	Good	VG	Fine	VF	XF	Unc
ND(1714) 2 known	—	—	—	—	—	—	—

Note: Garrett $36,000

HIBERNIA-VOCE POPULI

FARTHING

KM#Tn21.1 **Composition:** Copper. **Note:** Large letters

Date	AG	Good	VG	Fine	VF	XF	Unc
1760	90.00	150	275	450	750	1,550	—

COLONIAL COINAGE

KM#Tn21.2 Composition: Copper. **Note:** Small letters

Date	AG	Good	VG	Fine	VF	XF	Unc
1760 extremely rare	—	—	—	—	—	—	—

Note: Norweb $5,940.

HALFPENNY

KM#Tn22 Composition: Copper.

Date	AG	Good	VG	Fine	VF	XF
1700 Extremely rare	—	—	—	—	—	—

Note: Date is in error; ex-Roper $575. Norweb $577.50. Stack's Americana, VF, $2,900

1760 varieties	10.00	30.00	50.00	100.00	185	350
1760	20.00	35.00	60.00		110	200	400

Note: legend VOOE POPULI

HIGLEY OR GRANBY

KM#Tn16 Composition: Copper.**Obverse Legend:** CONNECTICVT. **Note:** THE VALVE OF THREE PENCE.

Date	AG	Good	VG	Fine	VF	XF	Unc
1737	—	—	—	—	—	—	—

Note: Garrett $16,000

KM#Tn17 Composition: Copper.**Obverse Legend:** THE VALVE OF THREE PENCE. **Reverse Legend:** I AM GOOD COPPER.

Date	AG	Good	VG	Fine	VF	XF	Unc
1737 2 known	—	—	—	—	—	—	—

Note: ex-Norweb $6,875

KM#Tn18.1 Composition: Copper.**Obverse Legend:** VALUE ME AS YOU PLEASE. **Reverse Legend:** I AM GOOD COPPER.

Date	AG	Good	VG	Fine	VF	XF	Unc
1737	6,500	8,500	10,500	14,500	25,000	—	—

KM#Tn18.2 Composition: Copper.**Obverse Legend:** VALVE ME AS YOU PLEASE.. **Reverse Legend:** I AM GOOD COPPER..

Date	AG	Good	VG	Fine	VF	XF	Unc
1737 2 known	—	—	—	—	—	—	—

KM#Tn19 Composition: Copper.**Reverse:** Broad axe.

Date	AG	Good	VG	Fine	VF	XF	Unc
ND(1737)	—	—	—	—	—	—	—

Note: Garrett $45,000

1739 5 known	—	—	—	—	—	—	—

Note: Eliasberg $12,650. Oechsner $9,900. Steinberg (holed) $4,400.

KM#Tn20 Composition: Copper.**Obverse Legend:** THE WHEELE GOES ROUND. **Reverse:** J CUT MY WAY THROUGH.

Date	AG	Good	VG	Fine	VF	XF	Unc
ND(1737) unique	—	—	—	—	—	—	—

Note: Roper $60,500

NEW YORKE

KM#Tn9 **Composition:** Brass. **Note:** The 1700 date is circa.

Date	AG	Good	VG	Fine	VF	XF	Unc
1700	650	1,250	2,850	4,500	7,500	—	—

KM#Tn9a **Composition:** White Metal.

Date	AG	Good	VG	Fine	VF	XF	Unc
1700	4 known	—	—	—	—	—	—

PITT

FARTHING

KM#Tn23 **Composition:** Copper.

Date	AG	Good	VG	Fine	VF	XF	Unc
1766	—	—	—	1,350	2,850	6,000	—

HALFPENNY

KM#Tn24 **Composition:** Copper.

Date	AG	Good	VG	Fine	VF	XF	Unc
1766	45.00	85.00	175	350	700	1,500	—

ROYAL PATENT COINAGE

HIBERNIA

FARTHING

KM#20 **Composition:** Copper. **Note:** Pattern.

Date	AG	Good	VG	Fine	VF	XF	Unc
1722	25.00	50.00	125	220	325	700	—

KM#24 **Composition:** Copper. **Obverse:** 1722 obverse. **Obverse Legend:** ...D:G:REX..

Date	AG	Good	VG	Fine	VF	XF	Unc
1723	20.00	40.00	60.00	90.00	150	350	—

KM#25 **Composition:** Copper. **Obverse Legend:** DEI • GRATIA • REX •.

Date	AG	Good	VG	Fine	VF	XF	Unc
1723	10.00	20.00	40.00	65.00	90.00	200	—

KM#25a **Composition:** Silver.

Date	Good	VG	Fine	VF	XF	Unc	Proof
1723	—	—	—	800	1,600	—	2,700
1724	45.00	75.00	125	250	485	—	—

HALFPENNY

KM#21 **Composition:** Copper. **Reverse:** Harp left, head right.

Date	AG	Good	VG	Fine	VF	XF	Unc
1722	—	15.00	35.00	65.00	135	350	—

KM#22 **Composition:** Copper. **Obverse:** Harp left, head right. **Note:** Pattern.

Date	AG	Good	VG	Fine	VF	XF	Unc
1722	7.00	—	—	1,150	1,750	3,000	—

KM#23.1 **Composition:** Copper.**Reverse:** Harp right.

Date	AG	Good	VG	Fine	VF	XF	Unc
1722	2.00	15.00	35.00	60.00	125	250	—
1723	7.00	15.00	25.00	40.00	80.00	175	—
1723/22	10.00	20.00	45.00	90.00	185	375	—
1724	7.00	15.00	35.00	60.00	125	265	—

KM#23.2 **Composition:** Copper. **Obverse:** DEII error in legend.

Date	AG	Good	VG	Fine	VF	XF	Unc
1722	40.00	90.00	180	300	500	750	—

KM#26 **Composition:** Copper.**Reverse:** Large head. **Note:** Rare. Generally mint state only. Probably a pattern.

Date	AG	Good	VG	Fine	VF	XF	Unc
1723	—	—	—	—	—	—	—

KM#27 **Composition:** Copper.**Reverse:** Continuous legend over head.

Date	AG	Good	VG	Fine	VF	XF	Unc
1724	30.00	65.00	150	300	475	750	—

ROSA AMERICANA

HALFPENNY

KM#1 **Composition:** Copper.**Obverse Legend:** D • G • REX •.

Date	AG	Good	VG	Fine	VF	XF	Unc
1722	20.00	40.00	60.00	100.00	220	475	—

KM#2 **Composition:** Copper. **Obverse:** Uncrowned rose. **Obverse Legend:** DEI GRATIA REX.. **Note:** Several varieties exist.

Date	AG	Good	VG	Fine	VF	XF	Unc
1722	18.00	35.00	55.00	100.00	200	475	—
1723	285	525	750	1,350	2,250	—	—

KM#3 **Composition:** Copper.**Reverse Legend:** VTILE DVLCI.

Date	AG	Good	VG	Fine	VF	XF	Unc
1722	250	450	650	1,100	—	—	—

KM#9 **Composition:** Copper.**Reverse:** Crowned rose.

Date	AG	Good	VG	Fine	VF	XF	Unc
1723	18.00	35.00	55.00	100.00	200	450	—

PENNY

KM#4 **Composition:** Copper.**Reverse Legend:** UTILE DULCI. **Note:** Several varieties exist.

Date	AG	Good	VG	Fine	VF	XF	Unc
1722	18.00	35.00	55.00	100.00	175	385	—

KM#5 **Composition:** Copper. **Note:** Several varieties exist. Also known in two rare pattern types with long hair ribbons, one with V's for U's on the obverse.

Date	AG	Good	VG	Fine	VF	XF	Unc
1722	18.00	35.00	55.00	100.00	220	475	—

KM#10 **Composition:** Copper. **Note:** Several varieties exist.

Date	AG	Good	VG	Fine	VF	XF	Unc
1723	18.00	35.00	55.00	100.00	200	420	—

KM#12 Composition: Copper. **Note:** Pattern.

Date	AG	Good	VG	Fine	VF	XF	Unc
1724 2 known	—	—	—	—	—	—	—

KM#13 Composition: Copper.

Date	AG	Good	VG	Fine	VF	XF	Unc
ND(1724) 5 known	—	—	—	—	—	—	—

Note: Norweb $2,035

KM#14 Composition: Copper. **Obverse:** George II. **Note:** Pattern.

Date	AG	Good	VG	Fine	VF	XF	Unc
1727 2 known	—	—	—	—	—	—	—

2 PENCE

KM#6 Composition: Copper. **Reverse:** Motto with scroll.

Date	AG	Good	VG	Fine	VF	XF	Unc
ND(1722)	35.00	60.00	110	200	350	700	—

KM#7 Composition: Copper. **Reverse:** Motto without scroll.

Date	AG	Good	VG	Fine	VF	XF	Unc
ND(1722) 3 known	—	—	—	—	—	—	—

KM#8.1 Composition: Copper. **Obverse:** Period after REX. **Reverse:** Dated.

Date	AG	Good	VG	Fine	VF	XF	Unc
1722	25.00	40.00	70.00	125	265	500	—

KM#8.2 Composition: Copper. **Obverse:** Without period after REX

Date	AG	Good	VG	Fine	VF	XF	Unc
1722	22.00	40.00	70.00	125	275	525	—

KM#11 Composition: Copper. **Obverse:** No stop after REX. **Reverse:** Stop after 1723. **Note:** Several varieties exist.

Date	AG	Good	VG	Fine	VF	XF	Unc
1723	25.00	45.00	75.00	140	285	550	—

KM#15 Composition: Copper. **Note:** Pattern. Two varieties exist; both extremely rare.

Date	AG	Good	VG	Fine	VF	XF	Unc
1724	—	—	—	—	—	—	—

Note. ex-Garrett $5,775. Stack's Americana, XF, $10,925

KM#16 Composition: Copper. **Note:** Pattern.

Date	AG	Good	VG	Fine	VF	XF	Unc
1733 4 known	—	—	—	—	—	—	—

Note: Norweb $19,800

VIRGINIA HALFPENNY

KM#Tn25.1 Composition: Copper. **Reverse:** Small 7s in date.. **Note:** Struck on Irish halfpenny planchets.

Date	Good	VG	Fine	VF	XF	Unc	Proof
1773	—	—	—	—	—	—	3,500

KM#Tn25.2 Composition: Copper. **Obverse:** Period after GEORGIVS. **Reverse:** Varieties with 7 or 8 strings in harp.

Date	AG	Good	VG	Fine	VF	XF	Unc
1773	6.00	12.00	25.00	50.00	100.00	250	465

KM#Tn25.3 Composition: Copper. **Obverse:** Without period after GEORGIVS. **Reverse:** Varieties with 6, 7 or 8 strings in harp.

Date	AG	Good	VG	Fine	VF	XF	Unc
1773	7.00	15.00	30.00	60.00	135	275	525

KM#Tn25.4 Composition: Copper. **Obverse:** Without period after GEORGIVS. **Reverse:** 8 harp strings, dot on cross.

Date	AG	Good	VG	Fine	VF	XF	Unc
1773	—	—	—	—	—	—	—

Note: ex-Steinberg $2,600

KM#Tn26 Composition: Silver. **Note:** So-called "shilling" silver proofs.

Date	AG	Good	VG	Fine	VF	XF	Unc
1774 6 known	—	—	—	—	—	—	—

Note: Garrett $23,000

REVOLUTIONARY COINAGE

CONTINENTAL "DOLLAR".

KM#EA1 Composition: Pewter **Obverse Legend:** CURRENCY.

Date	AG	Good	VG	Fine	VF	XF	Unc
1776	—	—	1,850	3,000	4,750	8,750	18,500

KM#EA2 Composition: Pewter **Obverse Legend:** CURRENCY, EG FECIT.

Date	AG	Good	VG	Fine	VF	XF	Unc
1776	—	—	1,750	2,850	4,250	7,750	16,000

KM#EA2a Composition: Silver **Obverse Legend:** CURRENCY, EG FECIT.

Date	AG	Good	VG	Fine	VF	XF	Unc
1776 2 known	—	—	—	—	—	—	—

KM#EA3 Composition: Pewter **Obverse Legend:** CURRENCY.

Date	AG	Good	VG	Fine	VF	XF	Unc
1776 extremely rare	—	—	—	—	—	—	—

KM#EA4 Composition: Pewter **Obverse Legend:** CURRENCY. **Reverse:** Floral cross.

Date	AG	Good	VG	Fine	VF	XF	Unc
1776 3 recorded	—	—	—	—	—	—	—

Note: Norweb $50,600. Johnson $25,300

KM#2 **Composition:** Copper **Obverse:** "African head."

Date	AG	Good	VG	Fine	VF	XF	Unc
1785	25.00	45.00	85.00	200	450	1,500	—

KM#3.1 **Composition:** Copper **Obverse:** Bust facing left.

Date	AG	Good	VG	Fine	VF	XF	Unc
1785	60.00	100.00	150	275	400	750	—
1786	20.00	30.00	50.00	90.00	185	465	—
1787	22.00	35.00	60.00	110	125	350	—
1788	20.00	30.00	50.00	100.00	220	500	—

KM#EA5 **Composition:** Pewter **Obverse Legend:** CURENCY.

Date	AG	Good	VG	Fine	VF	XF	Unc
1776	—	—	1,650	2,750	4,000	8,000	16,000

KM#EA5a **Composition:** Brass **Obverse Legend:** CURENCY. **Note:** Two varieties exist.

Date	AG	Good	VG	Fine	VF	XF	Unc
1776	—	—	—	—	13,500	17,500	—

KM#EA5b **Composition:** Silver **Obverse Legend:** CURENCY.

Date	AG	Good	VG	Fine	VF	XF	Unc
1776 unique	—	—	—	—	—	—	—

Note: Romano $99,000

KM#4 **Composition:** Copper **Obverse:** Small mailed bust facing left. **Reverse Legend:** ETLIB INDE.

Date	AG	Good	VG	Fine	VF	XF	Unc
1786	22.00	35.00	55.00	85.00	165	400	—

KM#5 **Composition:** Copper **Obverse:** Small mailed bust facing right. **Reverse Legend:** INDE ET LIB.

Date	AG	Good	VG	Fine	VF	XF	Unc
1786	30.00	55.00	75.00	115	225	475	—

STATE COINAGE

CONNECTICUT

KM#1 **Composition:** Copper **Obverse:** Bust facing right.

Date	AG	Good	VG	Fine	VF	XF	Unc
1785	20.00	30.00	50.00	85.00	190	450	—

KM#6 **Composition:** Copper **Obverse:** Large mailed bust facing right.

Date	AG	Good	VG	Fine	VF	XF	Unc
1786	30.00	50.00	90.00	165	350	850	—

COLONIAL COINAGE

KM#7 **Composition:** Copper **Obverse:** "Hercules head."

Date	AG	Good	VG	Fine	VF	XF	Unc
1786	25.00	40.00	75.00	135	300	700	—

KM#8.1 **Composition:** Copper **Obverse:** Draped bust.

Date	AG	Good	VG	Fine	VF	XF	Unc
1786	22.00	35.00	65.00	120	275	600	—

KM#9 **Composition:** Copper **Obverse:** Small head. **Reverse Legend:** ETLIB INDE.

Date	AG	Good	VG	Fine	VF	XF	Unc
1787	25.00	40.00	90.00	150	350	800	—

KM#10 **Composition:** Copper **Obverse:** Small head. **Reverse Legend:** INDE ET LIB.

Date	AG	Good	VG	Fine	VF	XF	Unc
1787	75.00	135	175	275	450	950	—

KM#11 **Composition:** Copper **Obverse:** Medium bust. **Note:** Two reverse legend types exist.

Date	AG	Good	VG	Fine	VF	XF	Unc
1787	50.00	80.00	140	200	325	625	—

KM#12 **Composition:** Copper **Obverse:** "Muttonhead" variety. **Note:** Extremely rare with legend INDE ET LIB.

Date	AG	Good	VG	Fine	VF	XF	Unc
1787	30.00	50.00	120	250	650	1,500	—

KM#3.3 **Composition:** Copper **Obverse:** Perfect date. **Reverse Legend:** IN DE ET.

Date	AG	Good	VG	Fine	VF	XF	Unc
1787	35.00	65.00	85.00	135	250	600	—

KM#13 **Composition:** Copper **Obverse:** "Laughing head"

Date	AG	Good	VG	Fine	VF	XF	Unc
1787	22.00	35.00	60.00	110	250	700	—

KM#14 **Composition:** Copper **Obverse:** "Horned head"

Date	AG	Good	VG	Fine	VF	XF	Unc
1787	15.00	25.00	40.00	70.00	175	475	—

KM#15 **Composition:** Copper **Reverse Legend:** IND ET LIB

Date	AG	Good	VG	Fine	VF	XF	Unc
1787/8	25.00	40.00	75.00	130	250	650	—
1787/ 1887	20.00	30.00	50.00	90.00	200	520	—

KM#16   Composition: Copper **Obverse Legend:**
CONNECT. **Reverse Legend:** INDE ET LIB. **Note:** Two
additional scarce reverse legend types exist.

Date	AG	Good	VG	Fine	VF	XF	Unc
1787	22.00	37.50	60.00	115	220	550	—

KM#8.2   Composition: Copper **Obverse:** Draped
bust. **Note:** Many varieties.

Date	AG	Good	VG	Fine	VF	XF	Unc
1787	12.00	20.00	40.00	80.00	135	275	—

KM#8.3   Composition: Copper **Obverse Legend:**
AUCIORI.

Date	AG	Good	VG	Fine	VF	XF	Unc
1787	15.00	25.00	50.00	110	250	600	—

KM#8.4   Composition: Copper **Obverse Legend:**
AUCTOPI.

Date	AG	Good	VG	Fine	VF	XF	Unc
1787	20.00	30.00	60.00	125	265	650	—

KM#8.5   Composition: Copper **Obverse Legend:**
AUCTOBI.

Date	AG	Good	VG	Fine	VF	XF	Unc
1787	15.00	25.00	50.00	110	225	550	—

KM#8.6   Composition: Copper **Obverse Legend:**
CONNFC.

Date	AG	Good	VG	Fine	VF	XF	Unc
1787	12.00	20.00	40.00	85.00	200	525	—

KM#8.7   Composition: Copper **Obverse Legend:**
CONNLC.

Date	AG	Good	VG	Fine	VF	XF	Unc
1787		30.00	60.00	125	265	650	—

KM#8.8   Composition: Copper **Reverse Legend:**
FNDE.

Date	AG	Good	VG	Fine	VF	XF	Unc
1787	15.00	25.00	45.00	90.00	210	535	—

KM#8.9   Composition: Copper **Reverse Legend:**
ETLIR.

Date	AG	Good	VG	Fine	VF	XF	Unc
1787	15.00	25.00	45.00	90.00	210	535	—

KM#8.10   Composition: Copper **Reverse Legend:**
ETIIB.

Date	AG	Good	VG	Fine	VF	XF	Unc
1787	20.00	30.00	50.00	100.00	225	550	—

KM#20   Composition: Copper **Obverse:** Mailed bust
facing right.

Date	AG	Good	VG	Fine	VF	XF	Unc
1788	15.00	25.00	45.00	90.00	200	425	—

KM#21   Composition: Copper **Obverse:** Small
mailed bust facing right.

Date	AG	Good	VG	Fine	VF	XF	Unc
1788	75.00	150	285	550	1,100	2,500	—

KM#3.4   Composition: Copper **Obverse Legend:**
CONNLC.

Date	AG	Good	VG	Fine	VF	XF	Unc
1788	15.00	25.00	40.00	80.00	175	400	—

KM#22.1   Composition: Copper **Obverse:** Draped
bust facing left. **Reverse Legend:** INDE ET LIB.

Date	AG	Good	VG	Fine	VF	XF	Unc
1788	12.00	20.00	35.00	55.00	135	375	—

KM#22.2   Composition: Copper **Reverse Legend:**
INDLET LIB.

Date	AG	Good	VG	Fine	VF	XF	Unc
1788	20.00	30.00	55.00	90.00	185	400	—

KM#22.3   Composition: Copper **Obverse Legend:**
CONNEC. **Reverse Legend:** INDE ET LIB.

Date	AG	Good	VG	Fine	VF	XF	Unc
1788	22.00	35.00	60.00	100.00	200	425	—

KM#22.4   Composition: Copper **Obverse Legend:**
CONNEC. **Reverse Legend:** INDL ET LIB.

Date	AG	Good	VG	Fine	VF	XF	Unc
1788	22.00	35.00	60.00	100.00	200	425	—

MASSACHUSETTS

CENT

HALFPENNY

KM# 17 **Composition:** Copper

Date	AG	Good	VG	Fine	VF	XF	Unc
1776 unique	—	—	—	—	—	—	—

Note: Garrett $40,000

PENNY

KM# 18 **Composition:** Copper

Date	AG	Good	VG	Fine	VF	XF	Unc
1776 unique	—	—	—	—	—	—	—

HALF CENT

KM# 19 **Composition:** Copper **Note:** Varieties exist; some are rare.

Date	AG	Good	VG	Fine	VF	XF	Unc
1787	30.00	50.00	90.00	175	350	800	—
1788	35.00	55.00	100.00	185	375	850	—

KM# 20.1 **Composition:** Copper **Reverse:** Arrows in right talon

Date	AG	Good	VG	Fine	VF	XF	Unc
1787 7 known	—	—	—	—	—	—	—

Note: Ex-Bushnell-Brand $8,800. Garrett $5,500

KM# 20.2 **Composition:** Copper **Reverse:** Arrows in left talon

Date	AG	Good	VG	Fine	VF	XF	Unc
1787	25.00	40.00	65.00	120	285	785	—

KM# 20.3 **Composition:** Copper **Reverse:** "Horned eagle" die break

Date	AG	Good	VG	Fine	VF	XF	Unc
1787	28.00	45.00	70.00	130	300	785	—

KM# 20.4 **Composition:** Copper **Reverse:** Without period after Massachusetts

Date	AG	Good	VG	Fine	VF	XF	Unc
1788	28.00	45.00	70.00	135	320	850	—

KM# 20.5 **Composition:** Copper **Reverse:** Period after Massachusetts, normal S's

Date	AG	Good	VG	Fine	VF	XF	Unc
1788	28.00	45.00	70.00	120	275	775	—

KM# 20.6   Composition: Copper **Reverse:** Period after Massachusetts, S's like 8's

Date	AG	Good	VG	Fine	VF	XF	Unc
1788	22.00	35.00	60.00	120	275	775	—

NEW HAMPSHIRE

KM# 1   Composition: Copper

Date	AG	Good	VG	Fine	VF	XF	Unc
1776 extremely rare	—	—	—	—	—	—	—

Note: Garrett $13,000

NEW JERSEY

KM# 8   Composition: Copper **Obverse:** Date below draw bar.

Date	AG	Good	VG	Fine	VF	XF	Unc
1786 extremely rare	—	—	—	—	—	—	—

Note: Garrett $52,000

KM# 9   Composition: Copper **Obverse:** Large horse head, date below plow, no coulter on plow.

Date	AG	Good	VG	Fine	VF	XF	Unc
1786	75.00	150	285	550	1,450	5,500	—

KM# 10   Composition: Copper **Reverse:** Narrow shield, straight beam.

Date	AG	Good	VG	Fine	VF	XF	Unc
1786	25.00	40.00	65.00	150	350	975	—

KM# 11.1   Composition: Copper **Reverse:** Wide shield, curved beam. **Note:** Varieties exist.

Date	AG	Good	VG	Fine	VF	XF	Unc
1786	28.00	45.00	85.00	180	425	1,000	—

COLONIAL COINAGE

KM# 11.2   Composition: Copper **Obverse:** Bridle variety (die break). **Note:** Reverse varieties exist.

Date	AG	Good	VG	Fine	VF	XF	Unc
1786	30.00	50.00	90.00	185	425	1,000	—

KM# 12.1   Composition: Copper **Reverse:** Plain shield. **Note:** Small planchet. Varieties exist.

Date	AG	Good	VG	Fine	VF	XF	Unc
1787	20.00	30.00	60.00	100.00	200	675	—

KM# 12.2   Composition: Copper **Reverse:** Shield heavily outlined. **Note:** Small planchet.

Date	AG	Good	VG	Fine	VF	XF	Unc
1787	22.00	35.00	75.00	125	285	800	—

KM# 13   Composition: Copper **Obverse:** "Serpent head."

Date	AG	Good	VG	Fine	VF	XF	Unc
1787	40.00	60.00	120	285	700	1,275	—

KM# 14   Composition: Copper **Reverse:** Plain shield. **Note:** Large planchet. Varieties exist.

Date	AG	Good	VG	Fine	VF	XF	Unc
1787	22.00	35.00	75.00	135	300	850	—

KM# 15   Composition: Copper **Reverse Legend:** PLURIBS.

Date	AG	Good	VG	Fine	VF	XF	Unc
1787	30.00	50.00	100.00	225	600	1,100	—

KM# 16   Composition: Copper **Obverse:** Horse's head facing right. **Note:** Varieties exist.

Date	AG	Good	VG	Fine	VF	XF	Unc
1788	20.00	30.00	65.00	125	375	750	—

KM# 17   Composition: Copper **Reverse:** Fox before legend. **Note:** Varieties exist.

Date	AG	Good	VG	Fine	VF	XF	Unc
1788	—	55.00	110	275	725	1,550	—

KM# 18   Composition: Copper **Obverse:** Horse's head facing left. **Note:** Varieties exist.

Date	AG	Good	VG	Fine	VF	XF	Unc
1788	65.00	125	285	575	1,150	3,000	—

NEW YORK

KM# 1   Composition: Copper **Obverse Legend:** NON VI VIRTUTE VICI.

Date	AG	Good	VG	Fine	VF	XF	Unc
1786	1,200	2,200	3,750	6,000	11,500	—	—

KM# 2   Composition: Copper **Obverse:** Eagle on globe facing right.

Date	AG	Good	VG	Fine	VF	XF	Unc
1787	175	750	1,250	3,500	6,500	12,750	—

KM#3   Composition: Copper **Obverse:** Eagle on globe facing left.

Date	AG	Good	VG	Fine	VF	XF	Unc
1787	350	700	1,200	3,250	6,000	12,000	—

MACHIN MILL

KM# 4   Composition: Copper **Reverse:** Large eagle, arrows in right talon.

Date	AG	Good	VG	Fine	VF	XF	Unc
1787 2 known	—	—	—	—	—	—	—

Note: Norweb $18,700

KM# 9   Composition: Copper **Obverse Legend:** NOVA EBORAC. **Reverse:** Figure seated right.

Date	AG	Good	VG	Fine	VF	XF	Unc
1787	40.00	75.00	125	260	525	1,100	—

KM# 5   Composition: Copper **Obverse:** George Clinton.

Date	AG	Good	VG	Fine	VF	XF	Unc
1787	2,250	4,000	5,500	9,500	20,000	—	—

KM# 10   Composition: Copper **Reverse:** Figure seated left.

Date	AG	Good	VG	Fine	VF	XF	Unc
1787	35.00	55.00	110	225	500	1,000	—

KM# 6   Composition: Copper **Obverse:** Indian. **Reverse:** New York arms.

Date	AG	Good	VG	Fine	VF	XF	Unc
1787	1,000	2,000	4,000	6,500	10,500	25,000	—

KM# 11   Composition: Copper **Obverse:** Small head, star above. **Obverse Legend:** NOVA FBORAC.

Date	AG	Good	VG	Fine	VF	XF	Unc
1787	300	600	1,750	3,000	4,500	6,500	—

KM# 7   Composition: Copper **Obverse:** Indian. **Reverse:** Eagle on globe.

Date	AG	Good	VG	Fine	VF	XF	Unc
1787	1,650	3,000	6,500	11,500	23,500	35,000	—

KM# 8   Composition: Copper **Obverse:** Indian. **Reverse:** George III.

Date	AG	Good	VG	Fine	VF	XF	Unc
1787	125	200	350	650	1,350	4,200	—

KM# 12   Composition: Copper **Obverse:** Large head, two quatrefoils left. **Obverse Legend:** NOVA EBORAC.

Date	AG	Good	VG	Fine	VF	XF	Unc
1787	200	300	400	650	1,150	2,500	—

COLONIAL COINAGE

KM#13   Composition: Copper **Note:** Crude, lightweight imitations of the British Halfpenny were struck at Machin's Mill in large quantities bearing the obverse legends: GEORGIVS II REX, GEORGIVS III REX, and GEORGIUS III REX, with the BRITANNIA reverse. There are many different mulings. These pieces, which have plain crosses in the shield of Britannia, are not to be confused with the very common British made imitations, which usually have outlined crosses in the shield. Some varieties are very rare.

Date	AG	Good	VG	Fine	VF	XF	Unc
ND(1747 -1788)	—	—	—	—	—	—	—

Note: Examples are dated: 1747, 1771, 1772, 1774, 1775, 1776, 1777, 1778, 1784, 1785, 1786, 1787 and 1788. Other dates may exist

VERMONT

KM#1   Composition: Copper **Reverse Legend:** IMMUNE COLUMBIA.

Date	AG	Good	VG	Fine	VF	XF	Unc
ND(1785)	1,250	2,000	3,000	5,000	9,000	—	—

KM#2   Composition: Copper **Obverse Legend:** VERMONTIS.

Date	AG	Good	VG	Fine	VF	XF	Unc
1785	120	200	300	600	1,150	—	—

KM#3   Composition: Copper **Obverse Legend:** VERMONTS.

Date	AG	Good	VG	Fine	VF	XF	Unc
1785	85.00	150	225	450	900	3,200	—

KM#4   Composition: Copper **Obverse Legend:** VERMONTENSIUM.

Date	AG	Good	VG	Fine	VF	XF	Unc
1786	75.00	125	200	450	950	3,250	—

KM#5   Composition: Copper **Obverse:** "Baby head." **Reverse:** AUCTORI: VERMONS.

Date	AG	Good	VG	Fine	VF	XF	Unc
1786	120	200	300	550	1,150	4,500	—

KM#6   Composition: Copper **Obverse:** Bust facing left. **Obverse Legend:** VERMON: AUCTORI:.

Date	AG	Good	VG	Fine	VF	XF	Unc
1786	60.00	100.00	185	300	750	2,250	—
1787 extremely rare	—	—	—	—	—	—	—

EARLY AMERICAN TOKENS

ALBANY CHURCH "PENNY"

KM#7   Composition: Copper **Obverse:** Bust facing right. **Note:** Varieties exist.

Date	AG	Good	VG	Fine	VF	XF	Unc
1787	—	—	—	—	—	—	—

KM#8   Composition: Copper **Note:** Britannia mule.

Date	AG	Good	VG	Fine	VF	XF	Unc
1787	25.00	40.00	65.00	140	285	950	—

KM#9.1   Composition: Copper **Reverse Legend:** INDE ET LIB **Note:** Varieties exist.

Date	AG	Good	VG	Fine	VF	XF	Unc
1788	40.00	65.00	120	220	550	1,850	—

KM#9.2   Composition: Copper **Obverse:** "C" backward in AUCTORI.

Date	AG	Good	VG	Fine	VF	XF	Unc
1788 extremely rare	—	—	—	—	—	—	—

Note: Stack's Americana, Fine, $9,775

KM#10   Composition: Copper **Reverse Legend:** ET LIB INDE.

Date	AG	Good	VG	Fine	VF	XF	Unc
1788	75.00	125	300	600	1,100	—	—

KM#11   Composition: Copper **Note:** George III Rex mule.

Date	AG	Good	VG	Fine	VF	XF	Unc
1788	85.00	145	325	650	1,250	2,750	—

ALBANY CHURCH "PENNY"

KM#Tn54.1   Composition: Copper **Obverse:** Without "D" above church. **Note:** Uniface.

Date	AG	Good	VG	Fine	VF	XF	Unc
5 known	—	—	3,500	7,000	14,000	—	—

KM#Tn54.2   Composition: Copper **Obverse:** With "D" above church. **Note:** Uniface.

Date	AG	Good	VG	Fine	VF	XF	Unc
rare	—	—	3,000	5,000	10,000	—	—

AUCTORI PLEBIS

KM#Tn50   Composition: Copper

Date	AG	Good	VG	Fine	VF	XF	Unc
1787	20.00	45.00	90.00	150	300	600	—

BAR "CENT"

KM#Tn49   Composition: Copper

Date	AG	Good	VG	Fine	VF	XF	Unc
ND(1785)	85.00	150	275	675	1,200	2,500	—

CASTORLAND "HALF DOLLAR"

KM#Tn87.1   Composition: Silver **Edge:** Reeded.

Date	AG	Good	VG	Fine	VF	XF	Unc
1796	—	—	—	—	—	3,550	—

KM#Tn87.1a   Composition: Copper **Edge:** Reeded.

Date	AG	Good	VG	Fine	VF	XF	Unc
1796 3 known	—	—	—	—	—	1,650	—

KM#Tn87.1b   Composition: Brass **Edge:** Reeded.

Date	AG	Good	VG	Fine	VF	XF	Unc
1796 unique	—	—	—	—	—	—	—

KM#Tn87.2   Composition: Copper **Edge:** Plain.
Note: Thin planchet.

Date	AG	Good	VG	Fine	VF	XF	Unc
1796 unique	—	—	—	—	—	—	—

KM#Tn87.3   Composition: Silver **Edge:** Reeded.
Note: Thin planchet. Restrike.

Date	Good	VG	Fine	VF	XF	Unc	Proof
1796	—	—	—	—	—	325	—

KM#Tn87.4   Composition: Silver **Edge:** Lettered.
Edge Lettering: ARGENT. **Note:** Thin planchet.
Restrike.

Date	Good	VG	Fine	VF	XF	Unc	Proof
1796	—	—	—	—	—	60.00	—

KM#Tn87.3a   Composition: Copper **Edge:** Reeded.
Note: Thin planchet. Restrike.

Date	Good	VG	Fine	VF	XF	Unc	Proof
1796	—	—	—	—	—	285	—

KM#Tn87.5   Composition: Copper **Edge:** Lettered.
Edge Lettering: CUIVRE. **Note:** Thin planchet.
Restrike.

Date	Good	VG	Fine	VF	XF	Unc	Proof
1796	—	—	—	—	—	40.00	—

CHALMERS

3 PENCE

KM#Tn45   Composition: Silver

Date	AG	Good	VG	Fine	VF	XF	Unc
1783	250	500	1,000	1,500	2,650	5,500	—

6 PENCE

KM#Tn46.1   Composition: Silver **Reverse:** Small date

Date	AG	Good	VG	Fine	VF	XF	Unc
1783	350	700	1,500	2,250	5,500	12,000	—

KM#Tn46.2   Composition: Silver **Reverse:** Large date

Date	AG	Good	VG	Fine	VF	XF	Unc
1783	300	600	1,300	2,000	4,000	10,000	—

SHILLING

KM#Tn47.1   Composition: Silver **Reverse:** Birds with long worm

Date	AG	Good	VG	Fine	VF	XF	Unc
1783	180	300	500	1,000	2,000	4,500	—

KM#Tn47.2   Composition: Silver **Reverse:** Birds with short worm

Date	AG	Good	VG	Fine	VF	XF	Unc
1783	150	250	475	900	1,850	4,500	—

KM#Tn48   Composition: Silver **Reverse:** Rings and stars

Date	AG	Good	VG	Fine	VF	XF	Unc
1783 4 known	—	—	—	—	—	—	—

Note: Garrett $75,000

COPPER COMPANY OF UPPER CANADA

HALFPENNY

KM#Tn86 **Composition:** Copper

Date	Good	VG	Fine	VF	XF	Unc	Proof
1796	—	—	—	—	—	—	3,750

FRANKLIN PRESS

KM#Tn73 **Composition:** Copper **Edge:** Plain.

Date	AG	Good	VG	Fine	VF	XF	Unc
1794	18.00	35.00	55.00	85.00	175	300	600

KENTUCKY TOKEN

KM#Tn70.1 **Composition:** Copper **Edge:** Plain.
Note: 1793 date is circa.

Date	AG	Good	VG	Fine	VF	XF	Unc
ND (1793)	12.00	25.00	40.00	60.00	100.00	265	575

KM#Tn70.2 **Composition:** Copper **Edge:** Engrailed.

Date	AG	Good	VG	Fine	VF	XF	Unc
ND (1793)	35.00	75.00	125	200	350	950	1,850

KM#Tn70.3 **Composition:** Copper **Edge:** Lettered.
Edge Lettering: PAYABLE AT BEDWORTH.

Date	AG	Good	VG	Fine	VF	XF	Unc
ND (1793) unique	—	—	—	—	—	1,980	—

KM#Tn70.4 **Composition:** Copper **Edge:** Lettered.
Edge Lettering: PAYABLE AT LANCASTER.

Date	AG	Good	VG	Fine	VF	XF	Unc
ND (1793)	14.00	28.00	45.00	65.00	110	285	725

KM#Tn70.5 **Composition:** Copper **Edge:** Lettered.
Edge Lettering: PAYABLE AT I.FIELDING.

Date	AG	Good	VG	Fine	VF	XF	Unc
ND(1793) unique	—	—	—	—	—	—	—

KM#Tn70.6 **Composition:** Copper **Edge:** Lettered.
Edge Lettering: PAYABLE AT W. PARKERS.

Date	AG	Good	VG	Fine	VF	XF	Unc
ND(1793) unique	—	—	—	—	1,800	—	—

KM#Tn70.7 **Composition:** Copper **Edge:**
Ornamented branch with two leaves.

Date	AG	Good	VG	Fine	VF	XF	Unc
ND(1793) unique	—	—	—	—	—	—	—

MOTT TOKEN

KM#Tn52.1 **Composition:** Copper **Note:** Thin planchet.

Date	AG	Good	VG	Fine	VF	XF	Unc
1789	30.00	60.00	120	220	350	850	—

KM#Tn52.2 **Composition:** Copper **Note:** Thick planchet. Weight generally about 170 grams.

Date	AG	Good	VG	Fine	VF	XF	Unc
1/89	25.00	50.00	100.00	175	300	700	—

KM#Tn52.3 **Composition:** Copper **Edge:** Fully engrailed. **Note:** Specimens struck with perfect dies are scarcer and generally command higher prices.

Date	AG	Good	VG	Fine	VF	XF	Unc
1789	40.00	85.00	175	350	600	1,250	—

MYDDELTON TOKEN

KM#Tn85 **Composition:** Copper

Date	Good	VG	Fine	VF	XF	Unc	Proof
1796	—	—	—	—	—	—	0,500

KM#Tn85a   Composition: Silver

Date	Good	VG	Fine	VF	XF	Unc	Proof
1796	—	—	—	—	—	—	5,500

NEW YORK THEATRE

KM#Tn28a   Composition: Brass**Obverse:** Wreath below ship.

Date	AG	Good	VG	Fine	VF	XF	Unc
1779	60.00	120	200	325	600	1,150	2,200

KM#Tn90   Composition: Copper **Note:** 1796 date is circa.

Date	AG	Good	VG	Fine	VF	XF	Unc
1796	—	—	300	900	2,000	3,250	8,000

NORTH AMERICAN

HALFPENNY

KM#Tn28b   Composition: Pewter **Obverse:** Wreath below ship.

Date	AG	Good	VG	Fine	VF	XF	Unc
1779	—	—	—	1,500	3,000	6,500	

KM#Tn29   Composition: Brass**Obverse:** VLUGTENDE below ship

Date	AG	Good	VG	Fine	VF	XF	Unc
1779 unique	—	—	—	—	—	—	—

Note: Garrett $16,000

KM#Tn30   Composition: Copper

Date	AG	Good	VG	Fine	VF	XF	Unc
1781	6.50	12.50	25.00	75.00	135	365	750

STANDISH BARRY

3 PENCE

RHODE ISLAND SHIP

KM#Tn55   Composition: Silver

Date	AG	Good	VG	Fine	VF	XF	Unc
1790	850	1,350	2,000	3,000	6,500	12,000	—

KM#Tn27a   Composition: Brass**Obverse:** Without wreath below ship.

Date	AG	Good	VG	Fine	VF	XF	Unc
1779	50.00	100.00	175	275	500	1,000	2,000

KM#Tn27b   Composition: Pewter **Obverse:** Without wreath below ship.

Date	AG	Good	VG	Fine	VF	XF	Unc
1779	—	—	—	—	1,250	2,500	5,500

TALBOT, ALLUM & LEE

CENT

KM#Tn71.1   Composition: Copper **Reverse:** NEW YORK above ship **Edge:** Lettered. **Edge Lettering:** PAYABLE AT THE STORE OF

Date	AG	Good	VG	Fine	VF	XF	Unc
1794	12.00	25.00	45.00	90.00	175	300	925

KM#Tn71.2   Composition: Copper **Reverse:** NEW YORK above ship **Edge:** Plain. **Note:** Size of ampersand varies on obverse and reverse dies.

Date	AG	Good	VG	Fine	VF	XF	Unc
1794 4 known	—	—	—	—	2,350	3,000	—

KM#Tn72.1   Composition: Copper **Reverse:** Without NEW YORK above ship **Edge:** Lettered. **Edge Lettering:** PAYABLE AT THE STORE OF

Date	AG	Good	VG	Fine	VF	XF	Unc
1794	100.00	200	350	650	1,000	2,250	4,550

KM#Tn72.2   Composition: Copper **Edge:** Lettered. **Edge Lettering:** WE PROMISE TO PAY THE BEARER ONE CENT.

Date	AG	Good	VG	Fine	VF	XF	Unc
1795	10.00	20.00	40.00	75.00	160	300	725

KM#Tn72.3   Composition: Copper **Edge:** Lettered. **Edge Lettering:** CURRENT EVERYWHERE.

Date	AG	Good	VG	Fine	VF	XF	Unc
1795 unique	—	—	—	—	—	—	—

KM#Tn72.4   Composition: Copper **Edge:** Olive leaf.

Date	AG	Good	VG	Fine	VF	XF	Unc
1795 unique	—	—	—	—	—	—	—

Note: Norweb $4,400

KM#Tn72.5   Composition: Copper **Edge:** Plain.

Date	AG	Good	VG	Fine	VF	XF	Unc
1795 plain edge; 2 known	—	—	—	—	—	—	—
1795 Lettered edge; unique	—	—	—	—	—	—	—

Note: Edge: Cambridge Bedford Huntington.X.X.; Norweb, $3,960

WASHINGTON PIECES

KM#Tn35   Composition: Copper **Obverse Legend:** GEORGIVS TRIUMPHO.

Date	AG	Good	VG	Fine	VF	XF	Unc
1783	25.00	40.00	65.00	150	325	750	—

KM#Tn36   Composition: Copper **Obverse:** Large military bust. **Note:** Varieties exist.

Date	AG	Good	VG	Fine	VF	XF	Unc
1783	8.00	15.00	25.00	50.00	110	280	—

KM#Tn37.1   Composition: Copper **Obverse:** Small military bust. **Edge:** Plain.

Date	AG	Good	VG	Fine	VF	XF	Unc
1783	10.00	20.00	35.00	65.00	125	300	—

Note: One proof example is known. Value: $12,500

KM#Tn37.2 **Composition:** Copper **Obverse:** Small military bust. **Edge:** Engrailed.

Date	AG	Good	VG	Fine	VF	XF	Unc
1783	18.00	35.00	50.00	80.00	175	345	—

KM#Tn38.1 **Composition:** Copper **Obverse:** Draped bust, no button on drapery, small letter.

Date	AG	Good	VG	Fine	VF	XF	Unc
1783	10.00	20.00	35.00	65.00	125	285	—

KM#Tn38.2 **Composition:** Copper **Obverse:** Draped bust, button on drapery, large letter.

Date	AG	Good	VG	Fine	VF	XF	Unc
1783	25.00	40.00	60.00	100.00	200	350	—

KM#Tn38.4 **Composition:** Copper **Edge:** Engrailed. **Note:** Restrike.

Date	Good	VG	Fine	VF	XF	Unc	Proof
1783	—	—	—	—	—	—	400

KM#Tn38.4a **Composition:** Copper **Note:** Bronzed. Restrike.

Date	Good	VG	Fine	VF	XF	Unc	Proof
1783	—	—	—	—	—	—	—

KM#Tn83.3 **Composition:** Copper **Obverse:** Large modern lettering. **Edge:** Plain. **Note:** Restrike.

Date	Good	VG	Fine	VF	XF	Unc	Proof
1783	—	—	—	—	—	—	500

KM#Tn83.4b **Composition:** Silver **Note:** Restrike.

Date	Good	VG	Fine	VF	XF	Unc	Proof
1783	—	—	—	—	—	—	1,000

KM#Tn83.4c **Composition:** Gold AGW. **Note:** Restrike.

Date	AG	Good	VG	Fine	VF	XF	Unc
1783 2 known	—	—	—	—	—	—	—

KM#Tn60.1 **Composition:** Copper **Obverse Legend:** WASHINGTON PRESIDENT. **Edge:** Plain.

Date	AG	Good	VG	Fine	VF	XF	Unc
1792	850	1,450	3,250	5,000	7,500	—	—

Note: Steinberg $12,650. Garrett $15,500

KM#Tn60.2 **Composition:** Copper **Obverse Legend:** WASHINGTON PRESIDENT. **Edge:** Lettered. **Edge Lettering:** UNITED STATES OF AMERICA.

Date	AG	Good	VG	Fine	VF	XF	Unc
1792	1,350	2,250	4,500	7,500	12,500	—	—

KM#Tn61.1 **Composition:** Copper **Obverse Legend:** BORN VIRGINIA. **Note:** Varieties exist.

Date	AG	Good	VG	Fine	VF	XF	Unc
ND(1792)	250	500	1,000	2,200	3,750	7,500	—

KM#Tn61.2 **Composition:** Silver **Edge:** Lettered. **Edge Lettering:** UNITED STATES OF AMERICA.

Date	AG	Good	VG	Fine	VF	XF	Unc
ND(1792) 2 known	—	—	—	—	—	—	—

KM#Tn61.1a **Composition:** Silver **Edge:** Plain.

Date	AG	Good	VG	Fine	VF	XF	Unc
ND(1792) 4 known	—	—	—	—	—	—	—

Note: Roper $16,500

KM#Tn62 **Composition:** Silver **Reverse:** Heraldic eagle. 1792 half dollar. **Note:** Mule.

Date	AG	Good	VG	Fine	VF	XF	Unc
ND(1792) 3 known	—	—	—	—	—	—	—

COLONIAL COINAGE

KM#Tn77.1 **Composition:** Copper **Obverse
Legend:** LIBERTY AND SECURITY. **Edge:** Lettered.
Note: "Penny."

Date	AG	Good	VG	Fine	VF	XF	Unc
ND(1795)	25.00	40.00	75.00	135	275	625	2,000

KM#Tn77.2 **Composition:** Copper **Edge:** Plain.
Note: "Penny."

Date	AG	Good	VG	Fine	VF	XF	Unc
ND(1795) extremely rare	—	—	—	—	—	—	—

KM#Tn77.3 **Composition:** Copper **Note:** "Penny."
Engine-turned borders.

Date	AG	Good	VG	Fine	VF	XF	Unc
ND(1795) 12 known	—	—	—	—	—	—	3,750

KM#Tn78 **Composition:** Copper **Note:** Similar to
"Halfpenny" with date on reverse.

Date	AG	Good	VG	Fine	VF	XF	Unc
1795 very rare	—	—	—	—	—	—	—

Note: Roper $6,600

HALFPENNY

KM#Tn56 **Composition:** Copper **Obverse Legend:**
LIVERPOOL HALFPENNY

Date	AG	Good	VG	Fine	VF	XF	Unc
1791	300	450	550	850	1,650	2,350	—

KM#Tn66.1 **Composition:** Copper **Reverse:** Ship
Edge: Lettered.

Date	AG	Good	VG	Fine	VF	XF	Unc
1793	20.00	30.00	60.00	110	235	500	—

KM#Tn66.2 **Composition:** Copper **Reverse:** Ship
Edge: Plain.

Date	AG	Good	VG	Fine	VF	XF	Unc
1793 5 known	—	—	—	—	2,000	—	—

KM#Tn75.1 **Composition:** Copper **Obverse:** Large
coat buttons **Reverse:** Grate **Edge:** Reeded.

Date	AG	Good	VG	Fine	VF	XF	Unc
1795	12.00	20.00	30.00	60.00	120	265	575

KM#Tn75.2 **Composition:** Copper **Reverse:** Grate
Edge: Lettered

Date	AG	Good	VG	Fine	VF	XF	Unc
1795	45.00	85.00	165	225	300	625	1,200

KM#Tn75.3 **Composition:** Copper **Obverse:** Small
coat buttons **Reverse:** Grate **Edge:** Reeded.

Date	AG	Good	VG	Fine	VF	XF	Unc
1795	10.00	35.00	60.00	100.00	175	375	850

KM#Tn76.1 **Composition:** Copper **Obverse
Legend:** LIBERTY AND SECURITY. **Edge:** Plain.

Date	AG	Good	VG	Fine	VF	XF	Unc
1795	18.00	35.00	60.00	100.00	175	435	975

KM#Tn76.2 **Composition:** Copper **Edge:** Lettered.
Edge Lettering: PAYABLE AT LONDON ...

Date	AG	Good	VG	Fine	VF	XF	Unc
1795	12.00	20.00	30.00	60.00	125	375	800

KM#Tn76.3 **Composition:** Copper **Edge:** Lettered.
Edge Lettering: BIRMINGHAM ...

Date	AG	Good	VG	Fine	VF	XF	Unc
1795	14.00	22.00	35.00	70.00	150	425	950

COLONIAL COINAGE

KM#Tn76.4   Composition: Copper **Edge:** Lettered.
Edge Lettering: AN ASYLUM ...

Date	AG	Good	VG	Fine	VF	XF	Unc
1795	18.00	35.00	60.00	100.00	225	450	1,000

KM#Tn76.5   Composition: Copper **Edge:** Lettered.
Edge Lettering: PAYABLE AT LIVERPOOL ...

Date	AG	Good	VG	Fine	VF	XF	Unc
1795 unique	—	—	—	—	—	—	—

KM#Tn76.6   Composition: Copper **Edge:** Lettered.
Edge Lettering: PAYABLE AT LONDON-LIVERPOOL.

Date	AG	Good	VG	Fine	VF	XF	Unc
1795 unique	—	—	—	—	—	—	—

KM#Tn81.1   Composition: Copper **Reverse
Legend:** NORTH WALES **Edge:** Plain.

Date	AG	Good	VG	Fine	VF	XF	Unc
(ca.1795)	25.00	45.00	85.00	145	250	550	1,450

KM#Tn82   Composition: Copper **Reverse:** Four
stars at bottom **Reverse Legend:** NORTH WALES

Date	AG	Good	VG	Fine	VF	XF	Unc
ND(1795)	200	400	700	1,500	2,850	5,500	—

KM#Tn81.2   Composition: Copper **Reverse
Legend:** NORTH WALES **Edge:** Lettered.

Date	AG	Good	VG	Fine	VF	XF	Unc
	120	250	400	600	950	2,000	4,500

KM#Tn39   Composition: Copper **Obverse Legend:**
UNITY STATES

Date	AG	Good	VG	Fine	VF	XF	Unc
1783	12.00	22.00	40.00	70.00	160	325	—

KM#Tn40   Composition: Copper **Note:** Double
head.

Date	AG	Good	VG	Fine	VF	XF	Unc
ND(1783)	10.00	20.00	35.00	65.00	135	300	—

KM#Tn41   Composition: Copper **Obverse:** "Ugly
head." **Note:** 3 known in copper, 1 in white metal.

Date	AG	Good	VG	Fine	VF	XF	Unc
1784	—	—	—	—	—	—	—

Note: Roper $14,850

KM#Tn57   Composition: Copper **Reverse:** Small
eagle

Date	AG	Good	VG	Fine	VF	XF	Unc
1791	30.00	60.00	125	250	335	675	—

KM#Tn58 Composition: Copper **Reverse:** Large eagle

Date	AG	Good	VG	Fine	VF	XF	Unc
1791	35.00	65.00	145	275	375	725	—

KM#Tn65 Composition: Copper **Obverse:** "Roman" head

Date	Good	VG	Fine	VF	XF	Unc	Proof
1723	—	—	—	—	—	17,600	

HALF DOLLAR

KM#Tn59.1 Composition: Copper **Edge:** Lettered. **Edge Lettering:** UNITED STATES OF AMERICA

Date	AG	Good	VG	Fine	VF	XF	Unc
1792							
2 known	—	—	—	—	—	—	—

Note: Roper $2,860. Benson, EF, $48,300

KM#Tn59.2 Composition: Copper **Edge:** Plain.

Date	AG	Good	VG	Fine	VF	XF	Unc
1792							
3 known	—	—	—	—	—	—	—

KM#Tn59.1a Composition: Silver **Edge:** Lettered. **Edge Lettering:** UNITED STATES OF AMERICA

Date	AG	Good	VG	Fine	VF	XF	Unc
1792 rare	—	—	—	—	—	—	—

Note: Roper $35,200

KM#Tn59.2a Composition: Silver **Edge:** Plain.

Date	AG	Good	VG	Fine	VF	XF	Unc
1792 rare	—	—	—	—	—	—	—

KM#Tn59.1b Composition: Gold AGW. **Edge:** Lettered. **Edge Lettering:** UNITED STATES OF AMERICA

Date	AG	Good	VG	Fine	VF	XF	Unc
1792 unique	—	—	—	—	—	—	—

KM#Tn63.1 Composition: Silver **Reverse:** Small eagle **Edge:** Plain.

Date	AG	Good	VG	Fine	VF	XF	Unc
1792	4,500	7,000	9,000	12,500	20,000	37,500	—

KM#Tn63.2 Composition: Silver **Edge:** Ornamented, circles and squares.

Date	AG	Good	VG	Fine	VF	XF	Unc
1792							
5 known	—	—	—	—	—	—	—

KM#Tn63.1a Composition: Copper **Edge:** Plain.

Date	AG	Good	VG	Fine	VF	XF	Unc
1792	750	1,500	3,500	5,750	8,500	—	—

Note: Garrett $32,000

KM#Tn63.3 Composition: Silver **Edge:** Two olive leaves.

Date	AG	Good	VG	Fine	VF	XF	Unc
1792 unique	—	—	—	—	—	—	—

KM#Tn64 Composition: Silver **Reverse:** Large heraldic eagle

Date	AG	Good	VG	Fine	VF	XF	Unc
1792 unique	—	—	—	—	—	—	—

Note: Garrett $16,500

EARLY AMERICAN PATTERNS

CONFEDERATIO

KM# EA22   Composition: Copper **Reverse:** Small circle of stars.

Date	AG	Good	VG	Fine	VF	XF	Unc
1785	—	—	—	—	8,800	16,500	—

KM# EA23   Composition: Copper **Reverse:** Large circle of stars. **Note:** The Confederatio dies were struck in combination with 13 other dies of the period. All surviving examples of these combinations are extremely rare.

Date	AG	Good	VG	Fine	VF	XF	Unc
extremely rare	—	—	—	—	—	—	—

IMMUNE COLUMBIA

KM# EA20   Composition: Copper **Obverse:** George III.

Date	AG	Good	VG	Fine	VF	XF	Unc
1785	750	1,250	1,850	2,250	5,000	9,000	—

KM# EA21   Composition: Copper **Obverse:** Vermon.

Date	AG	Good	VG	Fine	VF	XF	Unc
1785	600	1,000	1,650	2,000	4,750	8,500	—

KM# EA17a   Composition: Silver **Reverse Legend:** CONSTELLATIO.

Date	AG	Good	VG	Fine	VF	XF	Unc
—	—	—	—	—	20,700	—	

KM# EA19a   Composition: Gold AGW. **Reverse Legend:** CONSTELATIO.

Date	AG	Good	VG	Fine	VF	XF	Unc
1785 unique	—	—	—	—	—	—	—

KM# EA17   Composition: Copper **Reverse Legend:** CONSTELLATIO.

Date	AG	Good	VG	Fine	VF	XF	Unc
1785	—	—	—	—	—	14,375	—

KM# EA18   Composition: Copper **Obverse Legend:** Extra star in border. **Reverse Legend:** CONSTELLATIO.

Date	AG	Good	VG	Fine	VF	XF	Unc
1785	—	—	—	—	—	—	—

Note: Caldwell $4,675

KM# EA19   Composition: Copper **Reverse:** Blunt rays.

Date	AG	Good	VG	Fine	VF	XF	Unc
1785 2 known	—	—	—	—	—	—	—

Note: Norweb $22,000

KM# EA28   Composition: Copper **Obverse Legend:** IMMUNIS COLUMBIA. **Reverse:** Eagle.

Date	AG	Good	VG	Fine	VF	XF	Unc
1786 3 known	—	—	—	—	—	—	—

KM# EA24   Composition: Copper **Obverse:** Washington.

Date	AG	Good	VG	Fine	VF	XF	Unc
1786 3 known	—	—	—	—	—	—	—

Note: Garrett $50,000. Steinberg $12,650

KM# EA25   Composition: Copper **Obverse:** Eagle.

Date	AG	Good	VG	Fine	VF	XF	Unc
1786 unique	—	—	—	—	—	—	—

Note: Garrett $37,500

KM# EA26   Composition: Copper **Obverse:** Washington. **Reverse:** Eagle.

Date	AG	Good	VG	Fine	VF	XF	Unc
1786 2 known	—	—	—	—	—	—	—

KM# EA27   Composition: Copper **Obverse Legend:** IMMUNIS COLUMBIA.

Date	AG	Good	VG	Fine	VF	XF	Unc
1786 extremely rare	—	—	—	—	—	—	—

Note: Rescigno, AU, $33,000. Steinberg, VF, $11,000

NOVA CONSTELLATIO

KM# EA6.1   Composition: Copper **Obverse:** Pointed rays. **Obverse Legend:** CONSTELLATIO. **Reverse:** Small "US".

Date	AG	Good	VG	Fine	VF	XF	Unc
1783	20.00	35.00	65.00	125	255	585	—

KM# EA6.2   Composition: Copper **Obverse:** Pointed rays. **Obverse Legend:** CONSTELLATIO. **Reverse:** Large "US".

Date	AG	Good	VG	Fine	VF	XF	Unc
1783	20.00	35.00	70.00	140	285	650	—

KM# EA7   Composition: Copper **Obverse:** Blunt rays. **Obverse Legend:** CONSTELATIO.

Date	AG	Good	VG	Fine	VF	XF	Unc
1783	22.00	40.00	80.00	150	350	750	—

KM# EA8   Composition: Copper **Obverse:** Blunt rays. **Obverse Legend:** CONSTELATIO.

Date	AG	Good	VG	Fine	VF	XF	Unc
1785	22.00	40.00	80.00	160	375	775	—

KM# EA9   Composition: Copper **Obverse:** Pointed rays. **Obverse Legend:** CONSTELLATIO.

Date	AG	Good	VG	Fine	VF	XF	Unc
1785	20.00	35.00	70.00	140	285	650	—

KM# EA10   Composition: Copper **Note:** Contemporary circulating counterfeit. Similar to previously listed coin.

Date	AG	Good	VG	Fine	VF	XF	Unc
1786 extremely rare	—	—	—	—	—	—	—

5 UNITS

KM#EA12 **Composition:** Copper

Date	AG	Good	VG	Fine	VF	XF	Unc
1783 unique	—	—	—	—	—	—	—

100 (BIT)

KM#EA13.1 **Composition:** Silver **Edge:** Leaf.

Date	AG	Good	VG	Fine	VF	XF	Unc
1783 2 known	—	—	—	—	—	—	—

Note: Garrett $97,500. Stack's auction, May 1991, $72,500

KM#EA13.2 **Composition:** Silver **Edge:** Plain.

Date	AG	Good	VG	Fine	VF	XF	Unc
1783 unique	—	—	—	—	—	—	—

500 (QUINT)

KM#EA14 **Composition:** Silver **Obverse Legend:** NOVA CONSTELLATIO

Date	AG	Good	VG	Fine	VF	XF	Unc
1783 unique	—	—	—	—	—	—	—

Note: Garrett $165,000

KM#EA15 **Composition:** Silver **Obverse:** Without legend

Date	AG	Good	VG	Fine	VF	XF	Unc
1783 unique	—	—	—	—	—	—	—

Note: Garrett $55,000

1000 (MARK)

KM#EA16 **Composition:** Silver

Date	AG	Good	VG	Fine	VF	XF	Unc
1783 unique	—	—	—	—	—	—	—

Note: Garrett $190,000

EARLY AMERICAN PATTERNS

EARLY FEDERAL COINAGE

BRASHER

KM#Tn51.1 **Composition:** Gold AGW. **Obverse:** Sunrise over mountains. **Reverse:** Displayed eagle with shield on breast, EB counterstamp on wing.

Date	AG	Good	VG	Fine	VF	XF	Unc
1787 6 known	—	—	—	—	—	—	—

Note: Heritage FUN Sale, January 2005, AU-55, $2.415 million.

KM#Tn51.2 **Composition:** Gold AGW. **Obverse:** Sun rise over mountains **Reverse:** Displayed eagle with shield on breast. EB counterstamp on breast.

Date	AG	Good	VG	Fine	VF	XF	Unc
1787 unique	—	—	—	—	—	—	—

Note: Heritage FUN Sale, January 2005, XF-45, $2.99 million

FUGIO "CENT"

KM# EA30.1 Composition: Copper **Obverse:** Club rays, round ends.

Date	AG	Good	VG	Fine	VF	XF	Unc
1787	40.00	75.00	150	375	850	1,600	—

KM# EA30.2 Composition: Copper **Obverse:** Club rays, concave ends.

Date	AG	Good	VG	Fine	VF	XF	Unc
1787	250	700	1,800	2,750	5,000	—	—

KM# EA30.3 Composition: Copper **Obverse Legend:** FUCIO.

Date	AG	Good	VG	Fine	VF	XF	Unc
1787	—	750	1,850	2,850	55,000	—	—

KM# EA31.1 Composition: Copper **Obverse:** Pointed rays. **Reverse:** UNITED above, STATES below.

Date	AG	Good	VG	Fine	VF	XF	Unc
1787	100.00	250	550	1,000	1,500	3,500	—

KM# EA31.2 Composition: Copper **Reverse:** UNITED STATES at sides of ring.

Date	AG	Good	VG	Fine	VF	XF	Unc
1787	20.00	45.00	90.00	175	300	650	—

KM# EA31.3 Composition: Copper **Reverse:** STATES UNITED at sides of ring.

Date	AG	Good	VG	Fine	VF	XF	Unc
1787	25.00	55.00	110	220	350	700	—

KM# EA31.4 Composition: Copper **Reverse:** Eight-pointed stars on ring.

Date	AG	Good	VG	Fine	VF	XF	Unc
1787	30.00	65.00	120	250	400	800	—

KM# EA31.5 Composition: Copper **Reverse:** Raised rims on ring, large lettering in center.

Date	AG	Good	VG	Fine	VF	XF	Unc
1787	35.00	75.00	135	275	450	950	—

KM# EA32.1 Composition: Copper **Obverse:** No cinquefoils, cross after date. **Obverse Legend:** UNITED STATES.

Date	AG	Good	VG	Fine	VF	XF	Unc
1787	50.00	110	250	425	650	1,250	—

KM# EA32.2 Composition: Copper **Obverse:** No cinquefoils, cross after date. **Obverse Legend:** STATES UNITED.

Date	AG	Good	VG	Fine	VF	XF	Unc
1787	60.00	110	250	425	650	1,250	—

KM# EA32.3 Composition: Copper **Obverse:** No cinquefoils, cross after date. **Reverse:** Raised rims on ring.

Date	AG	Good	VG	Fine	VF	XF	Unc
1787	—	—	—	—	2,600	—	—

KM# EA33 Composition: Copper **Obverse:** No cinquefoils, cross after date. **Reverse:** With rays. **Reverse Legend:** AMERICAN CONGRESS.

Date	AG	Good	VG	Fine	VF	XF	Unc
1787 extremely rare	—	—	—	—	—	—	—

Note: Norweb $63,800

KM# EA34   Composition: Brass **Note:** New Haven restrike.

Date	AG	Good	VG	Fine	VF	XF	Unc
1787	—	—	—	—	—	—	500

KM# EA34a   Composition: Copper **Note:** New Haven restrike.

Date	AG	Good	VG	Fine	VF	XF	Unc
1787	—	—	—	—	—	500	—

KM# EA34b   Composition: Silver **Note:** New Haven restrike.

Date	AG	Good	VG	Fine	VF	XF	Unc
1787							
(ca.1858)	—	—	—	—	—	—	1,850

KM# EA34c   Composition: Gold AGW. **Note:** New Haven restrike.

Date	AG	Good	VG	Fine	VF	XF	Unc
1787(ca.1858)							
2 known	—	—	—	—	—	—	—

Note: Norweb (holed) $1,430

ISSUES OF 1792

CENT

KM# PnE1   Composition: Copper Around Silver **Note:** Silver plug in center.

Date	AG	Good	VG	Fine	VF	XF	Unc
1792							
12 known	—	—	—	—	—	—	—

Note: Norweb, MS-60, $143,000

KM# PnF1   Composition: Copper **Note:** No silver center.

Date	AG	Good	VG	Fine	VF	XF	Unc
1792							
8 known	—	—	—	—	—	—	—

Note: Norweb, EF-40, $35,200; Benson, VG-10, $57,500

KM# PnG1   Composition: Copper **Edge:** Plain **Note:** Commonly called "Birch cent."

Date	AG	Good	VG	Fine	VF	XF	Unc
1792 unique	—	—	—	—	—	—	—

KM# PnH1   Composition: Copper **Obverse:** One star in edge legend **Note:** Commonly called "Birch cent."

Date	AG	Good	VG	Fine	VF	XF	Unc
1792 2 known	—	—	—	—	—	—	—

Note: Norweb, EF-40, $59,400

KM# PnI1   Composition: Copper **Obverse:** Two stars in edge legend **Note:** Commonly called "Birch cent."

Date	AG	Good	VG	Fine	VF	XF	Unc
1792 6 known	—	—	—	—	—	—	—

Note: Hawn, strong VF, $57,750

KM# PnJ1   Composition: White Metal **Reverse:** "G.W.Pt." below wreath tie **Note:** Commonly called "Birch cent."

Date	AG	Good	VG	Fine	VF	XF	Unc
1792 unique	—	—	—	—	—	—	—

Note: Garrett, $90,000

HALF DISME

KM#5 **Composition:** Silver

Date	AG	Good	VG	Fine	VF	XF	Unc
1792	1,250	—	3,500	6,500	8,500	16,500	—

KM#PnA1 **Composition:** Copper

Date	AG	Good	VG	Fine	VF	XF	Unc
1792	unique	—	—	—	—	—	—

DISME

KM#PnB1 **Composition:** Silver

Date	AG	Good	VG	Fine	VF	XF	Unc
1792	3 known	—	—	—	—	—	—

Note: Norweb, EF-40, $28,600

KM#PnC1 **Composition:** Copper **Edge:** Reeded

Date	AG	Good	VG	Fine	VF	XF	Unc
1792	14 known	—	—	—	—	—	—

Note: Hawn, VF, $30,800; Benson, EF-45, $109,250

KM#PnD1 **Composition:** Copper **Edge:** Plain

Date	AG	Good	VG	Fine	VF	XF	Unc
1792	2 known	—	—	—	—	—	—

Note: Garrett, $45,000

QUARTER

KM#PnK1 **Composition:** Copper **Edge:** Reeded
Note: Commonly called "Wright quarter."

Date	AG	Good	VG	Fine	VF	XF	Unc
1792	2 known	—	—	—	—	—	—

KM#PnL1 **Composition:** White Metal **Edge:** Plain
Note: Commonly called "Wright quarter."

Date	AG	Good	VG	Fine	VF	XF	Unc
1792	2 known	—	—	—	—	—	—

Note: Norweb, VF-30 to EF-40, $28,600

KM#PnM1 **Composition:** White Metal **Note:**
Commonly called "Wright quarter."

Date	AG	Good	VG	Fine	VF	XF	Unc
1792	die trial	—	—	—	—	—	—

Note: Garrett, $12,000

COLONIAL COINAGE

US TERRITORIAL GOLD

Territorial gold pieces (also referred to as "Private" and "Pioneer" gold) are those struck outside the U.S. Mint and not recognized as official issues by the federal government. The pieces so identified are of various shapes, denominations, and degrees of intrinsic value, and were locally required because of the remoteness of the early gold fields from a federal mint and/or an insufficient quantity of official coinage in frontier areas.

The legality of these privately issued pieces derives from the fact that federal law prior to 1864 prohibited a state from coining money, but did not specifically deny that right to an individual, providing that the privately issued coins did not closely resemble those of the United States.

In addition to coin-like gold pieces, the private minters of the gold rush days also issued gold in ingot and bar form. Ingots were intended for circulation and were cast in regular values and generally in large denominations. Bars represent a miner's deposit after it had been assayed, refined, cast into convenient form (generally rectangular), and stamped with the appropriate weight, fineness, and value. Although occasionally cast in even values for the convenience of banks, bars were more often of odd denomination, and when circulated were rounded off to the nearest figure. Ingots and bars are omitted from this listing.

CALIFORNIA

Fractional and Small Size Gold Coinage

During the California gold rush a wide variety of U.S. and foreign coins were used for small change, but only limited quantities of these coins were available. Gold dust was in common use, although this offered the miner a relatively low value for his gold.

By 1852 California jewelers had begun to manufacture 25¢, 50¢ and $1 gold pieces in round and octagonal shapes. Makers included M. Deriberpe, Antoine Louis Nouizillet, Isadore Routhier, Robert B. Gray, Pierre Frontier, Eugene Deviercy, Herman J. Brand, and Herman and Jacob Levison. Reuben N. Hershfield and Noah Mitchell made their coins in Leavenworth, Kansas and most of their production was seized in August 1871. Herman Kroll made California gold coins in New York City in the 1890s. Only two or three of these companies were in production at any one time. Many varieties bear the makers initials. Frontier and his partners made most of the large Liberty Head, Eagle reverse, and Washington Head design types. Most of the small Liberty Head types were made first by Nouizillet and later by Gray and then the Levison brothers and lastly by the California Jewelry Co. Coins initialed "G.G." are apparently patterns made by Frontier and Deviercy for the New York based firm of Gaime, Guillemot & Co.

Most of the earlier coins were struck from gold alloys and had an intrinsic value of about 50-60 percent of face value. They were generally struck from partially hubbed dies and with reeded collars. A few issues were struck with a plain collar or a collar with reeding on only 7 of the 8 sides. Many issues are too poorly struck or too thin to have a clear and complete image of the collar. The later coins and some of the earlier coins were struck from laminated or plated gold planchets, or from gold plated silver planchets. Most of the last dates of issue are extremely thin and contain only token amounts of gold.

Circumstantial evidence exists that the coins issued through 1856 circulated as small change. The San Francisco mint was established in 1854, and by 1856 it had ramped up its production enough to satisfy the local need for small change. However, some evidence exists that these small gold coins may have continued to circulate on occasion through to 1871. After 1871, the gold content of the coins dramatically decreases and it is very unlikely that any of these last issues circulated.

Although the Private Coinages Act of 1864 outlawed all private coinage, this law was not enforced in California and production of small denominated gold continued through 1882. In the spring of 1883, Col. Henry Finnegass of the U.S. Secret Service halted production of the denominated private gold pieces. Non-denominated tokens (lacking DOLLARS, CENTS or the equivalent) were also made during this latter period, sometimes by the same manufacturing jeweler using the same obverse die and the same planchets as the small denomination gold coins. Production of these tokens continues to this day, with most issues made after the 1906 earthquake and fire being backdated to 1847-1865 and struck from brass or gold plated brass planchets.

Approximately 25,000 pieces of California small denomination gold coins are estimated to exist, in a total of over 500 varieties. A few varieties are undated, mostly gold rush era pieces; and a few of the issues are backdated, mostly those from the 1880's. This listing groups varieties together in easily identified categories. The prices quoted are for the most common variety in each group. UNC prices reflect the median auction prices realized of MS60 to MS62 graded coins. BU prices reflect the median auction prices realized of MS63 to MS64 graded coins. Pre-1871 true MS-65 coins are rare and sell for substantial premiums over the prices on this list. Post-1871 coins are rarely found with wear and often have a cameo proof appearance. Auction prices realized are highly volatile and it is not uncommon to find recent records of sales at twice or half of the values shown here. Many of the rarity estimates published in the 1980s and earlier have proven to be too high, so caution is advised when paying a premium for a rare variety. In addition, many varieties that have a refined appearance command higher prices than equivalent grade but scarcer varieties that have a more crude appearance.

Several counterfeits of California Fractional Gold coins exist. Beware of 1854 and 1858 dated round 1/2 dollars, and 1871 dated round dollars that have designs that do not match any of the published varieties. Beware of reeded edge Kroll coins being sold as originals (see the listings below).

For further information consult "California Pioneer Fractional Gold" by W. Breen and R.J. Gillio and "The Brasher Bulletin" the official newsletter of The Society of Private and Pioneer Numismatists.

CALIFORNIA

1/4 DOLLAR (OCTAGONAL)

KM# 1.1   Obverse: Large Liberty head, left **Reverse:** Value and date within beaded circle

Date	Fine	VF	XF	Unc	BU
1853	—	—	100	200	300
1854	—	—	100	250	350
1855	—	—	100	250	350
1856	—	—	100	260	375

KM# 1.2   Obverse: Liberty head, left **Reverse:** Value and date within wreath

Date	Fine	VF	XF	Unc	BU
1859	—	—	65.00	200	450
1864	—	—	75.00	250	400
1866	—	—	75.00	250	400
1867	—	—	65.00	250	400
1868	—	—	70.00	200	350
1869	—	—	70.00	200	350
1870	—	—	65.00	200	350
1871	—	—	65.00	200	350

KM# 1.3   Obverse: Large Liberty head, left, above date **Reverse:** Value and "CAL" within wreath

Date	Fine	VF	XF	Unc	BU
1872	—	—	65.00	250	400
1873	—	—	50.00	175	300

KM# 1.4   Obverse: Small Liberty head, left **Reverse:** Value and date within beaded circle

Date	Fine	VF	XF	Unc	BU
1853	—	—	125	325	425

KM# 1.5   Obverse: Small Liberty head, left, above date **Reverse:** Value within wreath

Date	Fine	VF	XF	Unc	BU
1854	—	—	125	300	350

KM# 1.6   Obverse: Small Liberty head, left **Reverse:** Value and date within wreath

Date	Fine	VF	XF	Unc	BU
1855	—	—	—	—	—
1856	—	—	—	—	—
1857 Plain edge	—	—	—	—	—
Note: Kroll type date					
1857 Reeded edge	—	—	—	—	—
Note: Kroll type date					
1860	—	—	—	—	—
1870	—	—	—	—	—

KM# 1.7   Obverse: Liberty head, left **Reverse:** Value in shield and date within wreath

Date	Fine	VF	XF	Unc	BU
1863	—	—	150	500	—
1864	—	—	65.00	240	—
1865	—	—	85.00	250	550
1866	—	—	85.00	250	400
1867	—	—	75.00	200	400
1868	—	—	75.00	200	—
1869	—	—	75.00	190	300
1870	—	—	75.00	200	350

KM# 1.8   Obverse: Small Liberty head, left, above date **Reverse:** Value and "CAL" within wreath

Date	Fine	VF	XF	Unc	BU
1870	—	—	65.00	200	300
1871	—	—	65.00	175	250
1871	—	—	65.00	175	250
1873	—	—	175	400	—
1874	—	—	65.00	175	275
1875/3	—	—	350	1,000	—
1876	—	—	65.00	200	300

KM# 1.9   Obverse: "Goofy" Liberty head, left **Reverse:** Value and date within wreath

Date	Fine	VF	XF	Unc	BU
1870	—	—	85.00	200	300

KM# 1.10   Obverse: "Oriental" Liberty head, left, above date **Reverse:** "1/4 CALDOLL" withn wreath

Date	Fine	VF	XF	Unc	BU
1881	—	—	—	1,000	3,000

KM# 1.11   Obverse: Large Liberty head, left, above 1872 **Reverse:** Value and 1871 within wreath

Date	Fine	VF	XF	Unc	BU
1872-71	—	—	—	1,000	3,000

KM# 2.1   Obverse: Large indian head, left, above date **Reverse:** Value within wreath

Date	Fine	VF	XF	Unc	BU
1852	—	—	100	240	450
Note: Back dated issue					
1868	—	—	100	240	450
Note: Back dated issue					
1874	—	—	85.00	220	400
Note: Back dated issue					
1876	—	—	85.00	220	400
1880	—	—	75.00	200	350
1881	—	—	85.00	220	400

KM# 2.2   Obverse: Large indian head, left, above date **Reverse:** Value within wreath

Date	Fine	VF	XF	Unc	BU
1872	—	—	65.00	210	300
1873/2	—	—	200	550	800
1873	—	—	90.00	250	350
1874	—	—	65.00	210	300
1875	—	—	90.00	250	350
1876	—	—	90.00	250	350

KM# 2.3   Obverse: Small indian head, left, above date **Reverse:** Vallue and CAL within wreath

Date	Fine	VF	XF	Unc	BU
1875	—	—	90.00	250	350
1876	—	—	90.00	250	500
1881	—	—	—	500	1,100

KM# 2.4   Obverse: "Aztec" indian head, left, above date **Reverse:** Value and CAL within wreath

Date	Fine	VF	XF	Unc	BU
1880	—	—	65.00	210	300

KM# 2.6   Obverse: "Dumb" indian head, left, above date **Reverse:** Value and CAL within wreath

Date	Fine	VF	XF	Unc	BU
1881	—	—	—	650	—

KM# 2.7   Obverse: "Young" indian head, left, above date **Reverse:** Value within wreath

Date	Fine	VF	XF	Unc	BU
1881	—	—	—	450	—

KM# 2.8   Obverse: Indian head, left, above date **Reverse:** Value and "CAL" within wreath

Date	Fine	VF	XF	Unc	BU
1882	—	—	—	500	750

KM# 3   Obverse: Washington head, left, above date **Reverse:** Value and CAL within wreath

Date	Fine	VF	XF	Unc	BU
1872	—	—	—	400	950

1/4 DOLLAR (ROUND)

KM# 4   Obverse: Defiant eagle above date **Reverse:** "25¢" within wreath

Date	Fine	VF	XF	Unc	BU
1854	—	—	11,000	33,000	44,000

KM# 5.1   Obverse: Large Liberty head, left **Reverse:** Value and date within wreath

Date	Fine	VF	XF	Unc	BU
1853	—	—	400	1,000	1,500
1854	—	—	150	400	600
1859	—	—	70.00	225	275
1865	—	—	90.00	250	350
1866	—	—	—	200	300
1867	—	—	—	200	300
1868	—	—	—	200	300
1870	—	—	—	200	300
1871	—	—	—	200	300

KM# 5.2   Obverse: Large Liberty head, left, above date **Reverse:** Value and CAL within wreath

Date	Fine	VF	XF	Unc	BU
1871	—	—	—	200	275
1872	—	—	—	200	275
1873	—	—	—	180	260

KM# 5.3   Obverse: Small Liberty head, left **Reverse:** "25¢" in wreath

Date	Fine	VF	XF	Unc	BU
	—	—	1,000	2,450	3,500

KM# 5.4   Obverse: Small Liberty head, left **Reverse:** "1/4 DOLL." or "DOLLAR" and date in wreath

Date	Fine	VF	XF	Unc	BU
	—	—	90.00	200	350
Note: Rare counterfeit exists					
1853	—	—	500	1,200	2,500
1853 10 stars	—	—	120	275	365
Note: Kroll type					
1855 11 stars	—	—	—	50.00	100
Note: Kroll type					
1856	—	—	100	250	350
1860	—	—	65.00	175	275
1864	—	—	75.00	200	300
1865	—	—	90.00	225	350
1866	—	—	125	600	350
1867	—	—	65.00	175	350
1869	—	—	65.00	175	300
1870	—	—	125	250	450

KM# 5.5 **Obverse:** Small Liberty head, left **Reverse:** Value in shield and date within wreath

Date	Fine	VF	XF	Unc	BU
1863	—	—	80.00	200	—

KM# 6.3 **Obverse:** Small indian head, left, above date **Reverse:** Value within wreath

Date	Fine	VF	XF	Unc	BU
1875	—	—	75.00	250	400
1876	—	—	65.00	200	350
1881 Rare	—	—	—	—	—

KM# 5.6 **Obverse:** Small Liberty head, left, above date **Reverse:** Value and "CAL" within wreath

Date	Fine	VF	XF	Unc	BU
	—	—	100	500	—
1870	—	—	80.00	200	250
1871	—	—	80.00	200	250
1871	—	—	—	210	350
1873	—	—	—	300	500
1874	—	—	—	300	500
1875	—	—	—	250	475
1876	—	—	—	225	450

KM# 6.4 **Obverse:** "Young" indian head, left, above date **Reverse:** Value and CAL within wreath

Date	Fine	VF	XF	Unc	BU
1882	—	—	400	1,225	1,750

KM# 7 **Obverse:** Washington head, left, above date **Reverse:** Value and CAL within wreath

Date	Fine	VF	XF	Unc	BU
1872	—	—	—	600	900

KM# 5.7 **Obverse:** "Goofy" Liberty head, left **Reverse:** Value and date within wreath

Date	Fine	VF	XF	Unc	BU
1870	—	—	110	220	250

1/2 DOLLAR (OCTAGONAL)

KM# 5.8 **Obverse:** Liberty head, left, with "H" and date below **Reverse:** Value and "CAL" in wreath

Date	Fine	VF	XF	Unc	BU
1871	—	—	80.00	160	250

KM# 8.1 **Obverse:** Liberty head, left, above date **Reverse:** "1/2 DOLLAR" in beaded circle, "CALIFORNIA GOLD" around circle

Date	Fine	VF	XF	Unc	BU
1853	—	—	165	350	450
1854	—	—	110	285	350

Note: Rare counterfeit exists

1854	—	—	165	350	450
1856	—	—	165	365	450

KM# 6.1 **Obverse:** Large indian head, left, above date **Reverse:** Value within wreath

Date	Fine	VF	XF	Unc	BU
1852	—	—	—	200	300
Note: Back dated issue					
1868	—	—	—	250	375
Note: Back dated issue					
1874	—	—	—	190	275
Note: Back dated issue					
1876	—	—	—	200	325
1878/6	—	—	—	200	300
1880	—	—	—	200	325
1881	—	—	—	200	325

KM# 8.2 **Obverse:** Liberty head, left **Reverse:** Small eagle with rays ND("peacock")

Date	Fine	VF	XF	Unc	BU
1853	—	—	400	1,000	1,500

KM# 8.3 **Obverse:** Large Liberty head, left **Reverse:** Large eagle with date

Date	Fine	VF	XF	Unc	BU
1853	—	—	750	2,250	—

KM# 6.2 **Obverse:** Large indian head, left, above date **Reverse:** Value and "CAL" within wreath

Date	Fine	VF	XF	Unc	BU
1872/1	—	—	—	200	300
1873	—	—	—	180	275
1874	—	—	—	180	275
1875	—	—	—	200	300
1876	—	—	—	200	300

KM# 8.4 **Obverse:** Liberty head, left **Reverse:** Value and date within wreath

Date	Fine	VF	XF	Unc	BU
1859	—	—	—	200	275
1866	—	—	—	300	400

TERRITORIAL GOLD

Date	Fine	VF	XF	Unc	BU
1867	—	—	—	225	300
1868	—	—	—	225	300
1869	—	—	—	250	350
1870	—	—	—	250	350
1871	—	—	—	225	300

KM# 8.5   Obverse: Large Liberty head, left, above date **Reverse:** Value and "CAL" within wreath

Date	Fine	VF	XF	Unc	BU
1872	—	—	—	250	350
1873	—	—	—	225	300

KM# 8.6   Obverse: Liberty head, left **Reverse:** Date in wreath, "HALF DOL. CALIFORNIA GOLD" around wreath

Date	Fine	VF	XF	Unc	BU
1854	—	—	100	350	500
1855	—	—	90.00	300	400
1856	—	—	90.00	265	325
1856	—	—	165	1,100	—
Note: Back date issue struck in 1864					
1868	—	—	60.00	185	275
Note: Kroll type date					

KM# 8.7   Obverse: Small Liberty head, left **Reverse:** "HALF DOLLAR" and date in wreath

Date	Fine	VF	XF	Unc	BU
1864	—	—	—	275	350
1870	—	—	—	275	—

KM# 8.8   Obverse: Liberty head, left **Reverse:** "CAL. GOLD HALF DOL" and date in wreath

Date	Fine	VF	XF	Unc	BU
1869	—	—	—	200	350
1870	—	—	—	200	350

KM# 8.9   Obverse: Small Liberty head, left, above date **Reverse:** Value and "CAL" in wreath

Date	Fine	VF	XF	Unc	BU
1870	—	—	55.00	200	300
1871	—	—	55.00	200	250
1871	—	—	55.00	165	250
1873	—	—	85.00	300	600
1874	—	—	85.00	300	600
1875	—	—	250	1,000	—
1876	—	—	55.00	200	250

KM# 8.10   Obverse: "Goofy" Liberty head, left **Reverse:** Value and date within wreath

Date	Fine	VF	XF	Unc	BU
1870	—	—	55.00	200	300

KM# 8.11   Obverse: "Oriental" Liberty head, left, above date **Reverse:** "1/2 CALDOLL" within wreath

Date	Fine	VF	XF	Unc	BU
1881	—	—	250	750	1,150

KM# 9.1   Obverse: Large indian head, left above date **Reverse:** Value within wreath

Date	Fine	VF	XF	Unc	BU
1852	—	—	—	500	900
Note: Back dated issue					
1868	—	—	—	650	1,000
Note: Back dated issue					
1874	—	—	—	500	900
Note: Back dated issue					
1876	—	—	—	300	400
1880	—	—	—	300	400
1881	—	—	—	300	400

KM# 9.2   Obverse: Large indian head, left, above date **Reverse:** Value and "CAL" within wreath

Date	Fine	VF	XF	Unc	BU
1852	—	—	—	450	700
Note: Back dated issue					
1868	—	—	—	260	550
Note: Back dated issue					
1872	—	—	—	200	300
1873/2	—	—	—	200	400
1873	—	—	—	200	300
1874/3	—	—	—	250	350
1874	—	—	—	200	300
1875	—	—	—	250	425
1876	—	—	—	250	400
1878/6	—	—	—	250	400
1880	—	—	—	500	1,000
1881	—	—	—	250	400

KM# 9.3   Obverse: Small indian head, left above date **Reverse:** Value and CAL within wreath

Date	Fine	VF	XF	Unc	BU
1875	—	—	—	225	350
1876	—	—	—	225	350

KM# 9.4   Obverse: "Young" indian head, left above date **Reverse:** Value and CAL within wreath

Date	Fine	VF	XF	Unc	BU
1881	—	—	—	550	850
1882 Rare	—	—	—	—	—

1/2 DOLLAR (ROUND)

KM# 10   Obverse: Arms of California and date **Reverse:** Eagle and legends

Date	Fine	VF	XF	Unc	BU
1853	—	—	1,250	4,500	5,500

KM# 11.1   Obverse: Liberty head, left **Reverse:** Large eagle and legends

Date	Fine	VF	XF	Unc	BU
1854	—	—	1,000	6,000	—

KM# 11.2   Obverse: Liberty head, left, above date **Reverse:** "HALF DOL. CALIFORNIA GOLD" around wreath

Date	Fine	VF	XF	Unc	BU
1854	—	—	175	300	450

KM# 11.3   Obverse: Liberty head, left **Reverse:** Date in wreath, value and "CALIFORNIA GOLD" around wreath

Date	Fine	VF	XF	Unc	BU
1852	—	—	145	275	400
1852	—	—	145	275	400
1853	—	—	145	275	400
1853	—	—	165	300	425
1853	—	—	165	300	425
1853 Date on reverse	—	—	125	225	300
Note: Kroll type					
1854 Large head	—	—	300	1,000	1,600
1854 Small head	—	—	—	100	200
Note: Common counterfeits exist					
1855 Date on reverse	—	—	175	325	550
Note: Kroll type					
1856	—	—	100	225	325
1860/56	—	—	125	250	400

KM# 11.4   Obverse: Liberty head, left **Reverse:** Small eagle and legends

Date	Fine	VF	XF	Unc	BU
1853 Rare	—	—	—	—	—
1853	—	—	5,000	10,000	15,000

KM# 11.5   Obverse: Liberty head, left **Reverse:** Value in wreath; "CALIFORNIA GOLD" and date around wreath

Date	Fine	VF	XF	Unc	BU
1853	—	—	150	750	1,500

KM# 11.6   Obverse: Liberty head, left **Reverse:** Value and date within wreath

Date	Fine	VF	XF	Unc	BU
Rare	—	—	—	—	—
1854	—	—	850	—	
Note: Common counterfeit without "FD" beneath truncation					
1855	—	—	155	450	600
1859	—	—	140	350	500
1859	—	—	—	175	250
1865	—	—	—	225	350
1866	—	—	—	250	400
1867	—	—	—	225	350
1868	—	—	—	250	400
1869	—	—	—	250	400
1870	—	—	—	225	350
1871	—	—	—	200	300
1873	—	—	—	250	450

KM# 11.7   Obverse: Liberty head, left, above date **Reverse:** Value and "CAL" within wreath

Date	Fine	VF	XF	Unc	BU
1870	—	—	—	250	400
1871	—	—	—	250	400
1871	—	—	—	400	—
1872	—	—	—	250	400
1873	—	—	—	400	1,000
1874	—	—	—	250	750
1875	—	—	—	300	800
1876	—	—	—	250	—

KM# 11.8   Obverse: Liberty head, left **Reverse:** Value and date within wreath, "CALIFORNIA GOLD" outside

Date	Fine	VF	XF	Unc	BU
1863	—	—	265	675	950

Note: This issue is a rare Kroll type. All 1858 dates of this type are counterfeits

KM# 11.9   Obverse: Liberty head, left **Reverse:** "HALF DOLLAR" and date in wreath

Date	Fine	VF	XF	Unc	BU
1864	—	—	100	250	350
1866	—	—	200	500	700
1867	—	—	100	250	350
1868	—	—	100	250	350
1869	—	—	125	300	—
1870	—	—	—	350	—

KM# 11.11   Obverse: "Goofy" Liberty head, left **Reverse:** Value and date within wreath

Date	Fine	VF	XF	Unc	BU
1870	—	—	125	400	700

KM# 11.12   Obverse: Liberty head, left, with "H" and date below **Reverse:** Value and "CAL" within wreath

Date	Fine	VF	XF	Unc	BU
1871	—	—	90.00	200	275

KM# 12.1   Obverse: Large indian head, left, above date **Reverse:** Value within wreath

Date	Fine	VF	XF	Unc	BU
1852	—	—	—	350	675
1868	—	—	—	300	600
1874	—	—	—	300	600
1876	—	—	—	200	250
1878/6	—	—	—	300	450
1880	—	—	—	250	400
1881	—	—	—	250	400

KM# 12.2   Obverse: Large indian head, left, above date **Reverse:** Value and CAL within wreath

Date	Fine	VF	XF	Unc	BU
1872	—	—	—	200	300
1873/2	—	—	—	350	650
1873	—	—	—	200	300
1874/3	—	—	—	300	450
1874	—	—	—	200	300
1875/3	—	—	—	200	300
1875	—	—	—	300	500
1876/5	—	—	—	200	300
1876	—	—	—	340	600

KM# 12.3   Obverse: Small indian head, left, above date **Reverse:** Value and CAL within wreath

Date	Fine	VF	XF	Unc	BU
1875	—	—	100	250	450
1876	—	—	75.00	200	300

KM# 12.4   Obverse: "Young" indian head, left, above date **Reverse:** Value and CAL within wreath

Date	Fine	VF	XF	Unc	BU
1882	—	—	—	850	—

DOLLAR (OCTAGONAL)

KM# 13.1   Obverse: Liberty head, left **Reverse:** Large eagle and legends

Date	Fine	VF	XF	Unc	BU
	—	—	1,000	2,000	4,000
1853	—	—	3,000	5,500	—
1854	—	—	1,000	2,000	4,000

KM# 13.2   Obverse: Liberty head, left **Reverse:** Value and date in beaded circle; "CALIFORNIA GOLD", initials around circle

Date	Fine	VF	XF	Unc	BU
1853	—	—	275	750	1,100
1853	—	—	450	1,100	—
1853	—	—	300	900	—
1853	—	—	275	750	1,200
1854	—	—	450	1,100	—
1854	—	—	300	900	1,600
1855	—	—	350	900	—
1856	—	—	2,100	5,000	—
1863 Reeded edge	—	—	150	325	500
1863 Plain edge	—	—	—	40.00	80.00

Note: Reeded edge 1863 dates are Kroll types, while plain edge examples are Kroll restrikes

KM# 13.3   Obverse: Liberty head, left **Reverse:** Value and date inside wreath; legends outside wreath

Date	Fine	VF	XF	Unc	BU
1854 Rare	—	—	—	—	—

Note: Bowers and Marena sale 5-99, XF $9,775

Date	Fine	VF	XF	Unc	BU
1854	—	—	275	750	1,100
1855	—	—	275	750	1,100
1858	—	—	150	350	600

Note: 1858 dates are Kroll types

Date	Fine	VF	XF	Unc	BU
1859	—	—	1,900	—	—
1860	—	—	—	750	100
1868	—	—	—	750	1,100
1869	—	—	—	6,600	900

TERRITORIAL GOLD

Date	Fine	VF	XF	Unc	BU
1870	—	—	—	600	900
1871	—	—	—	400	850

KM# 13.4 Obverse: "Goofy" Liberty head, left
Reverse: Value and date within wreath

Date	Fine	VF	XF	Unc	BU
1870	—	—	—	1,000	1,500

KM# 13.5 Obverse: Liberty head, left, above date
Reverse: Value and date within wreath;
"CALIFORNIA GOLD" around wreath

Date	Fine	VF	XF	Unc	BU
1871	—	—	—	600	900
1874	—	—	—	—	—
1875	—	—	—	—	—
1876	—	—	—	—	—

KM# 14.1 Obverse: Large indian head, left, above
date **Reverse:** "1 DOLLAR" within wreath;
"CALIFORNIA GOLD" around wreath

Date	Fine	VF	XF	Unc	BU
1872	—	—	—	600	900
1073/2	—	—	—	700	1,100
1873	—	—	—	750	—
1874	—	—	—	850	1,300
1075	—	—	—	600	1,000
1876/5	—	—	—	1,000	1,300

KM# 14.2 Obverse: Small indian head, left, above
date **Reverse:** "1 DOLLAR CAL" within wreath

Date	Fine	VF	XF	Unc	BU
1875	—	—	700	1,200	—
1876	—	—	—	1,400	—

KM# 14.3 Obverse: Indian head, left, above date
Reverse: "1 DOLLAR" within wreath; "CALIFORNIA
GOLD" around wreath

Date	Fine	VF	XF	Unc	BU
1876	—	—	—	750	—

DOLLAR (ROUND)

KM# 15.1 Obverse: Liberty head, left **Reverse:**
Large eagle and legends

Date	Fine	VF	XF	Unc	BU
1853 Rare	—	—	—	—	—

Note: Superior sale Sept. 1987 MS-63 $35,200

KM# 15.2 Obverse: Liberty head, left **Reverse:**
Value and date within wreath; "CALIFORNIA GOLD"
around wreath

Date	Fine	VF	XF	Unc	BU
1854	—	—	3,000	—	—
1854	—	—	5,000	—	—
1854 Rare	—	—	—	—	—

Note: Superior sale Sept. 1988 Fine $13,200

1857 2 known	—	—	—	—	—
1870	—	—	500	2,000	—
18/1	—	—	850	2,500	ー

Note: Coutnerfeits reported

KM# 15.3 Obverse: Liberty head, left, above date
Reverse: Value within wreath; "CALIFORNIA GOLD"
around wreath

Date	Fine	VF	XF	Unc	BU
1870	—	—	500	1,400	2,000
1871	—	—	500	1,400	2,000

KM# 15.4 Obverse: "Goofy" Liberty head, left
Reverse: Value and date within wreath;
"CALIFORNIA GOLD" around wreath

Date	Fine	VF	XF	Unc	BU
1870	—	—	400	1,500	—

KM# 16 Obverse: Large indian head, left, above
date **Reverse:** Value within wreath; "CALIFORNIA
GOLD" outside wreath

Date	Fine	VF	XF	Unc	BU
1872	—	—	650	1,800	2,400

U.S. Territorial Gold Coinage
Private Assay Office Issues

CALIFORNIA

Norris, Grieg & Norris produced the first territorial gold coin struck in California, a $5 piece struck in 1849 at Benicia City, though it bears the imprint of San Francisco. The coining facility was owned by Thomas H. Norris, Charles Greig, and Hiram A. Norris, members of a New York engineering firm. A unique 1850 variety of this coin has the name STOCKTON beneath the date, instead of SAN FRANCISCO.

Early in 1849, John Little Moffat, a New York assayer, established an assay office at San Francisco in association with Joseph R. Curtis, Philo H. Perry, and Samuel Ward. The first issues of the **Moffat & Co.** assay office consisted of rectangular $16 ingots and assay bars of various and irregular denominations. In early August, the firm began striking $5 and $10 gold coins which resemble those of the U.S. Mint in design, but carry the legend S.M.V. (Standard Mint Value) CALIFORNIA GOLD on the reverse. Five-dollar pieces of the same design were also issued in 1850.

On Sept. 30, 1850, Congress directed the Secretary of the Treasury to establish an official Assay Office in California. Moffat & Co. obtained a contract to perform the duties of the U.S. Assay Office. **Augustus Humbert**, a New York watchcase maker, was appointed U.S. Assayer of Gold in California. Humbert stamped the first octagonal coin-ingots of the Provisional Government Mint on Jan. 31, 1851. The $50 pieces were accepted at par with standard U.S. gold coins, but were not officially recognized as coins. Officially, they were designated as "ingots." Colloquially, they were known as slugs, quintuple eagles, or 5-eagle pieces.

The $50 ingots failed to alleviate the need of California for gold coins. The banks regarded them as disadvantageous to their interests and utilized them only when compelled to do so by public need or convenience. Being of sound value, the ingots drove the overvalued $5, $10, and $20 territorial gold coins from circulation, bringing about a return to the use of gold dust for everyday transactions. Eventually, the slugs became so great a nuisance that they were discounted 3 percent when accepted. This unexpected turn of events forced Moffat & Co. to resume the issuing of $10 and $20 gold coins in 1852. The $10 piece was first issued with the Moffat & Co. imprint on Liberty's coronet, and later with the official imprint of Augustus Humbert on reverse. The $20 piece was issued with the Humbert imprint.

On Feb. 14, 1852, John L. Moffat withdrew from Moffat & Co. to enter the diving bell business, and Moffat & Co. was reorganized as the **United States Assay Office of Gold**, composed of Joseph R. Curtis, Philo H. Perry, and Samuel Ward. The U.S. Assay Office of Gold issued gold coins in denominations of $50 and $10 in 1852, and $20 and $10 in 1853. With the exception of the $50 slugs, they carry the imprint of the Assay Office on reverse. The .900 fine issues of this facility reflect an attempt to bring the issues of the U.S. Assay Office into conformity with the U.S. Mint standard.

The last territorial gold coins to bear the imprint of Moffat & Co. are $20 pieces issued in 1853, after the retirement of John L. Moffat. These coins do not carry a mark of fineness, and generally assay below the U.S. Mint standard.

Templeton Reid, previously mentioned in connection with the private gold issues of Georgia, moved his coining equipment to California when gold was discovered there, and in 1849 issued $10 and $25 gold pieces. No specimens are available to present-day collectors. The only known $10 piece is in the Smithsonian Collection. The only known specimen of the $25 piece was stolen from the U.S. Mint Cabinet Collection in 1858 and was never recovered.

Little is known of the origin and location of the **Cincinnati Mining & Trading Co.** It is believed that the firm was organized in the East and was forced to abandon most of its equipment while enroute to California. A few $5 and $10 gold coins were struck in 1849. Base metal counterfeits exist.

The **Massachusetts & California Co.** was organized in Northampton, Mass., in May 1849 by Josiah Hayden, S. S. Wells, Miles G. Moies, and others. Coining equipment was taken to San Francisco where $5 gold pieces were struck in 1849. The few pieces extant are heavily alloyed with copper.

Wright & Co., a brokerage firm located in Portsmouth Square, San Francisco, issued an undated $10 gold piece in the autumn of 1849 under the name of **Miners' Bank**. Unlike most territorial gold pieces, the Miners' Bank eagle was alloyed with copper. The coinage proved to be unpopular because of its copper-induced color and low intrinsic value. The firm was dissolved on Jan. 14, 1850.

In 1849, Dr. **J. S. Ormsby** and Major William M. Ormsby struck gold coins of $5 and $10 denominations at Sacramento under the name of Ormsby & Co. The coinage, which is identified by the initials J. S. O., is undated. Ormsby & Co. coinage was greatly over-valued, the eagle assaying at as little as $9.37.

The **Pacific Co.** of San Francisco issued $5 and $10 gold coins in 1849. The clouded story of this coinage is based on conjecture. It is believed that the well-struck pattern coins of this type were struck in the East by the Pacific Co. that organized in Boston and set sail for California on Feb. 20, 1849, and that the crudely hand-struck pieces were made by the jewelry firm of Broderick and Kohler after the dies passed into their possession. In any event, the intrinsic value of the initial coinage exceeded face value, but by the end of 1849, when they passed out of favor, the coins had been debased so flagrantly that the eagles assayed for as little as $7.86.

Dubosq & Co., a Philadelphia jewelry firm owned by Theodore Dubosq Sr. and Jr. and Henry Dubosq, took melting and coining equipment to San Francisco in 1849, and in 1850 issued $5 and $10 gold coins struck with dies allegedly made by U.S. Mint Engraver James B. Longacre. Dubosq & Co. coinage was immensely popular with the forty-niners because its intrinsic worth was in excess of face value.

The minting equipment of David C. Broderick and Frederick D. Kohler (see Pacific Co.) was acquired in May 1850 by San Francisco jewelers George C. Baldwin and Thomas S. Holman, who organized a private minting venture under the name of **Baldwin & Co.** The firm produced a $5 piece of Liberty Head design and a $10 piece with Horseman device in 1850. Liberty Head $10 and $20 pieces were coined in 1851. Baldwin & Co. produced the first $20 piece issued in California.

Schultz & Co. of San Francisco, a brass foundry located in the rear of the Baldwin & Co. establishment, and operated by Judge G. W. Schultz and William T. Garratt, issued $5 gold coins from early 1851 until April of that year. The inscription "SHULTZ & CO." is a misspelling of SCHULTZ & CO.

Dunbar & Co. of San Francisco issued a $5 gold piece in 1851, after Edward E. Dunbar, owner of the California Bank in San Francisco, purchased the coining equipment of the defunct Baldwin & Co.

The San Francisco-based firm of **Wass, Molitor & Co.** was owned by 2 Hungarian exiles, Count S. C. Wass and A. P. Molitor, who initially founded the firm as a gold smelting and assaying plant. In response to a plea from the commercial community for small gold coins, Wass, Molitor & Co. issued $5 and $10 gold coins in 1852. The $5 piece was coined with small head and large head varieties, and the $10 piece with small head, large head, and small close-date varieties. The firm produced a second issue of gold coins in 1855, in denominations of $10, $20, and $50.

The U.S. Assay Office in California closed its doors on Dec. 14, 1853, to make way for the newly established San Francisco Branch Mint. The Mint, however, was unable to start immediate quantity production due to the lack of refining acids. During the interim, John G. Kellogg, a former employee of Moffat & Co., and John Glover Richter, a former assayer in the U.S. Assay Office, formed **Kellogg & Co.** for the purpose of supplying businessmen with urgently needed coinage. The firm produced $20 coins dated 1854 and 1855, after which Augustus Humbert replaced Richter and the enterprise reorganized as Kellogg & Humbert Melters, Assayers & Coiners. Kellogg & Humbert endured until 1860, but issued coins, $20 pieces, only in 1855.

BALDWIN & COMPANY

5 DOLLARS

KM# 17 Obverse: Liberty head, left, above date **Reverse:** Eagle

Date	Fine	VF	XF	Unc	DU
1850	4,000	6,500	10,000	25,000	—

10 DOLLARS

KM# 18 Obverse: Equestrian, right, swinging rope, above date and value **Reverse:** Eagle

Date	Fine	VF	XF	Unc	BU
1850	15,000	22,500	48,500	85,000	—

Note: Bass Sale May 2000, MS-64 $149,500

KM# 19 Obverse: Coronet head, left, within circle of stars, date below **Reverse:** Eagle

Date	Fine	VF	XF	Unc	BU
1851	9,000	14,500	28,500	50,000	—

20 DOLLARS

KM# 20 Obverse: Coronet head, left, within circle of stars, date below **Reverse:** Eagle

Date	Fine	VF	XF	Unc	BU
1851	—	—	—	—	—

Note: Stack's Superior Sale Dec. 1988, XF-40 $52,800; Beware of copies cast in base metals

BLAKE & COMPANY

20 DOLLARS

KM# 21 Obverse: Value within small center circle, legend around **Reverse:** Coining screw press above date and value

Date	Fine	VF	XF	Unc	BU
1855 Rare	—	—	—	—	—

Note: Many modern copies exist

J. H. BOWIE

5 DOLLARS

KM# 22 **Obverse:** Tree above date **Reverse:** Value

Date	Fine	VF	XF	Unc	BU
1849 Rare	—	—	—	—	—

Note: Americana Sale Jan. 2001, AU-58 $253,000

CINCINNATI MINING AND TRADING COMPANY

5 DOLLARS

KM# 23 **Obverse:** Draped bust with headdress, left **Reverse:** Eagle with shield, left, date below

Date	Fine	VF	XF	Unc	BU
1849 Rare	—	—	—	—	—

10 DOLLARS

KM# 24 **Obverse:** Draped bust with headdress, left **Reverse:** Eagle with shield, left, date below

Date	Fine	VF	XF	Unc	BU
1849 Rare	—	—	—	—	—

Note: Brand Sale 1984, XF $104,500

DUBOSQ & COMPANY

5 DOLLARS

KM# 26

Date	Fine	VF	XF	Unc	BU
1850	25,000	42,500	—	—	—

10 DOLLARS

KM# 27 **Obverse:** Coronet head, left, within circle of stars, date below **Reverse:** Eagle

Date	Fine	VF	XF	Unc	BU
1850	25,000	45,000	65,000	—	—

DUNBAR & COMPANY

5 DOLLARS

KM# 28 **Obverse:** Coronet head, left, within circle of stars, date below **Reverse:** Eagle

Date	Fine	VF	XF	Unc	BU
1851	22,500	32,500	55,000	—	—

Note: Spink & Son Sale 1988, AU $62,000

AUGUSTUS HUMBERT / UNITED STATES ASSAYER

10 DOLLARS

KM# 29.1 **Obverse:** Eagle, ribbon, value **Reverse:** Inscription, date **Note:** "AUGUSTUS HUMBERT" imprint.

Date	Fine	VF	XF	Unc	BU
1852/1	2,000	3,500	5,500	15,000	—
1852	1,500	2,500	4,750	11,500	—

KM# 29.2   **Note:** Error: IINITED.

Date	Fine	VF	XF	Unc	BU
1852/1 Rare	—	—	—	—	—
1852 Rare	—	—	—	—	—

20 DOLLARS

KM# 30   **Obverse:** Eagle, ribbon, banner and value **Reverse:** Inscription, date

Date	Fine	VF	XF	Unc	BU
1852/1	4,500	6,000	9,500	—	—

Note: Mory Sale June 2000, AU-53 $13,800; Garrett Sale March 1980, Humbert's Proof $325,000; Private Sale May 1989, Humbert's Proof ND(PCGS Pr-65) $1,350,000; California Sale Oct. 2000, Humbert's Proof ND(PCGS Pr-65) $552,000

50 DOLLARS

KM# 31.1   **Obverse:** "50 D C 880 THOUS", eagle **Reverse:** "50" in center

Date	Fine	VF	XF	Unc	BU
1851	9,500	12,000	22,000	—	—

KM# 31.1a   **Obverse:** 887 THOUS **Reverse:** 50 in center

Date	Fine	VF	XF	Unc	BU
1851	6,000	9,000	17,500	37,500	—

KM# 31.2   **Obverse:** "880 THOUS" **Reverse:** Without "50"

Date	Fine	VF	XF	Unc	BU
1851	5,000	8,000	16,500	35,500	—

KM# 31.2a   **Obverse:** 887 THOUS

Date	Fine	VF	XF	Unc	BU
1851	—	14,500	25,000	—	—

KM# 31.3   **Note:** "ASSAYER" inverted.

Date	Fine	VF	XF	Unc	BU
1851 Unique	—	—	—	—	—

KM# 31.4   **Obverse:** "880 THOUS" **Reverse:** Rays from central star

Date	Fine	VF	XF	Unc	BU
1851 Unique	—	—	—	—	—

TERRITORIAL GOLD

KELLOGG & COMPANY

20 DOLLARS

KM# 32.1   Obverse: "880 THOUS" **Reverse:** "Target"

Date	Fine	VF	XF	Unc	BU
1851	5,000	8,000	16,000	35,000	—

KM# 33.1   Obverse: Thick date **Reverse:** Short arrows

Date	Fine	VF	XF	Unc	BU
1854	1,200	2,000	4,000	17,500	—

KM# 33.2   Obverse: Medium date

Date	Fine	VF	XF	Unc	BU
1854	1,200	2,000	4,000	17,500	—

KM# 33.3   Obverse: Thin date **Reverse:** Short arrows

Date	Fine	VF	XF	Unc	BU
1854	1,200	2,000	4,000	17,500	—

KM# 32.1a   Obverse: "887 THOUS" **Reverse:** "Target"

Date	Fine	VF	XF	Unc	BU
1851	5,000	8,000	16,000	35,000	—

Note: Garrett Sale March 1980, Humberts Proof $500,000

KM# 32.2   Reverse: Small design

Date	Fine	VF	XF	Unc	BU
1851	5,000	8,000	16,000	—	—
1852	4,500	7,500	18,500	40,000	—

Note: Bloomfield Sale December 1996, BU $159,500

TERRITORIAL GOLD

KM# 33.4 Obverse: Thick date **Reverse:** Long arrows

Date	Fine	VF	XF	Unc	BU
1854	1,200	2,000	4,000	17,500	—
1855	1,200	2,250	4,250	18,500	—

Note: Garrett Sale March 1980 Proof $230,000

KM# 33.5 Obverse: Thick date **Reverse:** Medium arrows

Date	Fine	VF	XF	Unc	BU
1855	1,200	2,250	4,250	18,500	—

KM# 33.6 Reverse: Short arrows

Date	Fine	VF	XF	Unc	BU
1855	1,200	2,250	4,250	18,500	—

50 DOLLARS

KM# 34 Obverse: Coronet head, left, within circle of stars **Reverse:** Banner above eagle, written value in legend

Date	Fine	VF	XF	Unc	BU
1855	—	—	—	—	—

Note: Heritage ANA Sale August 1977, Proof $156,500

MASSACHUSETTES AND CALIFORNIA COMPANY

5 DOLLARS

KM# 35 Obverse: Rearing equestrian within shield, flanked by upright bear and deer **Reverse:** Value within wreath, date below

Date	Fine	VF	XF	Unc	BU
1849	40,000	65,000	—	—	—

TERRITORIAL GOLD

MINERS BANK

10 DOLLARS

Date	Fine	VF	XF	Unc	BU
ND(1849)	—	8,500	17,500	45,000	—

Note: Garrett Sale March 1980, MS-65 $135,000

Date	Fine	VF	XF	Unc	BU
ND(1849)	—	—	—	—	—

Note: Rare, as most specimens have heavy copper alloy

MOFFAT & COMPANY

5 DOLLARS

KM# 37.1 Obverse: Coronet head, left, within circle of stars, date below **Reverse:** Eagle, shield on breast

Date	Fine	VF	XF	Unc	BU
1849	1,000	1,500	3,500	12,000	—

KM# 37.2 Obverse: Coronet head, left, within circle of stars, date below **Reverse:** Die break at "DOL"

Date	Fine	VF	XF	Unc	BU
1849	1,000	1,500	3,500	12,000	—

KM# 37.3 Obverse: Coronet head, left, within circle of stars, date below **Reverse:** Die break on shield

Date	Fine	VF	XF	Unc	BU
1849	1,000	1,500	3,500	12,000	—

KM# 37.4 Obverse: Coronet head, left, within circle of stars, date below **Reverse:** Small letters

Date	Fine	VF	XF	Unc	BU
1850	1,100	1,650	4,200	14,000	—

KM# 37.5 Obverse: Coronet head, left, within circle of stars, date below **Reverse:** Large letters

Date	Fine	VF	XF	Unc	BU
1850	1,100	1,650	4,200	14,000	—

Note: Garrett Sale March 1980, MS-60 $21,000

10 DOLLARS

KM# 38.1 Obverse: Coronet head, left, within circle of stars, date below **Reverse:** Value: "TEN DOL.", arrow below period

Date	Fine	VF	XF	Unc	BU
1849	1,650	3,500	6,000	15,000	—

KM# 38.2 Obverse: Coronet head, left, within circle of stars, date below **Reverse:** Arrow above period

Date	Fine	VF	XF	Unc	BU
1849	1,650	3,500	6,000	15,000	—

KM# 38.3 Obverse: Coronet head, left, within circle of stars, date below **Reverse:** Value: "TEN D.", large letters

Date	Fine	VF	XF	Unc	BU
1849	2,250	5,000	7,500	16,500	—

KM# 38.4 Obverse: Coronet head, left, within circle of stars, date below **Reverse:** Small letters

Date	Fine	VF	XF	Unc	BU
1849	—	5,000	7,500	16,500	—

KM# 39.1 Obverse: Coronet head, left, within circle of stars, date below **Reverse:** Banner above eagle **Note:** "MOFFAT & CO." imprint, wide date

Date	Fine	VF	XF	Unc	BU
1852	2,500	5,500	10,000	20,000	—

TERRITORIAL GOLD

KM# 39.2 Obverse: Coronet head, left, within circle of stars, date below **Reverse:** 880 thous. in banner above eagle **Note:** Close date. Struck by Augustus Humbert.

Date	Fine	VF	XF	Unc	BU
1852	2,000	4,250	9,000	18,500	—

20 DOLLARS

KM# 40 Obverse: Coronet head, left, within circle of stars, date below **Reverse:** Circle of stars and rays above eagle **Note:** Struck by Curtis, Perry, & Ward.

Date	Fine	VF	XF	Unc	BU
1853	2,150	3,750	6,000	16,500	—

NORRIS, GREIG, & NORRIS

HALF EAGLE

KM# 41.1 Obverse: Date in center of circle of stars and legend **Reverse:** Period after "ALLOY"

Date	Fine	VF	XF	Unc	BU
1849	2,250	3,750	7,250	20,000	—

KM# 41.2 Obverse: Date in center of circle of stars and legend **Reverse:** Period after "ALLOY"

Date	Fine	VF	XF	Unc	BU
1849	2,250	3,750	7,250	20,000	—

KM# 41.3 Obverse: Date in center of circle of stars and legend **Reverse:** Period after "ALLOY"

Date	Fine	VF	XF	Unc	BU
1849	1,750	3,000	6,750	20,000	—

KM# 41.4 Obverse: Date in center of circle of stars and legend **Reverse:** Without period after "ALLOY"

Date	Fine	VF	XF	Unc	BU
1849	1,750	3,000	6,750	20,000	—

KM# 42 Obverse: "STOCKTON" beneath date

Date	Fine	VF	XF	Unc	BU
1850 Unique	—	—	—	—	—

J. S. ORMSBY

5 DOLLARS

KM# 43.1 Obverse: "J.S.O." in center **Reverse:** Value within circle of stars

Date	Fine	VF	XF	Unc	BU
ND(1849) Unique	—	—	—	—	—

KM# 43.2 Obverse: "J.S.O." in center **Reverse:** Value within circle of stars

Date	Fine	VF	XF	Unc	BU
ND(1849) Unique	—	—	—	—	—

Note: Superior Auction 1989, VF $137,500

10 DOLLARS

KM# 44 Obverse: "J.S.O." in center **Reverse:** Value in center circle of stars

Date	Fine	VF	XF	Unc	BU
ND(1849) Rare	—	—	—	—	—

Note: Garrett Sale March 1980, F-12 $100,000; Ariagno Sale June 1999, AU-50 $145,000

PACIFIC COMPANY

5 DOLLARS

KM# 45 **Obverse:** Stars within rays of Liberty cap, value below **Reverse:** Eagle

Date	Fine	VF	XF	Unc	BU
1849 Rare	—	—	—	—	—

Note: Garrett Sale March 1980, VF-30 $180,000

10 DOLLARS

KM# 46.1 **Obverse:** Stars within rays of Liberty cap, value below **Reverse:** Eagle, date below

Date	Fine	VF	XF	Unc	BU
1849 Rare	—	—	—	—	—

Note: Waldorf Sale 1964, $24,000

KM# 46.2 **Obverse:** Stars within rays of Liberty cap, value below **Reverse:** Eagle

Date	Fine	VF	XF	Unc	BU
1849 Rare	—	—	—	—	—

1 DOLLAR

KM# A45 **Obverse:** Stars within rays of Liberty cap, value below **Reverse:** Eagle

Date	Fine	VF	XF	Unc	BU
ND(1849) Unique	—	—	—	—	—

Note: Mory Sale June 2000, EF-40 $57,500

TEMPLETON REID

10 DOLLARS

KM# 47 **Obverse:** Date in center **Reverse:** Value in center

Date	Fine	VF	XF	Unc	BU
1849 Unique	—	—	—	—	—

20 DOLLARS

KM# 48

Date	Fine	VF	XF	Unc	BU
1849 Unknown	—	—	—	—	—

Note: The only known specimen was stolen from the U.S. Mint in 1858 and has never been recovered. For additional listings of Templeton Reid, see listings under Georgia

SCHULTZ & COMPANY

5 DOLLARS

KM# 49 **Obverse:** Coronet head, left, within circle of stars, date below **Reverse:** Eagle, shield on breast, value below

Date	Fine	VF	XF	Unc	BU
1851	—	36,800	50,000	—	—

UNITED STATES ASSAY OFFICE OF GOLD

10 DOLLARS

KM# 50.1 **Obverse:** TEN DOLS 884 THOUS **Reverse:** "O" of "OFFICE" below "I" of "UNITED"

Date	Fine	VF	XF	Unc	BU
1852	—	—	—	—	—

Note: Garrett Sale March 1980, MS-60 $18,000

20 DOLLARS

KM# 51.2   Obverse: TEN DOLS, 884 THOUS
Reverse: "O" below "N", strong beads

Date	Fine	VF	XF	Unc	BU
1852	1,750	2,500	3,850	9,500	—

KM# 51.3   Obverse: TEN DOLS, 884 THOUS
Reverse: Weak beads

Date	Fine	VF	XF	Unc	BU
1852	1,750	2,500	3,850	9,500	—

KM# 53   Obverse: 884/880 THOUS **Reverse:**
Inscription, date

Date	Fine	VF	XF	Unc	BU
1853	8,500	12,500	17,500	23,500	—

KM# 52   Obverse: TEN D, 884 THOUS **Reverse:**
Inscription, date

Date	Fine	VF	XF	Unc	BU
1853	5,000	7,750	14,500	—	—

KM# 52a   Obverse: 900 THOUS **Reverse:**
Inscription, date

Date	Fine	VF	XF	Unc	BU
1853	2,700	4,200	6,500	—	—

Note: Garrett Sale March 1980, MS-60 $35,000

KM# 53a   Obverse: 900/880 THOUS **Reverse:**
Inscription, date

Date	Fine	VF	XF	Unc	BU
1853	1,550	2,750	4,250	10,000	—

Note: 1853 Liberty Head listed under Moffat & Company

TERRITORIAL GOLD

50 DOLLARS

WASS, MOLITOR & COMPANY

5 DOLLARS

KM# 55.1 **Obverse:** Small head, rounded bust **Reverse:** Eagle, shield on breast

Date	Fine	VF	XF	Unc	BU
1852	2,000	4,000	6,750	16,500	—

KM# 55.2 **Obverse:** Coronet head, left, within circle of stars **Reverse:** Eagle, shield on breast **Note:** Thick planchet.

Date	Fine	VF	XF	Unc	BU
1852 Unique	—	—	—	—	—

KM# 56 **Obverse:** Large head, pointed bust **Reverse:** Eagle, shield on breast

Date	Fine	VF	XF	Unc	BU
1852	2,000	4,500	8,500	17,500	—

10 DOLLARS

KM# 57 **Obverse:** Long neck, large date **Reverse:** Eagle, shield on breast

Date	Fine	VF	XF	Unc	BU
1852	2,750	5,000	8,500	15,500	—

KM# 58 **Obverse:** Short neck, wide date **Reverse:** Eagle, shield on breast

Date	Fine	VF	XF	Unc	BU
1852	1,500	2,650	5,500	13,500	—

KM# 54 **Obverse:** 887 THOUS **Reverse:** "Target"

Date	Fine	VF	XF	Unc	BU
1852	4,000	6,500	13,500	26,500	—

KM# 54a **Obverse:** 900 THOUS **Reverse:** "Target"

Date	Fine	VF	XF	Unc	BU
1852	5,000	7,000	14,500	28,500	—

KM# 59.1 **Obverse:** Short neck, small date **Reverse:** Eagle, shield on breast

Date	Fine	VF	XF	Unc	BU
1852 Rare	—	—	—	—	—

Note: Eliasberg Sale May 1996, EF-45 $36,300; S.S. Central America Sale December 2000, VF-30 realized $12,650

KM# 59.2 **Obverse:** Plugged date **Reverse:** Eagle, shield on breast

Date	Fine	VF	XF	Unc	BU
1855	6,000	8,000	12,500	28,500	—

20 DOLLARS

KM# 60 **Obverse:** Large head **Reverse:** Eagle, shield on breast, value in banner above

Date	Fine	VF	XF	Unc	BU
1855 Rare	—	—	—	—	—

KM# 61 **Obverse:** Small head **Reverse:** Eagle, shield on breast, value in banner above

Date	Fine	VF	XF	Unc	BU
1855	7,000	11,000	20,000	—	—

50 DOLLARS

KM# 62 **Obverse:** Coronet head, left, within circle of stars, date below **Reverse:** Value within wreath

Date	Fine	VF	XF	Unc	BU
1855	—	—	—	—	—

Note: Bloomfield Sale December 1996, BU $170,500

COLORADO

The discovery of gold in Colorado Territory was accompanied by the inevitable need for coined money. Austin M. Clark, Milton E. Clark, and Emanuel H. Gruber, bankers of Leavenworth, Kansas, moved to Denver where they established a bank and issued $2.50, $5, $10, and $20 gold coins in 1860 and 1861. To protect the holder from loss by abrasion, **Clark, Gruber & Co.** made their coins slightly heavier than full value required. The 1860 issues carry the inscription PIKE'S PEAK GOLD on reverse. CLARK, GRUBER & CO. appears on the reverse of the 1861 issues, and PIKE'S PEAK on the coronet of Liberty. The government purchased the plant of Clark, Gruber & Co. in 1863 and operated it as a federal Assay Office until 1906.

In the summer of 1861, **John Parsons**, an assayer whose place of business was located in South Park at the Tarryall Mines, Colorado, issued undated gold coins in the denominations of $2.50 and $5. They, too, carry the inscription PIKE'S PEAK GOLD on reverse.

J. J. Conway & Co., bankers of Georgia Gulch, Colorado operated the Conway Mint for a short period in 1861. Undated gold coins in the denominations of $2.50, $5, and $10 were issued. A variety of the $5 coin does not carry the numeral 5 on reverse. The issues of the Conway Mint were highly regarded for their scrupulously maintained value.

CLARK, GRUBER & COMPANY

2-1/2 DOLLARS

KM# 63   Obverse: Coronet head, left, within circle of stars, date below **Reverse:** Eagle, shield on breast

Date	Fine	VF	XF	Unc	BU
1860	750	1,300	2,500	8,500	—

Note: Garrett Sale March 1980, MS-65 $12,000

KM# 64.1   Obverse: Coronet head, left, within circle of stars, date below **Reverse:** Eagle, shield on breast

Date	Fine	VF	XF	Unc	BU
1861	850	1,500	2,750	11,500	—

KM# 64.2   Obverse: Coronet head, left, within circle of stars, date below **Reverse:** Eagle, shield on breast
Note: Extra high edge.

Date	Fine	VF	XF	Unc	BU
1861	850	1,750	3,500	12,500	—

5 DOLLARS

KM# 65   Obverse: Coronet head, left, within circle of stars, date below **Reverse:** Eagle, shield on breast

Date	Fine	VF	XF	Unc	BU
1860	1,000	1,750	3,000	9,200	—

Note: Garrett Sale March 1980, MS-63 $9,000

KM# 66   Obverse: Coronet head, left, within circle of stars, date below **Reverse:** Eagle, shield on breast

Date	Fine	VF	XF	Unc	BU
1861	1,500	2,500	4,500	13,500	—

10 DOLLARS

KM# 67   Obverse: Mountain above value **Reverse:** Eagle, shield on breast

Date	Fine	VF	XF	Unc	BU
1860	2,750	3,750	8,000	21,500	—

KM# 68   Obverse: Coronet head, left, within circle of stars, date below **Reverse:** Eagle, shield on breast

Date	Fine	VF	XF	Unc	BU
1861	1,500	2,500	4,500	15,500	—

20 DOLLARS

KM# 69   Obverse: Mountain above value **Reverse:** Eagle, shield on breast

Date	Fine	VF	XF	Unc	BU
1860	25,000	55,000	75,000	100,000	—

Note: Eliasberg Sale May 1996, AU $90,200; Schoonmaker Sale June 1997, VCF $62,700

KM# 70   **Obverse:** Coronet head, left, within circle of stars, date below **Reverse:** Circle of stars and rays above eagle

Date	Fine	VF	XF	Unc	BU
1861	7,000	10,000	21,500	—	—

J. J. CONWAY

2-1/2 DOLLARS

KM# 71   **Obverse:** & CO. in center **Reverse:** Value in center

Date	Fine	VF	XF	Unc	BU
ND(1861)	—	45,000	70,000	—	—

5 DOLLARS

KM# 72.1   **Obverse:** & CO in center **Reverse:** Value in center

Date	Fine	VF	XF	Unc	BU
ND(1861) Rare	—	—	—	—	—

Note: Brand Sale June 1984, XF-40 $44,000

KM# 72.2   **Obverse:** & CO. in center **Reverse:** Numeral 5 omitted

Date	Fine	VF	XF	Unc	BU
ND(1861) Unique	—	—	—	—	—

10 DOLLARS

KM# 73   **Obverse:** & CO. within circle **Reverse:** Numeral value within circle of stars

Date	Fine	VF	XF	Unc	BU
ND(1861) Rare	—	60,000	—	—	—

JOHN PARSONS

2-1/2 DOLLARS

KM# 74   **Obverse:** Minting press **Reverse:** Eagle, shield on breast, value below

Date	Fine	VF	XF	Unc	BU
ND(1861) Rare	—	—	—	—	—

Note: Garrett Sale March 1980, VF-20 $85,000

5 DOLLARS

KM# 75   **Obverse:** Minting press **Reverse:** Eagle, shield on breast, value below

Date	Fine	VF	XF	Unc	BU
ND(1861) Rare	—	—	—	—	—

Note: Garrett Sale March 1980, VF-20 $100,000

GEORGIA

The first territorial gold pieces were struck in 1830 by **Templeton Reid**, a goldsmith and assayer who established a private mint at Gainesville, Georgia, at the time gold was being mined on a relatively large scale in Georgia and North Carolina. Reid's pieces were issued in denominations of $2.50, $5, and $10. Except for an undated variety of the $10 piece, all are dated 1830.

CHRISTOPHER BECHTLER

2-1/2 DOLLARS

KM# 76.1   **Obverse:** "2.50" in center **Reverse:** "GEORGIA", "64 G, 22 CARATS"

Date	Fine	VF	XF	Unc	BU
	1,650	2,650	5,000	10,000	—

KM# 76.2   **Obverse:** 2.50 in center **Reverse:** "GEORGIA", "64 G, 22 CARATS", even 22

Date	Fine	VF	XF	Unc	BU
	1,850	2,850	5,500	11,500	—

5 DOLLARS

KM# 77   Obverse: "RUTHERF" **Reverse:** "128 G", "22 CARATS" below

Date	Fine	VF	XF	Unc	BU
	2,000	3,500	5,500	11,500	—

KM# 78.1   Obverse: "RUTHERFORD" **Reverse:** "128 G", "22 CARATS" below

Date	Fine	VF	XF	Unc	BU
	2,000	3,750	6,000	12,500	—

KM# 78.2   Obverse: Value in center **Reverse:** Colon after "128 G:"

Date	Fine	VF	XF	Unc	BU
	—	20,000	30,000	—	—

Note: Akers Pittman Sale October 1997, VF-XF $26,400

TEMPLETON REID

2-1/2 DOLLARS

KM# 79   Obverse: Date in center **Reverse:** "2.50" in center

Date	Fine	VF	XF	Unc	BU
1830	12,500	32,500	55,000	—	—

5 DOLLARS

KM# 80   Obverse: "$ 5" in center above date **Reverse:** "$ 5" in center

Date	Fine	VF	XF	Unc	BU
1830 Rare	—	—	—	—	—

Note: Garrett Sale November 1979, XF-40 $200,000

10 DOLLARS

KM# 81   Obverse: With date **Reverse:** Written value

Date	Fine	VF	XF	Unc	BU
1830 Rare	—	—	—	—	—

KM# 82   Obverse: Undated **Reverse:** Written value

Date	Fine	VF	XF	Unc	BU
ND(1830) Rare	—	—	—	—	—

Note: Also see listings under California

NORTH CAROLINA

The southern Appalachians were also the scene of a private gold minting operation conducted by Christopher Bechtler Sr., his son August, and nephew Christopher Jr. The Bechtlers, a family of German metallurgists, established a mint at Rutherfordton, North Carolina, which produced territorial gold coins for a longer period than any other private mint in American history. Christopher Bechtler Sr. ran the Bechtler mint from July 1831 until his death in 1842, after which the mint was taken over by his son August who ran it until 1852.

The Bechtler coinage includes but 3 denominations -- $1, $2.50, and $5 - but they were issued in a wide variety of weights and sizes. The coinage is undated, except for 3 varieties of the $5 piece which carry the inscription "Aug. 1, 1834" to indicate that they conform to the new weight standard adopted by the U.S. Treasury for official gold coins. **Christopher Bechtler Sr.** produced $2.50 and $5 gold coins for Georgia, and $1, $2.50, and $5 coins for North Carolina. The dollar coins have the distinction of being the first gold coins of that denomination to be produced in the United States. While under the supervision of **August Bechtler**, the Bechtler mint issued $1 and $5 coins for North Carolina.

AUGUST BECHTLER

KM# 83.1 **Obverse:** Numeral "1" in center **Reverse:** "CAROLINA, 27 G. 21C."

Date	Fine	VF	XF	Unc	BU
ND(1842-52)	450	650	1,150	2,950	—

KM# 83.2 **Obverse:** Numeral "1" in center **Reverse:** "CAROLINA, 27 G. 21C."

Date	Fine	VF	XF	Unc	BU
ND(1842-52)	450	650	1,150	2,950	—

5 DOLLARS

KM# 84 **Obverse:** Value in center **Reverse:** "CAROLINA", "134 G. 21 CARATS"

Date	Fine	VF	XF	Unc	BU
ND(1842-52)	1,750	3,500	6,000	12,500	—

KM# 85 **Obverse:** Value in center **Reverse:** "CAROLINA", "128 G. 22 CARATS"

Date	Fine	VF	XF	Unc	BU
ND(1842-52)	3,000	5,500	8,000	15,000	—

KM# 86 **Obverse:** Value in center **Reverse:** "CAROLINA", "141 G: 20 CARATS"

Date	Fine	VF	XF	Unc	BU
ND(1842-52)	2,750	4,850	7,500	14,500	—

Note: Proof restrikes exist from original dies; in the Akers Pittman Sale October 1997, an example sold for $14,300

CHRISTOPHER BECHTLER

DOLLAR

KM# 87 **Obverse:** 28 G. **Reverse:** CAROLINA, N reversed

Date	Fine	VF	XF	Unc	BU
ND(1831-42)	900	1,200	1,700	3,750	—

KM# 88.1 **Obverse:** 28. G. centered without star **Reverse:** N. CAROLINA

Date	Fine	VF	XF	Unc	BU
ND(1831-42)	1,500	2,200	3,500	8,000	—

KM# 88.2 **Obverse:** N CAROLINA **Reverse:** 28 G high without star

Date	Fine	VF	XF	Unc	BU
ND(1831-42)	2,500	4,500	6,500	12,000	—

KM# 89 **Obverse:** 30 G. **Reverse:** N. CAROLINA

Date	Fine	VF	XF	Unc	BU
ND(1831-42)	850	1,200	2,750	5,500	—

2-1/2 DOLLARS

KM# 90.1 **Obverse:** 250 in center **Reverse:** CAROLINA, 67 G. 21 CARATS

Date	Fine	VF	XF	Unc	BU
ND(1831-42)	1,250	2,250	5,500	11,500	—

KM# 90.2 **Obverse:** 250 in center **Reverse:** 64 G 22 CARATS, uneven 22

Date	Fine	VF	XF	Unc	BU
ND(1831-42)	1,450	2,850	6,000	12,000	—

KM# 90.3 **Reverse:** Even 22

Date	Fine	VF	XF	Unc	BU
ND(1831-42)	1,650	3,000	6,500	12,500	—

KM# 91   Obverse: 250 in center **Reverse:**
CAROLINA, 70 G. 20 CARATS

Date	Fine	VF	XF	Unc	BU
ND(1831-42)	1,650	3,000	6,750	18,500	—

Note: Bowers and Merena Long Sale May 1995, MS-63
$31,900

KM# 92.1   Obverse: RUTHERFORD in a circle,
border of large beads **Reverse:** NORTH CAROLINA,
250, 20 C. 75 G.

Date	Fine	VF	XF	Unc	BU
ND(1831-42)	—	7,500	11,500	25,000	—

KM# 92.2   Obverse: RUTHERFORD in circle
Reverse: NORTH CAROLINA, 250, without 75 G,
wide 20 C.

Date	Fine	VF	XF	Unc	BU
ND(1831-42)	2,800	5,000	7,000	14,500	—

KM# 92.3   Obverse: Narrow 20 C

Date	Fine	VF	XF	Unc	BU
ND(1831-42)	2,800	5,000	7,000	14,500	—

KM# 93.1   Obverse: RUTHERFORD in a circle
Reverse: NORTH CAROLINA without 75 G,
CAROLINA above 250 instead of GOLD

Date	Fine	VF	XF	Unc	BU
ND(1831-42) Unique	—	—	—	—	—

KM# 93.2   Obverse: NORTH CAROLINA, 20 C
Reverse: 75 G, border finely serrated

Date	Fine	VF	XF	Unc	BU
ND(1831-42)	4,500	7,500	10,500	—	—

5 DOLLARS

KM# 94   Obverse: Numeral value in center **Reverse:**
CAROLINA, 134 G., star, 21 CARATS

Date	Fine	VF	XF	Unc	BU
ND(1831-42)	1,650	3,250	6,000	11,000	—

KM# 95   Obverse: Numeral value in center **Reverse:**
21 above CARATS, without star

Date	Fine	VF	XF	Unc	BU
ND(1831-42) Unique	—	—	—	—	—

KM# 96.1   Obverse: RUTHERFORD **Reverse:**
CAROLINA, 140 G. 20 CARATS

Date	Fine	VF	XF	Unc	BU
1834	1,750	3,750	6,500	11,500	—

KM# 96.2   Obverse: Numeral value in center
Reverse: 140 .C., 20 CARATS

Date	Fine	VF	XF	Unc	BU
1834	2,000	4,000	7,000	12,500	—

KM# 97.1   Obverse: RUTHERF **Reverse:**
CAROLINA. 140 G. 20 CARATS; 20 close to CARATS

Date	Fine	VF	XF	Unc	BU
1834	1,800	3,850	6,750	12,000	—

KM# 97.2   Obverse: Written value in center
Reverse: 20 away from CARATS

Date	Fine	VF	XF	Unc	BU
1834	2,500	6,500	11,500	—	—

KM# 98   Obverse: RUTHERF **Reverse:** CAROLINA, 141 G, 20 CARATS

Date	Fine	VF	XF	Unc	BU
ND(1831-42)					
Proof restrike	—	—	—	15,500	—

KM# 99.1   Obverse: RUTHEFER in a circle **Reverse:** NORTH CAROLINA, 150 G, below 20 CARATS

Date	Fine	VF	XF	Unc	BU
ND(1831-42)	2,800	4,500	8,500	18,500	—

KM# 99.2   Obverse: RUTHEFER in a circle **Reverse:** Without 150 G

Date	Fine	VF	XF	Unc	BU
ND(1831-42)	3,200	6,000	10,000	20,000	—

OREGON

The Oregon Exchange Co., a private mint located at Oregon City, Oregon Territory, issued $5 and $10 pieces of local gold in 1849. The initials K., M., T., A., W. R. C. (G on the $5 piece), and S. on the obverse represent the eight founders of the **Oregon Exchange Co.**: William Kilborne, Theophilus Magruder, James Taylor, George Abernathy, William Willson, William Rector, John Campbell, and Noyes Smith. Campbell is erroneously represented by a G on the $5 coin. For unknown reasons, the initials A and W are omitted from the $10 piece. O.T. (Oregon Territory) is erroneously presented as T.O. on the $5 coin.

OREGON EXCHANGE COMPANY

5 DOLLARS

KM# 100   Obverse: Beaver above date and sprigs **Reverse:** Value

Date	Fine	VF	XF	Unc	BU
1849	10,000	18,500	33,350	—	—

10 DOLLARS

KM# 101   Obverse: Beaver above date and sprigs **Reverse:** Value

Date	Fine	VF	XF	Unc	BU
1849	20,000	40,000	65,000	—	—

UTAH

MORMON ISSUES

2-1/2 DOLLARS

KM# 102   Obverse: Design above eye **Reverse:** Clasped hands above date

Date	Fine	VF	XF	Unc	BU
1849	4,000	7,000	13,500	24,500	—

5 DOLLARS

KM# 103   Obverse: Design above eye **Reverse:** Clasped hands above date

Date	Fine	VF	XF	Unc	BU
1849	4,000	7,000	12,000	23,500	—

KM# 104   Obverse: Designs above eye and stars **Reverse:** Clasped hands above date

Date	Fine	VF	XF	Unc	BU
1850	4,500	7,500	15,000	25,500	—

TERRITORIAL GOLD

KM# 105   Obverse: Lion facing left above date
Reverse: Design on eagle breast

Date	Fine	VF	XF	Unc	BU
1860	6,500	12,000	25,000	37,500	—

10 DOLLARS

KM# 106   Obverse: Design above eye **Reverse:**
Clasped hands above date

Date	Fine	VF	XF	Unc	BU
1849 Rare	—	—	—	—	—

Note: Heritage ANA Sale July 1988, AU $93,000

20 DOLLARS

KM# 107   Obverse: Design above eye **Reverse:**
Clasped hands above date

Date	Fine	VF	XF	Unc	BU
1849	22,500	47,500	85,000	—	—

TERRITORIAL GOLD

HAWAII

KM# 1a CENT
Copper **Ruler:** Kamehameha III **Obv:** Uniformed bust, facing **Obv. Legend:** KAMEHAMEHA III.KA.MOI. **Rev:** Value within wreath **Rev. Legend:** AUPUNI HAWAII

Date	Mintage	VG	F	VF	XF	Unc
1847 Plain 4, 13 berries (6 left, 7 right)	100,000	200	275	400	600	1,000

KM# 1b CENT
Copper **Ruler:** Kamehameha III **Obv:** Uniformed bust, facing **Obv. Legend:** KAMEHAMEHA III.KA.MOI. **Rev:** Value within wreath **Rev. Legend:** AUPUNI HAWAII

Date	Mintage	VG	F	VF	XF	Unc
1047	Inc. above	200	275	400	600	1,000

Note: Plain 4, 15 berries (8 left, 7 right)

KM# 1f CENT
Copper **Ruler:** Kamehameha III **Obv:** Uniformed bust, facing **Obv. Legend:** KAMEHAMEHA III.KA.MOI. **Rev:** Value within wreath **Rev. Legend:** AUPUNI HAWAII

Date	Mintage	VG	F	VF	XF	Unc
1847	Inc. above	550	800	1,500	2,000	—

Note: Plain 4, 15 berries (7 left, 8 right)

KM# 1c CENT
Copper **Ruler:** Kamehameha III **Obv:** Uniformed bust, facing **Obv. Legend:** KAMEHAMEHA III.KA.MOI. **Rev:** Value within wreath **Rev. Legend:** AUPUNI HAWAII

Date	Mintage	VG	F	VF	XF	Unc
1847	Inc. above	200	275	400	600	1,200

Note: Plain 4, 17 berries (8 left, 9 right)

KM# 1d CENT
Copper **Ruler:** Kamehameha III **Obv:** Uniformed bust, facing **Obv. Legend:** KAMEHAMEHA III.KA.MOI. **Rev:** Value within wreath **Rev. Legend:** AUPUNI HAWAII

Date	Mintage	VG	F	VF	XF	Unc
1847	Inc. above	200	275	400	600	1,000

Note: Crosslet 4, 15 berries (7 left, 8 right)

KM# 1e CENT
Copper **Ruler:** Kamehameha III **Obv:** Uniformed bust, facing **Obv. Legend:** KAMEHAMEHA III.KA.MOI. **Rev:** Value within wreath **Rev. Legend:** AUPUNI HAWAII

Date	Mintage	VG	F	VF	XF	Unc
1847	Inc. above	250	400	550	850	3,500

Note: Crosslet 4, 18 berries (9 left, 9 right)

KM# 2 5 CENTS (Pattern)
Nickel **Ruler:** Kalakaua I **Obv:** Head left, date below **Obv. Legend:** KALAKAUA KING OF SANDWICH ISLANDS **Rev:** Value within crowned belt

Date	Mintage	VG	F	VF	XF	Unc
1881		200	4,500	5,500	7,500	12,000	17,000

Note: All original specimens of this pattern were struck on thin nickel planchets, presumably in Paris and have "MAILLECHORT" stamped on the edge. In the early 1900's, deceptive replicas of the issue were produced in Canada, on thick and thin nickel and aluminum, and thin copper planchets (thick about 2.7 to 3.1mm; thin about 1.4 to 1.7mm). The original patterns can be easily distinguished from the replicas, because on the former, a small cross surmounts the crown on the reverse; on the replicas the

KM# 3 10 CENTS (Umi Keneta)
2.5000 g., 0.9000 Silver 0.0723 oz. ASW **Ruler:** Kalakaua I **Obv:** Head right, date below **Obv. Legend:** KALAKAUA I KING OF HAWAII **Rev:** Crown and value within wreath

Date	Mintage	VG	F	VF	XF	Unc
1883	250,000	45.00	60.00	95.00	250	1,000
1883 Proof	26	Value: 7,500				

KM# 4a 1/8 DOLLAR (Hapawalu)
Copper **Ruler:** Kalakaua I **Obv:** Head right **Obv. Legend:** KALAKAUA I KING OF HAWAII **Note:** Pattern issue.

Date	Mintage	VG	F	VF	XF	Unc
1883 Proof	18	Value: 20,000				

KM# 4 1/8 DOLLAR (Hapawalu)
0.9000 Silver **Ruler:** Kalakaua I **Obv:** Head right **Obv. Legend:** KALAKAUA I KING OF HAWAII **Note:** Pattern issue.

Date	Mintage	VG	F	VF	XF	Unc
1883 Proof	20	Value: 50,000				

KM# 5   1/4 DOLLAR (Hapaha)

6.2200 g., 0.9000 Silver 0.1800 oz. ASW   **Ruler:** Kalakaua I
Obv: Head right, date below **Obv. Legend:** KALAKAUA I KING
OF HAWAII **Rev:** Crowned arms divides value **Rev. Legend:**
UA MAU KE...

Date	Mintage	VG	F	VF	XF	Unc
1883	500,000	40.00	55.00	70.00	100	200
1883/1383	Inc. above	45.00	65.00	95.00	150	300
1883 Proof	26	Value: 10,000				

KM# 5a   1/4 DOLLAR (Hapaha)

Copper   **Ruler:** Kalakaua I **Obv:** Head right, date below **Obv.
Legend:** KALAKAUA I KING OF HAWAII **Rev:** Crowned arms
divides value **Rev. Legend:** UA MAU KE... **Note:** Pattern issue.

Date	Mintage	VG	F	VF	XF	Unc
1883 Proof	18	Value: 8,500				

KM# 6   1/2 DOLLAR (Hapalua)

12.5000 g., 0.9000 Silver 0.3617 oz. ASW   **Ruler:** Kalakaua I
Obv: Head right, date below **Obv. Legend:** KALAKAUA I KING
OF HAWAII **Rev:** Crowned arms divides value **Rev. Legend:**
UA MAU KE...

Date	Mintage	VG	F	VF	XF	Unc
1883	700,000	100	125	175	300	1,200
1883 Proof	26	Value: 12,000				

KM# 6a   1/2 DOLLAR (Hapalua)

Copper   **Ruler:** Kalakaua I **Obv:** Head right, date below **Obv.
Legend:** KALAKAUA I KING OF HAWAII **Rev:** Crowned arms
divides value **Rev. Legend:** UA MAU KE... **Note:** Pattern issue.

Date	Mintage	VG	F	VF	XF	Unc
1883 Proof	18	Value: 10,000				

KM# 7   DOLLAR (Akahi Dala)

26.7300 g., 0.9000 Silver 0.7734 oz. ASW   **Ruler:** Kalakaua I
Obv: Head right, date below **Obv. Legend:** KALAKAUA I KING
OF HAWAII **Rev:** Crowned arms with supporters within
crowned mantle **Rev. Legend:** UA MAU KE...

Date	Mintage	VG	F	VF	XF	Unc
1883	500,000	250	300	450	750	4,000
1883 Proof	26	Value: 15,000				

KM# 7a   DOLLAR (Akahi Dala)

Copper   **Ruler:** Kalakaua I **Obv:** Head right, date below **Obv.
Legend:** KALAKAUA I KING OF HAWAII **Rev:** Crowned arms
with supporters within crowned mantle **Rev. Legend:** UA MAU
KE... **Note:** Pattern issue.

Date	Mintage	VG	F	VF	XF	Unc
1883 Proof	18	Value: 15,000				

Note: Official records indicate the following quantities of the
above issues were redeemed and melted: KM#1 - 88,405;
KM#3 - 79; KM#5 - 257,400; KM#6 - 612,245; KM#7 - 453,652.
That leaves approximate net mintages of: KM#1 - 11,600;
KM#3 - 250,000; KM#5 (regular date) - 242,600, (unknown)
40,000; KM#6 - 87,700; KM#7 - 46,300.

PHILIPPINES

UNITED STATES ADMINISTRATION

DECIMAL COINAGE

KM# 162   1/2 CENTAVO
Bronze **Obv:** Man seated beside hammer and anvil **Rev:** Eagle above stars and striped shield

Date	Mintage	F	VF	XF	Unc	BU
1903	12,084,000	0.50	1.00	2.00	12.00	20.00
1903 Proof	2,558	Value: 60.00				
1904	5,654,000	0.50	1.25	3.00	15.00	25.00
1904 Proof	1,355	Value: 75.00				
1905 Proof	471	Value: 300				
1906 Proof	500	Value: 200				
1908 Proof	500	Value: 250				

KM# 163   CENTAVO
4.7000 g., Bronze **Obv:** Man seated beside hammer and anvil **Rev:** Eagle above stars and striped shield

Date	Mintage	F	VF	XF	Unc	BU
1903	10,790,000	0.50	1.00	2.50	15.00	30.00
1903 Proof	2,558	Value: 75.00				
1904	17,040,000	0.50	1.00	2.50	17.50	32.50
1904 Proof	1,355	Value: 75.00				
1905	10,000,000	0.50	1.00	2.50	20.00	40.00
1905 Proof	471	Value: 200				
1906 Proof	500	Value: 175				
1908 Proof	500	Value: 190				
1908S	2,187,000	2.50	5.00	12.50	50.00	80.00
1909S	1,738,000	7.50	12.50	30.00	90.00	140
1910S	2,700,000	2.00	5.00	10.00	50.00	80.00
1911S	4,803,000	1.00	4.00	7.50	40.00	60.00
1912S	3,000,000	3.00	6.50	12.50	90.00	120
1913S	5,000,000	1.00	2.50	7.50	50.00	85.00
1914S	5,000,000	1.00	2.50	5.00	40.00	65.00
1915S	2,500,000	20.00	40.00	90.00	600	975
1916S	4,330,000	6.00	12.50	25.00	110	175
1917/6S	7,070,000	22.00	30.00	75.00	300	425
1917S	Inc. above	2.50	5.00	10.00	40.00	80.00
1918S	11,660,000	2.00	4.00	10.00	60.00	125
1918S Large S	Inc. above	75.00	150	325	1,300	1,800
1919S	4,540,000	0.75	2.00	6.00	35.00	65.00
1920S	2,500,000	4.00	9.00	20.00	125	265
1920	3,552,000	1.00	3.50	8.50	45.00	70.00
1921	7,283,000	0.75	3.50	7.50	40.00	70.00
1922	3,519,000	0.50	1.50	6.00	40.00	65.00
1925M	9,332,000	0.50	1.50	6.00	40.00	60.00
1926M	9,000,000	0.50	1.50	6.00	35.00	50.00
1927M	9,270,000	0.35	2.00	6.00	40.00	75.00
1928M	9,150,000	0.35	1.00	5.00	25.00	40.00
1929M	5,657,000	1.00	3.00	8.00	40.00	75.00
1930M	5,577,000	0.50	1.50	4.00	30.00	45.00
1931M	5,659,000	0.50	1.50	5.00	40.00	55.00
1932M	4,000,000	0.75	2.50	6.00	45.00	65.00
1933M	8,393,000	0.25	1.50	3.00	15.00	30.00

Date	Mintage	F	VF	XF	Unc	BU
1934M	3,179,000	0.75	2.00	3.00	40.00	75.00
1936M	17,455,000	0.25	1.00	3.00	35.00	50.00

KM# 164   5 CENTAVOS
Copper-Nickel, 21.3 mm. **Obv:** Man seated beside hammer and anvil **Rev:** Eagle above stars and striped shield

Date	Mintage	F	VF	XF	Unc	BU
1903	8,910,000	0.50	1.25	3.00	25.00	35.00
1903 Proof	2,558	Value: 75.00				
1904	1,075,000	0.75	1.50	3.50	27.00	35.00
1904 Proof	1,355	Value: 85.00				
1905 Proof	471	Value: 200				
1906 Proof	500	Value: 175				
1908 Proof	500	Value: 175				
1916S	300,000	25.00	60.00	95.00	600	850
1917S	2,300,000	2.00	5.00	10.00	125	175
1918/7S	—	3.00	9.00	18.50	120	—
1918S	2,780,000	1.50	5.00	10.00	100	150
1919S	1,220,000	2.50	7.50	15.00	150	200
1920	1,421,000	3.00	10.00	20.00	125	150
1921	2,132,000	2.00	7.00	10.00	90.00	125
1925M	1,000,000	5.00	15.00	30.00	175	225
1926M	1,200,000	3.00	8.00	15.00	90.00	125
1927M	1,000,000	2.00	5.00	10.00	60.00	75.00
1928M	1,000,000	3.00	6.00	11.00	60.00	75.00

KM# 173   5 CENTAVOS
Copper-Nickel **Obv:** Man seated beside hammer and anvil **Rev:** Eagle above stars and striped shield **Note:** Mule.

Date	Mintage	F	VF	XF	Unc	BU
1918S	—	200	600	1,450	2,500	4,500

KM# 175   5 CENTAVOS
4.7500 g., Copper-Nickel, 19 mm. **Obv:** Man seated beside hammer and anvil **Rev:** Eagle above stars and striped shield

Date	Mintage	F	VF	XF	Unc	BU
1930M	2,905,000	1.00	2.00	4.00	40.00	50.00
1931M	3,477,000	1.00	2.50	6.00	75.00	90.00
1932M	3,956,000	1.00	2.00	4.00	50.00	65.00
1934M	2,154,000	1.00	2.50	10.00	60.00	100
1935M	2,754,000	1.00	2.00	6.00	95.00	125

KM# 165 10 CENTAVOS

2.6924 g., 0.9000 Silver 0.0779 oz. ASW **Obv:** Female standing beside hammer and anvil **Rev:** Eagle above stars and striped shield

Date	Mintage	F	VF	XF	Unc	BU
1903	5,103,000	1.25	3.50	5.00	35.00	60.00
1903 Proof	2,558	Value: 80.00				
1903S	1,200,000	8.00	15.00	35.00	350	500
1904	11,000	10.00	15.00	35.00	75.00	125
1904 Proof	1,355	Value: 100				
1904S	5,040,000	1.50	2.50	6.00	40.00	75.00
1905 Proof	471	Value: 225				
1906 Proof	500	Value: 200				

KM# 169 10 CENTAVOS

2.0000 g., 0.7500 Silver 0.0482 oz. ASW **Obv:** Female standing beside hammer and anvil **Rev:** Eagle above stars and striped shield

Date	Mintage	F	VF	XF	Unc	BU
1907	1,501,000	1.50	3.00	5.00	50.00	75.00
1907S	4,930,000	1.00	2.00	4.00	40.00	55.00
1908 Proof	500	Value: 200				
1908S	3,364,000	1.00	2.00	4.00	60.00	90.00
1909S	312,000	15.00	35.00	60.00	350	450
1910S	—	—	—	—	—	—

Note: Unknown in any collection. Counterfeits of the 1910S are commonly encountered

1911S	1,101,000	3.00	4.00	12.50	75.00	125
1912S	1,010,000	2.25	4.00	12.00	75.00	125
1913S	1,361,000	1.50	3.00	10.00	50.00	75.00
1914S	1,180,000	3.00	5.50	15.00	150	225
1915S	450,000	7.50	17.50	35.00	250	425
1917S	5,991,000	1.00	2.00	3.50	50.00	75.00
1918S	8,420,000	0.85	1.50	2.00	27.50	35.00
1919S	1,630,000	1.00	2.50	4.00	45.00	55.00
1920	520,000	3.50	5.00	15.00	75.00	150
1921	3,863,000	0.85	1.50	2.50	30.00	40.00
1929M	1,000,000	0.85	1.50	2.50	20.00	35.00
1935M	1,280,000	0.85	1.50	2.00	20.00	30.00

KM# 166 20 CENTAVOS

5.3849 g., 0.9000 Silver 0.1558 oz. ASW **Obv:** Female standing beside hammer and anvil **Rev:** Eagle above stars and striped shield

Date	Mintage	F	VF	XF	Unc	BU
1903	5,353,000	2.50	3.00	5.00	35.00	70.00
1903 Proof	2,558	Value: 125				
1903S	150,000	8.00	15.00	50.00	450	750
1904	11,000	15.00	25.00	35.00	100	150
1904 Proof	1,355	Value: 125				
1904S	2,060,000	2.75	3.50	9.00	100	150
1905 Proof	471	Value: 275				
1905S	420,000	7.50	12.00	25.00	150	200
1906 Proof	500	Value: 250				

KM# 170 20 CENTAVOS

4.0000 g., 0.7500 Silver 0.0964 oz. ASW **Obv:** Female standing beside hammer and anvil **Rev:** Eagle above stars and striped shield

Date	Mintage	F	VF	XF	Unc	BU
1907	1,251,000	2.00	3.00	10.00	65.00	100
1907S	3,165,000	2.00	2.50	7.50	40.00	60.00
1908 Proof	500	Value: 250				
1908S	1,535,000	2.00	3.00	12.50	50.00	75.00
1909S	450,000	6.00	22.00	45.00	300	400
1910S	500,000	6.00	20.00	45.00	350	500
1911S	505,000	5.00	15.00	35.00	225	400
1912S	750,000	4.00	7.50	25.00	200	225
1913S/S	949,000	8.00	20.00	35.00	225	325
1913S	Inc. above	3.00	7.00	15.00	150	200
1914S	795,000	3.50	6.00	20.00	140	225
1915S	655,000	10.00	15.00	30.00	250	450
1916S	1,435,000	3.00	8.00	17.50	85.00	125
1917S	3,151,000	1.65	2.50	4.00	50.00	70.00
1918S	5,560,000	1.50	2.50	4.00	40.00	50.00
1919S	850,000	1.75	4.00	7.00	75.00	125
1920	1,046,000	1.75	5.00	8.00	90.00	120
1921	1,843,000	1.50	2.50	4.00	50.00	75.00
1929M	1,970,000	1.50	2.50	4.00	40.00	50.00

KM# 174 20 CENTAVOS

4.0000 g., 0.7500 Silver 0.0964 oz. ASW **Obv:** Female standing beside hammer and anvil **Rev:** Eagle above stars and striped shield **Note:** Mule.

Date	Mintage	F	VF	XF	Unc	BU
1928M	100,000	5.00	13.00	35.00	550	800

KM# 167 50 CENTAVOS

13.4784 g., 0.9000 Silver 0.3900 oz. ASW **Obv:** Female standing beside hammer and anvil **Rev:** Eagle above stars and striped shield

Date	Mintage	F	VF	XF	Unc	BU
1903	3,102,000	6.50	8.50	12.00	75.00	110
1903 Proof	2,558	Value: 150				
1903S 2 Known	—	—	—	—22,000	—	—
1904	11,000	25.00	32.00	50.00	150	200
1904 Proof	1,355	Value: 175				
1904S	2,160,000	6.50	9.50	15.00	100	140
1905 Proof	471	Value: 325				
1905S	852,000	8.00	15.00	35.00	600	1,200
1906 Proof	500	Value: 275				

KM# 171   50 CENTAVOS
10.0000 g., 0.7500 Silver 0.2411 oz. ASW **Obv:** Female standing beside hammer and anvil **Rev:** Eagle above stars and striped shield

Date	Mintage	F	VF	XF	Unc	BU
1907	1,201,000	5.00	10.00	30.00	175	225
1907S	2,112,000	4.00	10.00	20.00	125	150
1908 Proof	500	Value: 250				
1908S	1,601,000	4.00	9.00	25.00	250	500
1909S	528,000	5.00	15.00	45.00	275	350
1917S	674,000	5.00	10.00	25.00	125	200
1918S	2,202,000	3.75	6.00	9.00	100	125
1919S	1,200,000	3.75	5.50	10.00	150	150
1920	420,000	3.75	4.50	8.00	35.00	75.00
1921	2,317,000	BV	3.75	5.00	20.00	50.00

KM# 172   PESO
20.0000 g., 0.8000 Silver 0.5144 oz. ASW **Obv:** Female standing beside hammer and anvil **Rev:** Eagle above stars and striped shield

Date	Mintage	F	VF	XF	Unc	BU
1907 Proof, 2 known	—	—	—	—	—	—
1907S	10,276,000	8.00	9.00	12.00	60.00	100
1908 Proof	500	Value: 700				
1908S	20,955,000	8.00	9.00	12.00	60.00	90.00
1909S	7,578,000	8.00	9.00	15.00	70.00	100
1910S	3,154,000	8.00	10.00	20.00	250	400
1911S	463,000	12.00	20.00	45.00	700	1,000
1912S	680,000	12.00	25.00	75.00	750	1,200

UNITED STATES ADMINISTRATION
Commonwealth

DECIMAL COINAGE

KM# 179   CENTAVO
5.3000 g., Bronze, 25 mm. **Obv:** Male seated beside hammer and anvil **Rev:** Eagle above shield

Date	Mintage	F	VF	XF	Unc	BU
1937M	15,790,000	0.25	1.00	4.00	12.50	25.00
1938M	10,000,000	0.25	0.75	3.00	20.00	35.00
1939M	6,500,000	0.25	2.00	4.00	15.00	30.00
1940M	4,000,000	0.25	0.75	2.00	13.00	35.00
1941M	5,000,000	0.25	2.00	5.00	20.00	35.00
1944S	58,000,000	—	0.15	0.25	2.25	5.00

KM# 168   PESO
26.9568 g., 0.9000 Silver 0.7800 oz. ASW **Obv:** Female standing beside hammer and anvil **Rev:** Eagle above stars and striped shield

Date	Mintage	F	VF	XF	Unc	BU
1903	2,791,000	13.50	17.50	25.00	150	200
1903 Proof	2,558	Value: 300				
1903S	11,361,000	12.50	15.00	20.00	125	150
1904	11,000	65.00	85.00	110	250	325
1904 Proof	1,355	Value: 350				
1904S	6,600,000	12.50	15.00	25.00	125	165
1905S straight serif on 1	—	17.50	25.00	45.00	300	450
1905 Proof	471	Value: 900				
1905S curved serif on 1	6,056,000	14.00	20.00	30.00	200	350
1906 Proof	500	Value: 800				
1906S	201,000	750	1,200	2,500	12,000	20,000

Note: Counterfeits of the 1906S exist

KM# 180   5 CENTAVOS
4.8000 g., Copper-Nickel **Obv:** Male seated beside hammer and anvil **Rev:** Eagle with wings open above shield

Date	Mintage	F	VF	XF	Unc	BU
1937M	2,494,000	1.00	2.50	5.50	45.00	75.00
1938M	4,000,000	0.50	1.00	2.50	15.00	30.00
1941M	2,750,000	1.00	2.50	8.00	40.00	75.00

HAWAII, PHILLIPINES, PUERTO RICO

KM# 180a 5 CENTAVOS

4.9200 g., Copper-Nickel-Zinc, 19 mm. **Obv:** Male seated beside hammer and anvil **Rev:** Eagle with wings open above shield

Date	Mintage	F	VF	XF	Unc	BU
1944	21,198,000	—	0.20	0.50	2.00	4.00
1944S	14,040,000	—	0.20	0.25	1.00	2.00
1945S	72,796,000	—	0.20	0.25	1.00	2.00

KM# 181 10 CENTAVOS

2.0000 g., 0.7500 Silver 0.0482 oz. ASW, 16.7 mm. **Obv:** Female standing beside hammer and anvil **Rev:** Eagle with wings open above shield

Date	Mintage	F	VF	XF	Unc	BU
1937M	3,500,000	0.85	2.00	4.00	20.00	30.00
1938M	3,750,000	BV	0.85	2.00	10.00	15.00
1941M	2,500,000	BV	1.25	2.50	15.00	35.00
1944D	31,592,000	—	—	BV	1.25	2.50
1945D	137,208,000	—	—	BV	1.00	2.25

Note: 1937, 1938, and 1941 dated strikes have inverted W's for M's

KM# 182 20 CENTAVOS

4.0000 g., 0.7500 Silver 0.0964 oz. ASW, 21 mm. **Obv:** Female standing beside hammer and anvil **Rev:** Eagle with wings open above shield

Date	Mintage	F	VF	XF	Unc	BU
1937M	2,665,000	BV	1.75	3.50	15.00	30.00
1938M	3,000,000	BV	1.50	2.50	12.50	20.00
1941M	1,500,000	1.50	2.00	3.00	11.00	20.00
1944D	28,596,000	—	—	BV	1.75	2.50
1944D/S	—	12.00	16.50	20.00	50.00	75.00
1945D	82,804,000	—	—	BV	1.50	2.50

KM# 176 50 CENTAVOS

10.0000 g., 0.7500 Silver 0.2411 oz. ASW, 27.5 mm. **Subject:** Establishment of the Commonwealth **Obv:** Busts facing each other **Rev:** Eagle above shield **Designer:** Ambrosia Morales

Date	Mintage	F	VF	XF	Unc	BU
1936	20,000	—	30.00	45.00	75.00	110

KM# 183 50 CENTAVOS

10.0000 g., 0.7500 Silver 0.2411 oz. ASW, 27.5 mm. **Obv:** Female standing beside hammer and anvil **Rev:** Eagle with wings open above shield

Date	Mintage	F	VF	XF	Unc	BU
1944S	19,187,000	—	—	BV	4.50	6.50
1945S	18,120,000	—	—	BV	4.50	6.50

KM# 177 PESO

20.0000 g., 0.9000 Silver 0.5787 oz. ASW, 35 mm. **Subject:** Establishment of the Commonwealth **Obv:** Conjoined busts left **Rev:** Eagle with wings open above shield **Designer:** Ambrosia Morales

Date	Mintage	F	VF	XF	Unc	BU
1936	10,000	—	50.00	75.00	175	225

KM# 22   20 CENTAVOS
5.0000 g., 0.9000 Silver 0.1447 oz. ASW **Ruler:** Alfonso XIII
Obv: Young head left **Rev:** Crowned arms, pillars

Date	Mintage	F	VF	XF	Unc	BU
1895 PGV	3,350,000	45.00	80.00	165	400	—

KM# 178   PESO
20.0000 g., 0.9000 Silver 0.5787 oz. ASW, 35 mm. **Subject:**
Establishment of the Commonwealth **Obv:** Conjoined busts
left **Rev:** Eagle with wings open above shield **Designer:**
Ambrosia Morales

Date	Mintage	F	VF	XF	Unc	BU
1936	10,000	—	50.00	75.00	175	225

KM# 23   40 CENTAVOS
10.0000 g., 0.9000 Silver 0.2893 oz. ASW **Ruler:** Alfonso XIII
Obv: Young head left **Rev:** Crowned arms, pillars

Date	Mintage	F	VF	XF	Unc	BU
1896 PGV	725,000	250	350	850	2,850	—

PUERTO RICO

DECIMAL COINAGE

KM# 20   5 CENTAVOS
1.2500 g., 0.9000 Silver 0.0362 oz. ASW **Ruler:** Alfonso XIII
Obv: Value, date **Rev:** Crowned arms, pillars

Date	Mintage	F	VF	XF	Unc	BU
1896 PGV	600,000	30.00	50.00	90.00	225	—

KM# 21   10 CENTAVOS
2.5000 g., 0.9000 Silver 0.0723 oz. ASW **Ruler:** Alfonso XIII
Obv: Young head left **Rev:** Crowned arms, pillars

Date	Mintage	F	VF	XF	Unc	BU
1896 PGV	700,000	35.00	70.00	150	375	—

KM# 24   PESO
25.0000 g., 0.9000 Silver 0.7234 oz. ASW **Ruler:** Alfonso XIII
Obv: Young head left **Rev:** Crowned arms, pillars

Date	Mintage	F	VF	XF	Unc	BU
1895 PGV	8,500,000	300	450	900	2,500	3,250

INDEX

A

B

C

D

E

F

G

H

I

J

K

L

M

INDEX

W

Y

INDEX

2008 U.S. Mint Issues

PRESIDENTS OF THE UNITED STATES SERIES

This program is for a circulating dollar coin. Four presidents will be honored each year. 2008 issues will include: Andrew Jackson, John Quincy Adams, Martin Van Buren, and James Madison. The size, weight and composition are the same as the Sacagawea dollar.

STATE QUARTER PROGRAM

FIRST LADIES OF THE UNITED STATES SERIES

This program will honor the First Ladies of the United States with a ten dollar, one-half ounce .9999 fine gold coin. 2008 will see issues honoring Elizabeth Monroe, Louisa Adams, Martin Van Buren's Liberty (no spouse), Andrew Jackson's Liberty (no spouse).

HOW TO USE THE DVD

This DVD is PC and Macintosh® compatible when used with Adobe Acrobat Reader® version 6.0 or later. A step-by-step free download of Adobe Acrobat Reader® 8 is available at www.adobe.com. Adobe Reader® 8 was used in creating the instructions that follow.

To help you successfully navigate through the PDF document, several types of searches are available.

USING BOOKMARKS

Click on the Bookmarks icon to open the Bookmarks window. Use these links to go to specific points of interest. To scroll through pages in each section, use the arrows at the top of the screen (see next page for instructions to find page navigators).

USING THE FIND BOX

Locate the find box in the tool bar and enter the word(s) you are searching for.

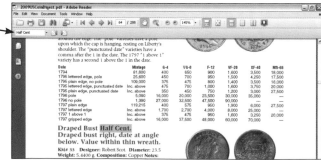

To navigate through the results of your search, use the Find Next icon.

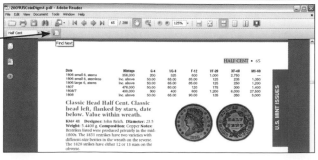

USING THE SEARCH OPTION

Locate the Search button by choosing Customize Toolbars in the Tools pull-down menu. Check Search (binocular icon) to have the Search option available in the toolbar.

Click on the Search icon to open the Search dialog box.

In the Search dialog box, enter the word(s) you are searching for and click on the Search button.

The list of results will appear in the dialog box. Click on the listings to view each page that contains your searched word(s).

To begin a new word search, click on the New Search button.

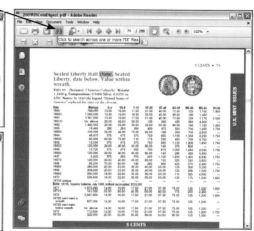

USING PAGE NAVIGATORS

Activate the Page Navigator Toolbar by choosing Customize Toolbars in the Tools pull-down menu. Check each tool as shown at right. You are now able to page through the PDF document by using the arrows at the top of the screen or by entering a page number you wish to view.

The Table of Contents is on page 3 and the Index is on pages 266 - 277.

You may also enlarge the images of the coins up to 400% for easy viewing